SHELLY CASHMAN SERIES®

Discovering
THE INTERNET

COMPLETE

Fifth Edition

Jennifer T. Campbell

 Cengage

SHELLY CASHMAN SERIES®

Australia • Brazil • Canada • Mexico • Singapore • United Kingdom • United States

Cengage

Discovering the Internet: Complete,
Fifth Edition
Jennifer T. Campbell

Senior Product Team Manager: Lauren Murphy

Content Developer: Jon Farnham

Associate Content Developer: Crystal Parenteau

Product Assistant: Rachael Starbard

Development Editor: Amanda Brodkin

Director of Production: Patty Stephan

Senior Content Project Manager: Matthew Hutchinson

Manufacturing Planner: Julio Esperas

Market Development Manager: Kristie Clark

Market Development Manager: Gretchen Swann

QA Manuscript Reviewers: Jeffrey Schwartz, John Freitas, Danielle Shaw

Cover Design: Lisa Kuhn, Curio Press, LLC

Cover Photo: © Tom Kates/Cengage Learning

Library of Congress Control Number: 2014951791

ISBN: 978-1-285-84540-1

Cengage
200 Pier 4 Boulevard
Boston, MA 02210
USA

Cengage is a leading provider of customized learning solutions with employees residing in nearly 40 different countries and sales in more than 125 countries around the world. Find your local representative at: **www.cengage.com.**

To learn more about Cengage platforms and services, register or access your online learning solution, or purchase materials for your course, visit **www.cengage.com.**

Printed at CLDPC, USA, 09-23

Contents

Chapter 4

Communicating Online

Chapter 5

Getting More Out of the Internet

Preface

The Shelly Cashman Series® offers the finest textbooks in computer education. We are proud of the fact that our textbook series has been the most widely used series in educational instruction. *Discovering the Internet: Complete, Fifth Edition* continues with the innovation, quality, and reliability that you have come to expect from the Shelly Cashman Series.

In *Discovering the Internet: Complete, Fifth Edition*, you will find an educationally sound, highly visual, and easy-to-follow pedagogy that combines Internet concepts with step-by-step projects and corresponding screens. The Internet and the World Wide Web have changed the way people find information, communicate with others, and conduct business activities. The chapters and exercises in this book are designed to help students understand how the Internet and the web have changed today's world, understand the structure of the Internet and the web, and understand how to use both technologies to enrich their personal and professional lives.

Objectives of This Textbook

Discovering the Internet: Complete, Fifth Edition is intended for a course that provides comprehensive coverage of Internet and web concepts. No experience with the Internet or the web is assumed. The objectives of this book are:

- To teach Internet and web history and concepts
- To demonstrate how to use a browser and online search tools
- To introduce different types of online communication tools
- To develop an exercise-oriented approach that allows learning by doing
- To encourage independent study and help those who are working alone

Organization of This Textbook

Discovering the Internet: Complete, Fifth Edition provides basic coverage of Internet and web concepts. The material is divided into four chapters and three appendices.

CHAPTER 1 — INTO THE INTERNET   In Chapter 1, students are introduced to basic Internet and web terminology, taught how the Internet and web are used, and familiarized with the history of the Internet and the web.

CHAPTER 2 — BROWSING THE WEB   In Chapter 2, students are introduced to websites, webpages, web portals, web servers, and web browsers. Students learn to use web browser features, such as tabbed browsing, and learn about online risks and safeguards.

CHAPTER 3 — SEARCHING THE WEB   In Chapter 3, students learn how to perform the search process and use various search tools to do basic and advanced web searches.

CHAPTER 4 — COMMUNICATING ONLINE   In Chapter 4, students learn how to send and receive email using both an email client and a web-based email service. Students also learn about participating in other types of online communication, such as mailing lists, newsgroups, wikis, and web-based discussion groups. Students are introduced to a variety of social media, such as blogs and social networks.

CHAPTER 5 — GETTING MORE OUT OF THE INTERNET   In Chapter 5, students explore getting more out of the Internet and the web including: visiting consumer, vertical, and industry portals; getting news, weather, and sports information; experiencing streaming media; using online reference tools; exploring special interest sites; managing their personal finances; and downloading and uploading files.

CHAPTER 6 — UNDERSTANDING INTERNET TECHNOLOGIES AND SECURITY   In Chapter 6, students learn about the networking technologies and communication services that make communicating over the Internet and accessing the web possible. Students also learn more about online security risks and safeguards.

CHAPTER 7 — UNDERSTANDING E-BUSINESS   In Chapter 7, students use real-world e-business examples to explore different e-business models.

APPENDIX A — EXPLORING OTHER BROWSERS   This appendix discusses the functionality differences among four additional browsers: Google Chrome, Firefox, Opera, and Safari. It also addresses the general differences in mobile browsers for tablets and smartphones.

APPENDIX B — UNDERSTANDING WEB DESIGN   This new appendix provides a brief presentation of the website planning and designing process.

APPENDIX C — EXPLORING THE CLOUD   This new appendix provides a brief presentation of web apps, storage, cloud security, and how cloud services can extend one's usage of the web.

Instructor Resources

The Instructor Resources include both teaching and testing aids and can be accessed online at www.cengage.com/login.

INSTRUCTOR'S MANUAL   Includes lecture notes summarizing the chapter sections, figures and boxed elements found in every chapter, teacher tips, classroom activities, lab activities, and quick quizzes in Microsoft Word files.

SYLLABUS   Contains easily customizable sample syllabi that cover policies, assignments, exams, and other course information.

FIGURE FILES   Illustrations for every figure in the textbook are available in electronic form. Figures are provided both with and without callouts.

POWERPOINT PRESENTATIONS   A one-click-per-slide presentation system provides PowerPoint slides for every subject in each chapter. Presentations are based on chapter objectives.

SOLUTIONS TO EXERCISES   Includes solutions for all end-of-chapter and chapter reinforcement exercises.

TEST BANKS   Test Banks include questions for every chapter, feature objective-based and critical-thinking question types, and include page number references and figure references, when appropriate.

DATA FILES FOR STUDENTS   Includes all the files that are required by students to complete the exercises.

ADDITIONAL ACTIVITIES FOR STUDENTS   Consists of Chapter Reinforcement Exercises, which are true/false, multiple-choice, and short answer questions that help students gain confidence in the material learned.

About Our Covers

The Shelly Cashman Series is continually updating our approach and content to reflect the way today's students learn and experience new technology. This focus on student success is reflected on our covers, which feature real students from The University of Rhode Island using the Shelly Cashman Series in their courses, and reflect the varied ages and backgrounds of the students learning with our books. When you use the Shelly Cashman Series, you can be assured that you are learning computer skills using the most effective courseware available.

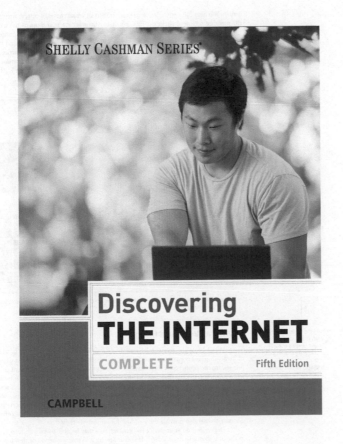

Textbook Walk-Through

DOWNLOADING AND UPLOADING FILES One of the most useful Internet activities is downloading files from a server or uploading files to a server. A **server** is a computer on a network used to store files. As you learned earlier, a web server stores webpages. Other server examples are a mail server that stores email messages and a file server that stores electronic files. To **download** is to copy or transfer files from a server to your computer or device; to **upload** is to copy, post, or transfer files from your computer or device to a server. The Internet standard or protocol that you use to upload or download music, software, word processing, picture, and other files to a server is the **File Transfer Protocol (FTP)**.

FACTS @HAND Peer-to-peer media file sharing became popular in the late 1990s by websites such as Napster that allowed individual users to upload music files and share them with others, without permission from, or reimbursement for, the copyright holder. Companies such as Rhapsody and Pandora offer subscription-based radio and downloadable music files that are licensed by the copyright holders and available to individual users.

CLOUD COMPUTING Remote data access, storage, software access, and collaboration technologies are all aspects of **cloud computing**. Users of cloud computing can access a variety of software and storage methods by using a computer or mobile device with Internet access and browser software. Google Drive™ is an example of cloud computing. Google Drive includes Google Docs, a group of software products available online, including word processing (Figure 1-10), spreadsheet, and presentation software. When logged on to Google Drive, a user can use the software to create a document, such as a spreadsheet, save and store the document online, and share the document with others to collaborate on changes — all without installing software on the user's computer or device.

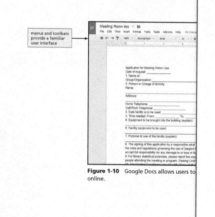

menus and toolbars provide a familiar user interface

Figure 1-10 Google Docs allows users to [...] online.

Facts@Hand
Each chapter contains multiple Facts@Hand tips that provide industry statistics or usage information relevant to the Internet and web concepts discussed in the chapter.

article. You also can copy a link and paste it into an email message or text message. When the message recipient clicks the link, his or her browser starts and opens the webpage.

Most browsers and websites enable you to share webpages and web content to social media and content sharing websites, such as Facebook, Twitter, Pinterest, and more. You can post a link to an article using the sharing or connectivity icons in the article or on the webpage (Figure 2-66). If you are using Pinterest, you can select which graphic on the webpage to display on your Pinterest board. You also can copy and paste a URL directly into a Facebook post or Twitter tweet.

sharing icons

© 2014 Microsoft

Figure 2-66 Sharing or connectivity icons enable you to share web content with your friends, family, or contacts.

Saving a Webpage Image

While browsing the web, you might find an image that you want to save. Be aware of ownership and copyrights when saving and using webpage images. Most webpage images are the property of their owners. U.S. copyright laws protect content owners from unauthorized copying and sharing of text, images, and other media. You cannot use copyright-protected images without permission from the owner or source. Some images, such as many images found at U.S. government websites, are in the public domain. You can use images in the public domain freely. You generally need to provide credit or source information about the source of public domain images. Many websites that offer public domain images also provide the wording for an image credit line.

Depending on your device or browser, you may be able to save an image, such as the one shown in Figure 2-67. If you are using a Windows laptop or desktop, right-click the image and then click the 'Save picture as' command on the shortcut menu. If you are using a Macintosh or mobile device, your steps will vary. For example, many mobile devices or computers with a touch screen will open a menu of commands, including the option to save web content or media if you press and hold the image or other content.

@SOURCE For more information on U.S. copyright laws and how to ensure you are following them when saving or sharing web content and media, use a search engine to search for *U.S. copyright laws web content*.

@Source
Each chapter includes multiple @Source tips that encourage students to find more information on topics by providing keywords on which to search.

Step-By-Step Instruction

Step-by-step hands-on instructions provide a context beyond the point-and-click. Each step provides information on why students are performing each task, or what will occur as a result.

Q&A

Q&A boxes identify questions students may have when working through the steps and provide additional information about what they are doing, right where they need it.

2
- Tap or click Bookmarks, or another similar command.
- Tap or click the Other folder link to open a new folder (Figure 2-42)
- In the Label text box, type **Textbook links** as the favorite name.

3
- Choose where to add the bookmark, if possible.
- Enter **Discovering the Internet** as the folder name.
- Tap or click the Create or Save button to create the new Discovering the Internet folder.
- Tap or click the Save or Add button or another appropriate button to add the favorite to the new Discovering the Internet folder.

Figure 2-42

To Delete a Favorites Subfolder and Its Contents

When you no longer need a Favorites or Bookmarks subfolder or an individual favorite, you can delete it. The following steps delete the Discovering the Internet folder and its contents.

1
- Click the Favorites button or Bookmarks button, or open your browser and open the browser menu if you are using a mobile device.
- Display your list of favorites and subfolders.

60   Chapter 2   Browsing the Web

2
- Right-click the folder if necessary, then tap or click Delete, or a similar command (Figure 2-44).
- Click the Yes button, if necessary, to confirm the deletion.
- Close the browser.

Q&A
Can I organize my favorites or bookmarks? Depending on your device or browser, you likely can reorganize them. Use a search engine to search for steps to organize favorites or bookmarks for your browser or device.

Figure 2-44

History

Another easy way to revisit a webpage is to use a history of the websites and webpages you have visited during a specific number of days.

A **History list** displays a list of past browsing data. Your History list might contain icons for websites visited several weeks ago, last week, and every day of the current week, including today, depending on your settings. When you tap or click one of these icons, a list of webpage folders might appear, or the website may open automatically. Each folder represents a website visited during that time period. You can expand each website folder to view links to the individual webpages viewed at the website.

You also can reorganize your view of the History list. Depending on your device or browser, you might have options to view the History list by website, most visited, order visited today, or more. Additionally, you may be able to search for previously viewed webpages.

Using a Webpage Search Feature and Clicking Links

Many websites include a keyword search feature to allow you to find a specific webpage within a website. You can enter keywords in the search feature's text box and then tap or click a Search button to find webpages at the website that contain those keywords. You will learn more about keyword searches in Chapter 3. Some websites, such as The Weather Channel, have special search tools designed to find information organized by common categories, such as ZIP code, city, or state (Figure 2-17). Others, such as Cengage.com, allow you to enter general information, such as a topic or author name, or narrow your results to be more specific, such as by typing an ISBN, which is the unique number assigned to every book.

Figure 2-17

@ISSUE   Web Ads

As you browse the web or use web or mobile apps, you may notice a barrage of advertisements. Web advertisements can appear in pop-up windows in front of the webpage or app currently displayed or in pop-under windows that appear behind the browser window or app. Although advertising revenue does offset many costs associated with creating webpages, ads are generally considered inconvenient and bothersome by web users. Some advertisements with attention-grabbing sounds and animation, called **rich media ads**, even appear right in the middle of or floating across the webpage or app you are viewing. Most visitors consider these approaches to web advertising increasingly invasive, distracting, and bothersome.

For these reasons, you may want to block ads. Blocking or filtering ads is important particularly for children. According to research by Dr. Jakob Nielsen, a web usability pioneer, children are less able than adults to distinguish between web ads and content. When a child sees a cartoon character in an ad, for example, he or she likely will click the ad expecting to see more cartoons. Using an ad filter or blocker can help reduce the likelihood that children will click ads and navigate to webpages selling products and services. Many ads contain malicious content that can introduce viruses, spyware, or other harmful programs or apps onto your computer or device.

Most current browsers include a feature that blocks pop-up ads; however, other kinds of ads, including rich media ads, may still appear. Ch... to turn o...

@Issue
Each chapter includes one or more @Issue sections that provide additional discussion of important Internet and web issues.

Chapter Review
A review of the Internet and web concepts discussed in the chapter.

Like other types of Internet connections, digital satellite has some disadvantages. Snow, rain, wind, or even clouds may affect the clarity of the signal. Furthermore, the lengthy distance to the orbiting satellites can create a significant lag in the response time. The lag is not noticeable while browsing webpages; but for communications such as instant messaging or chat, which take place simultaneously, or in **real time**, the lag may be noticeable.

Chapter Review

The Internet is a worldwide network of networks that individuals, institutions, and businesses use to communicate, share information, and conduct business transactions. Using the Internet enables people to acquire useful information; send and receive email and text messages; exchange thoughts, photos, files, and links with others using social media; and take advantage of the convenience e-commerce allows them when shopping and paying for items. Businesses conduct business transactions with their customers, vendors, and employees over the Internet, and use social media to build a community and share information.

The World Wide Web, also known as the web, is a subset of the Internet that supports webpages, which can include text, graphics, animation, sound, or video. A website is a collection of related webpages. Webpages connect to each other through hyperlinks, which enable a user to move from one webpage to another, on the same or another website. A browser allows users to access and view webpages, while a search tool allows users to find specific web-based resources.

The Internet has its roots in ARPANET, a research and defense initiative of the U.S. government in collaboration with technology firms and universities. In 1990, NSFNet superseded ARPANET as the main government network linking universities and research facilities. The U.S. Congress opened the Internet to commercial use in 1992. Tim Berners-Lee's development of the Web in 1991 caused Internet usage to explode. Berners-Lee developed the use of hyperlinks between different files, HTML to create web documents, the addressing scheme, and the original WorldWideWeb browser. In 1994, the first commercial web browser allowed businesses and individuals to discover the possibilities available online, and the use of the Internet expanded rapidly.

Individuals and businesses use cable broadband, phone lines, or wireless connections to access the Internet through a wide array of methods with varying speeds and costs.

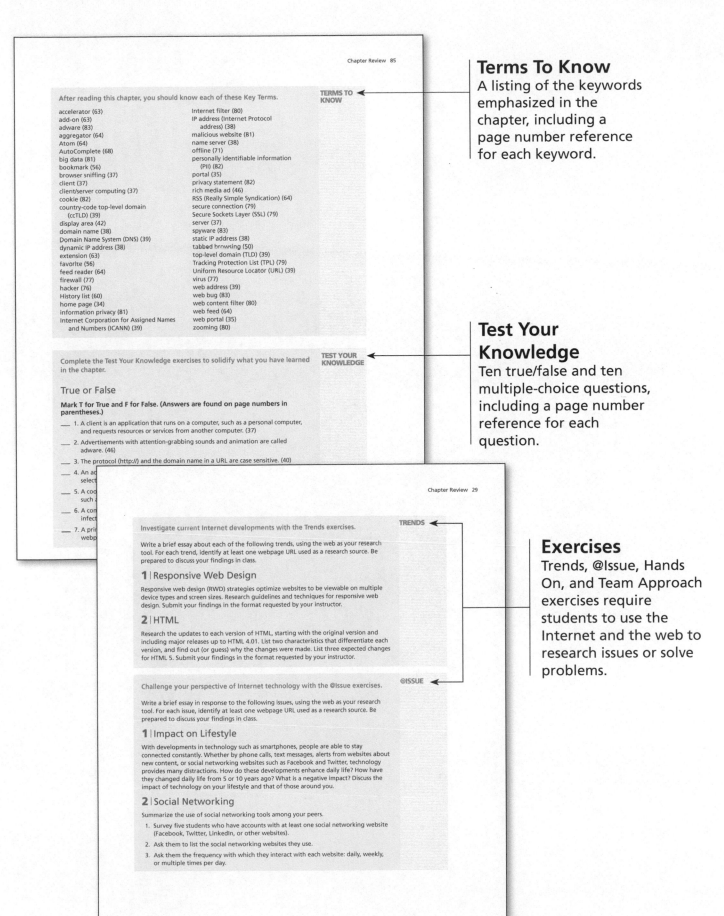

After reading this chapter, you should know each of these Key Terms.

TERMS TO KNOW

accelerator (63)
add-on (63)
adware (83)
aggregator (64)
Atom (64)
AutoComplete (68)
big data (81)
bookmark (56)
browser sniffing (37)
client (37)
client/server computing (37)
cookie (82)
country-code top-level domain
    (ccTLD) (39)
display area (42)
domain name (38)
Domain Name System (DNS) (39)
dynamic IP address (38)
extension (63)
favorite (56)
feed reader (64)
firewall (77)
hacker (76)
History list (60)
home page (34)
information privacy (81)
Internet Corporation for Assigned Names
    and Numbers (ICANN) (39)

Internet filter (80)
IP address (Internet Protocol
    address) (38)
malicious website (81)
name server (38)
offline (71)
personally identifiable information
    (PII) (82)
portal (35)
privacy statement (82)
rich media ad (46)
RSS (Really Simple Syndication) (64)
secure connection (79)
Secure Sockets Layer (SSL) (79)
server (37)
spyware (83)
static IP address (38)
tabbed browsing (50)
top-level domain (TLD) (39)
Tracking Protection List (TPL) (79)
Uniform Resource Locator (URL) (39)
virus (77)
web address (39)
web bug (83)
web content filter (80)
web feed (64)
web portal (35)
zooming (80)

Terms To Know
A listing of the keywords emphasized in the chapter, including a page number reference for each keyword.

Complete the Test Your Knowledge exercises to solidify what you have learned in the chapter.

TEST YOUR KNOWLEDGE

True or False

Mark T for True and F for False. (Answers are found on page numbers in parentheses.)

____ 1. A client is an application that runs on a computer, such as a personal computer, and requests resources or services from another computer. (37)

____ 2. Advertisements with attention-grabbing sounds and animation are called adware. (46)

____ 3. The protocol (http://) and the domain name in a URL are case sensitive. (40)

____ 4. An ad
       select

____ 5. A coo
       such

____ 6. A con
       infect

____ 7. A pri
       webp

Test Your Knowledge
Ten true/false and ten multiple-choice questions, including a page number reference for each question.

Investigate current Internet developments with the Trends exercises.

TRENDS

Write a brief essay about each of the following trends, using the web as your research tool. For each trend, identify at least one webpage URL used as a research source. Be prepared to discuss your findings in class.

1 | Responsive Web Design

Responsive web design (RWD) strategies optimize websites to be viewable on multiple device types and screen sizes. Research guidelines and techniques for responsive web design. Submit your findings in the format requested by your instructor.

2 | HTML

Research the updates to each version of HTML, starting with the original version and including major releases up to HTML 4.01. List two characteristics that differentiate each version, and find out (or guess) why the changes were made. List three expected changes for HTML 5. Submit your findings in the format requested by your instructor.

Challenge your perspective of Internet technology with the @Issue exercises.

@ISSUE

Write a brief essay in response to the following issues, using the web as your research tool. For each issue, identify at least one webpage URL used as a research source. Be prepared to discuss your findings in class.

1 | Impact on Lifestyle

With developments in technology such as smartphones, people are able to stay connected constantly. Whether by phone calls, text messages, alerts from websites about new content, or social networking websites such as Facebook and Twitter, technology provides many distractions. How do these developments enhance daily life? How have they changed daily life from 5 or 10 years ago? What is a negative impact? Discuss the impact of technology on your lifestyle and that of those around you.

2 | Social Networking

Summarize the use of social networking tools among your peers.

1. Survey five students who have accounts with at least one social networking website (Facebook, Twitter, LinkedIn, or other websites).

2. Ask them to list the social networking websites they use.

3. Ask them the frequency with which they interact with each website: daily, weekly, or multiple times per day.

Exercises
Trends, @Issue, Hands On, and Team Approach exercises require students to use the Internet and the web to research issues or solve problems.

Discovering
THE INTERNET

COMPLETE

1 | Into the Internet

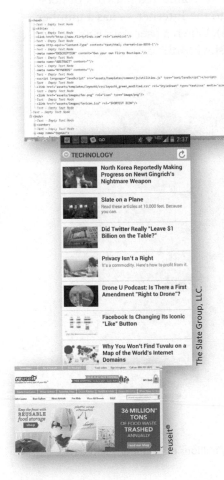

FlirtyFinds

The Slate Group, LLC.

reuseit®

Introduction

Internet. Email. Web. Wi-Fi. RSS. VoIP. GPS. Hotspots. Blog. Cloud computing. Social network. You most likely have heard and used many of these terms and technologies. New developments constantly are emerging that affect the way people communicate and collaborate with others, access information, and purchase products and services.

In this chapter, you will learn the meaning of these and many other Internet-related terms. You will discover some of the many ways people and businesses use the Internet. You also will review the history of the Internet and learn about the companies, technologies, and organizations that control the Internet. Finally, you will learn how individuals and businesses connect to the Internet.

Objectives

After completing this chapter, you will be able to:

1. Define the Internet

2. Describe how individuals, businesses, educational institutions, and organizations use the Internet

3. Discuss the developments of the Internet and the World Wide Web

4. Explain how individuals and businesses connect to the Internet

Defining the Internet

The **Internet** is a global network of computers and mobile devices that allows individuals and businesses around the world to share information and other resources and conduct business transactions. More specifically, the Internet is an interconnected network of networks, where each **host** — a computer directly connected to the Internet — has a number of other computers and devices connected to it (Figure 1-1). When a user connects to the Internet to access or share information and services, he or she is **online**.

Figure 1-1   The Internet is the largest computer network, connecting millions of computers and devices around the world.

© Cengage Learning; © Mmaxer/Shutterstock.com; © Alfonso de Tomas/Shutterstock.com; © SSSCCC/Shutterstock. com; © iStockphoto/Petar Chernaev; © amfoto/Shutterstock.com; © iStockphoto.com/scanrail; ©iStockphoto.com/Oleksiy Mark/scanrail; © iStockphoto/sweetym; Source: Microsoft; © Oleksiy Mark/Shutterstock.com; Source: Cengage Learning; © iStockphoto/Stephen Krow; © Cengage Learning; © iStockphoto/Skip O'Donnell; Source: Apple Inc; © iStockphoto/Skip O'Donnell; Source: Nutrition Blog Network; © iStockphoto/Ayaaz Rattansi; Source: Microsoft; © Oleksiy Mark/Shutterstock.com; Source: Microsoft; © Cengage Learning;

All computers and mobile devices, including smartphones, tablets, home and business personal computers, and supercomputers used by government and researchers, share a common method of communicating known as a protocol. A **protocol** is a standard or set of rules that computer network devices follow when transmitting and receiving data. Every computer and device connected to the Internet uses **Transmission Control Protocol/ Internet Protocol (TCP/IP)**. TCP/IP makes it possible for data to be transmitted to any Internet-connected computer or device, regardless of operating system or device type. You will learn more about TCP/IP and other Internet technologies in later chapters.

Internet communications travel across high-speed networks that connect networks around the world using fiber-optic cables, satellites, and other technologies. Communication carriers operate these high-speed networks, which provide the Internet framework.

Q&A | **Who owns the Internet?**

No single organization owns or controls the Internet. Several groups, such as the Internet Corporation for Assigned Names and Numbers (ICANN), the Internet Assigned Numbers Authority (IANA), and the Internet Society (ISOC), oversee and standardize the development of Internet technologies and manage some Internet processes. To learn more about each of these organizations, use a search engine to search for ICANN, IANA, or ISOC.

Using the Internet

The Internet and the web significantly have influenced the way the world communicates, educates, entertains, and conducts business. People use the Internet to search for information, conduct academic or scientific research, conduct business, communicate, share information or media, check news or weather, keep up with sports statistics, participate in online training, shop, play games, and download books, music, or videos (Figure 1-2).

access information

send email

converse
with others

Figure 1-2 People around the world use the Internet in daily activities, such as accessing information, sending and receiving email messages, and conversing with others from their computers and mobile devices.

© Alex Staroseltsev / Shutterstock.com; Source: Microsoft; © iStockphoto / Petar Chernaev; Source: WeatherBug; © artjazz / Shutterstock.com; Source: WebMD, LLC; © iStockphoto / Mikkel William Nielsen; © Jochen Tack / Alamy; © iStockphoto / pictafolio

Who Uses the Internet?

People in all occupations and stages of life use the Internet: students and teachers, businesspeople and professionals, homemakers, children, and retirees. Individuals can use the Internet to search for information on almost any topic — entertainment, sports, politics, science, art, history, and so forth. Medical professionals use the Internet to research new drugs and current treatments, as well as to communicate with patients and to transfer records electronically to other physicians. Families synchronize electronic calendars, send text messages, find recipes, and schedule appointments. Politicians, celebrities, and other public figures use social media and webpages to share news, events, and other information with a community of followers. Consumers shop online, pay bills, make bank deposits and transfers, and complete and submit their taxes online. Businesspeople and professionals use the Internet to communicate with clients and colleagues whether at home or on the road using email, text, chat, social networking, or video conferencing; work on office computers from their laptops or mobile devices while traveling or telecommuting; view up-to-the-minute business news; and check stock prices.

FACTS @HAND As part of research to mark the 25th anniversary of the World Wide Web, in 2014 the Pew Research published the following statistics: Nearly all Americans who meet one or more of the following criteria have access to the Internet: those who live in households earning $75,000 or more, young adults ages 18–29, and those with college degrees.

Q&A

Is the Internet's societal influence all good?
Being constantly connected has its price. In the past, employees' workdays were finished when they physically left the office, but now they can be expected to keep on top of work-related communication during what used to be personal, family, or leisure time. The compulsion to constantly check social media, sports scores, or text messages can have a negative effect on human relationships. To learn more, use a search engine to search for *Internet's negative effect.*

People also use the Internet to publish **blogs**. Blogs can cover any topic, such as humor or news. Many corporations and organizations use blogs to share news with interested parties. Individuals or groups of individuals create general interest blogs to share humorous stories or pictures, or write about current events. Millions of people go online to share ideas and information by hosting and participating in blogs — a process called **blogging**. Many blogs enable and encourage users to add comments to posts. **Video sharing** websites, sometimes called **video blogging** websites, such as YouTube and Vimeo, allow users to share and comment on personal and professional videos. **Microblogging** is sending brief text messages to subscribers, such as by using Twitter or other services to share status updates, links to articles, photos, and more.

New uses of the Internet continually are evolving, providing new and improved technologies for individuals and businesses.

Internet Activities

The Internet supports a wide range of activities, including the following:

- Browsing and searching for information
- Communicating with others through email, text or video chat, social networking, instant messaging, mailing lists, blogs and microblogs, and other media
- Downloading and uploading files
- Accessing remote computers or servers
- Conducting business activities
- Online shopping and bill payment

The following sections define and describe each of these activities:

THE WORLD WIDE WEB   The **World Wide Web**, commonly called the **web**, is a subset of the Internet. The web includes a vast collection of documents called **webpages**, which can include text, pictures, sound, animation, or video. A **website** is a collection of related webpages. Website examples (Figure 1-3) include college and university websites; corporate websites; websites for companies that sell products or services, such as Thirty-One; websites for nonprofit organizations, such as the Red Cross; and personal websites such as blogs.

@SOURCE Although some people use the terms *Internet* and *web* interchangeably, the Internet and the web are not one and the same. The Internet is a worldwide public network that links private networks. The Internet gives users access to a variety of resources for communication, research, file sharing, and commerce. The web, a subset of the Internet, is just one of those resources.

retail website   nonprofit website

Figure 1-3   Websites include college and university, corporate, retail, nonprofit, and personal sites.

A **markup language** is a coding system that uses tags to provide instructions about the appearance, structure, and formatting of a document. Webpages use markup languages to define the layout and/or content of the pages. Web designers use **Hypertext Markup Language (HTML)** codes to define the layout and structure of a webpage. The HTML markup language uses predefined codes called **HTML tags** to define the format and organization of webpage elements (Figure 1-4). For example, the <html> ....</html> tag pair indicates the beginning and the end of a webpage, respectively. The <b> ....</b> HTML tag pair indicates the text between the tags is set in bold.

website in browser

HTML markup for website

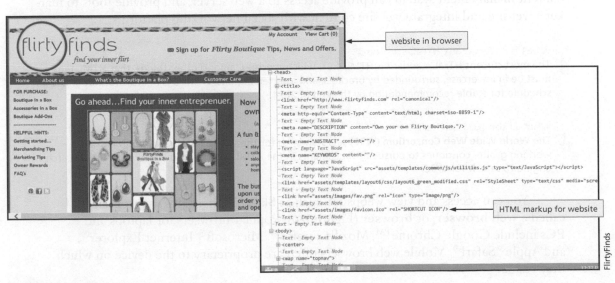

Figure 1-4   HTML tags define webpage elements.

When a webpage downloads into a browser, the browser reads and interprets the HTML tags to display the page with organized and formatted text, images, and links. **Cascading style sheets (CSS)** are documents that specify design aspects of a webpage, such as fonts and colors. Other markup languages include XML, XHTML, and WML (Figure 1-5).

Markup Languages

Language	Description
Extensible Markup Language (XML)	Uses both predefined and customized tags to facilitate the consistent sharing of information, especially within large groups. Whereas HTML defines the appearance and organization of webpage content, XML defines the content itself. For example, using XML, a programmer can define the custom tag <serialnum> to indicate that the information following the tag is a product serial number.
Extensible Hypertext Markup Language (XHTML)	A family of XML markup languages that mirrors or extends versions of HTML. Webpages created using XHTML look better than HTML-coded webpages when viewed on smartphones or other handheld computers, or by users of assistive technologies.
Wireless Markup Language (WML)	An XML-based markup language used to design webpages specifically for mobile browsers. WML uses Wireless Application Protocol (WAP) to allow Internet access by wireless devices.

© Cengage Learning®

Figure 1-5 Additional webpage markup languages.

You can create a webpage using a simple text editor program, such as Notepad, or using WYSIWYG (What You See Is What You Get) **web authoring software**, such as Adobe Dreamweaver or an online content management system, such as WordPress. Web authoring software automatically generates the appropriate HTML and CSS tags as the user creates individual webpages that become part of a websites. To share a webpage or website with others, you must upload, or **publish**, it to a web server so that other users may access it. A **web server** is a computer that stores webpages. A content management system, like web authoring software, also provides tools to generate webpages without requiring the web designer to know how to code using HTML and CSS. In addition, a content management system can provide access to a web server, and provide tools to market a website and integrate website content with social networking platforms.

Q&A | **What is the current HTML standard?**
The most current HTML standard is HTML 4.01, which specifies, among other things, that HTML tags must be in lowercase, surrounded by brackets, and inserted in pairs. HTML 5 is in draft format and is on schedule for stable recommendation by the end of 2014.

Q&A | **What is the role of the W3C?**
The **World Wide Web Consortium (W3C)** sets standards for the web. The W3C, through an HTML working group, continues to pursue advancements in the HTML standard. To learn more, use a search engine to search for *W3C*.

You can access and view webpages, such as Slate, using a software program called a **web browser**, or **browser** (Figure 1-6). Popular browsers for laptops and PCs include Google Chrome™, Mozilla Firefox®, Microsoft® Internet Explorer®, and Apple® Safari®. Mobile web browsers often are proprietary to the device on which they reside.

Figure 1-6   The same webpage viewed in different browsers.

Q&A

What is RWD?
Responsive web design (RWD) is a web design strategy. The goal of RWD is to create websites that adjust layout and, in some cases, content, to the device and screen displaying the webpages.

Webpages connect to other webpages using hyperlinks. A **hyperlink**, or **link**, is text or a picture on a webpage, such as Gourmet.com, that you tap or click to view a different location on the same webpage, another webpage at the same website (Figure 1-7), a webpage at a different website, or to an email address, or PDF document.

Figure 1-7   Webpages at the same website or across different websites are connected by links.

Exploring the web by moving from one webpage to another is sometimes called **browsing** or **surfing the web**. For example, when planning a trip, you might first visit an airline webpage and book a flight. Quite possibly, the airline webpage contains links to other travel-related websites, so you could tap or click a link on the airline webpage to visit a hotel webpage and book your accommodations. Finally, you tap or click a link on the hotel webpage to view a webpage containing yet more links to restaurants and entertainment venues near the hotel. When reading an article on a webpage, you often can find background information or articles on related topics by tapping or clicking links within the text of the article, or in a sidebar or list beside or below the article. In Chapter 2 you will learn how to use a web browser to access webpages and how to tap or click hyperlinks to view other webpages.

Q&A | **What is a scripting language?**
Scripting languages are programming languages used to write short programs, called scripts, that execute in real time at the server or in the web browser when a webpage downloads. **Scripts** make webpages dynamic and interactive by adding such features as multimedia, animation, and forms or by connecting webpages to underlying databases.

Q&A | **What is an app?**
An **app** (short for application) is a software program. The term, app, typically refers to programs that run on mobile devices (mobile apps), or the web (web apps). Apps are an integral part of Internet technology.

Q&A | **What is Web 2.0?**
Web 2.0 technologies and practices are designed to make users' web experiences interactive by incorporating social media and user-driven content into web pages.

A **search tool** is a web-based resource that helps you find specific information on the web. One type of search tool is a search engine, such as Google or Bing, which you can use to search for webpages that contain specific keywords or phrases. Figure 1-8 illustrates a Google search results webpage. You will learn how to use search tools in Chapter 3.

Figure 1-8 Search tools allow users to find information on the web.

EMAIL AND OTHER COMMUNICATIONS TOOLS Individuals and organizations of all types use websites to communicate ideas and information. Web communication technologies include email, blogging, social networking, social bookmarking, chat, instant messaging, virtual meetings and collaborative workspaces, video sharing, VoIP, interactive gaming, and 3D virtual worlds. **Email** allows Internet users to send and receive messages and files over a local computer network or the Internet. Sending an email message is inexpensive, fast, and useful when compared to sending print mail or making a phone call. You can send email when it is convenient for you, and the recipient can read it and respond when it is convenient for him or her. You use an **email program**, such as Microsoft Outlook® or web-based email, such as Gmail™ to create, send, receive, and manage email.

In addition to email, the Internet offers several other ways for individuals and groups to communicate (Figure 1-9), including texting, instant messaging (IM), mobile instant messaging (MIM), Internet Relay Chat (IRC), mailing lists, wikis, collaborative workspaces, massively multiplayer online games (MMOGs), social networking, and social bookmarking. These communications tools allow Internet users to connect with others online to converse about a topic or an activity of interest, share information, conduct business, and play games. You will learn more about email and other online communications tools, including various online tools categorized as social media, in Chapter 4.

Internet Communication Methods

Online Communication	Description	Must users be online at the same time?
Email	Users send and receive text with or without attached files	No
Instant messaging (IM) and mobile instant messaging (MIM)	Two or more users take turns exchanging brief messages	Yes
Internet Relay Chat (IRC) or chatting	Users type text into a chat window; all users can see what other users type	Yes
Massive multiplayer online games (MMOGs)	Many users play online games simultaneously, and can compete and interact with people all over the world	Yes
Newsgroups and mailing lists	Users subscribe to a newsgroup discussion or mailing list on a certain topic and receive messages about that topic	No
Social bookmarking	Users share web links to articles, videos, photographs, and webpages, and can use tags to organize their bookmarks	No
Social networking	Users share status updates, microblogs, photos and video, links, and personal commentary using a variety of online tools	No

© Cengage Learning®

Figure 1-9 The Internet offers many ways for people to communicate.

Perhaps the first person to send an email message who was not a computer scientist was Queen Elizabeth II, who sent an email message on March 26, 1976 from an Army base.

FACTS @HAND

DOWNLOADING AND UPLOADING FILES   One of the most useful Internet activities is downloading files from a server or uploading files to a server. A **server** is a computer on a network used to store files. As you learned earlier, a web server stores webpages. Other server examples are a mail server that stores email messages and a file server that stores electronic files. To **download** is to copy or transfer files from a server to your computer or device; to **upload** is to copy, post, or transfer files from your computer or device to a server. The Internet standard or protocol that you use to upload or download music, software, word processing, picture, and other files to a server is the **File Transfer Protocol (FTP)**.

FACTS @HAND   Peer-to-peer media file sharing became popular in the late 1990s by websites such as Napster that allowed individual users to upload music files and share them with others, without permission from, or reimbursement for, the copyright holder. Companies such as Rhapsody and Pandora offer subscription-based radio and downloadable music files that are licensed by the copyright holders and available to individual users.

CLOUD COMPUTING   Remote data access, storage, software access, and collaboration technologies are all aspects of **cloud computing**. Users of cloud computing can access a variety of software and storage methods by using a computer or mobile device with Internet access and browser software. Google Drive™ is an example of cloud computing. Google Drive includes Google Docs, a group of software products available online, including word processing (Figure 1-10), spreadsheet, and presentation software. When logged on to Google Drive, a user can use the software to create a document, such as a spreadsheet, save and store the document online, and share the document with others to collaborate on changes — all without installing software on the user's computer or device.

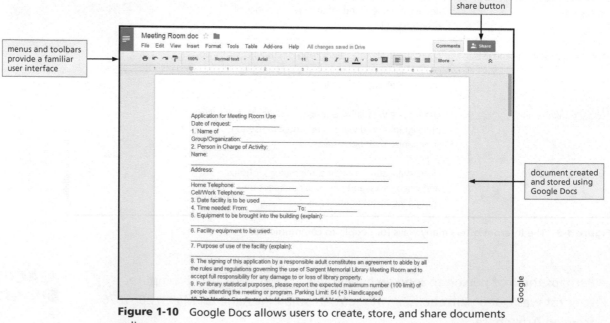

Figure 1-10   Google Docs allows users to create, store, and share documents online.

Businesses can take advantage of many remote computing technologies to keep employees productive while they travel, work from home, or interact with colleagues located around the world. One technology is a **virtual private network (VPN)**. A VPN provides a secure, encrypted connection between a remote user and a local area network. **Web conferencing** or **video calling** allows remote employees to participate in meetings, training sessions, and more. Web conferencing is a broad term that can include using the web to view slide show presentations, use live or streaming video, participate in surveys and polls, communicate using text chat, or view the presenter's screen using screen sharing.

Q&A

What is Telnet?

Telnet is a standard or protocol that allows users to log in and to access a remote computer, usually one with significantly higher processing power. While the public typically does not use Telnet, it still has many valuable uses. Computer system administrators, for example, can use Telnet to log in to a remote computer to troubleshoot problems.

CONDUCTING BUSINESS ACTIVITIES Businesses and organizations that use the Internet to generate a profit, promote their goods and services, or maintain goodwill with their partners, members, or customers are engaged in **e-business**. E-business is a broad term that includes electronically transmitted financial transactions, such as placing orders, sending invoices, or paying by credit card online. E-business also includes the functions of supporting and enhancing business relationships by sharing information with customers, suppliers, and employees. Although people often use the terms e-business and e-commerce interchangeably, e-business can refer to any use of the Internet to conduct a company's business, whereas **e-commerce** refers to Internet use for the purpose of generating sales of goods or services, or creating and maintaining customer relations.

E-commerce websites can be categorized by the participants involved in the transactions (Figure 1-11), such as businesses and consumers. **Business-to-consumer (B2C)** is

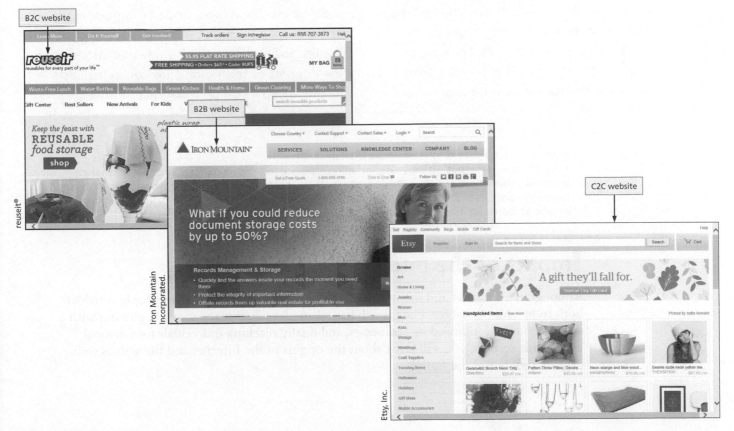

Figure 1-11 E-commerce involves all business transactions that use the Internet.

when a consumer uses the Internet to interact with an online business, such as an individual purchasing environmentally friendly items on Reuseit. One business using the Internet to purchase goods and services or complete other transactions with another business is an example of **business-to-business (B2B)** e-commerce. One example of B2B is Iron Mountain, which provides document and file storage, among other services, to other businesses. An organization might also use the Internet for **business-to-employee (B2E)** functions, such as connecting its employees to its human resources system. **Consumer-to-consumer (C2C)** occurs when a consumer uses the Internet to conduct business with another consumer. A collector purchasing a collectible item from another individual through an auction website, or purchasing a handmade item directly from the artisan on Etsy, are examples of C2C e-business activity. B2B transactions make up the majority of e-business dollars spent.

@ISSUE

The Dark Side of the Internet

The qualities that make the Internet and the web so powerful also make them vulnerable to misuse. Because anyone can publish webpages or web content, even ideas, videos, photos, and other content that may be illegitimate, biased, or unfounded can garner a huge audience.

The vast informational resources of the web also include adult-oriented websites and hate websites. Adults and children may stumble across them or other webpages with objectionable material. The ease of communicating over the Internet also makes it easy for destructive computer programs

to spread quickly and widely. The anonymity provided by the Internet makes it possible for criminals to steal credit card numbers, break into computers, engage in identity theft, or frighten others by **cyberstalking**, which is threatening or harassing people over the Internet.

In addition, there are health concerns with using the Internet, including physical problems such as vision, neck, or fingers/hands due to poor posture, or prolonged use without breaks. Societal concerns include addictions to the Internet or technology devices, as well as a negative impact on personal relationships.

Q&A   How can I keep safe while using the Internet?
Using the Internet is not without risks, including exposure to computer viruses, accidentally sharing personal information, and more. Be aware that others could share anything you type and any video or photo you post, even if you consider the exchange to be private. For more information, use a search engine to search for *Internet safety tips*.

Impact of the Internet

Although the Internet and the web are evolving continually, millions of people consider both to be indispensable. The growth has taken place over many years, beginning with the government, followed by businesses, and finally reaching individuals for personal use. In this section, you will learn about the origins of the Internet and the web as well as explore trends and the future.

Origins in ARPANET

The Internet traces its origins to a collaboration among academia, industry, and government that started in the early 1960s. At that time, computers had existed for only a few years, and were not available to the general public. Roughly 10,000 computers existed, many of which were mainframes used by the U.S. government to perform specific work for government agencies, such as the Census Bureau and the Pentagon.

Government officials were concerned that the United States was falling behind its Cold War competitors in the realm of science and technology, and worried that existing computer systems were vulnerable to nuclear attack. The government, including those involved in security and defense, decided that it was important to connect computers to distribute computing power and data to more than one location. Decentralizing computing resources would make them less vulnerable to attack.

To achieve these goals, the government tasked the Department of Defense (DoD) with creating the **Advanced Research Projects Agency (ARPA)**. In 1962, J.C.R. Licklider became the head of ARPA's computer and information processing research efforts. Licklider wrote a series of memos outlining his vision of a Galactic Network of interconnected computers, wherein users could share data and resources from around the world. His memos were the first published references to the idea of the Internet.

In the early 1960s, the phone system's vast network of cabling was the only available method of connecting two or more remote computers and exchanging data. Phone systems work by using a technology known as circuit switching. **Circuit switching** allows a caller to dial a number to establish and maintain a private circuit across the wires. One negative aspect of circuit switching is that, while a connection exists between two computers, no other resource can move data through the circuit, even while no data is travelling through the connection.

FACTS @HAND

The **Public Switched Telephone Network (PSTN)** used to be the main way all users connected to the Internet. PSTN still uses high-speed phone access, despite developments in mobile and broadband systems. Although initially built to handle voice communications, the phone network also is an integral part of computer communications. Data, instructions, and information can travel over the phone network over dial-up lines or dedicated lines. No longer a popular connectivity method because of its low bandwidth, PSTN remains in use in remote locations where other connection methods are not available.

In 1961, Leonard Kleinrock, a scholar at the University of California, Los Angeles (UCLA), wrote his doctoral dissertation and outlined the idea of data networking and packet switching. **Packet switching** involves separating data from a sending computer or device into small units known as **packets**, sending each packet independently over cables, and then reassembling the packets on the receiving computer or device. Each packet even can follow different routes to its destination. According to Kleinrock, packet switching would make the network more robust and less vulnerable to attack because the data would move in individual packets over different routes, rather than over a single dedicated connection. Figure 1-12 compares packet and circuit switching.

Circuit switching versus packet switching

Aspect	Circuit Switching	Packet Switching
Call setup	Required	Not required
Cost	Minimal; cost is per call	Cost is per packet
Bandwidth	Static between two computers; can cause wasted bandwidth	Dynamic; uses different paths to transfer packets separately
Congestion	Only at setup; once connection is established, data flows freely	Can occur on every packet because each is trying to find a separate path

Figure 1-12 Comparison of circuit and packet switching.

In 1966, ARPA, as part of the DoD, funded a new network of computers, called **ARPANET**, based on a plan developed by Lawrence G. Roberts at ARPA. Because of Kleinrock's research, the team chose the computer at UCLA to be the first computer on ARPANET. The team then selected the computer at the Stanford Research Institute (SRI) in Menlo Park, California, headed by Douglas Engelbart, as the second. Next, the government awarded a contract to Bolt Beranek and Newman (BBN), a company in Cambridge, Massachusetts, to create the programming, design, and hardware for the refrigerator-sized switches called IMPs (Interface Message Processors) to send the packets of data.

On September 2, 1969, representatives from BBN delivered the first IMP to the UCLA lab. About 20 people from the government, the phone company, and the university watched as a gray cable connected the mainframe to the IMP, and the packets flowed perfectly. Kleinrock said later, "We didn't think of this as a key event in any historical sense. We didn't even have a camera."

On October 29 of the same year, the second IMP arrived at SRI. At UCLA, a student named Charley Kline began to log on, as Kleinrock watched. Kline typed the letters, L-O-G — and then the new network crashed. After a quick fix, the first packets flowed from computer to computer.

By December 1969, the University of California Santa Barbara and the University of Utah joined the ARPANET network, making these four university connections the foundation of the global network known today as the Internet.

Growth and Development of ARPANET

As quickly as BBN could create the necessary hardware, more computers, or hosts, connected to ARPANET. Thirteen research centers were part of ARPANET by the end of 1970. It grew steadily during the next 15 years, roughly doubling in size every year. The first international connections were to England and Norway in 1973. Other nations came online in the late 1980s and early 1990s.

During those early years, programmers had to make constant changes to programs and hosts on the new network because no common communications protocol was in use. In 1972, Robert Kahn and Vinton Cerf developed two new protocols for ARPANET, TCP and IP, which solved these and other problems. **Transmission Control Protocol (TCP)** provided flow control over the network and error checking for lost packets. **Internet Protocol (IP)** addressed and sent the packets. In 1983, DARPA (Defense

Advanced Research Projects Agency) mandated the use of this suite of communications protocols, referred to as TCP/IP. Since then, every computer and device connected to the Internet has used TCP/IP to communicate.

Originally, researchers used ARPANET to log in to and use the computing power of remote computers and to share files. Soon the network's main use became interpersonal communication. In 1971, the first live computer-to-computer chat took place between Stanford University in California and BBN in Massachusetts. Late in 1971, Ray Tomlinson, a scientist at BBN, developed the first email program that could send and receive messages to and from remote computers. Email instantly became popular among researchers because it allowed them to collaborate on the continual development of ARPANET. By 1973, email constituted 75 percent of the data traffic over ARPANET.

1975 brought the first mailing list, titled SF-Lovers, for science fiction fans among the ARPA community. A **mailing list** allows participants to send a single message to the list, which then automatically routes the message to every other participant. Originally, ARPA tried to shut down mailing lists and other nonessential uses of the Internet, but later allowed them as they were a good test of predicting and managing Internet traffic and use.

Beyond Research, to the Public

Several factors led to the burgeoning growth of the new network. The academic community established networks, such as Usenet (1979) and BITNET (1981), which were open to all members of the academic community, not just the computer science researchers involved in the Internet. With the introduction of the Apple II, Macintosh, and IBM PC computers, many more members of the general public began to use computers daily. Computer use mostly was for business, although home personal computers started becoming popular. Most people had no access to the Internet until 1979, when CompuServe first offered a subscription service for sending email. The following year, CompuServe also made real-time chat available to subscribers.

In 1985, the National Science Foundation (NSF) established a new network called NSFNet. NSFNet connected five regional supercomputer centers at Princeton University; University of Pittsburgh; University of California, San Diego; University of Illinois; and Cornell University using high-speed connections. In 1987, then-Senator Al Gore called for a national computer network for research. Gore sponsored a bill to fund research to enhance the speed of the Internet **backbone**, the main long-distance lines and the hardware that connect computers to the Internet. By 1990, the success of the NSFNet led to the shutdown of ARPANET. NSFNet became the main network linking universities and research facilities. The military portion of ARPANET became a separate network called MILNET, which is now known as NIPRNET (Nonsecure Internet Protocol Router Network). When NSFNet opened to the entire academic community, the number of universities, K–12 schools, and community colleges connected to the Internet increased significantly.

The U.S. Congress overturned a ban on commercial activity on NSFNet in 1992. From that point, commercial activity over the network exploded. In 1995, the NSF moved the connections from the original NSFNet backbone to a commercial Internet backbone supported by commercial network providers, including MCI and AT&T. In the mid-1990s it became common to use English-language names, such as www.cengage.com, to identify computer hosts, rather than the long series of numbers originally used. Figure 1-13 provides a timeline of Internet milestones.

History of the Internet

Date	Milestone
1961	Leonard Kleinrock outlined the idea of data networking and packet switching.
1962	J.C.R. Licklider, head of ARPA, published memos that were the first references to the Internet.
1966	ARPA funded a new network of computers, called ARPANET, and BBN to create IMPs to send data.
1969	BBN delivered two IMPs to the UCLA lab.
1970	Thirteen research centers were part of ARPANET.
1971	The first live computer-to-computer chat took place between Stanford University and BBN.
1971	Ray Tomlinson developed the first email program.
1972	Robert Kahn and Vinton Cerf developed the TCP and IP protocols.
1973	The first international connections made England and Norway.
1973	Email constituted 75 percent of the data traffic over ARPANET.
1975	Development of the first mailing list, SF-Lovers.
1979	The Usenet network was established.
1979	CompuServe first offered a subscription service for sending electronic mail.
1981	The BITNET network was established.
1983	DARPA mandated the use of TCP/IP.
1985	The NSF established a new network called NSFNet.
1987	Al Gore sponsored a bill to fund research to enhance the speed of the Internet backbone.
1990	NSFNet became the main network linking universities and research facilities.
1990	The military portion of ARPANET became a separate network called MILNET.
1992	Congress overturned a ban on commercial activity on NSFNet.
1995	The NSF moved to a commercial Internet backbone supported by commercial network providers.

© Cengage Learning®

Figure 1-13 Timeline of Internet developments.

The Beginnings and Rise of the Web

Two additional events that occurred in the early 1990s were pivotal in the commercial explosion of the Internet. Paul Lindner and Mark McCahill, graduate students at the University of Minnesota, invented a new protocol to form a hierarchical directory-based system to deliver information across the Internet. They named the system **Gopher** after the university's mascot. For the first time, users could navigate easily through online text resources by using directory links to open folders and access files stored in those folders

(Figure 1-14). Many universities quickly followed suit and created Gopher systems to catalog their online resources. Because Gopher created an index of the documents on the server, it was easy to extend Gopher's capabilities to enable searching using an early search engine.

Figure 1-14 Gopher, a directory-based system, made it easier to find documents on servers connected to the Internet.

During that same period, Tim Berners-Lee, who was working at CERN in Switzerland, envisioned the use of hyperlinks to make connections between related ideas in separate documents. **Hypertext**, which is a system of hyperlinks that allows users to tap or click on a word to jump to another location within the same file, was already in use. Hypertext also allowed users to link to different files in the same location, but only when an index of the links was kept in a central database. Frustrated with these limitations, Berners-Lee visualized a system in which all of the various projects at CERN could cross-reference each other easily. He wrote a proposal outlining his vision, suggesting that hyperlinked resources should not be restricted to text, but could include graphics, video, or other document elements.

With the help of his CERN colleague Robert Cailliau, Berners-Lee created three technologies to make his ideas about hyperlinked documents a reality. First, he created HTML, used to create documents that can include text, graphics, and links. Berners-Lee then created a special software program to read and display HTML documents, the first browser known as WorldWideWeb (spelled with no spaces). Finally, because document links had to refer to the specific server that stored the linked documents, Berners-Lee devised a web addressing system and **Hypertext Transfer Protocol (HTTP)**, a protocol that defines how HTML documents transmit to a browser. Figure 1-15 shows an early version of Berners-Lee's WorldWideWeb browser and HTML documents.

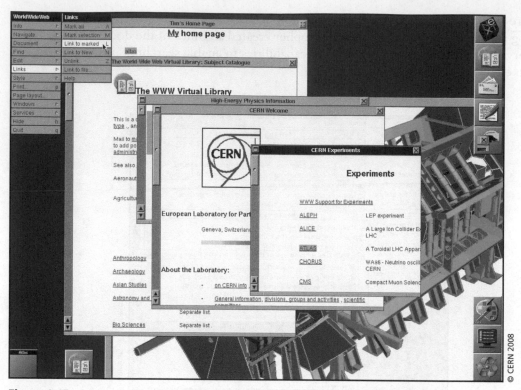

© CERN 2008

Figure 1-15   Berners-Lee's original WorldWideWeb browser and HTML documents.

Programmers began developing other browsers, but the one most widely used at universities and colleges was Mosaic™. Marc Andreessen and Eric Bina, two University of Illinois graduate students employed at the university's National Center for Supercomputing Applications (NCSA), created the Mosaic browser in March 1993. Mosaic was easy to install and use, and free to university faculty and students, so it instantly became popular.

The next year, with businesses clamoring for a browser to use, Andreessen broke ties with the University of Illinois, which claimed ownership of the Mosaic browser. He joined with Silicon Valley entrepreneur Jim Clark to found a new company, Netscape Communications. During the summer of 1994, the company created the first commercial browser, called Netscape Navigator.

By 1994, the Internet was growing exponentially, largely because of the new World Wide Web. Commercial and individual websites proliferated, radio stations began broadcasting over the Internet, and companies posted the first banner ads and sent the first bulk advertising by email, now called **spam**. By the end of 1994, the web had approximately 10 million users. Today, there are billions of worldwide Internet users with access to the web. Figure 1-16 illustrates highlights in the development of the web.

History of the WorldWideWeb

Date	Milestone
1991	Paul Lindner and Mark McCahill invented the Gopher protocol, which formed a hierarchical directory-based system to deliver information across the Internet.
1990	Tim Berners-Lee and Robert Cailliau established the use of hyperlinks and hypertext, and developed HTML and HTTP.
1991	Berners-Lee created the first browser, known as WorldWideWeb.
1993	Marc Andreessen and Eric Bina created the Mosaic browser.
1994	Andreessen and Jim Clark's Netscape Communications created the first commercial browser, Netscape Navigator.
1994	Companies posted the first banner ads and sent the first spam email, now called spam.
1994	The web had approximately 10 million users.
1995	Microsoft released its Internet Explorer browser for free.

© Cengage Learning®

Figure 1-16   Timeline of early web milestones.

FACTS @HAND

Microsoft released its Internet Explorer browser for free in 1995, launching what became known as the Browser War between Microsoft and Netscape. Microsoft had an edge because it was able to integrate its browser using its Windows operating system. When Netscape lost its market share to Microsoft, Netscape then made its code open-source and it became the foundation of Mozilla Firefox. To learn more, use a search engine to search for *browser wars*.

Q&A

What is Internet2?
Internet2 is a major cooperative initiative among academia, industry, and government agencies to increase the Internet's capabilities and solve some of its challenges. The nonprofit initiative has more than 300 university, corporate, government, and international members and sponsors devoted to developing and using new and emerging network technologies that facilitate research and education.

Connecting to the Internet

To enjoy all the benefits that the Internet and the web have to offer, individuals and businesses must first connect their computers and devices to the Internet. College and university students generally have access to the Internet through campus networks, computer labs, and wireless capabilities. Businesses provide their employees with connected computers and devices so that they can accomplish the tasks that have become essential to their jobs, including text, email, web conferencing, and file sharing.

Libraries, schools, businesses, and other organizations typically connect their computers and devices into a **local area network (LAN)**. A LAN connects computers using cables or wireless capabilities within a building or campus so users can share data and resources, such as printers. When an organization connects its LAN directly to the Internet, all of the computers and devices on the LAN have access to the Internet. Users can connect to the wireless Internet connections provided at airports, train stations, hotels, coffee shops, bookstores, and other businesses.

Internet Service Providers (ISPs)

An **Internet service provider (ISP)** is a business that has a permanent Internet connection and provides temporary Internet connections to individuals and companies. ISP service plans depend on speed, bandwidth, and other services, such as email, instant messaging, gaming, and online storage. A **mobile service provider,** sometimes called a wireless data provider, offers wireless Internet access to computers and mobile devices that have wireless capabilities.

ISPs are classified either as regional or national:

- A **regional ISP**, such as Windstream (Figure 1-17), provides Internet access for customers (individuals or businesses) in a specific geographic area.

- A **national ISP** provides Internet access in most major cities and towns nationwide. National ISPs may offer more services and generally have larger technical support staffs than regional ISPs. An example of a national ISP is EarthLink (Figure 1-18).

Figure 1-17 A regional ISP provides Internet access for homes and businesses in a specific geographical area.

Figure 1-18 A national ISP provides Internet access for homes and businesses across the United States.

A cable company, such as Verizon, can be an ISP and/or mobile service provider, as well as provide cable television and home phone access. Negotiating one price for all of those services can save you money and hassle, but can provide limited options if you are tied into one provider for all three because you can only choose from within the plans for each service offered by that provider.

An individual or a business must weigh several considerations when choosing an ISP, including the following:

- The speed or bandwidth of the connection
- The availability of wireless or mobile data service
- The type of connection and cost of service
- The availability of customer service and technical support

The speed of an Internet connection depends on **bandwidth**, which is the capacity of the communications channel. The speed at which data travels from one device to another is the **transfer rate**. Transfer rates measure the number of bits the line can transmit in one second (expressed as **bits per second**, or **Bps**). Transfer rates range from thousands of bits per second (**kilobits per second** or **KBps**) to millions of bits per second (**megabits per second** or **MBps**), and even billions of bits per second (**gigabits per second**, or **GBps**). A faster transfer rate translates into more expensive Internet access. Transfer rate has a direct impact on the user's experience with a website.

Q&A

What is a bit?
A **bit**, short for binary digit, is the smallest unit of electronic data. Bits are either the digit one (1) or zero (0). Thousands of bits flow each second, even over the slowest connection.

You also need to consider how you will physically connect your computer and other devices to the Internet, such as through wireless, DSL, or cable. Each Internet connection method has advantages and disadvantages related to speed, cost, features, and convenience.

Q&A

What do 3G and 4G mean?
Standards for mobile communications, including voice, mobile Internet access, video calls, and mobile TV, are classified by generation. **3G**, the third generation, provides mobile broadband access to devices such as laptop computers and smartphones. 3G devices support speech and data services, as well as data rates of at least 200 KBps (kilobits per second). **4G** systems improve on 3G standards by supporting services such as gaming and streamed multimedia.

Customer service and technical support offered by an ISP are always important factors and should be available 24 hours a day, 7 days a week.

Connection Methods

Users access the Internet and web using a variety of means. In the earliest days of the web, the most common way to access the Internet was using a dial-up phone line. Today, individuals and organizations use faster access methods, including digital dedicated lines, cable broadband, as well as wireless and cellular transmissions. Other connection methods include satellite, microwave, and wireless connections. In the following sections, you will learn about different ways to connect to the Internet.

Q&A

What is broadband?
The term, **broadband**, defines high-speed data transmissions over a communication channel that can transmit multiple signals at one time. ISDN, ADSL, and CATV Internet access are all examples of broadband Internet access.

CABLE Cable television (CATV) lines enable home or business users to connect to the Internet over the same coaxial cable that delivers television transmissions (Figure 1-19). Data can travel very rapidly through a cable modem connected to a CATV line. Then, using a splitter, the line from the cable company connects to both the television and computer. Cable Internet connections require a coaxial cable, a **line splitter** that divides the television signals from the data signals, a cable modem, and a network expansion card inside the computer. A **cable modem** is a particular type of modem used for high-speed cable connections.

Figure 1-19 Cable Internet access requires a line spli\er and cable modem.

©iStockphoto.com/tiridifilm; © image100/Alamy; © Erik S. Lesser/Landov; © iStockphoto/Stephen Krow; © Pablo Eder/Shutterstock.com; © Cengage Learning

Q&A | **What is Bluetooth?**
Bluetooth is a popular, short-range wireless connection that uses radio frequency to transmit data between two electronic devices, such as a smartphone and an earpiece.

Q&A | **What is a dial-up line?**
A **dial-up line** is a temporary connection that uses analog phone lines. Because of its slow access speed, dial-up access is the least popular Internet access method, and today is used only in remote areas where cable and other methods are not available. Similar to using the phone to make a call, a **modem** at the sending end dials the phone number of a modem at the receiving end. When the modem at the receiving end answers the call, it establishes a connection enabling data to transmit.

DIGITAL DEDICATED LINES Unlike a dial-up line in which the connection is reestablished each time it is used, a **dedicated line** is a constant connection between two communications devices that uses the local phone network. This permanent connection provides a high-quality connection suited for viewing or listening to **streaming media** — video or sound that downloads to a computer continuously to be watched or listened to in real time, such as watching TV programs, web conferencing, and gaming. Businesses sometimes use dedicated lines to connect geographically distant offices. Three popular types of digital dedicated lines are Integrated Services Digital Network (ISDN) lines, digital subscriber lines (DSL), and T-carrier lines.

Integrated Services Digital Network (ISDN) is a set of standards for digital transmission of data over standard copper phone lines. With ISDN, the same phone line that could carry only one computer signal now can carry three or more signals at once, through the same line, using a technique called **multiplexing**. Multiplexing allows for more data to transmit at the same time over the same line.

Digital subscriber line (DSL) is another digital line alternative for the small business or home user.

- A DSL transmits at fast speeds on existing standard copper phone wiring. Some of the DSL installations can provide a dial tone, so you can use the line for both voice and data.

- An **asymmetrical digital subscriber line (ADSL)** is a type of DSL that supports faster transmissions when receiving data than when sending data. ADSL is ideal for Internet access because users generally download more data from the Internet than they upload.

A **T-carrier line** is any of several types of digital lines that carry multiple signals over a single communications line. Whereas a standard dial-up phone line carries only one signal, digital T-carrier lines use multiplexing so that multiple signals can share the phone line. T-carrier lines provide extremely fast data transfer rates.

- The most popular T-carrier line is the **T-1 line**. Businesses often use T-1 lines to connect to the Internet.

- A **fractional T-1 line** is a less-expensive, slower connection option for home owners and small businesses. Instead of a single owner, multiple users share a fractional T-1.

A **T-3 line** is equal in speed to 28 T-1 lines. T-3 lines are the most expensive connection method. Main users of T-3 lines include large companies, phone companies, and service providers connecting to the Internet backbone.

WIRELESS FIDELITY People not physically connected to a network can use their computer or mobile device to access the Internet and web using **mobile wireless** technologies, which include radio signals, **wireless fidelity (Wi-Fi)** technologies, cellular phones, and wireless providers' broadband networks. Wi-Fi is a family of wireless networking standards that uses radio waves to allow a computer to communicate with other computers on a local area network or the Internet. A Wi-Fi network may be password protected or open to the public. A **hotspot** is a specific geographic location in which a wireless access point provides public Internet access. Hotspots can be found in hotels, airports, restaurants, coffee shops, convention centers, and other venues where people with notebook computers or handheld wireless devices are likely to need Internet access. A hotspot typically covers a 100-foot range from the wireless access point, although some may provide a greater range. A **wireless access point** (Figure 1-20) is a hardware device with an antenna that is connected to a wired network and is used to send and receive radio waves to and from notebook computers or other wireless devices. To connect to a wireless access point in a hotspot, a computer or device must be enabled with wireless capability, or have a Wi-Fi card or other wireless connectivity technology. The computer or device searches for a hotspot, and, if it finds one, connects to the Internet.

Figure 1-20 Wireless access point.

Satellite Internet access comes in two varieties: one-way and two-way (Figure 1-21). One-way satellite access uses the satellite for downloading data, and uses a slow, regular phone line and modem for uploading data. A better alternative is two-way satellite access, which uses the faster satellite connection for both uploading and downloading data. Satellite Internet access can be expensive both in monthly access fees and equipment costs, but satellite access may be the only alternative in rural areas.

communications satellite

earth-based station

earth-based station

© Cengage Learning®; © Mmaxer / Shutterstock.com; © Mmaxer / Shutterstock.com; © SSSCCC / Shutterstock.com

Figure 1-21 Communications satellites are placed about 22,300 miles above the Earth's equator.

Q&A

What is the difference between Wi-Fi and cellular?

A smartphone and some other computers and mobile devices may offer both Wi-Fi and cellular connection capabilities. Both enable a user to connect to the Internet without wires. To use a Wi-Fi connection, a computer or device must connect to a wireless router. The user must be within range of the router, and may require a password for access to the Wi-Fi connection. Users without immediate Wi-Fi access can rely on cellular coverage, which does not require access to a router. To learn more about how ISPs monitor cellular and Wi-Fi data charges, search the Internet for *ISP cellular versus Wi-Fi data charges*.

Like other types of Internet connections, digital satellite has some disadvantages. Snow, rain, wind, or even clouds may affect the clarity of the signal. Furthermore, the lengthy distance to the orbiting satellites can create a significant lag in the response time. The lag is not noticeable while browsing webpages; but for communications such as instant messaging or chat, which take place simultaneously, or in **real time**, the lag may be noticeable.

Chapter Review

The Internet is a worldwide network of networks that individuals, institutions, and businesses use to communicate, share information, and conduct business transactions. Using the Internet enables people to acquire useful information; send and receive email and text messages; exchange thoughts, photos, files, and links with others using social media; and take advantage of the convenience e-commerce allows them when shopping and paying for items. Businesses conduct business transactions with their customers, vendors, and employees over the Internet, and use social media to build a community and share information.

The World Wide Web, also known as the web, is a subset of the Internet that supports webpages, which can include text, graphics, animation, sound, or video. A website is a collection of related webpages. Webpages connect to each other through hyperlinks, which enable a user to move from one webpage to another, on the same or another website. A browser allows users to access and view webpages, while a search tool allows users to find specific web-based resources.

The Internet has its roots in ARPANET, a research and defense initiative of the U.S. government in collaboration with technology firms and universities. In 1990, NSFNet superseded ARPANET as the main government network linking universities and research facilities. The U.S. Congress opened the Internet to commercial use in 1992. Tim Berners-Lee's development of the Web in 1991 caused Internet usage to explode. Berners-Lee developed the use of hyperlinks between different files, HTML to create web documents, the addressing scheme, and the original WorldWideWeb browser. In 1994, the first commercial web browser allowed businesses and individuals to discover the possibilities available online, and the use of the Internet expanded rapidly.

Individuals and businesses use cable broadband, phone lines, or wireless connections to access the Internet through a wide array of methods with varying speeds and costs.

TERMS TO KNOW

After reading this chapter, you should know each of these key terms.

3G (21)
4G (21)
Advanced Research Projects Agency (ARPA) (13)
app (8)
ARPANET (14)
asymmetrical digital subscriber line (ADSL) (23)
backbone (15)
bandwidth (21)
bit (21)
bits per second (Bps) (21)
blog (4)
blogging (4)
Bluetooth (22)
broadband (21)
browser (6)
browsing the web (8)
business-to-business (B2B) (12)
business-to-consumer (B2C) (11)
business-to-employee (B2E) (12)
cable modem (22)
cable television (CATV) line (22)
cascading style sheet (CSS) (6)
circuit switching (13)
cloud computing (10)
consumer-to-consumer (C2C) (12)
cyberstalking (12)
dedicated line (22)
dial-up line (22)
digital subscriber line (DSL) (23)
download (10)
e-business (11)
e-commerce (11)
email (9)
email program (9)
Extensible Hypertext Markup Language (XHTML) (6)
Extensible Markup Language (XML) (6)
File Transfer Protocol (FTP) (10)
fractional T-1 line (23)
gigabits per second (GBps) (21)
Gopher (16)
host (2)
hotspot (23)
HTML tags (5)
hyperlink (7)
hypertext (17)
Hypertext Markup Language (HTML) (5)
Hypertext Transfer Protocol (HTTP) (17)
Integrated Services Digital Network (ISDN) (22)
Internet (2)
Internet Protocol (IP) (14)
Internet service provider (ISP) (20)
Internet2 (19)
kilobits per second (KBps) (21)

line splitter (22)
link (7)
local area network (LAN) (19)
mailing list (15)
markup language (5)
megabits per second (MBps) (21)
microblogging (4)
mobile service provider (20)
mobile wireless (23)
modem (22)
multiplexing (22)
national ISP (20)
online (2)
packet switching (13)
packets (13)
protocol (2)
Public Switched Telephone Network (PSTN) (13)
publish (6)
real time (25)
regional ISP (20)
responsive web design (RWD) (7)
satellite Internet access (24)
script (8)
scripting language (8)
search tool (8)
server (10)
spam (18)
streaming media (22)
surfing the web (8)
T-1 line (23)
T-3 line (23)
T-carrier line (23)
transfer rate (21)
Transmission Control Protocol (TCP) (14)
Transmission Control Protocol/Internet Protocol (TCP/IP) (2)
upload (10)
video blogging (4)
video calling (11)
video sharing (4)
virtual private network (VPN) (11)
web (5)
Web 2.0 (8)
web authoring software (6)
web browser (6)
web conferencing (11)
web server (6)
webpages (5)
website (5)
wireless access point (23)
wireless fidelity (Wi-Fi) (23)
World Wide Web (5)
World Wide Web Consortium (W3C) (6)

Complete the Test Your Knowledge exercises to solidify what you have learned in the chapter.

True or False

Mark T for True and F for False. (Answers are found on page numbers in parentheses.)

___ 1. The Internet is an interconnected network of computers and mobile devices. (2)

___ 2. Every computer or device connected to the Internet uses the Transmission Control Protocol/Internet Protocol (TCP/IP). (2)

___ 3. YouTube and Vimeo are examples of microblogging websites. (4)

___ 4. Cascading style sheets are documents that specify the layout of a webpage. (6)

___ 5. A server is a computer on a network used to store files. (10)

___ 6. The term, e-commerce, specifically refers to buying and selling goods over the Internet. (11)

___ 7. The person who first outlined the idea of packet switching was J.C.R. Licklider. (13)

___ 8. Tim Berners-Lee is credited with creating HTML and the first browser. (17)

___ 9. An ISP is a network that connects computers within a building or campus. (19)

___10. A dedicated line is a constant connection between two communications devices. (22)

Multiple Choice

Select the best answer. (Answers are found on page numbers in parentheses.)

1. A(n) _____ is a computer directly connected to the Internet. (2)
    a. ISP
    b. TCP/IP
    c. host
    d. server

2. A(n) _____ is a standard or set of rules that computer network devices follow when transmitting and receiving data. (2)
    a. protocol
    b. network
    c. LAN
    d. cascading style sheet

3. When you explore the web by tapping or clicking links to move between webpages, you are _____ the web. (8)
    a. browsing
    b. surfing
    c. linking
    d. Both A and B are true

4. FTP is used for _____. (10)

   a. email

   b. web conferencing

   c. uploading and downloading files

   d. All of the above

5. Remote data access, storage, software access, and collaboration techniques are all aspects of _____ computing. (10)

   a. web

   b. cloud

   c. virtual

   d. wireless

6. The B2B e-business model includes _____. (12)

   a. customers interacting with an online business

   b. firms conducting business online with other firms and businesses

   c. businesses staying in contact with consultants

   d. businesses connecting with their employees

7. _____ switching involves separating data from a sending computer or device into small units. (13)

   a. Packet

   b. Circuit

   c. Cable

   d. Wi-Fi

8. The main long-distance lines and the hardware that connect computers to the Internet are known as the Internet _____. (15)

   a. broadband

   b. network

   c. hotspot

   d. backbone

9. _____ is a protocol that defines how HTML documents transmit to a browser. (17)

   a. ISP

   b. HTTP

   c. ADSL

   d. XML

10. _____ refers to the capacity of a communications channel. (21)

    a. Bps

    b. Bandwidth

    c. Broadband

    d. Backbone

Investigate current Internet developments with the Trends exercises.

Write a brief essay about each of the following trends, using the web as your research tool. For each trend, identify at least one webpage URL used as a research source. Be prepared to discuss your findings in class.

1 | Responsive Web Design

Responsive web design (RWD) strategies optimize websites to be viewable on multiple device types and screen sizes. Research guidelines and techniques for responsive web design. Submit your findings in the format requested by your instructor.

2 | HTML

Research the updates to each version of HTML, starting with the original version and including major releases up to HTML 4.01. List two characteristics that differentiate each version, and find out (or guess) why the changes were made. List three expected changes for HTML 5. Submit your findings in the format requested by your instructor.

Challenge your perspective of Internet technology with the @Issue exercises.

Write a brief essay in response to the following issues, using the web as your research tool. For each issue, identify at least one webpage URL used as a research source. Be prepared to discuss your findings in class.

1 | Impact on Lifestyle

With developments in technology such as smartphones, people are able to stay connected constantly. Whether by phone calls, text messages, alerts from websites about new content, or social networking websites such as Facebook and Twitter, technology provides many distractions. How do these developments enhance daily life? How have they changed daily life from 5 or 10 years ago? What is a negative impact? Discuss the impact of technology on your lifestyle and that of those around you.

2 | Social Networking

Summarize the use of social networking tools among your peers.

1. Survey five students who have accounts with at least one social networking website (Facebook, Twitter, LinkedIn, or other websites).

2. Ask them to list the social networking websites they use.

3. Ask them the frequency with which they interact with each website: daily, weekly, or multiple times per day.

4. Ask them to list the purposes for which they use each website:

   a. To keep in touch with friends and family who are far away

   b. To post pictures, videos, and links

   c. To send email

   d. To chat or send instant messages

   e. To play games

   f. To post information about their thoughts, locations, or activities

   g. Other activities

5. Ask them what concerns they have about privacy, and what measures they take to protect themselves.

6. Ask them how they access the websites: smartphone, tablet, personal laptop, or school or library computers. Are there restrictions in their school or library computer labs regarding access to these websites?

7. Ask them whether their overall experiences have been positive or negative. If their experiences have been negative, what specific issues have come out of their social networking activities?

HANDS ON

Use the web to obtain more information about the concepts and skills in the chapter with the Hands On exercises.

1 | Connection Speeds

1. Use a search engine to search for connection speed tests. Choose one service offered by an ISP, such as Verizon.

2. Try the bandwidth tests and record the results. Write down what type of device you are using (laptop, smartphone, or tablet). If possible, try the bandwidth test on multiple devices connected to the same network.

3. Summarize the results of the tests and explain whether the connection speeds are considered slow, average, or fast, according to the bandwidth speed test websites.

4. At the direction of your instructor, repeat the tests at different times of the day over several days. Write a brief paragraph explaining any variation in connection speeds among the different days and times of day. Submit your findings in the format requested by your instructor.

2 | ISPs

1. Use a search engine to search for ISPs in your city or area code.

2. List four ISPs for your area that offer dedicated or high-speed connections. List one specializing in being a low-cost provider. For each provider, list which services they offer: phone, Internet, cable, and mobile. Identify which one has the best costs and most services.

3. Use a search engine to search for national ISPs that service your city or area code.

4. List four national ISPs for your area that offer dedicated or high-speed connections. For each provider, list which services they offer: phone, Internet, cable, and mobile. Identify which one has the best costs and most services.

5. Submit your findings in the format requested by your instructor.

Work collaboratively to reinforce the concepts and skills in the chapter with the Team Approach exercises.

1 | Internet History

1. Work as a team with three to four classmates. Each team member should research one or more of the technologies listed below and list at least three facts about each.

2. Research several of the following elements of the Internet and find its origin and purpose. Is it still used today? How?

   a. Usenet

   b. LISTSERV

   c. Firewalls

   d. IRC

   e. VoIP

   f. modem

3. Share your findings with your team. Discuss which technologies you were familiar with, and which you found interesting or learned new information about. Compile your results and submit in the format requested by your instructor.

2 | E-Commerce

1. Work as a team with three to four classmates.

2. As a team, decide which e-commerce business model you would like to learn more about: B2C, B2B, C2C, or B2E.

3. Answer the following questions about the e-commerce business model you chose.

   a. Who are the parties involved?

   b. List three possible applications. Have you used any of them? What were your experiences?

   c. Find four specific examples of websites using the business model.

4. Compile your results and submit in the format requested by your instructor.

2 | Browsing the Web

Introduction

Internet users rely on the web for access to a wealth of information, entertainment, and other resources. Chapter 1 introduced you to the basics of the web: websites, webpages, web servers, and browsers. In this chapter, you will explore websites and become familiar with the characteristics of webpages. You will learn about the role that IP addresses, domain names, and URLs play in accessing webpages stored on web servers around the world. You also will learn how to connect to the Internet or to a network, use a browser, and how to change browser options. Finally, you will discover the risks of browsing the web and safeguards you can employ to protect against those risks.

Objectives

After completing this chapter, you will be able to:

1. Describe a website, common webpage characteristics, and web servers

2. Explain the role IP addresses, domain names, and URLs play in locating webpages

3. Connect to the Internet or a network

4. Start a browser and view webpages

5. Visit webpages using browser shortcuts

6. Save online information for later use

7. Change browser options

8. Discuss the risks and safeguards related to using the web

Websites, Webpages, and Web Servers

The web consists of millions of websites and billions of webpages. Estimating the number of websites and webpages is impossible because of the dynamic nature of the web. Existing webpages continually add new pages and remove old webpages. New websites arise constantly. Websites create custom, on-demand webpages based on user interaction. In this section, you will learn about the types of webpages, the general characteristics of a webpage, and the role web servers play in making these websites and pages available to people around the world.

Websites

The number of webpages at a website varies based on the website's purpose as well as the content and services it provides. Websites can consist of a single webpage or thousands of pages. Businesses use websites to market and sell their products and services; to promote their standing in a specific industry; and to communicate with customers, business partners, and other stakeholders. Organizations of all types, from local youth sports programs to international charities, use websites to share information about ongoing activities, promote their programs, and solicit contributions. Personal websites might include content that highlights individual or family activities or interests, such as travel, cooking, sports, or genealogy research.

A **home page** is the primary webpage at a website. A personal website, for example, might consist of a single home page containing relevant information about an individual or a family. Alternatively, the website might also include additional webpages containing photos, links to blogs or social media, or other content. Visitors move among the webpages using links and navigation tools.

The home page of a news website, such as www.cnn.com, offers constantly evolving content based on the latest developments around the world, and sometimes provides different content based on a user's location or past browsing history. To provide a variety of updated content, a news home page uses features such as tabs so users can find information on more specific topics, and slide shows or carousels, which change content every few seconds (Figure 2-1).

slide show

Figure 2-1 A news website uses tabs and slide shows to make it easy for users to find the content they are looking for.

Typically, the website for a business or organization, such as American Red Cross, includes multiple webpages: a home page presents general, introductory information or news and provides links to a variety of related subsidiary webpages containing information about products and services, employment opportunities, the business or organization's history, contact information, and so forth (Figure 2-2). Most business or organizational websites include links to social media and networking websites that visitors can follow, visit, or share content.

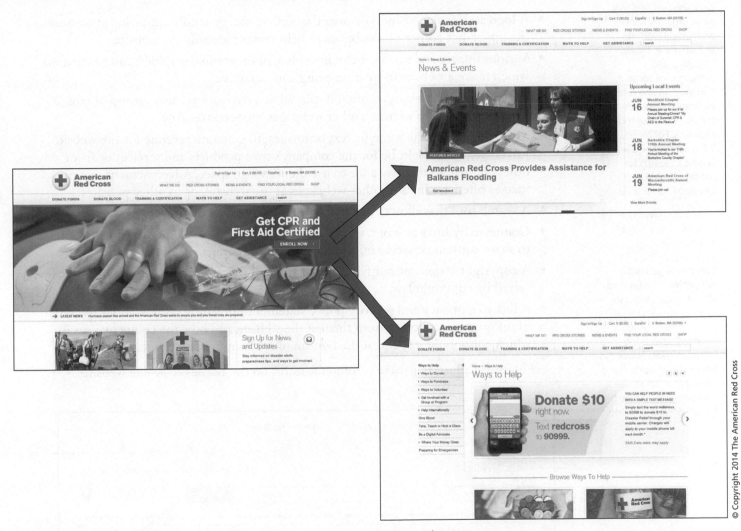

Figure 2-2 A multipage website consists of a home page and linked subsidiary webpages.

A **web portal**, or simply a **portal**, is a special type of website that offers access to a vast range of content and services. Some web portals serve as a starting point for visitors when they open their browsers. These types of portals generally offer trending or breaking local, national, and international news; weather and sports scores; access to reference tools, such as online white or yellow pages; market information and stock tickers; maps and driving instructions; links to other general-purpose websites; and a search tool. Websites such as Yahoo! and MSN are general-interest portals. Other portals, such as Golf.com or the Creativity Portal, focus on a more narrow range of information and services, and appeal to visitors with specific interests, such as golf or the creative arts.

@SOURCE Web designers use slide shows and galleries to provide a central focal point with content that changes automatically, or as a result of user intervention. Slide shows and galleries permit a website to feature several articles at once in a small amount of space.

Q&A

What is a hyperlocal portal?
A hyperlocal portal is a portal that features news, events, and articles about a specific geographic area.

Q&A

How can I evaluate web content?
As you browse the web, you will find that some organizational and topical websites lack accurate, timely, objective, and authoritative content. You must always carefully evaluate a website's content for these four elements. For more information, use a search engine to search for *critical evaluation of webpage content*.

Q&A

How do websites determine which ads to place on a webpage?
Sometimes you will notice that a website ad reflects recent searches or webpages you have visited. This is called targeted advertising. You will learn more about this later in the chapter. For more information, use a search engine to search for *targeted advertising*.

Webpages

A well-designed webpage will attract and hold a visitor's attention so that he or she will spend time viewing and interacting with the home page or other pages on the website. An effective webpage draws a visitor to items of potential interest and includes links that lead the visitor to investigate other webpages. Most commercial webpages (and many noncommercial webpages also) share some or all of the following characteristics that make them attractive, clearly identifiable, and easy to use:

- A logo and/or the business or organization's name, generally appearing at or near the upper-left corner of a webpage to help visitors identify the website.
- Various images and media, including video, photographs, graphics, and animations, which make a website more interesting and attractive.
- Links to related webpages, often displayed as a navigation bar or group of tabs, to make accessing the website's other webpages more convenient.
- Advertisements, which can be text or images, to generate revenue for the website. Advertisements might be for the company's own products and services or from other companies that pay a fee to use the webpage space. Advertisement text or images often are links to other webpages at the website, or to other websites.
- A search tool that allows visitors to locate specific information at the website.
- Connectivity links or icons, which enable a user to use social networking websites to share content or access information about the company or organization.
- A copyright statement notifying visitors that all the content at the website is protected by copyright law.
- A link to a privacy and security policy statement informing visitors about the type of information collected from them at the website and how the company uses it, which commonly is found at the bottom of a commercial webpage.

Figure 2-3 illustrates these common features on the Barnes & Noble website.

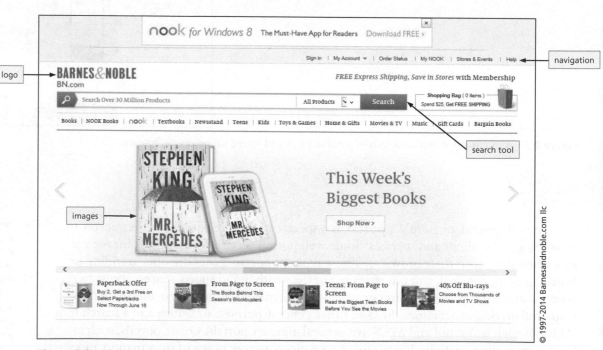

Figure 2-3 Most commercial webpages share common characteristics, such as logos, images, links, and search tools.

As you have learned, many websites and individual webpages are dynamic, meaning they can change content, layout, and design frequently. Because of the dynamic nature of the web, as well as use of responsive web design (RWD) to adjust content based on differences in browsers and mobile devices, the webpages you see on your screen as you work through the projects in this text might look somewhat different from the corresponding webpage figures in the book. Figure 2-4 shows differences in the *wired* magazine webpage when viewed on a laptop, an e-reader, and a smartphone.

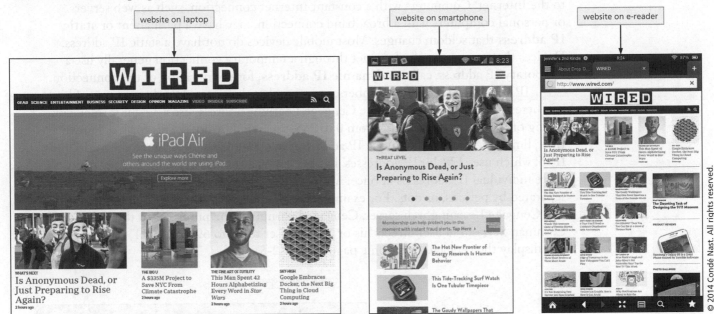

Figure 2-4 Responsive web design techniques adapt website content to different browsers, devices, and screen sizes.

Web Servers

Before a browser can display a webpage, it must first send a request for a copy of the page to the web server that hosts the webpage. The web server responds to the request by sending a copy of the webpage to the browser. This process is an example of **client/server computing**, in which a client — the browser — requests services from another computer — the web server.

Typically, a **client** is an application that runs on a computer or device, which requests resources or services from another computer or device. A **server** is a computer that "serves up," or provides, the requested resources or services. A server might be located in the same building, in a nearby building, or, in the case of a web server, anywhere in the world.

A single web server can store or host many small websites. For example, hundreds of students and instructors at a college or university can create personal websites and store them on the university's web server. Larger websites, such as those created by businesses or organizations, may be stored across multiple web servers.

Q&A

What is browser sniffing?
Browser sniffing is a technique websites use to determine the device and platform requesting the webpage information, to help the website deliver appropriate content and formatting for the device. For more information, use a search engine to search for *browser sniffing*.

Domain Names, IP Addresses, and URLs

When a browser sends a request for a webpage, the web server uses the domain name and URL to find the IP address of the webpage. In this section, you will learn the structure of an IP address, the function of the Domain Name System (DNS) and domain names, and the components of a Uniform Resource Locator (URL).

IP Addresses

An **IP address** (**Internet Protocol address**) is a unique number that identifies a computer or device connected to the Internet. Just as a postal service relies on mailing addresses to ensure correct mail delivery, the Internet relies on IP addresses to ensure that data goes to the correct computer or device.

A personal computer or mobile device must have an IP address while connected to the Internet. Computers with a constant Internet connection, such as web servers or personal computers with a broadband connection, may have a permanent or **static IP address** that seldom changes. Most mobile devices do not have a static IP address. Devices that connect to the Internet through a temporary connection generally use a temporary IP address, called a **dynamic IP address**, for the duration of the connection.

IP addresses use binary numbers, meaning that they correspond to a series of bits and bytes. IP addresses, such as the Cengage Learning address, use a 32-bit format, consisting of four numbers ranging from 0 to 255, separated by dots. This format, known as IPv4, limits the number of unique IP addresses to about 4.3 billion. Since the mid-2000s, IPv6, which uses 128-bit IP addresses, has been in widespread use, allowing for many more individual IP addresses at once. An IP address consists of groups of numbers, each separated by periods, or dots. For example, the IP address 69.32.133.11 is the IP address of a Cengage Learning web server. Cengage Learning is the publisher of the Shelly Cashman Series. If a user directs his or her browser to go to 69.32.133.11, the browser will display the cengage.com home page (Figure 2-5).

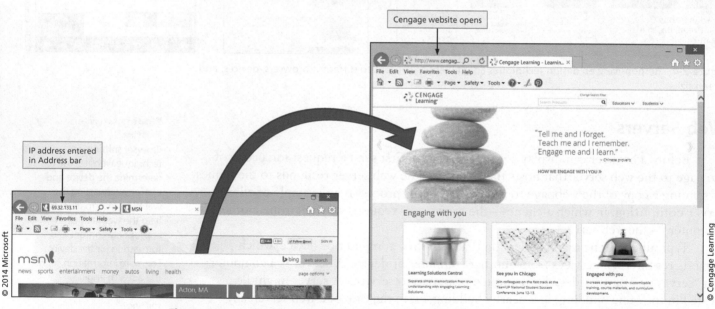

Figure 2-5 An IP address is the numeric equivalent of a URL.

© 2014 Microsoft

© Cengage Learning

Q&A

How can I find the numeric IP address for a domain name?

Both Windows and Macintosh computers use the *nslookup* command to determine a numeric IP address. To find out how to do this using your computer or device, use a search engine to search for *find numeric IP address* and your device and platform name.

Domain Names

Complex numeric IP addresses are difficult to remember. Because of this, it is common to use domain names to represent a web server's IP address. A **domain name** is a text alias for one or more IP addresses. The domain name cengage.com, for example, corresponds to the IP address 69.32.133.11. When a user enters a domain name such as cengage.com into a browser, the browser must look up the corresponding IP address by requesting the IP address from a name server. A **name server** is a server that contains databases with domain names and the numeric IP addresses to which they correspond. The DNS name server translates or "resolves" the domain name to its numeric IP address and returns the IP address to the browser. Then, the request for a webpage travels to the web server that hosts the webpage. Name servers are part of the **Domain Name System (DNS)**.

Because domain names must be unique, web designers must register domain names, much like trademarks. The organization that oversees naming and numbering functions in the DNS and controls the domain name registration system is the **Internet Corporation for Assigned Names and Numbers (ICANN)**. ICANN is a nonprofit organization that currently operates under the auspices of the U.S. Department of Commerce.

A **top-level domain (TLD)** identifies the type of organization associated with the domain. Originally, only seven generic top-level domains existed, including .com, .edu, and .org. Today, there are many more top-level domains, as shown in Figure 2-6. Many nations also have a **country-code top-level domain (ccTLD)**, such as .us for the United States, .ca for Canada, and .uk for the United Kingdom. New domain names include .vegas and .technology.

Top-Level Domains

TLD Abbreviation	Type of Domain	TLD Abbreviation	Type of Domain
.com	Commercial firms	.aero	Aviation industry
.edu	Educational institutions	.biz	Businesses
.gov	Government entities	.coop	Cooperatives
.mil	U.S. military	.info	All uses
.net	Major networking centers	.museum	Museums
.org	Nonprofit organizations	.name	Individuals
.int	International organizations	.pro	Credentialed professionals
.mobi	Mobile products and services	.jobs	Human resources professionals
.travel	Travel industry	.asia	Pan-Asian and Asia Pacific community
.tel	Business and individual contact information	.cat	Catalan linguistic community

© Cengage Learning®

Figure 2-6 Domains in the DNS are grouped by type of organization or sponsoring group.

Uniform Resource Locators (URLs)

Each webpage also has its own unique address. A **Uniform Resource Locator (URL)** is a unique address, sometimes called a **web address**, that identifies an individual webpage or other web-based resource. A URL has several components, as shown in Figure 2-7.

| protocol | host | domain name | path | webpage name |

http://www.website.com/path/webpage.htm

© Cengage Learning

Figure 2-7 A URL includes a protocol and a domain name. Some URLs also include the path and file name.

The first part of the URL is http://, the protocol or set of rules used to transmit a webpage from a web server to a browser. The second part of the URL is the name of the server hosting the webpage, generally the www web server designation, followed by the server's domain name and top-level domain, such as website.com. A URL also can contain the path to and the file name of a specific webpage. For example, in Figure 2-7 on the previous page, the path is /path/ and the file name is webpage.htm. When a user enters a URL in a browser, the http:// protocol and the www designation are optional. For example, entering either http://www.cengage.com or cengage.com in a browser loads the Cengage Learning home page in a browser. When a user enters a URL without a specific path and file name, the webpage returned to the browser generally is the website's home page.

Domain names are not case sensitive, meaning users can enter them in a browser in either uppercase or lowercase characters. For example, entering any of these three domain names — cengage.com, Cengage.Com, or CENGAGE.COM — in a browser accesses the same Cengage Learning home page. On some web servers, however, the path and file name might be case sensitive, which means the user must enter the path and file name correctly in the browser to locate the webpage.

Connecting to the Internet or a Network

Before you can browse the web, you first must connect your computer or device to the Internet. Smartphones and some other devices can use both cellular and wireless technology to connect to the Internet. If you have a smartphone or device that uses both technologies, you can conserve your cellular data usage (and save money) by connecting to a wireless network, if one is available and you have permission to do so. If you are using a desktop or laptop, you likely will have a built-in wireless network card or other technology that can locate available networks and allow you to access them. Alternatively, your desktop or laptop may have a physical connection to a network using cables.

Be cautious when accessing public or unsecured wireless networks; the information you send or access may not be secure. If you are not connected to a network whose source or host you know, such as your home or school's wireless network, be cautious about entering passwords, accessing financial or personal data, and other activities that may leave you vulnerable.

To Connect to the Internet

The following steps help you verify or establish a connection to the Internet or a network.

1

- If you are using a smartphone, check the upper-right or upper-left corner of your screen to see if you have bars, indicating that you are connected to the Internet using a cellular connection (Figure 2-8).

bars and 4G symbol indicate type and strength of cellular connection

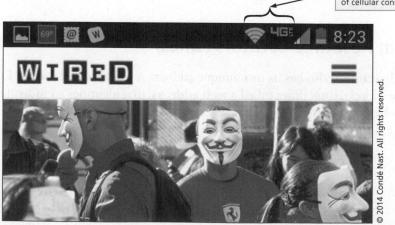

Figure 2-8

2

- If you are using a smartphone or other device, such as a tablet, and are within range of a secure wireless network, access your device's Settings menu or folder, and enable Wi-Fi if necessary.

- If you are using a laptop or desktop without a physical Internet connection, go to your computer's settings or Control Panel, find the network or Internet category, and enable Wi-Fi if necessary (Figure 2-9).

Figure 2-9

Browsers

As you learned in Chapter 1, a browser is software or an app used to access and view webpages. Popular browsers for personal computers in home and business settings are Google Chrome™, Mozilla Firefox®, Microsoft® Windows Internet Explorer®, Apple® Safari®, and Opera™. Mobile browsers often are proprietary to the device and platform, such as the Google Android browser. Other mobile browsers include Opera Mini, Safari, Google Chrome, Firefox Mobile, and Internet Explorer Mobile. Figure 2-10 illustrates the Windows® Internet Explorer® 11 browser window.

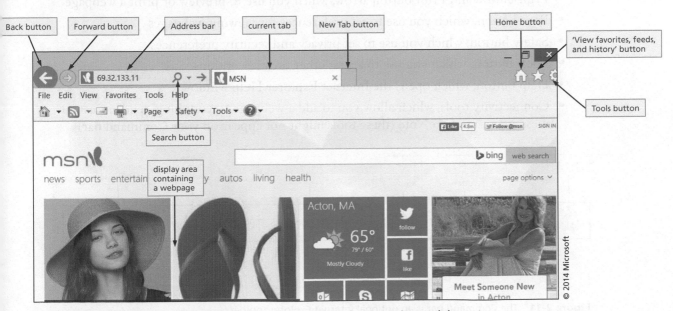

Figure 2-10 The Internet Explorer browser contains features for convenient web browsing.

The features within Internet Explorer 11 that help users browse the web include the:

- Home page, which is a single webpage or group of tabbed webpages that load when the browser starts
- **Display area**, which contains the webpage a web server requests
- Back and Forward buttons, which you can use to revisit recently viewed webpages
- Address bar, which contains the following: a text box into which users enter a URL or search keywords; the Search button, which initiates a search based on what the user enters in the Address text box; the Show Address bar; the AutoComplete button, which provides a drop-down menu of previously viewed and favorite websites; the Refresh button, which requests a fresh copy of the current webpage from the web server; the Compatibility View button, which appears only if there are compatibility issues and which you use to fix issues in webpages designed for previous browser versions; and the Stop button, which halts the download of a requested webpage
- Home button, which reopens the home page(s) or changes the home page setting
- 'View favorites, feeds, and history' button, which opens the Favorites Center pane, containing lists of frequently viewed webpages and a History list
- Tools button, which allows you to print, zoom, specify safety options, and set other browser settings
- Tabs for each open webpage
- New tab button, which you use to open an additional webpage in a new tab
- Scroll bar, which appears whenever a webpage is too long or wide to fit in the display area

The Command bar (Figure 2-11) is an optional, customizable Internet Explorer toolbar that contains the:

- Home button, which reopens the home page(s)
- Home button arrow, which changes the home page settings
- Add Feeds buttons, which you use to subscribe to web-based content
- Read mail button, which opens your email client software
- Print button and Print button arrow, which you use to preview or print a webpage
- Page button, which you use to set preferences for viewing webpages
- Safety button, which you use to set privacy and security preferences
- Tools button, which you use to access other browser options
- Help button, which opens the Internet Explorer Help window
- Connectivity tools, which allow you to add a webpage to your blog, send an instant message, or use OneNote (these tools might not appear on your Command bar)

Figure 2-11 The Command bar is an optional Internet Explorer toolbar.

If you are using a desktop or laptop with a different browser other than Internet Explorer, you will find similar features and capabilities, although they may have different names. Figure 2-12 lists differences among popular browsers for desktops and laptops. Appendix A covers browser features and differences in more detail.

Browser Features and Versions

Browser	Description	Mobile Version(s)
Google Chrome	Free browser for Windows and Mac OS. Must be downloaded and installed. Includes strong security features.	Google Chrome, Google Android
Mozilla Firefox	Free browser for Windows, Mac OS, and Linux computers. Must be downloaded and installed. Includes many plug-ins, privacy and security features, and a password manager.	Firefox Mobile
Microsoft Internet Explorer	Free browser, comes installed on Microsoft Windows computers. Offers protection against phishing and malware.	Internet Explorer Mobile
Apple Safari	The default browser for Mac OS computers. Includes built-in social networking sharing tools, and is known for its fast performance.	Safari Mobile
Opera	Used on both computers and mobile devices. Must be downloaded and installed. The second oldest browser.	Opera Mini

© Cengage Learning

Figure 2-12 List of common browsers.

Figure 2-13 shows the Google Android browser and the Silk browser found on Amazon Kindle e-book readers.

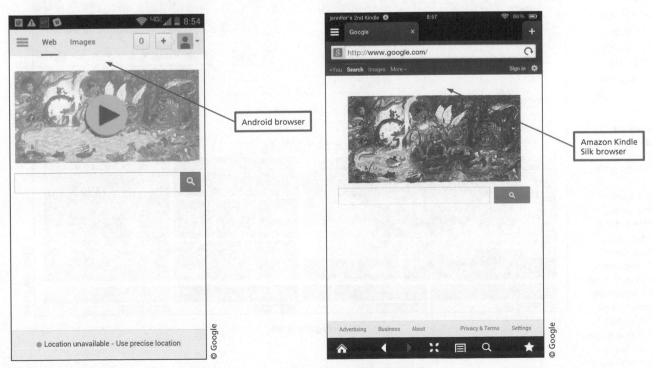

Figure 2-13 Websites viewed on mobile devices may differ from those on desktop or laptop computers.

Q&A

Why are some elements in my browser window different from the illustrations in this text?
The exercises in this book assume you are using a desktop or laptop to work through the steps. See each individual exercise for tips for users of mobile browsers or different browser versions. All efforts were made to ensure this book can be used with all browsers and devices.

Starting the Browser and Loading a Webpage

When you first open a browser, most likely it will open with its starting or home page. In some cases, the browser might display the most recently viewed webpage — this often occurs when using mobile devices. If your browser uses a home page, you can set the home or starting page to be any webpage you like. For example, many colleges, universities, and businesses use their organization's website home page as their home page. Many individuals use a portal website for their home page. The MSN portal webpage is the home page for illustrations in this text. You will learn more about changing the home page later in this chapter.

After the browser opens, you can enter the URL of the webpage you want to visit in the Address box on the Address bar. To complete the request, you might press the ENTER key, a Go button, or a similar command. Depending on the speed of your Internet connection and the contents of the webpage, it might load very quickly or it might take several seconds to load. For example, a webpage with numerous graphics might take longer to load than a webpage with few or no graphics or other media. In some cases, you may see a status bar at the bottom of the browser window that displays information about the loading process: the URL of the webpage, and a progress bar showing the duration of the loading process.

Note: The screenshots shown with the exercises in this chapter use the Internet Explorer v. 11 browser on a Windows 8 computer, but the instructions should work with all devices and browsers. Depending on your settings, Internet Explorer might not show the menu bar, and might display additional toolbars, tabs, and add-ons.

To Open Your Browser and Load a Webpage

The following steps open the browser, enter a URL in the Address box, and load a webpage in the browser window.

1

- Double-click the browser icon on the desktop, click the browser icon on the taskbar, or tap the browser icon on the home screen of your mobile device to open the browser (Figure 2-14).

Q&A

Why is my home page different?
If your browser uses a default home page, you will see the default home page when you first install the browser. Users typically replace this home page with one or more other webpages to suit their needs. You will learn more about changing the home page settings later in this chapter. Even if you have MSN as your home page, the content of this page will differ.

Figure 2-14

2

- Tap or click in the Address box on the Address bar. If necessary, select the current contents of the Address box.

- Enter **cengage.com** as the URL (Figure 2-15).

Q&A

Why do I see a list below the Address bar as I enter the URL? Many browsers remember URLs you have previously entered and also provide webpage suggestions based on the URL you currently are entering, both of which appear in the Address bar drop-down list. Your Address bar drop-down list might look different or display different results.

cengage.com URL entered in Address bar

Search button

© 2014 Microsoft

Figure 2-15

3

- Press the ENTER key, or tap or click the appropriate browser button to open the Cengage home page (Figure 2-16).

"The real voyage of discovery consists not in seeking new landscapes, but in having new eyes."

~ Marcel Proust

NATIONAL GEOGRAPHIC LEARNING »

Engaging with you

Learning Solutions Central

Separate simple memorization from true understanding with engaging Learning Solutions.

VIEW WALK-THROUGHS & TESTIMONIALS »

See you in Chicago

Join colleagues on the fast track at the TeamUP National Student Success Conference, June 12-13.

REGISTER TODAY »

Engaged with you

Increase engagement with customizable training, course materials, and curriculum development.

EXPERIENCE PERSONALIZED SERVICE »

© Cengage Learning

Figure 2-16

Using a Webpage Search Feature and Clicking Links

Many websites include a keyword search feature to allow you to find a specific webpage within a website. You can enter keywords in the search feature's text box and then tap or click a Search button to find webpages at the website that contain those keywords. You will learn more about keyword searches in Chapter 3. Some websites, such as The Weather Channel, have special search tools designed to find information organized by common categories, such as ZIP code, city, or state (Figure 2-17). Others, such as Cengage.com, allow you to enter general information, such as a topic or author name, or narrow your results to be more specific, such as by typing an ISBN, which is the unique number assigned to every book.

Figure 2-17

@ISSUE

Web Ads

As you browse the web or use web or mobile apps, you may notice a barrage of advertisements. Web advertisements can appear in pop-up windows in front of the webpage or app currently displayed or in pop-under windows that appear behind the browser window or app. Although advertising revenue does offset many costs associated with creating webpages, ads are generally considered inconvenient and bothersome by web users. Some advertisements with attention-grabbing sounds and animation, called **rich media ads**, even appear right in the middle of or floating across the webpage or app you are viewing. Most visitors consider these approaches to web advertising increasingly invasive, distracting, and bothersome.

For these reasons, you may want to block ads. Blocking or filtering ads is important particularly for children. According to research by Dr. Jakob Nielsen, a web usability pioneer, children are less able than adults to distinguish between web ads and content. When a child sees a cartoon character in an ad, for example, he or she likely will click the ad expecting to see more cartoons. Using an ad filter or blocker can help reduce the likelihood that children will click ads and navigate to webpages selling products and services. Many ads contain malicious content that can introduce viruses, spyware, or other harmful programs or apps onto your computer or device.

Most current browsers include a feature that blocks pop-up ads; however, other kinds of ads, including rich media ads, may still appear. Check your device and browser settings to turn on filters and ad blocking tools.

To Use a Search Box to Find Information

The following step uses a website search feature to find information about this book.

1

- Enter **Discovering the Internet** in the Search Products text box on the Cengage webpage.

- Press the ENTER key or tap or click the appropriate button to begin the search (Figure 2-18).

Q&A

Why am I prompted to specify what information I want?
If you are not logged into Cengage or do not have a Cengage account, you may see a window that asks if you are a student, instructor, or other options. Tap or click the Student option to continue.

- Tap or click the link for this text to open the webpage that contains product information for this book (Figure 2-19).

Figure 2-18

Figure 2-19

A simple way to load a different webpage in the browser window is to tap or click a link on the current webpage. Webpage links can be text, a graphic button, or an image. Text links generally appear underlined in a different color from other text on the webpage. It can be difficult to determine whether a graphic button or image is a link. If you are using a desktop or laptop, you can determine whether any webpage element — text, graphic button, or image — is a link by pointing to the element with the pointer. If the pointer changes to a pointing hand pointer and a URL appears in the status bar, the element is a link. It is harder to locate graphic links when using a mobile browser.

After a webpage loads in the browser, you then can click various links to locate additional information or use other features presented on the webpage. For example, the webpage for this book has links to additional materials you might find useful.

To View a Webpage

The following steps return you to Cengage's home page. You then use a scroll bar or gestures to view more information on the webpage.

1

- Tap or click the Cengage Learning logo to return to the home page, or enter `cengage.com` in the Address bar, and then the ENTER key or tap or click the appropriate button.

- Drag the scroll box on the vertical scroll bar down, or swipe your finger upward if using a mobile device with a touch screen, to view the content at the bottom of the webpage Figure 2-20, and then drag or swipe downward to view the top of the webpage.

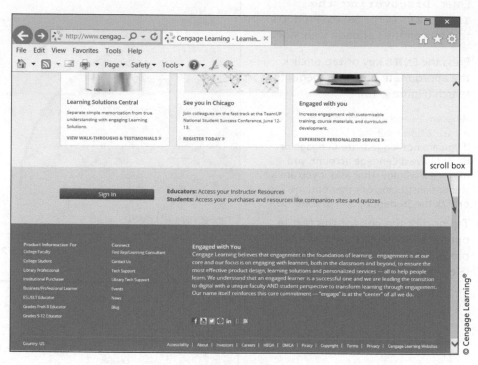

Figure 2-20

Navigating Recently Viewed Webpages

You can use browser or device buttons or icons to move back and forth between recently viewed webpages, reopen the default browser home page, reopen the current webpage, and stop the process of opening a webpage. In this section, you will learn about navigating recently viewed webpages. Later in this chapter and in Chapters 3 and 4, you will learn how to use other browser features.

MOVE BACKWARD AND FORWARD   If you have viewed multiple webpages in one browsing session, tapping or clicking a Back button returns you to the webpage you viewed immediately before the current webpage. Tapping or clicking a Forward button, if available, returns you to the webpage you viewed before you tapped or clicked the Back button. Some devices use a Back button to return to the previous app or to the home page, depending on the user's actions, and might not include options to move forward while browsing.

STOPPING AND REFRESHING   You might change your mind about viewing the webpage that is currently loading in the browser. For example, the page might take too long to load or the content may not seem appropriate. You can tap or click the browser's Stop button, which might be an X, include the word, Stop, or resemble a Stop Sign, to halt the process.

Refreshing or reloading a webpage opens an updated or current copy of the current webpage. The Refresh or Reload command is useful when you want to reopen a webpage for which you stopped the transfer or when you need to refresh webpages with content that changes every few minutes, such as stock quotes, weather, and news. Touch screen-enabled devices allow you to refresh content by tapping at the top of the window and swiping downward.

RETURNING TO THE HOME PAGE   When using a laptop or desktop browser, you can click the Home button to view the designated home page at anytime while you are browsing the web. The Home button also provides a list of options you can use to reset the browser's default home page. You will learn more about resetting the browser's home page options later in this chapter.

To Navigate Through Recently Viewed Pages

In the following steps, you navigate through webpages. Depending on your browser or device, your steps might differ, or you might be unable to complete all steps, such as forwarding or returning to the home screen.

1

- Enter **weather.com** in the Address box.

- Press the ENTER key or tap or click the appropriate button to open the weather.com webpage (Figure 2-21).

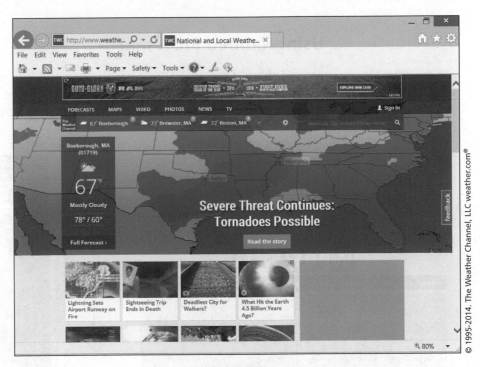

Figure 2-21

2

- Tap or click any link on The Weather Channel home page to open a new webpage in the same browser window and tab (Figure 2-22).

3

- Tap or click the Back button to return to The Weather Channel home page.

- Tap or click the Forward button, if available, to return to the webpage you were viewing before you clicked the Back button.

- Tap or click the Refresh button or menu command, or swipe at the top of the mobile browser window, to access the refreshed webpage to view the updated temperature or other new information on the webpage.

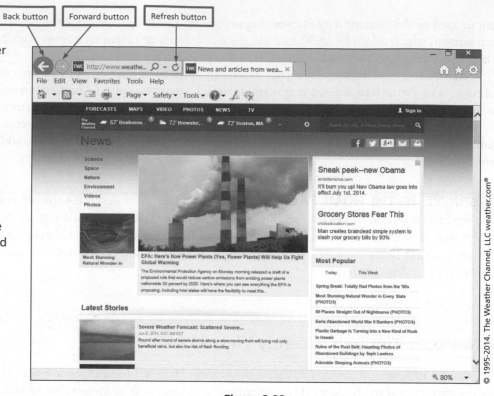

Figure 2-22

Using Tabbed Browsing

Tabbed browsing allows you to open multiple webpages in a single browser window, as shown in Figure 2-23. Each webpage you open appears in its own tab. The active tab appears in the foreground. If you are using a desktop or laptop browser, you likely will

Figure 2-23   Most browsers have tabbed browsing capabilities.

be able to see all tabs at once. If you are using a mobile device, you can view your open tabs using a menu command. You can bring a background webpage tab to the foreground for viewing by clicking the tab.

Most browsers and devices enable tabbed browsing by default. If the browser allows you to turn off tabbed browsing, each additional webpage you open will appear in a separate browser window.

Many browsers have a New tab button on the tab row that allows you display a blank tab and then enter a URL in the Address box, which then opens a webpage in the new tab. If you are using a mobile device, each URL you enter in the Address box may automatically open in a new tab. The new tab appears in the foreground.

Depending on your browser or device, when you open a new, blank tab, you may see icons for frequently visited websites, or an option to open tabs that you closed during your last browsing session.

To Open and Close Multiple Webpage Tabs

The following steps open multiple webpages in separate tabs using the Address bar and webpage links, view and close webpages, reopen webpages, and then close your browser. You also will reopen the browser and the webpages that you opened during the last work session (if possible). *Note:* These steps might not work with a mobile browser. If you are unable to complete the steps, read this section to learn how other browsers open multiple tabs.

1

- Open your browser, if necessary.

- Tap or click the New tab button on the tab row to open a new tab page (Figure 2-24).

Q&A

Where is my New tab button?
Depending on the browser or device you are using, your New tab button might have a different name. Look for a blank tab at the end of the tab row to locate the New tab button. If you do not see one, skip Step 1 and go to Step 2.

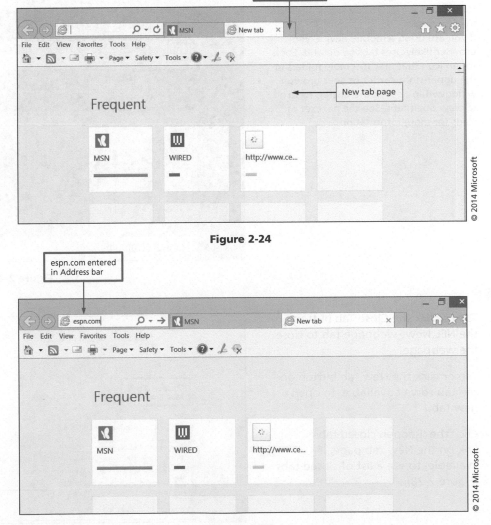

Figure 2-24

2

- Enter `espn.com` in the Address box (Figure 2-25).

Figure 2-25

3

- Press the ENTER key or tap or click the appropriate button to open the ESPN home page in a new tab.

- Tap or click the New tab button on the tab row to open a new tab page, if possible.

- Enter `nfl.com` in the Address box (Figure 2-26).

Figure 2-26

4

- Tap or click the necessary button to open the NFL.com home page (Figure 2-27).

Q&A

How can I verify that each website is in a new tab?

If you are using a mobile device, your browser likely uses tabs by default. Look for an icon that may resemble folders in the upper-right corner of your browser window. Tap or click the button to scroll to view open tabs. See the next set of steps for more information.

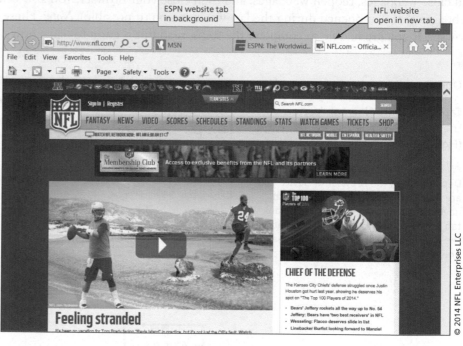

Figure 2-27

5

- Tap or click the Close Tab button on the NFL News webpage tab to close the webpage.

- Tap or click the New tab button on the tab row, if available, to open a new tab.

- Click the 'Reopen closed tabs' link on the New tab page, if available, to see a list of closed tabs (Figure 2-28).

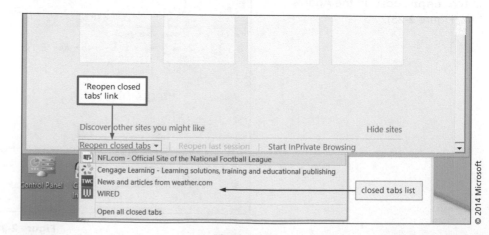

Figure 2-28

6

- Click the NFL News link to reopen the webpage in a new tab (Figure 2-29).

Why does the NFL News button not appear?
If NFL News does not appear on your New Tab page, or your browser or device does not have a New Tab page, enter **www.nfl.com/news** in the Address bar, and then press the ENTER key or tap or click the appropriate button.

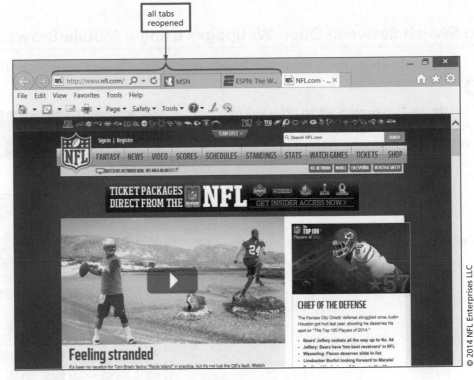

Figure 2-29

7

- Close the browser and close all tabs, if asked.

- Start the browser.

- Tap or click the New tab button on the tab row to open a new tab page if necessary (Figure 2-30).

Figure 2-30

8

- Click the 'Reopen last session' button, if available, to reopen the tabs that were open when you closed the browser (Figure 2-31).

Figure 2-31

To Switch Between Open Webpages using a Mobile Browser

The following steps demonstrate how to view open webpages using a mobile browser.

1

- Locate the Tabs button, which likely will look like folders and appear in the upper-right corner of your mobile browser window (Figure 2-32).

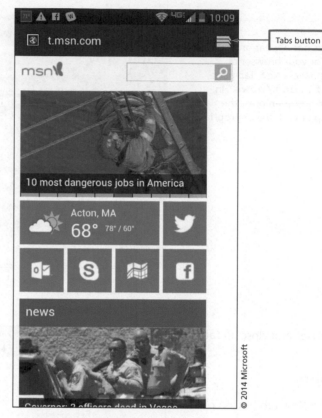

Figure 2-32

2

- Tap or click the Tabs button to display open tabs (Figure 2-33).

Q&A

Should I close tabs on my mobile browser when I am done using them?

Depending on your mobile device and browser, leaving tabs open may cause your battery to drain more quickly. Check your mobile device's Help feature and change your settings if necessary to close all tabs when you are done browsing.

Figure 2-33

3

- Swipe up or down, or use a scroll bar if
available, to view all open tabs (Figure 2-34).

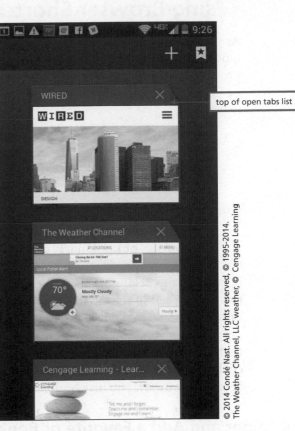

top of open tabs list

Figure 2-34

4

- Tap or click a tab to display it in the foreground
(Figure 2-35).

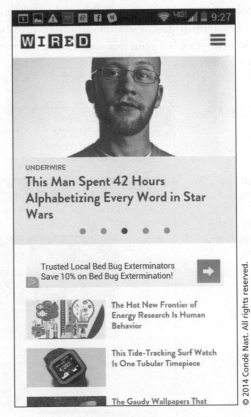

Figure 2-35

Using Browser Shortcuts to Visit Webpages

As you become more familiar with webpages and their content, you likely will want to quickly find useful webpage content, often by revisiting specific webpages. Most browsers provide shortcuts for accessing webpage content and revisiting webpages, including:

- Favorites
- History
- Accelerators
- Web feeds
- Address bar drop-down list
- Suggested websites

Favorites

A **favorite**, or **bookmark**, is a browser shortcut to a frequently viewed webpage. You can create a favorite, which includes the webpage's title and URL, for the current webpage by tapping or clicking a Favorites or Bookmark button, which, if available, may appear to the right or left of the tab row. A window should open that enables you to save the favorite or bookmark so that you can revisit it.

When you want to revisit the webpage, you simply open the Favorites or Bookmark folder, navigate or search for the favorite or bookmark you want you visit, and then tap or click the link. Favorites and bookmarks typically are stored in a folder. Depending on your device or browser, you may be able to create subfolders to better organize your favorites.

To Create a Subfolder and Add a Favorite or Bookmark

The following steps create a favorite for the Dell home page and save it in a new subfolder. *Note:* These steps work best with a desktop or laptop. Use a search engine to find how to create and use folders for favorites or bookmarks if these steps do not work for you. See the next set of steps for an example of how to use favorites or bookmarks on a mobile device.

- Close the browser and close all tabs, if asked.

- Start the browser.

- Start your browser and enter `dell.com` in the Address bar.

- Press the ENTER key, or tap or click the appropriate button to open the Dell home page (Figure 2-36).

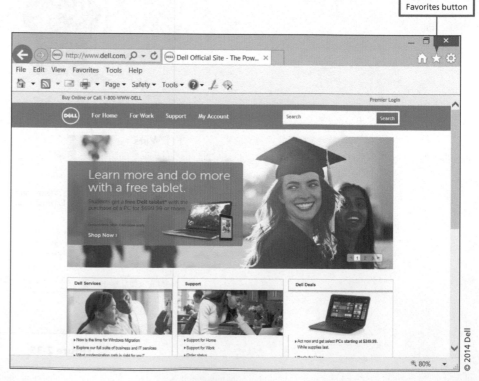

Favorites button

Figure 2-36

2

- Tap or click the Favorites or Bookmarks button, if available, to open the Favorites or Bookmarks pane (Figure 2-37).

- If necessary, navigate to view your list of favorites and subfolders.

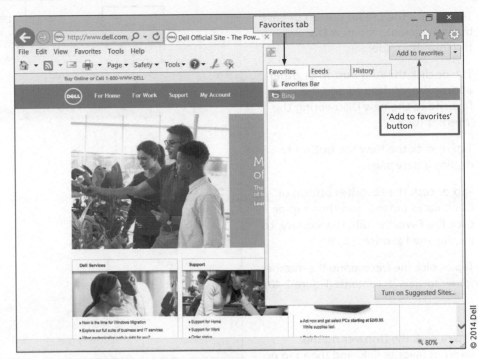

Figure 2-37

3

- Tap or click the 'Add to favorites' button or the Add Bookmark button, or use other similar command, to display the Add a Favorite dialog box.

- In the Name text box, type **Textbook links** as the favorite name (Figure 2-38).

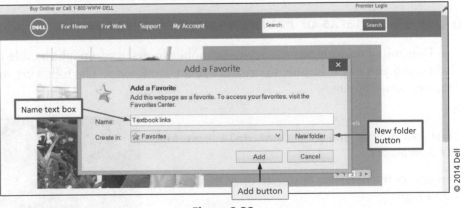

Figure 2-38

4

- Tap or click the New folder button, if available, to display the Create a Folder dialog box.

- In the Folder Name text box, type **Discovering the Internet** (Figure 2-39).

Figure 2-39

5

- Tap or click the Create button or Save button to create the new Discovering the Internet folder.

- Tap or click the Add button or other appropriate button to add the favorite to the new Discovering the Internet folder.

- Tap or click the New tab button to display a new page.

- Tap or click the Favorites button or Bookmarks button, and then tap or click the Favorites tab, if necessary, to display the Favorites pane.

- Tap or click the Discovering the Internet folder to view its contents (Figure 2-40).

6

- Tap or click the Discovering the Internet favorite link, and then tap or click the Textbook links link to open the Dell home page in the current tab.

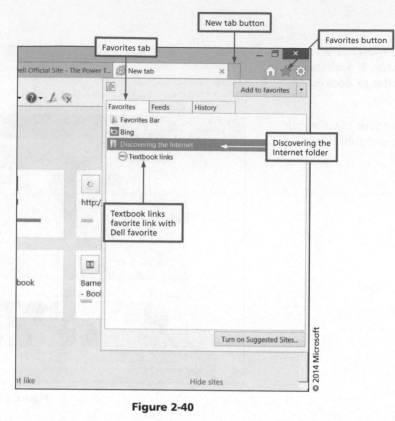

Figure 2-40

To Use Bookmarks or Favorites on a Mobile Device

Depending on your mobile device or mobile browser, you might be able to create bookmarks or favorites to websites, and you might be able to organize them into folders. The following steps create a bookmark and bookmark folder on a smartphone.

1

- Start your browser and enter **www.dell.com** in the Address bar.

- Tap or click the necessary button to open the Dell home page.

- Open your browser's menu to view options for the website (Figure 2-41).

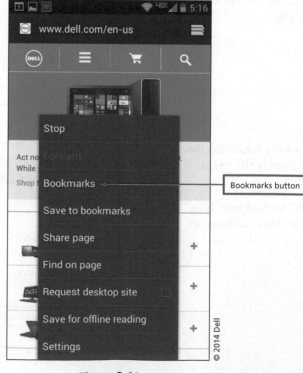

Figure 2-41

2

- Tap or click Bookmarks, or another similar command.

- Tap or click the Other folder link to open a new folder (Figure 2-42)

- In the Label text box, type **Textbook links** as the favorite name.

3

- Choose where to add the bookmark, if possible.

- Enter **Discovering the Internet** as the folder name.

- Tap or click the Create or Save button to create the new Discovering the Internet folder.

- Tap or click the Save or Add button or another appropriate button to add the favorite to the new Discovering the Internet folder.

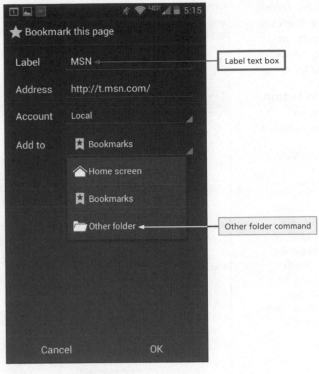

Figure 2-42

To Delete a Favorites Subfolder and Its Contents

When you no longer need a Favorites or Bookmarks subfolder or an individual favorite, you can delete it. The following steps delete the Discovering the Internet folder and its contents.

1

- Click the Favorites button or Bookmarks button, or open your browser and open the browser menu if you are using a mobile device.

- Display your list of favorites and subfolders.

- Tap or click the 'Discovering the Internet' folder to select it (Figure 2-43).

Figure 2-43

2

- Right-click the folder if necessary, then tap or click Delete, or a similar command (Figure 2-44).

- Click the Yes button, if necessary, to confirm the deletion.

- Close the browser.

Can I organize my favorites or bookmarks?
Depending on your device or browser, you likely can reorganize them. Use a search engine to search for steps to organize favorites or bookmarks for your browser or device.

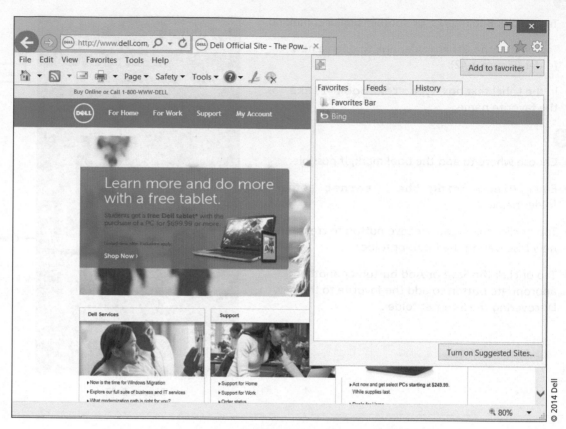

Figure 2-44

History

Another easy way to revisit a webpage is to use a history of the websites and webpages you have visited during a specific number of days.

A **History list** displays a list of past browsing data. Your History list might contain icons for websites visited several weeks ago, last week, and every day of the current week, including today, depending on your settings. When you tap or click one of these icons, a list of webpage folders might appear, or the website may open automatically. Each folder represents a website visited during that time period. You can expand each website folder to view links to the individual webpages viewed at the website.

You also can reorganize your view of the History list. Depending on your device or browser, you might have options to view the History list by website, most visited, order visited today, or more. Additionally, you may be able to search for previously viewed webpages.

To Revisit a Webpage Using the History List

The following steps use the History list to revisit a webpage.

1

- Start your browser.

- Tap or click the Favorites button, Customize button, or other option.

- Tap or click the History tab or History menu option to view the History list (Figure 2-45).

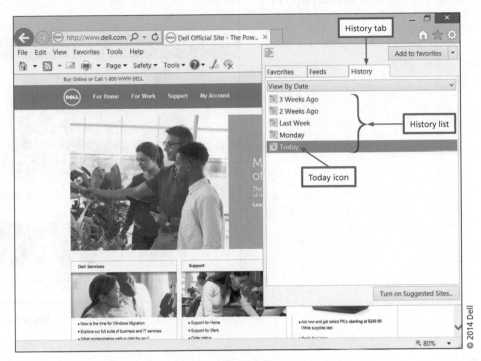

Figure 2-45

2

- Tap or click the Today icon, if necessary, to expand the list of webpages visited today (Figure 2-46).

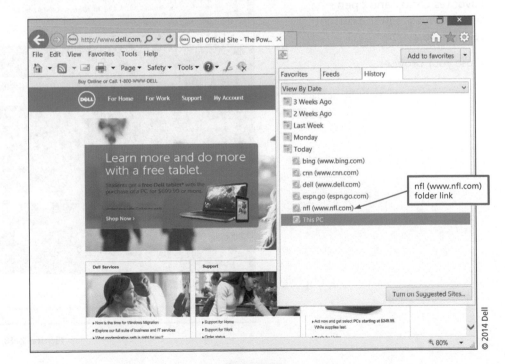

Figure 2-46

3

- Tap or click the NFL link in the History list to view links to individual webpages visited at the website, or to open the webpage in a new tab (Figure 2-47).

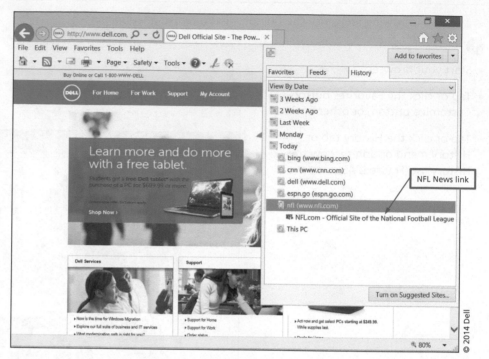

Figure 2-47

4

- Click any NFL link to close the Favorites Center and open the NFL website in the current tab (Figure 2-48).

- Close your browser.

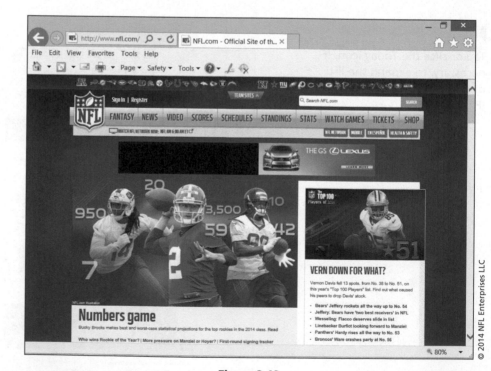

Figure 2-48

CLEAR THE BROWSER HISTORY You might want to clear your browser history for any number of reasons; for example, if you are working on a public or shared computer and want to protect your privacy. If your browser has this capability, it likely can be done using the History list or using browser settings (Figure 2-49). Clearing the browser history reduces the quantity of websites that the browser automatically suggests when you enter text into the Address bar, which can make returning to previously visited sites more tedious. You should decide whether to clear the history based on protecting your privacy. If you are using a computer or device to which only you have access, or which has password-protected user profiles, you may not need to clear your history.

Figure 2-49 Clearing your history can help protect your privacy.

Add-Ons

Add-ons, also called **accelerators** or **extensions**, allow you to access web content or take some action based on selected webpage text. For example, you can select webpage text and then open an online dictionary to see a definition of the word or translate the word into another language, or use it as a search keyword. Some add-ons are available for multiple platforms and devices, such as Evernote, which enables you to take notes and save web content to the cloud, and sync the data to your laptop, tablet, smartphone, and other devices (Figure 2-50).

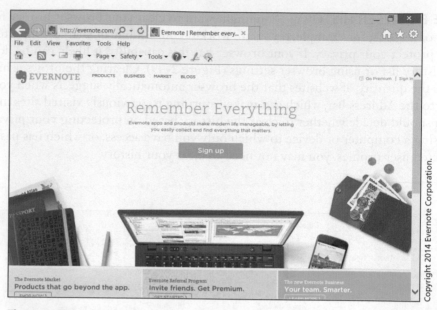

Figure 2-50 Add-ons extend the capability of your browser.

To install an add-on or see available add-ons, use a search engine to locate instructions and options by searching for add-ons for your specific device, browser, and/or platform.

Web Feeds

Figure 2-51 Websites commonly use this symbol to indicate you can subscribe to their web feed.

A **web feed** is a service that provides updates to web content for subscribers. **RSS (Really Simple Syndication)** and **Atom** are technologies that distribute web content to subscribers based on the websites and types of web content the user specifies (Figure 2-51). A **feed reader** is software or an app that collects the user's web feed content and provides it in a readable format for the user. Popular uses of web feeds include news headlines, links to website content, and blog postings to subscribers.

Sometimes called a news **aggregator**, a feed reader can be an email client or browser add-on. Most browsers have a built-in feed reader. You also can download stand-alone feed readers, such as NewzCrawler, or subscribe to online feed services, such as Bloglines (Figure 2-52). Feed readers generally are available for free.

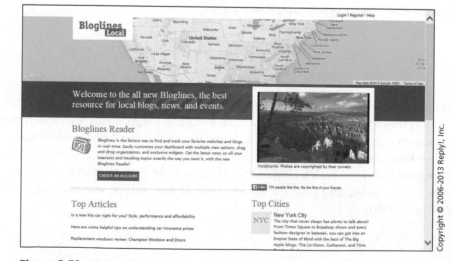

Figure 2-52 Online feed readers can gather all of the feeds to which you subscribe into one website, webpage, or app.

After you subscribe to a feed, you can open the feed webpage or open the feed reader software or app at anytime to view updated content, or to set feed preferences.

ACCESS OR INSTALL A FEED READER   Depending on your browser or device, you may have feed capabilities in your browser. If not, you can download and install a feed reader app, or sign up for a web-based feed reader service such as Feedly (Figure 2-53).

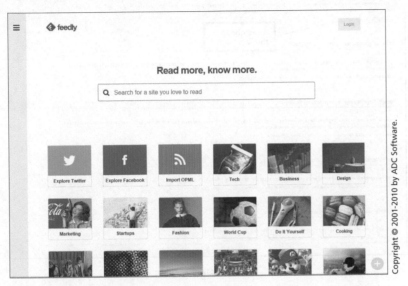

Figure 2-53   Use feed reader apps and web-based services if you do not have feed capability with your browser.

To Subscribe to a Web Feed

The following steps open the technology news webpage at a news-oriented website and subscribe to a news feed from the website.

1

- Start your browser.

- Type `cnn.com/tech` in the Address box and then press the ENTER key or tap or click the appropriate button to open the CNN.com technology webpage.

- Tap or click the Feeds button arrow to view the available feeds at the CNN website (Figure 2-54).

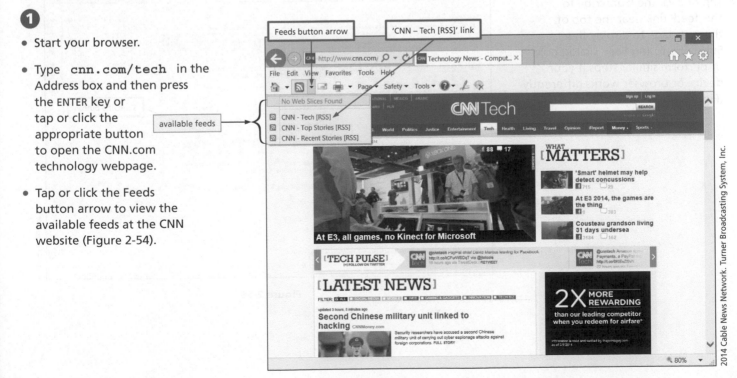

Figure 2-54

2

- Click 'CNN – Tech [RSS]' (or a different feed of your choice) to open the feed webpage in the same tab in Feed view (Figure 2-55).

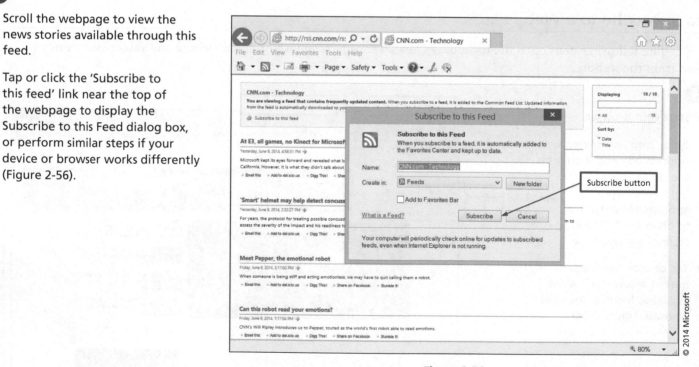

Figure 2-55

3

- Scroll the webpage to view the news stories available through this feed.

- Tap or click the 'Subscribe to this feed' link near the top of the webpage to display the Subscribe to this Feed dialog box, or perform similar steps if your device or browser works differently (Figure 2-56).

Figure 2-56

© 2014 Microsoft

4

- Tap or click the Subscribe button to display the confirmation webpage indicating that you have successfully subscribed to a CNN.com RSS feed (Figure 2-57).

5

- Tap or click the Close Tab button to close the confirmation webpage, if necessary.

Figure 2-57

Viewing and Deleting a Web Feed

Clicking the feed reader button on your browser displays a webpage that contains the web feeds to which you have subscribed. Figure 2-58 shows a list of feed subscriptions. If you have not subscribed to any feeds on the currently viewed webpage, your feed reader button likely will be gray, dimmed, or unavailable. Click a specific feed in the list to view its feed webpage in your browser. When you no longer want to subscribe to a web feed, you can unsubscribe by deleting the feed from the feed reader. Figure 2-59 shows a feed reader with feeds listed.

Q&A

Can I manage my feed preferences?
Yes. You can set preferences for how your browser or feed reader app handles web feeds. For example, you can change the frequency of feed updates or turn notifications for updates on or off.

Figure 2-58 Feed subscriptions

Figure 2-59 Listings of available web feeds.

Suggested Websites

Most browsers provide a list of suggested websites when you start typing in the Address bar. Using the text you enter as a basis, the browser uses **AutoComplete** feature (Figure 2-60) to suggest websites and search keywords and displays them in a list. AutoComplete suggestions come from your history of previously viewed webpages, as well as popular websites and common search terms. To visit a webpage, tap or click the URL that appears in the Address bar drop-down list. The list might also include suggested keywords for common and previously used searches. The Address bar drop-down list organizes its suggestions using AutoComplete suggestions, your browser history, and related search topics.

Figure 2-60   AutoComplete suggests websites and webpages based on popular searches and your search history.

Creating Shortcuts to a Website on the Desktop or Home Screen

A website shortcut on your computer or mobile device lets you open a website or webpage in your browser by tapping or clicking an icon. Windows and Mac desktop and laptop systems have a screen desktop, to which you can create shortcuts to websites. On a mobile device, such as a smartphone, you can create a shortcut icon for a website or webpage to the device's home screen.

To Create a Website Shortcut on the Desktop

The following steps create a shortcut to a website on the desktop, and then remove it. *Note:* These steps work best on a desktop or laptop computer. If you are using a mobile device, read these steps, and then use the next set of steps to create a website shortcut.

1

- Open your browser and navigate to msn.com if necessary.

- If necessary, minimize the browser window so that you can see the desktop.

- Tap or click the MSN icon in the Address bar, or select the URL in the Address bar (Figure 2-61).

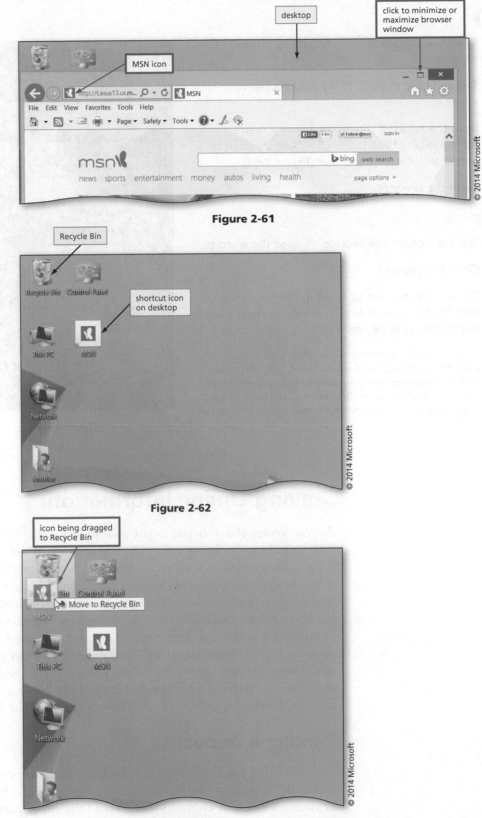

Figure 2-61

2

- Drag the icon or selected URL to the desktop to create a shortcut (Figure 2-62).

Figure 2-62

3

- Close the browser.

- Tap or click the icon on the desktop to open the website.

- Close the browser.

- To delete the shortcut icon, tap or click the icon to select it, and then drag the icon to the Recycle Bin or Trash (Figure 2-63).

Figure 2-63

To Create a Website Shortcut on a Mobile Device's Home Screen

The following steps create a shortcut icon to a website to a mobile device's home screen, and then remove it. *Note:* Depending on your device and browser, you may not be able to create website shortcuts. If that is the case, read the steps to understand the capabilities.

1

- Open your browser and navigate to msn.com if necessary.

- Tap and hold the URL in the Address bar to select it.

- Drag the selected URL to the home screen to open a menu, then tap or click 'Add shortcut to home' to create the shortcut (Figure 2-64).

- Close the browser.

2

- Tap the icon on the desktop to open the website.

- Close the browser.

- Tap or click the icon to select it, then drag the icon to the menu or area in which you remove items from your device.

Q&A

What if these steps do not work for me?
Depending on your browser or device, your steps may vary. For example, you may need to tap or click a Share button, and then tap or click the 'Add to Home Screen' command, or create a bookmark, and then add it to the home screen.

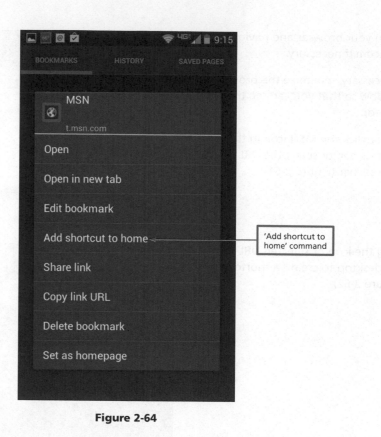

Figure 2-64

Saving Online Information

As you browse the web, you might want to print a hard copy of a webpage for later reference. Many websites offer printable versions of webpages or articles for this purpose. A printable version of a webpage eliminates features such as navigation bars along with other webpage content and elements unrelated to the article. Some websites offer the option to customize a printable copy of a web article, such as by adding or removing a header or footer, or eliminating ads or graphics. You also can save webpages in a variety of formats. For example, you can save a snapshot of the webpage or the complete HTML page with all of its associated files. You also can save just a webpage image. You can send the entire webpage or a link to the webpage to someone using email, text, or social media. You also can copy selected webpage content, including images, and then paste the selection into another document, such as a word processing document or the body of an email message.

Printing a Webpage

To print a webpage, you first must connect your computer or device to a printer wirelessly or using cables. To print a webpage, click the Print button, if available, on your browser's address or command bar to send the entire current webpage to the default printer. Depending on your computer or device, when you click the Print button you might see options that allow you to preview the webpage, and change paper size, page margins, and print orientation, header and footer content, and more.

Often, the hard copy printout of a webpage includes a header or footer on each page showing information such as the webpage title and page number, the URL, and the date on which the webpage was printed.

To print an article in a printer-friendly format, tap or click the Print link or button next to the article, if available, to open the article in a new tab, and then tap or click the Print button on your browser to open a new window with the printable article (Figure 2-65).

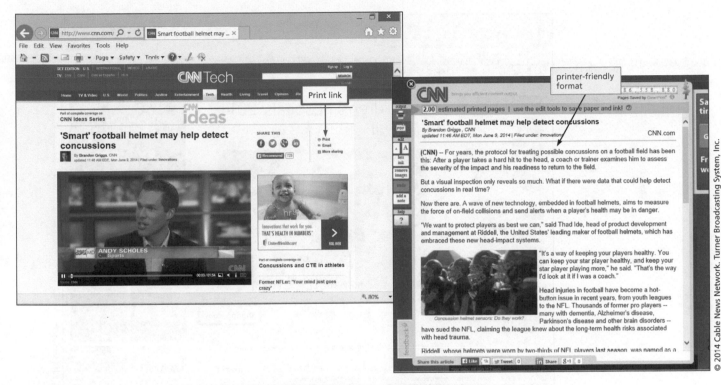

Figure 2-65 Many websites provide options to print articles in a printer-friendly format.

Saving a Webpage

Your computer or mobile device might support the ability to save a webpage as a file. When you save a webpage, you save a copy of its contents and, you might have various options for saving, including saving the entire webpage (HTML files and all graphics and style sheets), saving an archive file of a webpage, saving just the HTML file, or saving the webpage content as a text file. If you use either of the first two options, you can view the entire webpage, including graphics, while you are working offline. Working **offline** means that you are viewing previously loaded or saved webpages in the browser, but you are not connected to the Internet.

Sharing a Webpage

When you find a webpage that you think might interest someone else, you can share it by sending it to him or her by email or text. Many browsers have a 'Send page by email' command, and many websites have an Email or Text icon that, when tapped or clicked, opens a window that enables you to enter the recipient's email address or phone number and a short note. With either of these options, the recipient receives an email message with the webpage in the body of the message, or a text message with a link to the article. You also can copy a link and paste it into an email message or text message. When the message recipient clicks the link, his or her browser starts and opens the webpage.

Most browsers and websites enable you to share webpages and web content to social media and content sharing websites, such as Facebook, Twitter, Pinterest, and more. You can post a link to an article using the sharing or connectivity icons in the article or on the webpage (Figure 2-66). If you are using Pinterest, you can select which graphic on the webpage to display on your Pinterest board. You also can copy and paste a URL directly into a Facebook post or Twitter tweet.

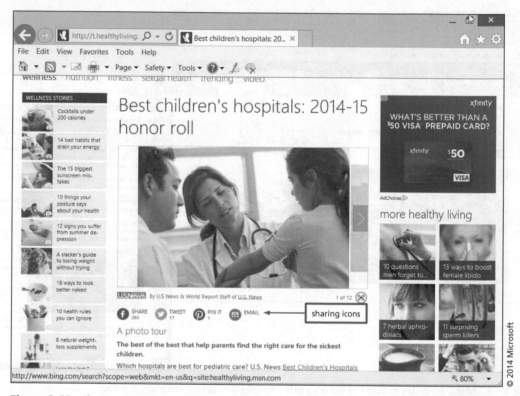

Figure 2-66 Sharing or connectivity icons enable you to share web content with your friends, family, or contacts.

For more information on U.S. copyright laws and how to ensure you are following them when saving or sharing web content and media, use a search engine to search for *U.S. copyright laws web content.*

Saving a Webpage Image

While browsing the web, you might find an image that you want to save. Be aware of ownership and copyrights when saving and using webpage images. Most webpage images are the property of their owners. U.S. copyright laws protect content owners from unauthorized copying and sharing of text, images, and other media. You cannot use copyright-protected images without permission from the owner or source. Some images, such as many images found at U.S. government websites, are in the public domain. You can use images in the public domain freely. You generally need to provide credit or source information about the source of public domain images. Many websites that offer public domain images also provide the wording for an image credit line.

Depending on your device or browser, you may be able to save an image, such as the one shown in Figure 2-67. If you are using a Windows laptop or desktop, right-click the image and then click the 'Save picture as' command on the shortcut menu. If you are using a Macintosh or mobile device, your steps will vary. For example, many mobile devices or computers with a touch screen will open a menu of commands, including the option to save web content or media if you press and hold the image or other content.

Figure 2-67 Be aware of copyright restrictions on saving or using images you find on the web.

Changing Browser Options

You can customize the browser window and some browser features in various ways. For example, you can show or hide commands, or change the display by zooming. As you have learned, with some computers or devices, you can change the browser's home page and select options for displaying the browser history.

Options to change or customize the browser commands you see depend on your computer, platform, and device. You should become familiar with your options, and what works best for your browsing needs. Figure 2-68 shows some options for customizing your browser.

Changing the Browser's Home Page

Depending on your browser, you can have either a single home page or multiple home pages open in tabs when the browser starts. If your computer or device opens by default with all open tabs from the last browsing session, with the most recent tab in the foreground, you may not be able to change your browser's home page.

Figure 2-68 You can customize your browser to fit your needs.

© 2014 Microsoft

To Add a Browser Home Page

The following steps change your browser's home page settings to add The Weather Channel home page to the current browser home page using Internet Explorer on a Windows computer. Then you remove the second home page to return to your original browser home page. *Note:* These steps assume you are using a Windows computer, and that you currently have only one browser home page. You may need to modify these steps to meet your specific needs. If your browser does not include the ability to specify a home page, or multiple home pages, read this set of steps to understand the capability of some browsers, but do not complete the steps.

1

- Start your browser.

- Enter `weather.com` in the Address bar and press the ENTER key or tap or click the appropriate button.

- Tap or click the Home button arrow on the Command bar to display the Home button menu (Figure 2-69).

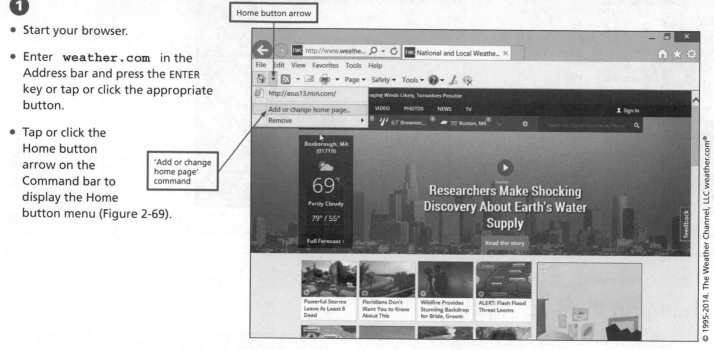

Figure 2-69

2

- Tap or click 'Add or change home page' to display the Add or Change Home Page dialog box.

- Tap or click the 'Add this webpage to your home page tabs' option button to add the current webpage as a home page tab (Figure 2-70).

3

- Tap or click the Yes button to add the webpage to your home page tabs.

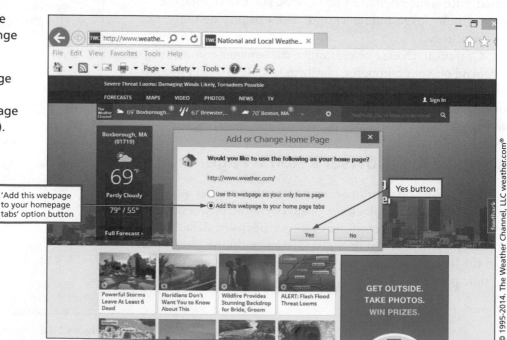

Figure 2-70

4

- Close your browser.

- Start your browser to view two home page tabs.

- Tap or click the Home button arrow on the Command bar to display the Home button menu.

- Tap or click Remove, then tap or click the weather.com icon on the menu.

Zooming a Webpage

You can change the view of the entire current webpage by enlarging or reducing it in a process called **zooming**. To zoom a webpage in or out using a browser for a laptop or desktop, look for a command on the right side of the status bar or Address bar that enables you to change browser display options. With a mobile device that is touch screen-enabled, pinch the screen to adjust the zoom. Zooming a webpage in to enlarge it can be especially helpful for people with vision problems, or to view web content on a mobile device. Zooming a webpage out enables you to see more webpage content (Figure 2-71).

© 2014 Microsoft

Figure 2-71 Zooming a website changes the amount you see on the screen.

Setting Other Browser Options

Depending on your browser or device, you may be able to further customize your browser. Options can include:

- Changing the browser's home page or pages
- Adding, deleting, organizing, and setting preferences for add-ons and plug-ins (Figure 2-72)
- Changing or restoring browser defaults, including zoom percentage and the default home page
- Managing your browsing history
- Changing how webpage tabs appear
- Modifying the settings for temporary Internet files (such as cookies)

- Establishing security and privacy controls
- Deleting temporary Internet files
- Changing settings that affect the browser's overall appearance

You will learn more about cookies and security and privacy options in the next section.

Figure 2-72 Managing your add-ons helps you extend your browser capability by adding security and convenience tools.

Using the Web: Risks and Safeguards

As you browse the web, you access information stored on servers located all over the world. Even as you use the web from the privacy of your home or office, you are venturing into a very public arena that connects millions of computers and people from around the globe. Although this global connectivity has many positive aspects, it also creates the possibility that you might encounter unethical people, objectionable material, or attacks from hackers. In the next few sections, you will learn about the risks of using the web and safeguards that can protect you from these risks.

Protecting Your Computer from Hackers

Anytime you connect to the Internet you should take precautions to protect your computer or device from hackers. A **hacker** is an individual who uses technology skills to access a network and the computers on that network without authorization. "Cracker" and "black hat hacker" are terms used to describe a criminal or unethical hacker. A hacker typically accesses a computer or device by connecting to it and then logging on as a legitimate user. Once logged on, the hacker can access data, programs, and apps; save or delete files or programs; or access the computer or device's power, all without the owner's knowledge or permission. The level of exposure is greater for users with an always-on Internet connection, or those who access the Internet using unsecured wireless networks.

A firewall (Figure 2-73) protects a computer or a network from unauthorized access by hackers. A **firewall**, which can be hardware or software, can examine network communications and then directly block or warn the user about those communications that do not meet a set of predetermined rules. For example, a firewall on a home computer connected to the Internet might be set to block certain outgoing communications from a specific software application or operating system utility, or it could prevent incoming communications from an unknown source without authorization.

Courtesy of NETGEAR; © Cengage Learning®; Courtesy of CheckPoint Software Technolcgies; © iStockphoto/ Skip Odonnell; Source: Nutrition Blog Network; © iStockphoto/123render; Source: Microsoft; © Iakov Filimonov/Shutterstock.com; © iStockphoto/Oleksiy Mark; Source: Microsoft; © iStockphoto/Ayaaz Rattansi; Source: Microsoft; © iStockphoto/Oleksiy Mark; Source: Microsoft; © Cengage Learning®

Figure 2-73

Your computer or device's operating system might provide a firewall. If you are running a home wireless network, you should purchase and install a firewall for the network, and use password protection to ensure that only authorized computers and devices can access the network. Many routers and other network devices used in small or home networks include firewalls. Businesses use a variety of sophisticated firewalls for their local area networks.

Virus Protection

A **virus** is a small, potentially damaging program or app that can infect a computer or device, which then can infect other computers or devices or the same network, or generate virus-enabled email or text messages or social networking posts and send the virus to the user's contacts. Browsing the web typically does not expose a computer or device to damaging viruses, and most browsers include filters and virus detection for your protection. When the user taps or clicks a link or opens an email message, text message, or file attachment that includes the virus, the computer or device becomes infected. Other risks include downloading software and apps from unsafe or unknown sources. One way to guard against viruses is to never access a link or open an email, text, or file unless you trust the source and you are expecting the communication or file. You will learn more about the risks of and safeguards for using email in Chapter 4. Another way to guard against viruses is to subscribe to virus protection software or apps, such as Norton™ AntiVirus (Figure 2-74) or McAfee® VirusScan, and enable the software or app to update automatically to keep the virus protection current.

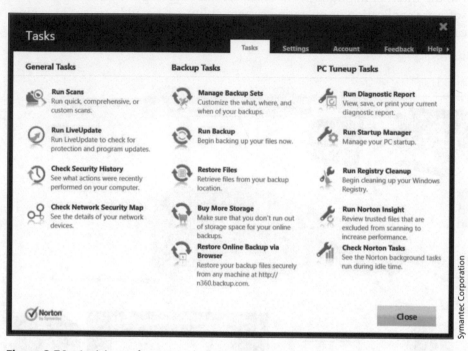

Figure 2-74 Antivirus software can help keep you safe when browsing the Internet.

Shopping Online Safely

Shopping online is convenient because consumers can read quickly about product features, view pictures, and compare prices. In most circumstances, shopping online is a safe activity; however, there are some risks. The risks of online shopping include not knowing with whom you are doing business, and the possibility of having your financial information stolen when providing payment information online. By following a few guidelines, you can enjoy safe and successful shopping online.

Before making a purchase from an online vendor, determine whether the business is reputable. For example, by purchasing products or services from well-known companies, such as Dell, Barnes & Noble, or Delta Air Lines, consumers can feel more confident about the purchase. Shoppers should read the company's security assurances on their website to confirm that the company will not use their customer information or payment information illegally. On the other hand, purchasing a collectible doll from an anonymous seller at an online auction website is inherently more risky because the seller may not have a well-known public reputation. The U.S. government website OnGuardOnline is a great resource for learning about shopping online safely and other computer and online safety issues.

In addition to choosing an online vendor carefully, consumers should be cautious when making payments over the Internet. Most online vendors accept credit cards, currently the most popular online payment method, which limits the consumer's liability. Other payment methods include electronic checks and third-party payment services, such as PayPal (Figure 2-75), which allow consumers to send money to anyone by email or money order. Third-party payment services are a popular means of paying for consumer-to-consumer (C2C) transactions.

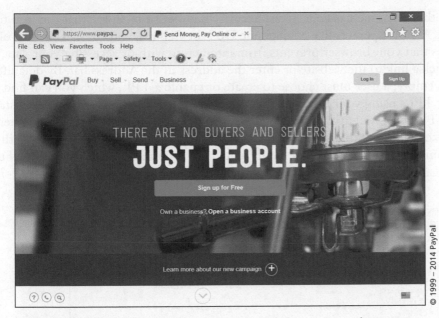

Figure 2-75   Third-party payment services are a popular way to send money using a secure Internet connection.

When paying for an online purchase using a credit card, be sure to access the website using a secure connection. A **secure connection** uses https:// rather than http:// as its connection protocol, and a locked padlock icon appears on the Security Status bar on the right side of the Address bar. The secure https:// protocol and the locked padlock icon signify that the website encrypts your data before sending it over a secure connection using Secure Sockets Layer. **Secure Sockets Layer (SSL)** is a commonly used protocol for managing the security of message transmissions on the Internet. Using a secure connection ensures the verifiable identity of the website based on information provided to an organization, called a certificate authority. You can click the padlock to view website verification information. You also can click a link below the verification information to view the Internet Explorer Help topic on trusted websites.

Finally, never send a credit card number or other personal or sensitive information by email or text. Hackers can use programs and apps to intercept email messages without your knowledge. Following these simple guidelines can help you shop online more safely and confidently.

Filtering Web Content

Web users sometimes mistakenly encounter objectionable material, such as offensive language, sexually explicit or violent material, or hate propaganda, while browsing the web. One of the web's greatest strengths is that it is unregulated and open to all; however, that also means that the web is an unprotected environment that contains material some may find objectionable. The prevalence of objectionable content can be particularly problematic for children using the Internet and browsing the web.

Tracking Protection Lists (TPLs) are one method to control websites that can access your content on the Internet. Every time you visit a website, the website potentially can take note of your searches, clicks, and other activity, and share that information with other websites. Those websites then use the information to personalize or target the ads and content you see, or other uses of your personal data. Adding a website to a TPL, or enabling a TPL from a third-party source can help you protect your personal data, such as passwords that enable hackers to access your account, sensitive data relating to your finances, or other data, such as your Social Security number or birthday, that can lead to identity theft. A TPL operates like a telephone Do Not Call list, and consists of a list of web addresses that your browser prevents from interacting with or accessing your data, unless you click a link to the website or enter the address in the Address bar. By default, a user's TPL is empty; a user must choose to create or enable a TPL, which you can find by searching for TPLs using your browser. You can create your own TPL, or you can install third-party TPLs that contain lists of known malicious or unscrupulous websites. When using TPLs, keep in mind that some websites rely on tracking, cookies, and other methods to fully function. By limiting their ability, you may be limiting the functionality of the website. You can add, delete, and manage TPLs using your browser settings (Figure 2-76).

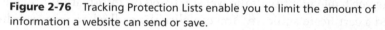

Figure 2-76 Tracking Protection Lists enable you to limit the amount of information a website can send or save.

Web content filters, also called **Internet filters**, are hardware and/or software that control the display of web content based on user settings. For example, parents can use a web content filter to protect their children from objectionable material. Employers can use a web content filter to prevent their employees from viewing objectionable material at work.

Some web content filters, such as iPrism® (for businesses), McAfee® SmartFilter (for schools), and Net Nanny® parental controls (for home use), might use specific filters that block certain webpages based on keywords or a predefined database of objectionable websites. In addition, browsers have built-in content filter features that can help block objectionable material. You can manage your web filters and set parental and other controls using your browser settings (Figure 2-77).

Figure 2-77 You can filter or block inappropriate webpage content by customizing your browser settings.

Protecting Against Malicious Websites

A **malicious website** is a website that is designed to look like a legitimate website, such as a website for downloading online games, but actually is owned by hackers or online thieves who use its content to capture your sensitive personal information, such as your name and password, or to distribute malicious software, such as a keystroke logger that records all your keystrokes. Most browsers have built-in filters for detecting malicious websites.

Keeping Your Personal Information Private

Information privacy refers to the right of individuals and companies to deny or restrict the collection and use of personal information. Websites track personal information entered in webpage forms and stored in the company databases. Although this information should be accessible only to authorized users, some people question whether this data really is private. Some companies and individuals collect and use your personal information and record your online activities without your authorization. Entities such as your employer, your Internet service provider (ISP), government agencies, the websites you visit, and third-party advertisers all might be tracking your online activities.

Some people are less concerned about protecting their personal information and enjoy the benefits of targeted marketing, personalized email messages, and direct mail, such as catalogs, as a result of information gathered about them while they browse the web. But many people are very concerned that their private information is vulnerable to entities such as third-party advertisers. The following sections discuss the entities that might be collecting and using your private information and the laws that protect your information privacy.

EMPLOYERS   An employer legally can monitor employee use of its computer equipment and time spent on the web at the workplace. Employers often publish policies explaining that they have the legal right to monitor employees' computer usage and require that their employees acknowledge that right before accepting employment. Most employers, however, do not abuse their right to monitor employees; employers only want to protect themselves from any illegal or harmful use of their network and computer systems.

INTERNET SERVICE PROVIDERS   An ISP is capable of tracking online usage because all of its customers' web traffic goes through the ISP's network. Unlike an employer, however, an ISP has no legitimate reason to track online behavior. Most ISP customers respond negatively to news of an ISP collecting their private information. Although an ISP has the ability to record online activities, many ISPs publish a privacy statement; a statement of their privacy policy specifically describing what information they collect, how they use it, and whether they share this information with third parties. The ISP makes the terms of such a privacy policy available to their customers in the form of a privacy statement, usually posted at the ISP's website.

GOVERNMENT AGENCIES   The concern about privacy has led to the passage of federal and state laws regarding the storage and disclosure of personal data. Several of these laws protect certain kinds of information, such as medical records and financial data, from access to anyone without the individual's permission. Other laws limit the U.S. government's right to track online activities to specific circumstances, such as to investigate crime or in cases of national defense.

PRIVACY ADVOCATES   Maintaining privacy is an important issue for web users. Organizations, such as the Electronic Privacy Information Center (EPIC), inform

Q&A

What is big data?
Big data refers to collection and sharing of data from various formats and sources, often without your knowledge. To learn more about big data issues, use a search engine to search for *big data*.

@SOURCE

To learn more about electronic privacy issues, use a search engine to search for *electronic privacy*.

government agencies and consumers about privacy issues and maintaining information about privacy issues at their websites. Government agencies use the information to protect its own data, create or change legislation, and inform the public about threats and how to avoid them. Consumers should keep aware of current security threats and be aware of each person's own role in protecting data.

BUSINESS WEBSITES   Business websites can collect personal information, such as names, addresses, telephone numbers, or credit card information, from shoppers or visitors and then store that information in a database. Consumers visiting websites should be aware of what information a business collects, how it uses the information, and what protection efforts the business takes. Consumers can learn how a company handles personal information collected at its website by reading the website's privacy statement.

Like ISPs, most businesses publish their privacy policies in an easily accessible **privacy statement** posted at their websites. You typically can find a link to a privacy statement at the bottom of a business's home page. Many companies demonstrate a commitment to privacy by becoming a member of the TRUSTe program. The TRUSTe program is a voluntary program that reviews a company's website and business practices to ensure that the website adheres to established privacy principles and complies with ongoing TRUSTe review and consumer resolution procedures. TRUSTe members can display the TRUSTe trustmark at their websites.

@SOURCE
To learn more about cookies, spyware, and adware, use a search engine to search for *cookies and spyware*.

To be an informed consumer and web user, you should make a habit of viewing the privacy statement at frequently visited websites to see exactly what information is collected and how the company or website will use it. The privacy statement should indicate how the company handles **personally identifiable information (PII)**, such as email addresses, names and addresses, or even more sensitive personal information, such as health, financial, political, or religious information.

Websites cannot collect personal information from children under the age of 13. The Children's Online Privacy Protection Act (COPPA) requires that websites get explicit permission from parents before marketing to or collecting personal data from children.

COOKIES   Businesses and other websites often rely on cookies to identify users and customize webpages. A **cookie** is a small text file stored on a computer or device that can contain data, such as a username, password, shipping address, or viewing preferences. Businesses then can use the information stored in cookies to deliver customized webpages, to remember a username and password, or to present targeted advertisements on a webpage. Businesses also use cookies to track which website pages users' visit most often and other website visitor statistics. Cookies can provide a positive visitor experience by speeding up the checkout or login process and by displaying recommended articles or sale items. Cookies still can be a cause for concern because the information is collected without the visitor's explicit consent and can be used by the website or sold to other websites without consent.

Most browsers allow you to set options for cookie handling when customizing your advanced privacy settings (Figure 2-78). When modifying browser privacy settings, you might not want to

Figure 2-78   You can set options for accepting or blocking cookies by customizing your browser's advanced privacy settings.

refuse all cookies. Some websites require the use of cookies; if you block all cookies, you may not be able to purchase merchandise, airline tickets, or services or benefit from customized content at such websites.

You can delete cookies from your computer or device. Be aware that deleting all cookies also deletes those that are useful, such as cookies that store personal profiles and preferences for frequently visited websites. Deleting cookies one at a time is preferable because it allows you to specify which ones to delete.

SPYWARE AND ADWARE   **Spyware** is a general term usually applied to any technology that accesses your computer system to gather information without your knowledge and approval. **Adware** is a form of spyware that gathers information and then uses that information to deliver targeted web advertising. Visitors sometimes unknowingly download adware when downloading other software. Another type of spyware is a web bug, also called a web beacon. A **web bug** is a tiny hidden graphic embedded in a webpage. Third-party advertisers sometimes use web bugs to collect information about website visitors. Web bugs gather information, such as a computer or device's IP address, the type of browser used to retrieve the bug, the web address of the webpage from which the user came, and the time and date the user viewed the webpage. Unlike cookies, which you can locate and delete, web bugs are invisible. Although web bugs can customize a user's experience or gather statistics on the website, the invisible nature of web bugs fuels privacy debates. To protect yourself from spyware, you can install spyware and adware protection software. Additionally, some virus protection software also checks for and removes spyware. Be sure to research any company before you download its software; some programs that claim to check for spyware are actually malicious programs. Even when downloading safe software, opt for a custom installation to ensure you are not downloading additional toolbars, apps, or programs that might come bundled with the program or app.

Opting Out

@ISSUE

Although website owners have a responsibility to post and adhere to privacy policies, consumers can take action to protect their own privacy. For example, consumers can take time to review the privacy policy statements posted at their favorite websites. To protect against third-party or other undesirable cookies on their computers, consumers can delete any unwanted cookies and set options to restrict cookie acceptance from third-party websites, or to prompt you to be able to accept cookies individually. Then they can check for opt-out instructions at websites and submit forms to opt out of receiving cookies, data collection, and advertising. Taking these actions can help protect and maintain privacy when browsing the web.

PROTECTING YOUR BROWSER HISTORY   As you learned earlier in this chapter, your browser records information about the websites you visit in the browsing history. In some circumstances, you might not want to record your browsing history during a specific browsing session (for example, when you share a computer and do not want others to see your browsing history). Some browsers offer an option to not store information about the websites you visit, such as Internet Explorer's InPrivate Browsing feature (Figure 2-79). Note that browser history protection does not prevent websites from gathering your personally identifiable information while you browse; it only prevents the browser from storing information about your browsing session.

Figure 2-79   Protecting your browser history can help protect your privacy when using a public or shared computer.

FILTERING WEBPAGE CONTENT   Earlier in this section, you learned about web beacons or bugs. As you browse the web, you view many webpages that contain content, such as advertising, provided by others, sometimes called content providers. When you visit a website containing content provided by third parties, the content providers might be capturing information about your browsing habits using web bugs. For example, content providers could display specific advertisements that might be of interest to you based on the types of websites you visit. To protect against this type of data gathering, you can access your browser's built-in filter, such as the Internet Explorer InPrivate Filtering feature. When a filtering feature is turned on, the browser analyzes each webpage you visit for suspicious third-party content. If the browser detects suspicious content, you will have the option of blocking the suspicious content. If desired, you can set an option to have the filtering feature automatically block any third-party content.

Chapter Review

Webpages typically include some or all of the following: a logo or name, images, links, advertisements, a search tool, sharing or connectivity icons, a copyright statement, and a link to a privacy policy statement.

An IP address is the unique numerical address of a computer on a network that you use to address and send data over a network, such as the Internet. A domain name is an easy-to-remember text alias for one or more IP addresses. A URL, also called a web address, is the unique address of a webpage; it consists of the http:// protocol, the server name, and the domain name, and can include the path and file name.

You can load webpages by typing each webpage's URL in the Address box on the Address bar and pressing the ENTER key or tapping or clicking the appropriate button. You also can load a webpage by clicking a webpage link. Depending on your browser and device, you can navigate among recently loaded webpages during the current browser session, load a fresh copy of the current webpage, stop loading a webpage, and load the browser's home page.

You can use several browser shortcuts to visit webpages, including favorites or bookmarks, a history list, web feeds, and suggested websites. Many websites enable you to print a printer-friendly copy of a webpage. You also can save a webpage in a variety of formats that include or exclude its related files, such as graphics. You can send or share a snapshot of or a link to a webpage to someone by email, text, or social media. Individual webpage images can be saved for private use in a variety of different formats.

You can change browser options, such as displaying and hiding toolbars and changing the home page to a new home page or a group of home pages that open in separate tabs, using the keyboard, a shortcut menu. You also can use a browser's privacy and security settings to browse the web more securely.

TERMS TO KNOW

After reading this chapter, you should know each of these Key Terms.

accelerator (63)
add-on (63)
adware (83)
aggregator (64)
Atom (64)
AutoComplete (68)
big data (81)
bookmark (56)
browser sniffing (37)
client (37)
client/server computing (37)
cookie (82)
country-code top-level domain
    (ccTLD) (39)
display area (42)
domain name (38)
Domain Name System (DNS) (39)
dynamic IP address (38)
extension (63)
favorite (56)
feed reader (64)
firewall (77)
hacker (76)
History list (60)
home page (34)
information privacy (81)
Internet Corporation for Assigned Names
    and Numbers (ICANN) (39)

Internet filter (80)
IP address (Internet Protocol
    address) (38)
malicious website (81)
name server (38)
offline (71)
personally identifiable information
    (PII) (82)
portal (35)
privacy statement (82)
rich media ad (46)
RSS (Really Simple Syndication) (64)
secure connection (79)
Secure Sockets Layer (SSL) (79)
server (37)
spyware (83)
static IP address (38)
tabbed browsing (50)
top-level domain (TLD) (39)
Tracking Protection List (TPL) (79)
Uniform Resource Locator (URL) (39)
virus (77)
web address (39)
web bug (83)
web content filter (80)
web feed (64)
web portal (35)
zooming (80)

TERMS TO KNOW

Complete the Test Your Knowledge exercises to solidify what you have learned in the chapter.

TEST YOUR KNOWLEDGE

True or False

Mark T for True and F for False. (Answers are found on page numbers in parentheses.)

____ 1. A client is an application that runs on a computer, such as a personal computer, and requests resources or services from another computer. (37)

____ 2. Advertisements with attention-grabbing sounds and animation are called adware. (46)

____ 3. The protocol (http://) and the domain name in a URL are case sensitive. (40)

____ 4. An add-on allows you to access web content or take some action based on selected webpage text. (63)

____ 5. A cookie is a small text file stored on a computer or device that can contain data, such as a username, password, shipping address, or viewing preferences. (82)

____ 6. A computer hacker is a small, potentially damaging computer program that can infect a computer and then be passed to other computers. (76)

____ 7. A printed webpage often has a header and footer containing the name of the webpage, the page number, the webpage's URL, and the date printed. (71)

___ 8. A filter is a security system that uses hardware and/or software to prevent unauthorized access to a computer on a network. (77)

___ 9. The secure https:// protocol and a padlock icon signify that your information is being sent over a secure connection. (79)

___10. A TPL consists of a list of web addresses that a browser will interact with only if the user clicks a link to the website or enters the address in the Address bar, limiting the amount of information a website can track. (79)

Multiple Choice

Select the best answer. (Answers are found on page numbers in parentheses.)

1. _____ is a tiny hidden graphic embedded in a webpage that third-party advertisers sometimes use to collect information about website visitors. (83)

    a. PII

    b. A web bug

    c. Spyware

    d. A virus

2. The organization that oversees naming and numbering functions in the DNS and controls the domain name registration system is _____. (39)

    a. ICANN

    b. SSL

    c. W3C

    d. TLD

3. A website that offers links to a wide range of content and services and is often used as a default starting webpage is called a(n) _____. (35)

    a. home page

    b. server

    c. web feed

    d. web portal

4. PII stands for _____. (82)

    a. Protocol Internet Index

    b. Personally Identifiable Information

    c. Protection of Internet Identity

    d. Private Internet Information

5. A browser may suggest websites when you type in the Address bar, including _____. (68)

    a. commonly visited websites

    b. your browser history

    c. search terms

    d. All of the above

6. _____ is a commonly used protocol for managing the security of message transmissions on the Internet. (79)

a. HTTP

b. URL

c. SSL

d. FTP

7. A web server with a permanent Internet connection needs a(n) _____ IP address. (38)

a. dynamic

b. private

c. static

d. assigned

8. Atom is an example of technology used to manage _____. (64)

a. web feeds

b. portals

c. virus protection

d. cookies

9. A(n) _____ examines network communications and then directly blocks or warns the user about those communications that do not meet a set of predetermined rules. (77)

a. cookie

b. firewall

c. filter

d. dynamic IP

10. _____ is a general name for any technology that accesses your computer system without your knowledge or approval to gather information. (83)

a. Adware

b. Gatherware

c. Privacyware

d. Spyware

Investigate current Internet developments with the Trends exercises.

TRENDS

Write a brief essay about each of the following trends, using the web as your research tool. For each trend, identify at least one webpage URL used as a research source. Be prepared to discuss your findings in class.

1 | Web Feeds

Visit a news website of your choice (a news portal, an entertainment or sports news website, or a general or local news website) and view the feeds available for the website. If none are available, choose a different website example. Subscribe to a feed on the website, and then view the feed content in your feed reader or browser. Is the content valuable to you? Where else might you obtain the information in the feed? What other information would you like to add to your web feed? Use a search engine to search for *web feed readers* for your device. Read at least one article that evaluates available feed readers, including, if available, the default or built-in feed reader for your browser. Would you continue to use the current feed reader to which you have access? Why or why not? What alternatives are available?

2 | Internet and Web Threats

1. Use a search engine to research the following Internet and web threats. Find a current example of at least one of these that is considered an active threat, or that made news because of its negative impact.

    a. criminal or unethical hackers

    b. viruses

    c. adware

    d. spyware

2. Using your research, write at least four paragraphs describing the threat and how to protect against it using browser and other tools and good judgment.

@ISSUE

Challenge your perspective of Internet technology with the @Issue exercises.

Write a brief essay in response to the following issues, using the web as your research tool. For each issue, identify at least one URL used as a research source. Be prepared to discuss your findings in class.

1 | Online Safety

1. Search for current articles on *shopping online safety*. Read at least two articles, and make a list of the identified threats and how to avoid them. Create a list of these tips to share with classmates.

2. Search for information about consumer privacy statistics. Create a list of three statistics that you found surprising. Research one of the statistics to find out how you could protect your privacy from that threat. Locate and print tips on online safety. Be prepared to discuss the tips with your classmates.

3. Search for information about threats to and protection of children online. Review recommendations for online child safety. Describe the risks to children using the Internet and the web, and suggest ways to protect children from those risks.

2 | Copyrights for Media on the Web

1. Search for information about media copyrights on the web. Read at least two articles or blog posts that discuss restrictions on using media posted by others on the web. Read at least two articles that outline how to protect your own media that you post online. Based on what you have read, answer the following questions:

    a. Who is responsible for protecting and enforcing copyright restrictions?

    b. If media or other content does not have a copyright disclaimer, can you use it freely?

    c. What methods should you take to protect your own media on the web?

Use the web to obtain more information about the skills taught in the chapter with the Hands On exercises.

1 | Share a Webpage

1. Start your browser, if necessary.

2. Visit a news website of your choice (a news portal, an entertainment or sports news website, or a general or local news website).

3. Tap or click on a link to an article you would like to send to a friend or share on social media.

   a. Make a note of the sharing icons available to you.

4. Use the sharing icons to send the article to yourself using text or email, or post a link to the article to one of your social media accounts, or if there is a social media group or page for your class, post it there. If possible, add a note as to why you are sharing the webpage.

   a. If you sent yourself the article, view the text message or email.

   b. If you posted the article to social media, view the post.

   c. If possible, take a screenshot of the post or email before deleting it.

5. Close your browser and submit your findings in the format requested by your instructor.

2 | Use the History List

1. View your browser's History list and then click the Today icon or text link in the History list, if necessary, to view a list of folders for websites visited by anyone using the computer or device today.

2. Click a folder in the Today list to expand it, if necessary, and view the links to individual webpages visited at that website today. Click a link to any webpage to revisit it.

3. Click the Last Week icon or text link, if available, to view the folders for websites visited last week. Click a link to any webpage to revisit it.

4. Find out how you would clear your browser history.

   a. Why would you want to clear your browser history?

   b. What would be the downside of clearing your browser history?

Work collaboratively to reinforce the concepts in the chapter with the Team Approach exercises.

1 | Privacy Policies

1. Work as a team with three to four classmates. Assign a team member to locate the privacy policy statement for at least one of the following companies.

   a. Amazon (www.amazon.com)

   b. Target (www.target.com)

   c. Hewlett-Packard (www.hp.com)

2. Answer the following privacy issue questions for each website:

   a. What information is collected from users? Is personally identifiable information collected?

   b. Why is the information collected?

   c. Does the company share the collected information with its business partners?

   d. How long is the information retained?

   e. Can a user opt out of the information collection; and if so, how?

   f. Does the website post any privacy guarantees, such as TRUSTe?

   g. Does the website use cookies or web bugs; and if so, why?

2. Compare your findings with your teammates, and as a group:

   a. List common policies or statements.

   b. List one unique issue for each website.

2 | Add-Ons

1. Join with three other students to create a team.

2. Select a browser or platform on which to focus your research.

3. Have each team member research a separate topic regarding add-ons:

   a. Negative or positive effect on security and privacy.

   b. Effect on the speed of your browser, computer, or device.

   c. Recommended add-ons for saving or sharing web content.

   d. Technologies used to create and manage add-ons.

3. Compare your findings with your teammates, and as a group come up with a summary of findings and recommendations regarding add-ons.

3 | Searching the Web

© 2014 Microsoft

© 2014 Infospace, LLC

Copyright © Google.

© 2014 Microsoft

Introduction

Searching for information is one of the most powerful and useful features of the web. In this chapter, you will learn how to describe and follow the steps in the search process, perform basic and advanced searches using general text-oriented and visual search tools, use browser search features, and use specialized search tools to locate people, businesses, current news stories, geographic information, video, social media content, hashtags, and products and services. You also will learn about online research alternatives to search tools.

Objectives

After completing this chapter, you will be able to:

1. Describe how search engines work, and understand the search process

2. Use different types of search tools and compare search results

3. Apply search tool shortcuts and advanced features, including Boolean operators

4. Perform searches using browser search features

5. Identify and use specialized search tools

6. Identify online research alternatives to standard search tools

The Search Process

Many people rely on the web to find specific information quickly. As you learned in Chapter 2, when you know the URL for a webpage, you can enter the URL in your browser's Address box, tap or click a link on the current webpage, or tap or click a favorite or bookmark to open the page. In this way, you can get the latest scores or team standings for your favorite sports teams, keep up with current news and trends, and purchase products or services from your preferred online stores.

At other times, you might need specific information but not know the webpage's URL, or you might require specific information but not know where to find it. For example, suppose you want to learn more about The White House by visiting webpages that provide that information. One way you could do so is to guess an appropriate URL — something like www.whitehouse.gov — and enter that guess in the browser's Address box. Alternatively, you can enter relevant search term keywords. When you start entering the URL or keywords, such as *The White House*, your browser will search for appropriate URLs and provide you with a suggested list. Figure 3-1 illustrates a specific process you can follow when searching the web. In the next sections, you will learn more about this process.

Step 1: Choose the best search tool	Enter the URL of a search engine, such as Bing, or a search directory, such as DMOZ, or enter your query in the Address box of your browser.
Step 2: Formulate the search query	Enter a possible URL or type search keywords. Enter more words for a more specific search that will return narrower results.
Step 3: Perform the search	Press ENTER key or tap or click a button to start the search process.
Step 4: Examine the search results	Determine which is the best result, keeping in mind that some links are paid.
Step 5: Evaluate the credibility of the search results	Make sure the links you choose are legitimate and objective, and contain the information that you need in a layout and design that are usable.

© Cengage Learning®

Figure 3-1   The web search process.

How Search Engines Work

When you use a search engine to find information, you are more likely to consider content among the first few results. Search engines use complicated, patented, ever-changing algorithms to create search rankings, which determine the order in which suggested content appears in the search results. **Search engine algorithms** instruct the search engine to locate and rank search results based on keywords and a variety of other factors. In addition to using programs called **crawlers** to locate webpages, search engines determine relevancy of search results based on page rankings, frequency of content updates, keywords and metadata, and number of inbound and outbound hyperlinks. In addition, search engines may use analytical tools to rank search results based on factors such as number of website visitors, trending topics, and more.

Google, Bing, Yahoo! and other search engines keep their search engine algorithms private. By not disclosing search engine algorithms, the search engines are attempting to prevent **search engine optimization (SEO)** marketers from manipulating web content to improve search rankings in order to have them appear higher in search results. Google updates its search algorithm approximately 500 times per year, requiring SEO marketers to follow best web content-writing practices rather than focusing exclusively on search engine rankings. Other trends and developments in search engine algorithms include:

- Personalized searches based on a user's previous search history
- Localized searches that provide results targeted to a user's geographic location
- Analysis of popular search terms in order to improve the algorithms
- Increased focus on social sharing by analyzing trending and commonly shared web content on social media platforms such as Facebook and Twitter
- Focus on **natural language searches** that use phrases or questions rather than keywords. For example, a keyword search might be: *SEO search engine rankings.* A natural language search for the same topic might be: *How can I use SEO to improve my website's search engine rankings?*
- Banning or removing webpages from the search engine index if they use manipulative or unethical SEO practices, ensuring the best search results for users

Choosing the Best Search Tool

Searching the web starts with selecting the most effective search tool to use for a particular search. Many different types of search tools, such as Google, StumbleUpon, Bing, and blinkx (Figure 3-2), are prevalent on the web. You will learn more about these and other search tools and how to use them later in the chapter. It is important to realize that search tool features and performance vary from tool to tool and change over time, and

© 2014 blinkx

Figure 3-2 You can access a variety of search tools, such as blinkx, on the web.

that new search tools continually become available. Also, a user's search needs might vary from one search to another, making one tool more appropriate for that type of search.

The best approach is to become familiar with and use multiple search tools, which allows you to evaluate search tools and then choose the tool best suited for a particular search. In general, when evaluating search tools, look for tools that:

- Are easy to use
- Return search results quickly
- Provide access to frequently updated large indexes of webpages and other web-based files
- Present the most relevant search results for a keyword search
- Clearly indicate paid or sponsored links in their search results list

Figure 3-3 lists some specialized search engine categories and options. Some of these categories and specific search engines are covered later in the chapter.

Search Engines

Content/Topic	Examples
Business	Business.com, GenieKnows, Justdial
Food/Recipes	RecipeBridge, Yummly
Job/Career	CareerBuilder, Hotjobs, Indeed, Glassdoor, Monster
Legal	Google Scholar, Lexis Nexis, WestLaw
Medical	Bing Health, Healthline, WebMD
Real Estate/Property	Realtor.com, Redfin, Trulia, Zillow
Maps	Google Maps, Mapquest, OpenStreetMap, Wikimapia
Question and Answer	Answers.com, eHow, wikiHow, WolframAlpha

© Cengage Learning®

Figure 3-3   Specialized search engines.

FACTS @HAND   According to the Pew Internet & American Life Project, 50 percent of Americans use the Internet as a main source of news. That number jumps to 71 percent for users under the age of 30.

Formulating the Search Query

The next step in the process of searching the web is to formulate a search query. A **search query** is a question that defines the information you seek. A query should include at least one **keyword**, a specific word that describes that information. To get the best results, choose keywords carefully and use specific rather than general keywords whenever appropriate. For example, suppose you recently visited an animal shelter and are considering adopting one of two dogs you saw at the shelter. But before you adopt your new pet, you want to use the web to learn more about the nature, characteristics, and care requirements of your two adoption possibilities: a sheltie and a golden retriever. Using the search keywords *sheltie* or *golden retriever* generates more relevant results than using the search keyword *dog*.

You enter search keywords in a search tool's **search text box** or in the Address box. The search tool then uses the keywords to identify relevant webpages and return a **search results list** containing the URL, title, and description of and links to webpages that the search tool determines to be the most relevant to the keywords. Each webpage item listed in a search results list is a **hit**. Figure 3-4 illustrates a search in the Bing search engine using the keyword *sheltie* and the resulting hits.

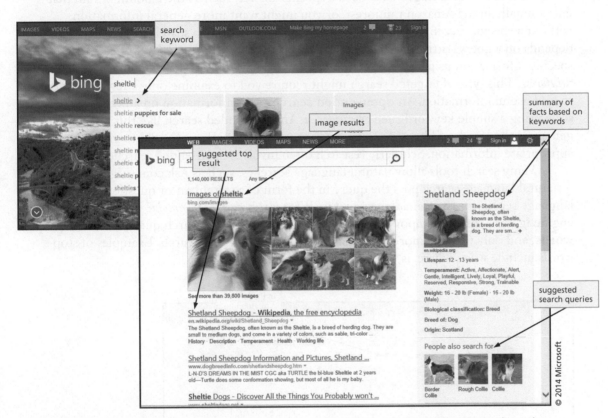

Figure 3-4 Search keywords entered in a search tool's search text box are used to return a search results list containing relevant webpage hits.

When you use multiple keywords, such as *golden retriever*, most search tools automatically assume the word, and, exists between keywords, meaning the webpages returned in the list of hits will contain *golden* and *retriever*. But assuming the word, and, exists between keywords does not guarantee that the keywords will appear close together on the webpages. Most search tools allow you to surround keywords with quotation marks when the keywords must appear together as a phrase. For example, a keyword search for *congressional bill* might return webpages containing the word, congressional, and the first name, Bill. Using quotation marks around the phrase *"congressional bill"* narrows the results to hits that contain that exact phrase.

The more keywords you include in a query, the more focused the results will be. For example, assume you are planning a vacation and want to find information about a specific national park. Searching for webpages using the keyword *park* will return a list of millions of pages, far more than you can or want to review and most of which are irrelevant to the information you seek. Using the phrase *"Grand Canyon National Park"* returns more relevant hits because the search process returns webpages that contain all of those keywords together and places the pages at or near the top of the list of hits. Omitting the quotation marks will likely produce slightly different search results — but webpages containing information about the Grand Canyon National Park still should be positioned at or near the top of the search results list.

Although it is always better to spell search keywords correctly, some search tools might either list search results for correctly spelled keywords or suggest the correct spelling. For example, searching for information about a musical instrument using the keyword *accordian* might return a list of webpages based on the correct spelling *accordion*, depending on which search tool is used.

Your search goal might be to seek a specific answer, such as the amount of rain that falls annually in the Amazon rainforest, or you might want more general information without a specific fact in mind. The number of hits returned in a search results list depends on a query's structure and keywords. For example, a **targeted search** seeks specific information using keyword combinations such as *"average rainfall" Amazon rainforest*. This type of targeted search might require you to examine only a few webpages to find useful information. An **open-ended search** seeks information on a broader scale using a simple keyword such as *rainforest*. An open-ended search like this typically generates thousands of hits and requires you to review multiple webpages to gather appropriate information. Scholarly research often involves open-ended searches.

Many search tools allow natural language searches, such as Ask.com (Figure 3-5). A natural language search puts the query in the form of a statement or question. A natural language search for the Canadian capital is: *What is the capital of Canada?* The search engine ignores small, unimportant words in a natural language search query, called **stop words**, and only uses the more important, specific words in the search. Examples of stop words include what, where, is, the, of, in, and how.

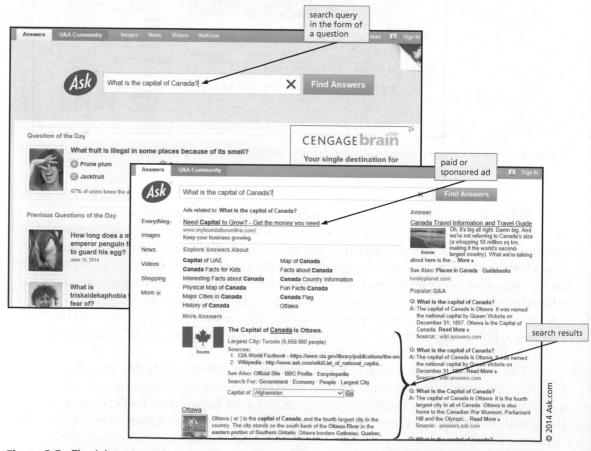

Figure 3-5 The Ask.com search tool with a complete question as the search query.

Because each search tool has its own method for evaluating keywords and determining what webpages are relevant to the keywords, it is a good idea to review a search tool's FAQ pages or Help section for information about the best way to formulate queries for that search tool.

Examining the Search Results

Different search tools perform searches and display hits in the search results list in various ways, so you should become familiar with and use a variety of search tools. As you have learned, a search engine lists the hits in a search results list in a certain order, usually with more relevant hits at or near the top of the list. Some search tools place hits for recommended websites at the top of a search results list because a human editor has determined that the sites are the most relevant to the keywords. Other search tools might place hits for paid placement or sponsored listings near or at the top of a search results list because these websites pay the search tools to do so. Although listed at or near the top, paid placement hits might or might not provide the best information for a query. For this reason, it is important to know how to identify any paid or sponsored hits that appear among the search results and, if necessary, scroll further down a search results list to review other, possibly more relevant, hits.

Because a web search can return thousands or millions of hits, most people typically look only at the first 10 or 20 hits in a search results list. If a user does not see any relevant webpages in the search results, the user might then reformulate the search query and search again using the same search tool or a different search tool. When a search engine returns a search results list with potentially relevant webpages, the user can tap or click links associated with relevant hits and review each webpage to find the desired information.

Evaluating the Credibility of Search Results

A key step in the search process is to evaluate the credibility of the webpages in the search results list. A search results list can contain an assortment of webpages. Although all webpages might contain information related to the query, there is no guarantee that they all will contain accurate or useful information. Because anyone can publish information to the Internet, it is important to carefully assess the credibility of the webpage content by looking at the authority of the source, the objectivity of the text, the scope and quality of the content, and the website's design and functionality.

AUTHORITY   The first step in determining the quality of the information on a webpage is to examine its authority. To do this, determine who owns or sponsors the website and, if possible, who authored the page content. Try to determine if the content's author and/or the website's sponsor has the appropriate expertise to present the information authoritatively. To do this, look for and read any background information posted about a webpage's author or the website's sponsoring organization.

Some search tools give extra weight to governmental and educational webpages, listing these hits at or near the top of a search results list. However, you should look past the top-level domain to the country-code top-level domain when evaluating the authority of these websites. For example, information presented by agencies of a totalitarian government that limits free speech or free access to the Internet and the web might not be unbiased or completely accurate. Websites with the .edu top-level domain represent educational institutions, but a webpage at an educational site might be the work of a student rather than a scholar. The highest quality and more authoritative results come from primary sources. A **primary source** is any document, item, or other data that provides firsthand information about a particular topic. For example, when searching for the history of the web, an authoritative primary source would be a webpage with an account written by Tim Berners-Lee, who participated in the development of the web firsthand.

Q&A   **Are wikis reliable web content sources?**
A **wiki** is a website that allows users to edit, update, and add content. When using wikis, keep in mind that biased or unauthorized authors or editors could be responsible for some articles. You should verify information you learn from a wiki with an outside source.

OBJECTIVITY   When examining a website's objectivity, determine whether the webpage information is presented fairly, whether the content contains any subtle or clear biases, or whether the information is skewed toward commercial or political interests. For example, when looking for information about vitamins or nutritional supplements, determine whether a webpage bases its recommendations on facts reported by other sources, or whether it is part of a commercial website that profits by promoting the sale of its particular formulas. One way to assess objectivity is to look on the webpage for links with recognizable, reputable domain names that link to other related websites.

SCOPE AND QUALITY   Evaluating the scope of webpage content — the depth of coverage and the amount of detail provided — can help determine its value. The intended audience — whether children or adults, professionals or enthusiasts — often determines the scope of a website. Additionally, high-quality webpage content should be accurate and up to date. Verifying facts and statements on a webpage with other web resources is a good way to verify accuracy. Look to see if the article or webpage has a time or date of posting listed to determine its timeliness.

One technique for determining scope and quality is to compare the information on several webpage sources that discuss the same topic. For example, in searching for the origin of pizza, the name Queen Margherita appears in a number of documents. If several webpages refer to her, but one page spells her name incorrectly or omits a reference to her entirely, you might consider that page to be a less valuable source of information. Some webpage authors publish information gathered from others without careful research. When a website author provides carefully researched webpage content, the content typically offers more details and depth, as well as contains citations or references to other sources, either as links or in a list at the end of the article or page. Comparing webpage coverage of the same topic can be helpful in evaluating the scope and quality of information on different pages. In addition, look for indications of publication or update dates and times on webpages, especially when researching trends or a developing story. Depending on the topic, an article published a year ago might contain still accurate information. For breaking news, currency is in hours or even minutes. Most search engines enable you to sort search results, such as by most recent entry. You will learn more about sorting results later in this chapter.

DESIGN AND FUNCTIONALITY   Your first impression of the website also offers insight to its credibility. Webpages with grammar or spelling errors, poor organization, missing images, or **broken links** — links that no longer work — at best indicate poor attention to detail, and at worst might indicate the page is a poor-quality source. An attractive and professional looking webpage does not guarantee high-quality, credible content on its own, however.

Figure 3-6 lists several key questions to ask as you evaluate the credibility of webpage content. Using these questions and the guidelines outlined earlier can help you identify valuable information resources from among the many hits listed in a search results list.

Evaluating the Credibility of Webpages

Area	Questions
Authority	• Is this a primary source document? • Is the webpage's sponsoring organization or author a noted authority? • Are the webpages up to date?
Objectivity	• Is the webpage objective? • Is any bias clearly stated?
Scope	• What is the intended audience for this website? • How does the information on the webpage compare with others on the same topic?
Design and functionality	• Does the webpage have a professional appearance? • Do all parts of the webpage work correctly?

© Cengage Learning®

Figure 3-6 Questions to ask when evaluating the credibility of webpages.

Search Tools

Web-based search tools help users around the world locate all types of information, including informational webpages, businesses, people, multimedia files, document databases, and more. Search tools used to find web-based information typically fall into one of the following broad categories: directories, search engines, and metasearch engines. In the following sections, you will learn how to identify directories, search engines, and metasearch engines; their characteristics; and how to use each to perform basic searches.

Directories

A **directory** is a human-compiled, hierarchical list of webpages organized by category. One of the first directories was created by Jerry Yang and David Filo (Figure 3-7 on the next page), two doctoral students at Stanford University, who began to keep a list of interesting webpages for their personal use. Their Stanford classmates and friends soon began asking to share the list, originally called Jerry's Guide to the Web. Soon the list became long and unwieldy, so Filo and Yang divided the list into categories and then later, as the number of webpages continued to grow, into subcategories. In 1995, the Jerry's Guide directory was renamed Yahoo!. The original Yahoo! directory has evolved to become the Yahoo! network of online tools and services, including Yahoo! Search, Yahoo! Directory, Yahoo! Mail, Yahoo! Shopping, and more.

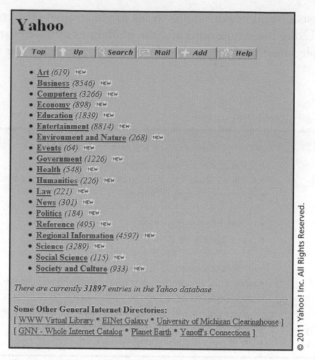

Figure 3-7 An early version of Yahoo!, the first widely popular web directory.

A staff of human editors compile directories and create an **index**, or list of webpages. Directories are useful search tools that present links to websites organized into easily understood categories. Directories offer a way to locate web-based information by browsing from a general category to an ever more specific category until you locate the desired information. For example, using the DMOZ Open Directory Project directory to locate a website that offers a trip planner and maps can involve clicking a number of links to move from a general category, such as Reference, through additional subcategories, to a useful webpage link and, finally, to the website (Figure 3-8). A user who locates information by tapping or clicking increasingly specific links is **drilling down** the directory categories.

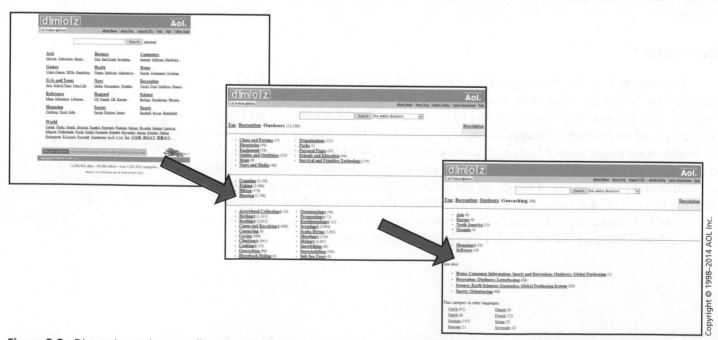

Figure 3-8 Directories use human editors to organize websites into hierarchical categories that can be browsed, or drilled down, by clicking links.

A **breadcrumb trail**, used by websites such as Gourmet.com (Figure 3-9), shows the hierarchical arrangement of categories and subcategories through which you have clicked. This list of category and subcategory links typically is located at the top of a webpage. You can click any link in the breadcrumb trail to move back and forth between categories and subcategories and return to the home page.

Figure 3-9   A breadcrumb trail indicates the hierarchy or path of the current webpage.

Using human editors to compile a directory's index of web resources is both a strength and a weakness. Human editors can organize lists of web resources in a logical way, making browsing or drilling down through a directory's categories an organized process. Using human editors also is a disadvantage, however, because of the time it takes for human editors to review new webpages and add them to a directory's index. Additionally, human editors determine what pages to accept for the index and what pages not to accept. Using a directory, therefore, might not provide links to a number of appropriate and useful webpages on any particular topic simply because the editors have rejected or not yet added the webpage to the index. In addition to the DMOZ Open Directory Project, other directories include Yahoo! Directory and Business.com.

To Use a Directory

The following steps drill down through DMOZ category links to find webpages that contain information about Grace Hopper, a computer programming pioneer. Then they return you to the DMOZ home page using the breadcrumb trail.

1

- Start your browser and enter **dmoz.org** in the Address bar.

- Press the ENTER key, or tap or click the necessary button to open the DMOZ home page (Figure 3-10).

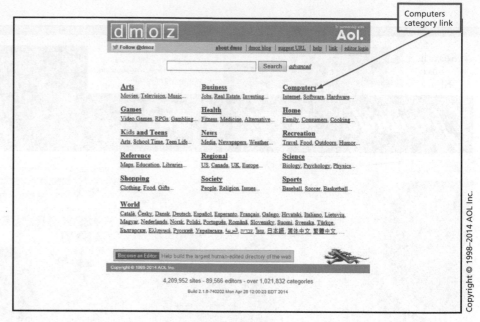

Figure 3-10

2

- Tap or click the Computers category link to view the Computers subcategories page in the same tab (Figure 3-11).

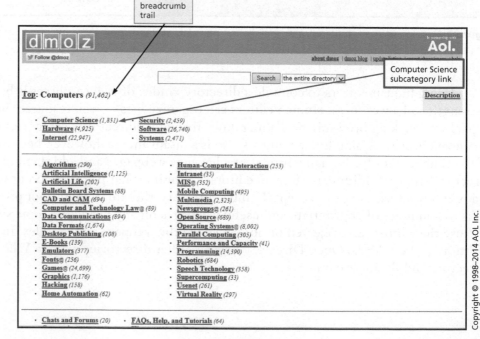

Figure 3-11

3

- Tap or click the Computer Science subcategory link to view the subcategory page.

- Tap or click the People subcategory link to view the subcategory page.

- Tap or click the Pioneers subcategory link to view the subcategory page (Figure 3-12).

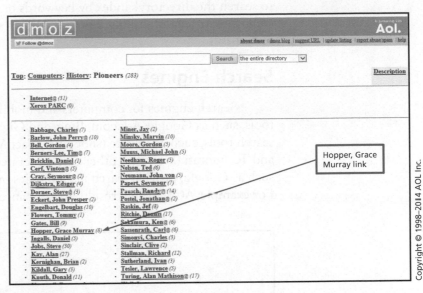

Figure 3-12

4

- Tap or click the Hopper, Grace Murray link to view the subcategory page (Figure 3-13).

Q&A

Why do I see a list of horizontal links above the category links?
You can see the path of the links you have clicked to reach the current webpage in the breadcrumb trail at the top of the page (Top: Computers: History: Pioneers). You can move back to a previously viewed webpage by clicking that page's link in the breadcrumb trail.

- Tap or click a Grace Murray Hopper link or another link of interest to view a webpage containing information about Grace Hopper (Figure 3-14).

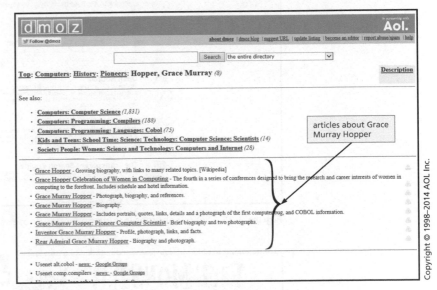

Figure 3-13

5

- Close the browser. If prompted, close all tabs.

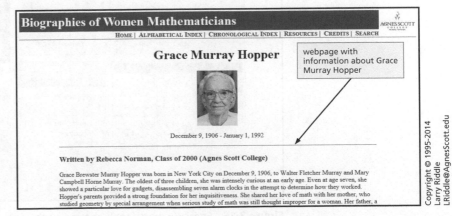

Figure 3-14

Most directories have strategic partnerships with search engines, to enable users to search the directory's index by keywords or use a partner search engine's index of webpages instead of drilling down. You will learn more about search engines in the next section.

Search Engines

Search engines for computers and mobile devices include general-purpose search tools, such as Google, Ask.com, Bing, and Gigablast (Figure 3-15). Additionally, specialty search tools, such as Bizrate (shopping), Fact Monster (kid-friendly searches; Figure 3-16), and Technorati (blogs and other user-generated media), abound. Some search engines, such as Google, provide search technologies or webpage indexes for other search engines. For example, AOL Search results are "enhanced" by Google.

Figure 3-15 Search engines include general-purpose search tools, such as Gigablast.

Figure 3-16 Specialty search tools abound on the web.

In contrast to directories, which humans compile, a **search engine** uses software called a **spider**, **bot** (short for robot), or **web crawler** that browses the web, automatically adding the URLs and other information about webpages to a searchable index. Yahoo! Slurp, Googlebot, and Bingbot are all examples of web crawlers. Web crawlers provide and categorize content for search engines. Users do not interact directly with web crawlers.

Different search engines collect different kinds of information about each webpage, but web crawlers typically scan for some or all of the following information to create their indexes:

- Page title — coded title that appears on the browser title bar when the webpage opens
- URL — specifically, the domain name (for example, cheaptickets.com)
- **Meta tag keywords** — descriptive keywords coded into the webpage's HTML code that are readable by the web crawler but invisible to the user
- Occurrence of keywords — both the frequency of use and where they appear on a webpage
- All of the words on the webpage, which is known as **full-text searching**
- Internal links within the webpage to other pages on the website (for example, site maps)
- Number and relevancy of other webpages that link to the page

Web servers store the webpage information retrieved by a web crawler in a database, creating an index similar to the index at the back of a book. Web crawlers continually browse the web to update their indexes with modified webpage content or new, previously unknown webpages. When a user interacts with a search engine, it accesses the results of the web crawler's searches, but doesn't interact with the web crawler directly.

When a user enters keywords into a search engine's search text box, the search engine compares the keywords with its index, compiles a list of webpages for which the keywords are relevant, and arranges the list in a specific order. Each search engine uses its own unique software and formula or algorithm to determine the relevance of a webpage to specific keywords, and the order in which to rank or list the pages in the search results.

Most search engines attempt to present the most useful and relevant results or hits at or near the top of a search results list to make their search engines more useful and to attract more users. As discussed earlier in this chapter, however, some search engines also accept payment from advertisers to prominently feature their webpages based on certain search keywords. These paid listings usually include a label that identifies them as paid or sponsored listings. Paid listings often appear in a prominent place on a search results webpage, such as at the top of the page or on the right side of the page.

Many search tools today have become hybrids — basing their results on indexes created both by web crawlers and by human editors. For the remainder of this book, the term, search engine, refers to various types of search tools.

To Use Search Engines

The following steps use four different search engines (Google, Ask.com, Yahoo! Search, and Bing) to find webpages that contain information about geotagging. As you use each search engine, carefully review each search results page to note the differences in the first 10 hits, the position of paid placement or sponsored listings, and any other features offered by the search engine.

Remember that because of the dynamic nature of webpages, as well as your specific device or platform, the content you see on your screen might vary from that in the figures in this chapter.

1

- Start your browser and enter `google.com` in the Address bar.

- Press the ENTER key, or tap or click the necessary button to open the Google home page.

- Enter `geo` in the search text box to display a list of options in the Search text box drop-down list, and to display search results in the Google window (Figure 3-17).

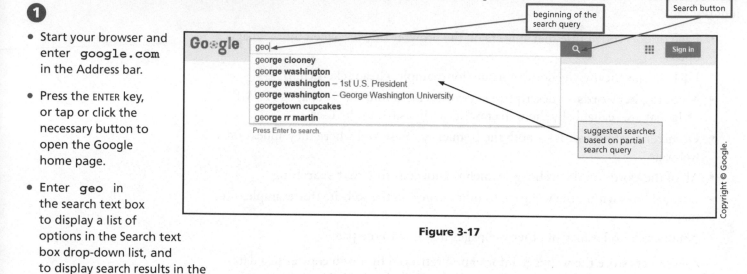

Figure 3-17

Copyright © Google.

Q&A **Why do I see a drop-down list below the Search text box?**
Some search engines suggest search queries based on the characters you enter in the Search text box. You can tap or click a suggested search query to use it, or close the list by pressing the ESC key or tapping or clicking a Close button or link.

2

- Enter `tagging` in the search text box to finish the keywords, and then tap or click the Search button to view the search results page.

- Scroll the search results page to view the top hits (Figure 3-18).

Figure 3-18

Copyright © Google.

3

- Open a new tab if necessary, and then enter `ask.com` in the Address bar.

- Press the ENTER key, or tap or click the necessary button to open the Ask.com home page

- Enter `geotagging` in the Ask search text box, and then tap or click the Find Answers button.

- Scroll the search results page to view suggested additional search options, sponsored ads, related searches, and the top hits (Figure 3-19).

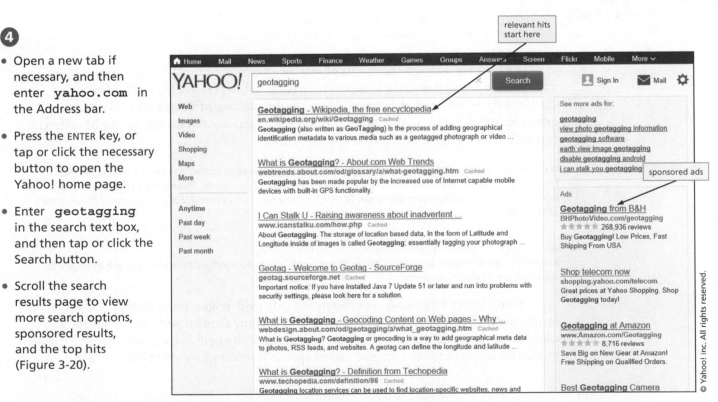

Figure 3-19

4

- Open a new tab if necessary, and then enter `yahoo.com` in the Address bar.

- Press the ENTER key, or tap or click the necessary button to open the Yahoo! home page.

- Enter `geotagging` in the search text box, and then tap or click the Search button.

- Scroll the search results page to view more search options, sponsored results, and the top hits (Figure 3-20).

Figure 3-20

5

- Open a new tab if necessary, and then enter **bing.com** in the Address bar.

- Press the ENTER key, or tap or click the necessary button to open the Bing home page.

- Enter **geotagging** in the search text box.

- Tap or click the Search button at the end of the text box.

- Scroll the search results page to view more search options, ads, and related searches links (Figure 3-21).

- Close the browser. If prompted, close all tabs.

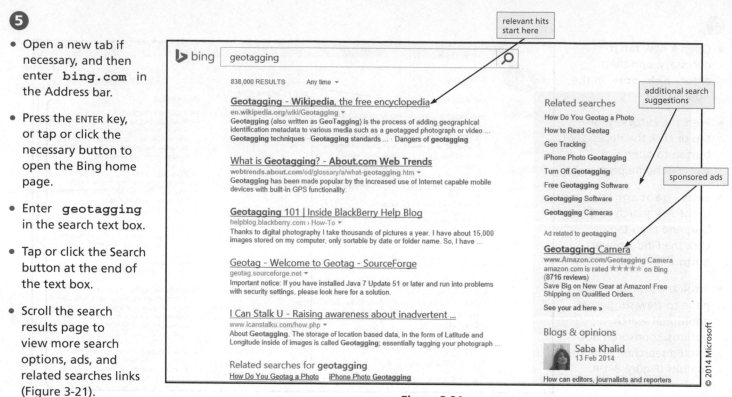

Figure 3-21

By looking through the results of searches performed in different search engines with the same search queries, you can see that the list of results likely will differ significantly — either in webpages listed or in the ranking of those pages — when using different search engines. Also, other features such as sponsored listings might be different, and each search engine might offer special features.

@SOURCE Some search providers, such as Google, Yahoo!, and Microsoft, allow users to download search toolbars as free browser plug-ins. Not all browsers include the ability to use search tool plug-ins. These toolbars are designed to make searching with a search provider's specific search engine easier and to provide access to some of the provider's other tools.

Q&A **Which search engines provide the most reliable results?**
Most major search engines provide reliable, unbiased search results. For more information, use a search engine to search for *search engine reliability*.

Some search engines do not clearly identify paid or sponsored listings on search results pages. Because of this, it is important to become familiar with and comfortable using more than one search engine. Reviewing a search engine's Help feature can provide insight for using the search engine and its special features more effectively.

FACTS @HAND According to a recent report by comScore, Google has more than 67 percent share of the desktop search engine market. Google is the most popular search engine in the United States, followed by Bing (18 percent), and Yahoo! (10 percent). AOL Search and Ask.com each have a small market share.

Kid-Friendly Searches

Using the web to help a child research a school project seems like a great idea, but allowing children to use a general search engine might result in some hits that link to objectionable content. A seemingly innocuous search query can result in hits that link to webpages that include offensive language, sexually explicit or violent material, or hate propaganda. Children may find it more difficult to evaluate sources for credibility, and can be attracted to colorfully designed webpages, which may or may not contain accurate and unbiased content.

Many search engines include a feature to block objectionable content. For example, Google, Yahoo! Search, and Bing provide a SafeSearch feature. Parents and teachers should enable these filtering options before children use a general search engine.

A number of other search engines have been created specifically for use by children. These search engines return search results that include only websites that are appropriate for children and young teens. They exclude from the results any websites that feature sexually explicit text or images, violence, hate speech, and gambling. Search engines for kids also might serve the needs of children and young teens better by offering search results focused on their level of reading and understanding. Some return only websites selected by an editorial staff that reviews the content of each site.

Some of the more widely used children's search engines include:

- Ask Kids
- Awesome Library
- CyberSleuth Kids
- Fact Monster
- Google Safe Search for Kids
- KidRex
- KidzSearch
- Mymunka
- SearchyPants
- Yippy

Metasearch Engines

Performing the same search multiple times using different search engines to get the best search results can be cumbersome. A **metasearch engine** is a special type of search tool that compiles the search results from multiple search engines into a single search results list, effectively performing multiple different searches at once. Metasearch engines include Dogpile, Mamma.com, Zoo (Figure 3-22), and Ixquick.

© 2014 Infospace, LLC

Figure 3-22 Metasearch engines, such as Zoo, submit a search query to multiple search engines and compile the hits in one search results list.

When you enter search query keywords in a metasearch engine's search text box, the metasearch engine submits the search query to a number of search engines at one time. It then compiles all of the results into a single list of hits. A good metasearch engine should eliminate duplicate entries, categorize the hits based on topic, order the hits by relevance, and indicate which search engines provided the search results. Metasearch engines typically rely heavily on sponsored listings, and some metasearch engines mix nonpaid and sponsored hits together in the same search results list; therefore, it is important that you carefully review the source of each hit returned by a metasearch engine to eliminate sponsored listings that might not be the most relevant to your search query.

To Use Metasearch Engines

The following steps use three metasearch engines to search for webpages containing information about mobile payment apps. As you complete each step, pay careful attention to each metasearch engine's features and the search engine indexes it uses to create the search results list. You will open each metasearch engine in a new window using a shortcut menu.

1

- Start your browser and enter `mamma.com` in the Address bar.

- Press the ENTER key, or tap or click the necessary button to open the Mamma home page.

- Enter `mobile payment apps` in the search text box, and then tap or click the Search button.

- Scroll the search results page to view the results (Figure 3-23).

- Identify the nonpaid and sponsored hits in the list.

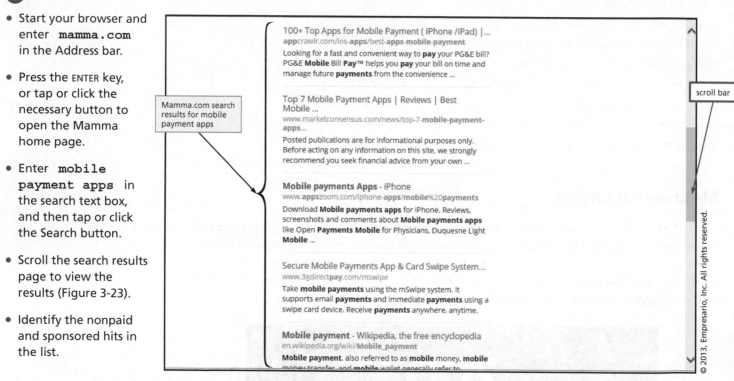

Mamma.com search results for mobile payment apps

scroll bar

Figure 3-23

②

- Open a new tab if necessary, and then enter **zoo.com** in the Address bar.

- Press the ENTER key, or tap or click the necessary button to open the zoo home page.

- Enter **mobile payment apps** in the search text box, and then tap or click the Search button.

- Scroll the search results in the list (Figure 3-24).

- Identify the nonpaid and sponsored hits in the list.

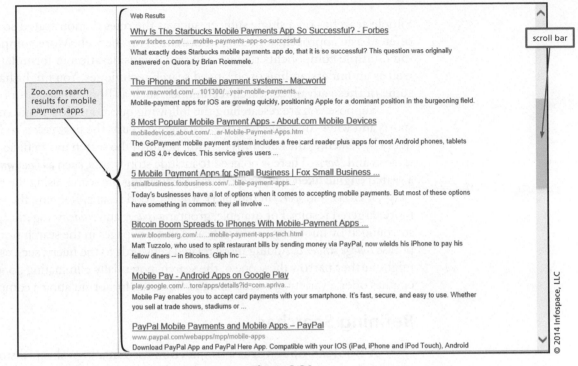

Zoo.com search results for mobile payment apps

Figure 3-24

© 2014 Infospace, LLC

③

- Open a new tab if necessary, and then enter **ixquick.com** in the Address bar.

- Press the ENTER key, or tap or click the necessary button to open the Ixquick home page.

- Enter **mobile payment apps** in the search text box, and then tap or click the Search button.

- Scroll the search results page to identify nonpaid and sponsored hits in the list (Figure 3-25).

- Close the browser. If prompted, close all tabs.

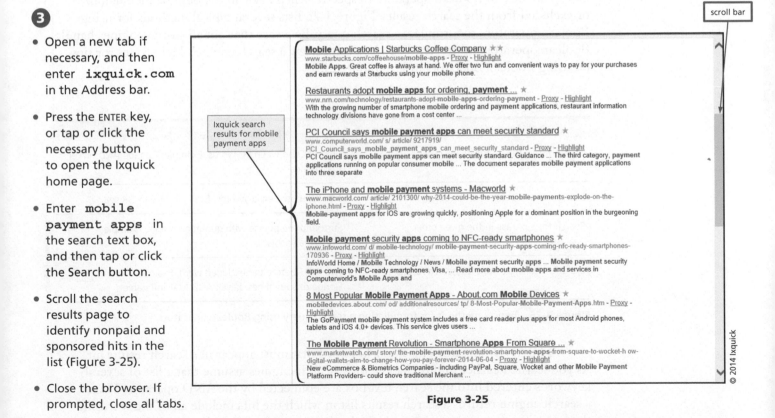

Ixquick search results for mobile payment apps

Figure 3-25

© 2014 Ixquick

Advanced Search Techniques

Simple searches on a single subject, such as the ones demonstrated so far in this chapter, offer a basic approach to finding information on the web. More complex searches involving multiple components require additional consideration in formulating the query, as well as an understanding of advanced search techniques. You might have already used some of these advanced search techniques, such as Boolean operators, without realizing it.

Suppose you are researching the following question: How many college students play sports and why? After selecting a search engine to use, the next task is to formulate the search query by selecting the keywords that will perform the search most efficiently — *college* and *students* and *sports*. There is no need to include stop words, such as *how*, *and*, and *why* because a search engine likely will ignore them. Performing the search using the three keywords *college*, *students*, and *sports* in the query will get good results. Refining the search will achieve more targeted results. For example, grouping *college* and *students* together in a single phrase surrounded by quotation marks indicates that webpages in the search results must contain the phrase *college students*. Adding more related keywords to the query, such as *intramural*, however, might further narrow the scope of the search, potentially eliminating good resources. Search engines offer a variety of search tips and shortcuts for formulating a complex search query.

Refining Searches

A **Boolean operator** is a conjunction used in a logical expression. When given multiple keywords in a query, a search engine uses the AND, OR, and NOT (typed in all capital letters) Boolean operators to specify which keywords should be included in or excluded from the search results. Figure 3-26 lists several typical methods for using Boolean operators to formulate a search query. Be aware that not all search engines handle Boolean operators in the same way. You can review a search engine's Help pages for tips on using Boolean operators in search queries.

Boolean Operators

Task	Procedure
Search for all the words in any order.	Type AND between keywords. Example: Canada AND nickel AND mines
Search for at least one of the words.	Type OR between keywords. Example: ocean OR sea
Search for a phrase in the given order.	Surround the phrase with quotation marks. Example: "Catalina yachts"
Exclude a concept from the search results.	Type NOT before the excluded word. Examples: orange NOT Florida or sometimes: kayak AND NOT inflatable

© Cengage Learning®

Figure 3-26   Typical methods for formulating a search query using Boolean operators.

The AND operator indicates a keyword that must appear in a search results hit. As you learned earlier in this chapter, most search engines assume that a list of several keywords entered into the search text box are connected by the AND operator. Thus, a search engine returns a search results list in which the hits include all of the words in the query. Some search engines permit the inclusion of multiple keywords in a query by preceding them with a plus sign instead of the AND operator.

Suppose you want the search results in the previous research example to include webpages that refer to students from either a university or a college. To find webpages that include either a university or a college, you must use an OR operator. To specify an either-or condition, you must specifically enter OR between the keywords to indicate that hits should include either of the keywords rather than both of the words.

To exclude a keyword from a search, some search engines require you to use the NOT operator before the excluded term (for example, diamonds NOT baseball). Other search engines might require a minus sign before the excluded term (for example, diamonds–baseball).

In addition to Boolean operators, major search engines also offer a number of searching shortcuts, such as the examples shown in Figure 3-27.

See your search engine's Help pages for more information about searching tips and shortcuts.

Sample Search Engine Shortcuts

Search Engine	To Do This:	Type This Search Query:
Yahoo! Search	Use the Yahoo! Maps feature to find a city map and have the map appear on your search results page	map! Boston
	Find a specific keyword as part of a webpage title	intitle:New York (no space following the colon)
Bing	Convert a specific number of dollars to euros or another currency	150 dollars in euros (or Canadian dollars, Mexican pesos, and so forth)
	Find a local business by location and type of business	Austin coffee shop (or other location and business)
Google	Get local weather information	weather: 78218 or weather: Chicago (or other ZIP code or location with or without the space after the colon)
	Perform an addition (+), subtraction (-), multiplication (*), or division (/) calculation	2598+1587 34687-25812 156798*7 2879/3
	Convert measurements	20 inches in cm (centimeters) 5,000 meters in miles

© Cengage Learning®

Figure 3-27   Major search engines also offer a number of searching shortcuts.

Major search providers continue to update their search engines with new features so that they can compete profitably with other search providers. For example, Google includes options for refining search results by adding more detail to each hit in a search results list. Additionally, search engines based on new or improved search technologies continue to appear. You should periodically survey available search engines to see what is new.

FACTS
@HAND

Advanced Search Forms

Many search engines provide an advanced search form you can use to structure a complex search query. An advanced search form typically prompts you to specify Boolean operators and other criteria, such as filtering the results by language, file type, or domain (such as .gov or .edu).

Creating a complex search in an advanced search form is a great way to learn more about how to use specific search engine shortcuts and Boolean operators. As you fill in the form, the search engine creates the search query based on the form's content, and then displays the completed search query at the top of the form and/or at the top of the search results page. You can review a completed search query to learn how to create similar searches by typing shortcuts and Boolean operators directly in the search engine's search text box.

To Use an Advanced Search Form

The following steps use the Google advanced search form to complete several searches. You first find webpages with information about the use of social media in political elections. Next, you find PDF files published at educational institutions that contain information about jobs or careers in economics. Finally, locate webpages that have been updated in the last month and contain either the word, galaxies, or the word, planets, in the page title. *Note:* An advanced search form typically is not a feature provided with mobile browsers. In the next section you will learn how to perform advanced searches in the Address bar in case your browser does not offer an advanced search form.

①

- Start your browser and enter `google.com` in the Address bar.

- Press the ENTER key, or tap or click the necessary button to open the Google home page.

Figure 3-28

- Enter `social media political elections` in the search text box (Figure 3-28).

②

- Tap or click the Search button to view the search results page, which shows the initial search query, social media political elections, in the text box at the top of the page.

- Scroll the page to view the search results list. The search results list might contain webpages from around the world. You want to refine the search to show only webpages from the United Kingdom.

Figure 3-29

- Tap or click the Settings button to open the Settings menu (Figure 3-29).

3

- Tap or click the Advanced search menu option to open the Advanced Search form (Figure 3-30).

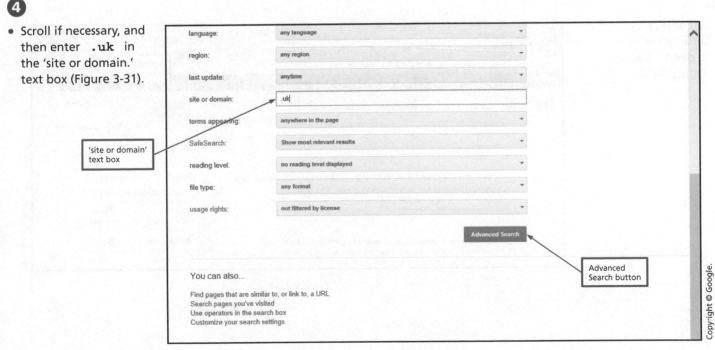

Figure 3-30

4

- Scroll if necessary, and then enter `.uk` in the 'site or domain.' text box (Figure 3-31).

Figure 3-31

⑤

- Tap or click the Advanced Search button to filter the search results for websites from the United Kingdom (Figure 3-32).

- View the search query, social media political elections site:.uk, in the Bing search text box at the top of the page.

- Scroll the search results page. The search results list only shows results from websites in the .uk domain.

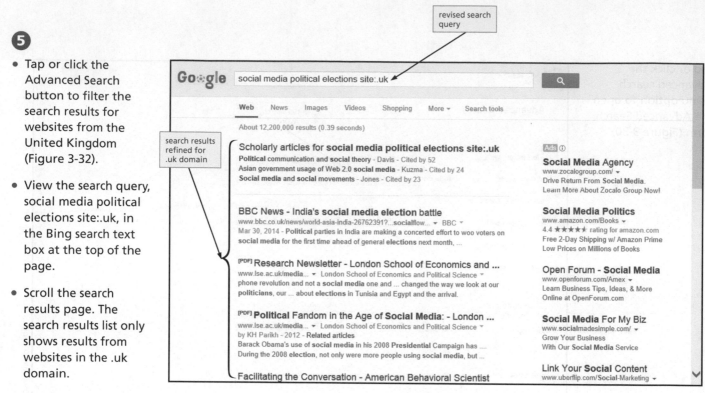

Figure 3-32

⑥

- Tap or click the Settings button to open a menu (Figure 3-33).

Figure 3-33

7

- Tap or click the Advanced search option to open the Advanced search form. Delete the previous search query and clear any selected options to clear the form.

- Enter `economics` in the 'this exact word or phrase' text box.

- Enter `jobs,` `careers` in the 'any of these words' text box.

- Enter `.edu` in the 'site or domain:' text box.

- Tap or click the file type arrow, and then tap or click Adobe Acrobat PDF (.pdf) in the list to specify that the search results must be PDF files (Figure 3-34).

'this exact word or phrase' text box

'any of these words' text box

all these words:	
this exact word or phrase:	economics
any of these words:	jobs, careers
none of these words:	
numbers ranging from:	to

Then narrow your results by...

language:	any language
region:	any region
last update:	anytime
site or domain:	.edu
terms appearing:	anywhere in the page
SafeSearch:	Show most relevant results
reading level:	no reading level displayed
file type:	Adobe Acrobat PDF (.pdf)

'site or domain' text box

file type list arrow

Figure 3-34

8

- Scroll if necessary, and then tap or click the Advanced Search button to start the search.

- Scroll the search results page to view the list of relevant PDF files published at educational institutions (Figure 3-35).

search query

Google   jobs, OR careers "economics" site:.edu filetype:pdf

Web   News   Images   Shopping   Videos   More ▾   Search tools

About 1,490,000 results (0.32 seconds)

[PDF] **JOBS** FOR **ECONOMICS** STUDENTS By - Central ...
www.cwu.edu/.../JOBS%20FOR%20ECO... ▾ Central Washington University ▾
For **economics** positions with our federal government, go to www.usajobs.gov; for positions with the State of Washington, go to www.careers.wa.gov. Also, if you ...

Jobs at LSE - London School of **Economics** and Political ...
www.lse.edu/intranet/staff/humanResources/.../jobsAtLSE/.../JSR0917PS.... ▾
Welcome to LSE. The School has all kinds of positions for people who can give us their best, from researchers to professors, accountants to security staff.

[PDF] Environmental **Economics** & Management - Career Center
career.uga.edu/.../EnvironmentalEconomicsMgmt.... ▾ University of Georgia ▾
Description of Environmental Economics and Management ... (View professionals speaking about their **careers** under the "Resources" tab and select "Online ...

[PDF] Agricultural and Applied **Economics** - Career Center
career.uga.edu/uploads/.../AgriculturalEconomics.p... ▾ University of Georgia ▾
Agricultural **economics** applies economic principles to food and fiber ... (View professionals speaking about their **careers** under the "Resources" ... Agriculture Consulting Positions- http://www.indeed.com/q-Agricultural-Consultant-**jobs**.html.

[PDF] "What Can I do With a Major in...**Economics**?" - Hofstra ...
www.hofstra.edu/.../what%20can%20i%20do%20...%... ▾ Hofstra University ▾
A major in **Economics** teaches you knowledge and skills that are useful in a variety ....
Whenever a large organization introduces a new job or reviews existing **jobs**, it also

indicates PDF file format

relevant PDF files published at educational institutions

Figure 3-35

9

- Tap or click the Settings button to open a menu.

- Tap or click the Advanced search option to open the Advanced search form. Delete the previous search query and clear any selected options to clear the form.

- Enter **galaxies planets** in the 'any of these words' text box.

- Tap or click the terms appearing list arrow, and click 'in the title of the page'.

- Tap or click the last update list arrow and click past month (Figure 3-36).

Figure 3-36

10

- Scroll if necessary, and then tap or click the Advanced Search button to start the search.

- Scroll the search results list to verify that the webpages returned meet the search criteria.

- Close the browser. If prompted, close all tabs.

Figure 3-37

Browser Searches

In the following sections, you will learn how to enter a search query in the Address bar, how to perform a keyword search on a webpage, how to search online reference sources, and how to sort and filter your search results.

Address Bar Searches

You can search the web by entering a search query in the Address box on the browser Address bar. After you enter the search query, you can press the ENTER key or tap or click the appropriate button to open the search results page in the current tab.

To Search Using the Address Box on the Address Bar

The following steps enter a search query in the Address box to search for kayaking vacations that do not include canoeing. Next, you search using the Address box searches for webpages containing information found on U.S. government websites about the U.S. Department of Agriculture MyPlate suggested food serving icon.

1

- Start your browser and enter **kayak AND vacation NOT canoe** in the Address box (Figure 3-38).

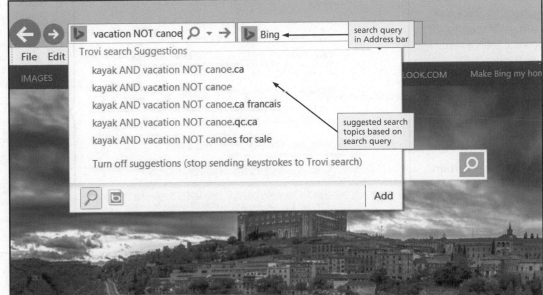

Figure 3-38

2

- Press the ENTER key, or tap or click the necessary button to view the search results (Figure 3-39).

- Scroll the page to review the search results list.

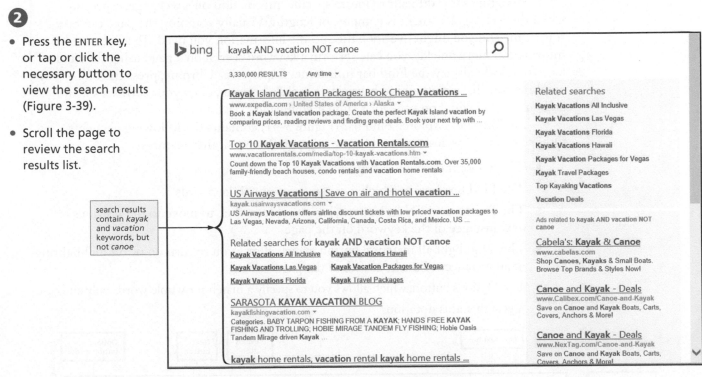

Figure 3-39

❸

- Enter **"MyPlate" usda .gov** in the Address box (be sure to enter the space between usda and .gov), and then press the ENTER key, or tap or click the necessary button to open the search results page (Figure 3-40).

- Scroll the page to confirm that the search results page lists webpages at U.S. government websites that contain information about the U.S. Department of Agriculture MyPlate food icon.

- Close the browser. If prompted, close all tabs.

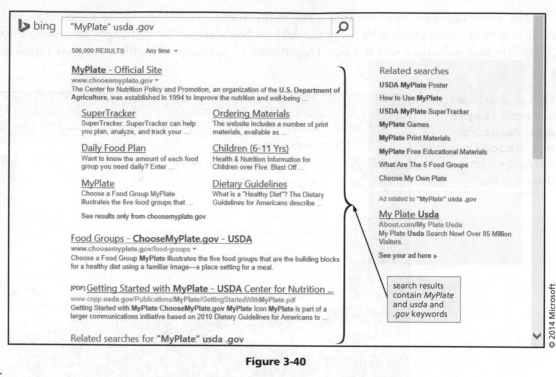

Figure 3-40

Webpage Searches

Sometimes it is difficult to locate specific information on a webpage, especially when the webpage's content is complex or lengthy. Visually scanning the page can take some time and you might overlook the specific information you need. To locate needed information more quickly, you can perform a keyword search on a page using the Find bar. To quickly display the Find bar in Internet Explorer or Chrome, press the CTRL+F key combination. To open the Find bar using a mobile browser, open your browser's menu and tap or click 'Find on page' or a similar command.

The Internet Explorer Find bar (Figure 3-41) contains the following elements. Other browsers for desktops and laptop computers have similar features.

- The 'Close the Find bar' button
- The Find text box, in which you can enter or edit keywords
- The Previous and Next buttons, which you can click to move to the previous or next instance of the keyword on the page
- The 'Highlight all matches' button, which allows you to turn on or off highlighting of all instances of the keyword on the page
- The Options button, which allows you to specify a match for whole words only and case
- A search status notation

Figure 3-41 The Internet Explorer Find bar

If you are using a mobile browser, open your browser menu, and tap or click 'Find on page' or a similar command to open your Find bar.

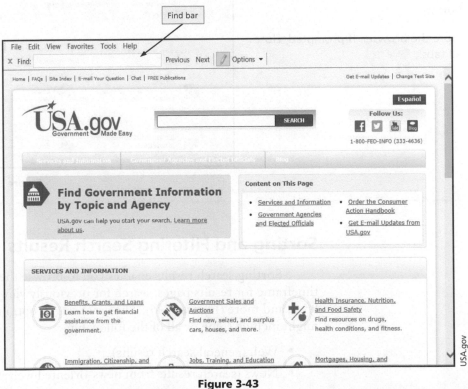

Figure 3-42 Mobile browsers often have webpage search features available from the browser menu.

To Search a Webpage Using the Find Bar

The following steps open a webpage in the browser, display the Find bar, and search the contents of the current page.

1

- Start your browser and enter **usa.gov** in the Address bar.

- Press the ENTER key, or tap or click the necessary button to open the webpage.

- Press CTRL+F or use your browser menu to open the Find bar (Figure 3-43).

Figure 3-43

2

- Enter `jobs` in the Find text box. The Find bar search status notation indicates two matches on the webpage (Figure 3-44).

Q&A

Why do I only see one match?
Your number or matches may differ. If you only get one match, skip the first two bullets of Step 3, or use another keyword of your choice.

Q&A

How do I view all of the matches?
You can continue to click the Next button to move from match to match. When no more matches are available, a search status notation indicating no more matches appears on the Find Bar.

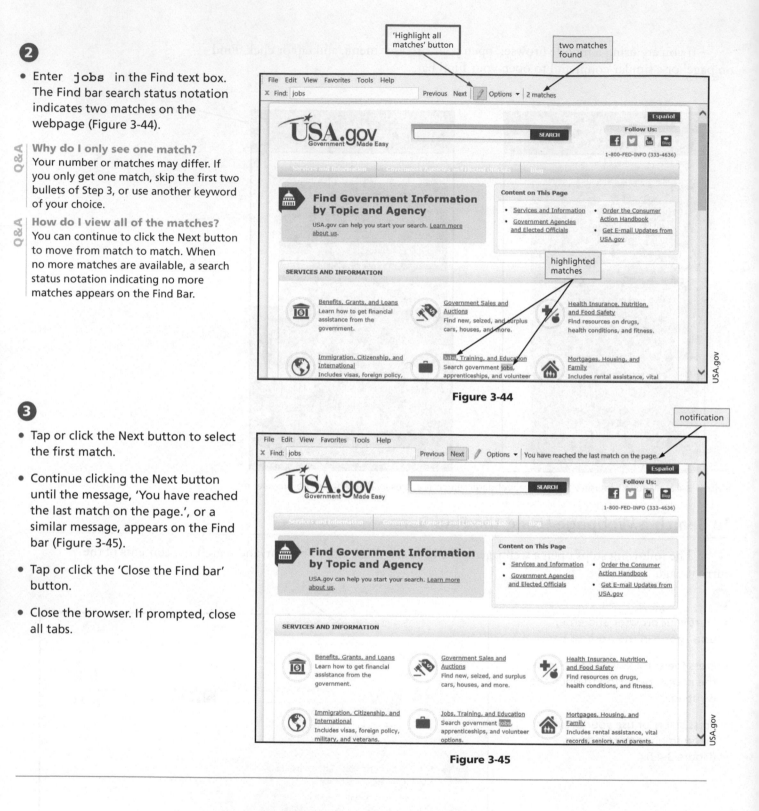

Figure 3-44

3

- Tap or click the Next button to select the first match.

- Continue clicking the Next button until the message, 'You have reached the last match on the page.', or a similar message, appears on the Find bar (Figure 3-45).

- Tap or click the 'Close the Find bar' button.

- Close the browser. If prompted, close all tabs.

Figure 3-45

Sorting and Filtering Search Results

Sorting search results enables you to browse the most recent results, specify a timeframe for results pages, search for previously viewed webpages, search by reading level, and more (Figure 3-46). The exact search options depend on your browser but might include some or all of the following:

- Web (general search results)
- News (search results from news-oriented websites)

- Images (images tagged with the search keyword(s))
- Shopping (links to purchase items related to the keyword
- Videos (videos tagged with the search keyword(s))

Figure 3-46 Google browser search for *mobile payment apps* filtered to show images.

Search Engine Privacy

@ISSUE

Search engines often use cookies to record search behavior. Although the search information typically does not correspond to personal information, such as name or address, it does correspond to the IP address of your computer. Because broadband users generally have a static IP address that seldom changes, this is tantamount to collecting personal identification. To learn more about search engine privacy issues, use a search engine to search for *search engine privacy*.

Specialized Searches

You can use specialized search engines to search for people, news, magazine or journal articles, videos, blogs and other social media, products, or services. The following section discusses a variety of search engines you can use to perform specialized searches. Additionally, this section introduces online sources you can use to find other types of information, such as company financial data.

@SOURCE

To locate search engines that focus on finding information about people and businesses, use a search engine to search for *people search engine* or *business search engine*.

People and Business Search

Web users often search for information about an individual or a business for either professional or personal reasons. One way to find webpages containing information about an individual or a business is to use the individual's name or the company name as search keywords. Looking for other information, such as an email address or telephone number, is more efficient when you use a specialized directory, such as an online **white pages directory** or **yellow pages directory**. Named for their similarity to telephone directories, white pages and yellow pages directories include free resources such as Pipl and Wink, and other directories, such as WhitePages and Superpages, that offer additional information for a fee (Figure 3-47). Some white pages and yellow pages directories offer additional services such as reverse lookup, which is useful when you know a telephone number and want to discover the name with which it is associated.

Figure 3-47 Superpages.com is one example of a business search engine.

Other specialized search engines provide links to sources for military records, alumni databases, criminal information, property transactions, and other types of data. To protect privacy, many of these records are open only to authorized people. For example, Classmates .com and other alumni databases require you to register and include yourself in the list, after which you may have access to the names of others who also have voluntarily made their information available. Several websites, such as Docusearch (Figure 3-48) and US Search, charge users a fee to access compiled information. Prices vary by type and length of report.

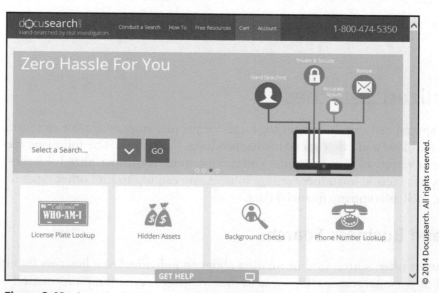

Figure 3-48 Some businesses provide database searches for individuals and businesses for a fee.

News and Current Events Search

Online news sources are diverse. Headlines often appear on the home pages of portal sites such as MSN and Yahoo!. Websites for broadcast television and radio stations publish current news. Search engines such as Bing (Figure 3-49) enable you to search for news. You can read the online version of various newspapers. Because most news is distributed through one of the major news wire services, such as the Associated Press (AP), United Press International (UPI), or Reuters, you will find the same or similar headlines and articles at various websites.

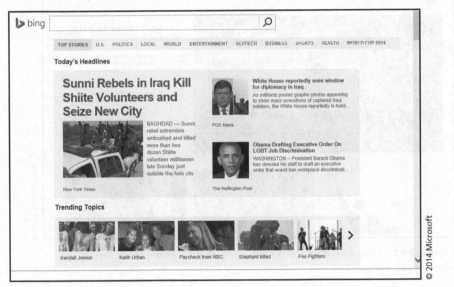

Figure 3-49 Bing News and other news search engines display trending topics and stories.

Video Search

Some search engines, such as ClipBlast, and Yahoo! Screen (Figure 3-50), specialize in indexing websites that offer video clips. Other search engines, such as Google, enable you to filter search results to show video or other specific media formats, as previously mentioned.

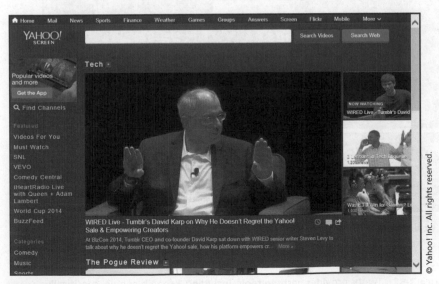

Figure 3-50 Yahoo! Screen is a video search engine.

Social Media Search

Another area of interest to Internet users is social media, which includes online tools used to communicate ideas, share links, contribute personal commentary, share photos, and interact online with other web users in various ways. You will learn more about social media in Chapter 4. You can use specialized search engines, sometimes called **social media aggregators**, such as Technorati, Google Blog Search, Digg (Figure 3-51), and Newsvine, to locate social media resources.

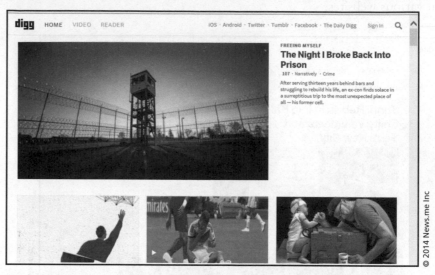

Figure 3-51 Digg and other social media aggregators locate social media resources and stories.

Hashtag Search

A **hashtag** is word or phrase (with spaces removed), preceded by the # sign. Hashtags are a form of metadata, and are used in social media platforms. Event promoters, politicians, social activists, entertainers, and more use hashtags to create and analyze trending topics. Hashtags effectively create a group of related posts or media on a specific platform, such as Twitter. Twitter and other social media platforms track hashtag trends. Web services exist that enable you to search for hashtags, create and register a hashtag, and more. Tagboard, Talkwalker, Rite Tag, and Twubs (Figure 3-52) are examples of hashtag search engines and tools.

Figure 3-52 Twubs provides hashtag tools, including a search engine, specifically for the Twitter platform.

To Search for a Hashtag

The following steps use the Tagboard hashtag search engine to search for and view text and media posts and articles using the hashtag #throwbackthursday, which is a popular hashtag used by people on Thursdays when posting photos and other media from the past.

1

- Start your browser and enter **tagboard.com** in the Address bar.

- Press the ENTER key, or tap or click the necessary button to open the Tagboard homepage.

- Enter **#throwbackthursday** in the Search text box (Figure 3-53).

Figure 3-53

Source: tagboard

2

- Press the ENTER key, or tap or click the necessary button to start the search.

- Click the #throwbackthursday list arrow to view links to tweets and other posts with the #throwbackthursday hashtag (Figure 3-54).

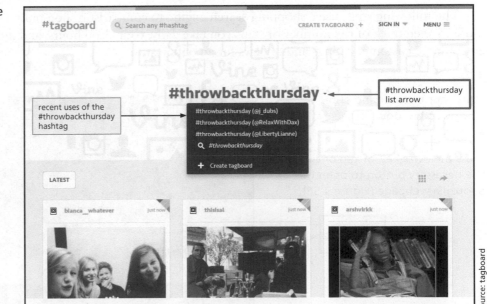

Figure 3-54

Source: tagboard

Shopping Search

Just about any product or service you can think of is for sale on the web. Shopping search engines, also known as **shopping bots** or **shopping aggregators**, include DealTime (Figure 3-55), Nextag, and Yahoo! Shopping. Shopping search engines aggregate, or collect, information about consumer products or services, and help online shoppers compare models, prices, shipping costs, and other variables from various sellers before they buy.

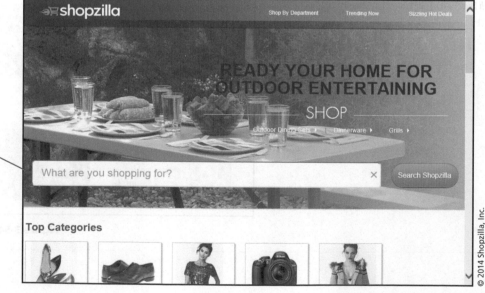

Figure 3-55 DealTime is an example of a shopping aggregator.

To Shop for a Fitness Tracker

The following steps use a shopping search engine to comparison shop online for a fitness tracker, which you can use to keep track of the number of steps you take daily, your sleep hours, and more. You narrow the search and then compare customer ratings and reviews for an online store.

1

- Start your browser and enter **shopzilla.com** in the Address bar.

- Press the ENTER key, or tap or click the necessary button to open the Shopzilla webpage (Figure 3-56).

What are you shopping for? text box

Figure 3-56

2

- Enter **fitness tracker** in the 'What are you shopping for?' text box, and then tap or click the Search Shopzilla button to view a list of available fitness trackers (Figure 3-57).

Sort By list arrow

'Strength & Fitness Training' link

price range options (yours may vary)

© 2014 Shopzilla, Inc.

Figure 3-57

3

- Tap or click the Sort By list arrow and tap or click 'Price Low-High' to sort the list by the lowest- to highest- priced fitness trackers.

- Scroll to view the results (Figure 3-58).

lowest option in the Price Range category

fitness trackers in the 'Strength & Fitness Training' category

© 2014 Shopzilla, Inc.

Figure 3-58

4

- Tap or click the 'Strength & Fitness Training' link to search within that department.

- Tap or click the first link under the Price Range heading to filter the list to only show the least expensive results (Figure 3-59).

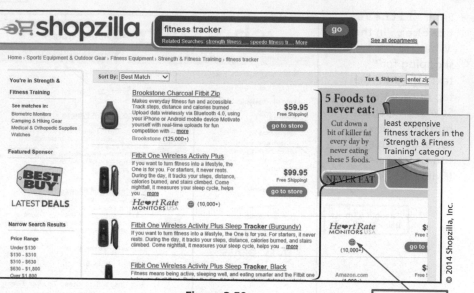

Figure 3-59

5

- Scroll if necessary, and then tap or click a green smiley face in the store list to review the store's rating details (Figure 3-60).

- Close the browser. If prompted, close all tabs.

Many online retailers, such as Amazon.com, integrate social media connectivity tools, enabling you to post a purchase notification or review of a product to your Facebook wall or Twitter feed.

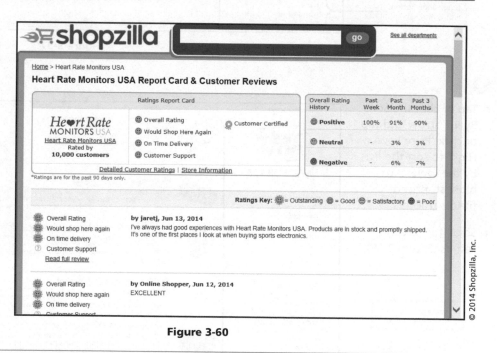

Figure 3-60

Research Alternatives to Search Engines

To review online tools that are useful for specific types of research, use a search engine to search for *research search engines.*

Search engines produce search results with links to vast resources. Depending on the keywords you enter for the search, it might take a while to sift through the results to find the specific information you seek. For in-depth or scholarly research, a more effective strategy is to access specialized collections of electronic resources. Although many such collections offer online access to information, finding them is not always so easy.

In this section, you will learn about a few of the more powerful and well-known services, such as LexisNexis, Proquest (Figure 3-61), ingentaconnect, FindLaw, Dun & Bradstreet, and Hoover's, which offer access to specialized information collections. These services are usually available only through paid subscriptions because of the specialized and proprietary information they contain and/or the efforts that go into compiling, obtaining, and updating the information they include. Many higher educational institutions subscribe to these services; therefore, students and faculty might have free access. If your school is not a subscriber, you still might be able to use these services through a public library that subscribes, by paying for an individual subscription, or with a pay-as-you-go fee.

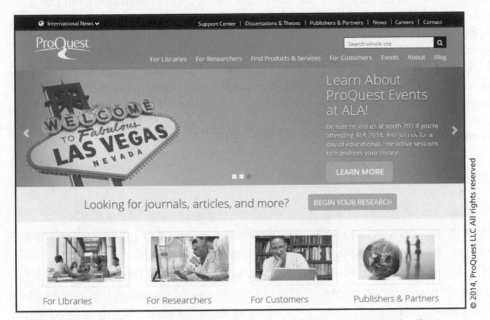

Figure 3-61   Several companies offer fee-based online access to specialized collections.

The LexisNexis service offers a web-based interface to find abstracts and articles on business, news, government, medical, and legal topics from a vast database of information. LexisNexis provides access to U.S. congressional and state government documents, statistics produced by governmental agencies and organizations, and primary and secondary sources of historical documents. It offers many sources of information on current issues and events, including organizational newsletters and governmental briefings not published commercially. Ideal for both academic scholars and students, LexisNexis is the first stop for many researchers.

The ingentaconnect service provides articles from academic and professional publications. Any researcher can search and view summaries of articles. A subscription or fee is required to obtain the full article online.

Hoover's and Dun & Bradstreet are two widely used resources for finding information on small and large businesses. Hoover's, a Dun & Bradstreet company, offers profiles on both public and private businesses, as well as extensive financial statements and analyses, management team information, and lists of competitors and market information. Dun & Bradstreet offers similar types of business and market information. It offers information that businesses of all sizes can use to find prospective customers, research suppliers, and check the credit risk of a potential partner or customer.

FindLaw is a portal for legal resources. It offers separate websites for the public and legal professionals. FindLaw is useful for finding information about laws and court cases, as well as for locating an attorney in your area or an attorney with a specific area of expertise. Whether you are dealing with a property complaint, a traffic ticket, criminal law, or a personal injury, this website offers an abundance of legal information.

Proquest provides information services to the business, scientific, engineering, financial, and legal communities over the Internet or an internal intranet. It offers in-depth information on news, business, chemistry, engineering, the environment, government, intellectual property, medicine, and pharmaceuticals. The depth of information comes from source materials, such as journals, dissertations, books,

@SOURCE

To access government resources, use a search engine to search for *government resources*.

newspapers, magazines, trade journals, newsletters, and citation bibliographies, as well as market research reports.

Government resources also can serve as excellent sources of information. For example, consumers can profit from information supplied by the Federal Citizen Information Center, while taxpayers can download forms and publications from the Internal Revenue Service website. The U.S. Census Bureau website supplies census statistics, the U.S. Bureau of Labor Statistics website offers government information on employment and labor economics, and the Library of Congress's website (named THOMAS, after Thomas Jefferson) provides searchable databases of legislative information. The U.S. Small Business Administration website has many resources for entrepreneurs and small business owners, and the U.S. National Park Service website contains excellent travel advice. An easy-to-use portal for the U.S. federal government is the USA.gov website, which you searched earlier in this chapter.

@ISSUE Citing Web Sources

In a research paper, scholars and students often quote or use facts found in another's writing and ideas. This practice is acceptable as long as you follow certain rules. The quotation must be set apart, either with quotation marks (if the quotation is short) or by indentation (if it is long). Furthermore, you must cite the author and source of the quote, using an appropriate citation. Using more than a few lines of a person's writing or not crediting the source constitutes plagiarism and is wrong. If using facts found in a source's research, you should use a footnote or endnote, or, if publishing your content electronically, you can use a hyperlink to the source.

This holds true not only for printed materials, such as books and magazines, but also for Internet sources, such as webpages or online books. The only exception is if you use information based on common knowledge or facts that appear in a number of sources. When this is the case, you do not need to cite the specific source from which you got the information.

Colleges and universities have differing requirements for citing sources, typically adhering to one of the following: *MLA Handbook for Writers of Research Papers* (MLA style), *Publication Manual of the American Psychological Association* (APA style), The *Chicago Manual of Style* (Chicago style), and *Scientific Style and Format: The CSE Manual for Authors, Editors, and Publishers* (CSE style).

To learn more about citing electronic resources, use a search engine to search for *citing electronic sources*.

Web-based resources that are invisible to the typical web user are called the **Invisible Web** or sometimes the **Deep Web**. These resources typically do not appear in search engine indexes because they exist only when generated dynamically by a search query, are not linked to other webpages, are not in HTML format (such as video or other media), or are private or password-protected. Elements of the Invisible Web include electronic books, product catalogs, library catalogs, government records, and other databases that users typically access directly from a specialized search engine within the resource. Search engines typically index only visual or accessible webpages, leaving a huge number of webpages untapped. Researchers continue to work on search technologies that will enable access to information currently hidden on the Invisible Web. Concerns about hidden web content include the possibility of criminal activity, such as sales of illegal firearms, funding of terrorist organizations, and distribution of instructional materials for dangerous activities, such as bomb making. The size of the Invisible Web is unknown, but researchers estimate it to be 4,000 to 5,000 times larger than the amount of accessible and searchable web content, known as the **Surface Web**.

Plagiarism

With a deadline approaching, many students turn to the web not only to do research on the topic, but also to take a shortcut right to the completed research paper. Some websites — referred to as paper mills — offer completed papers and assignments on a vast number of topics and from a variety of viewpoints. Some are free, some require an exchange (post a paper to take a paper), and some charge a fee based on the length of the paper.

Just as quoting a few lines without citing the source is plagiarism, so is turning in a paper from a paper mill. The consequences for plagiarism might be grave, including censure or expulsion. Instructors often can detect if a student turns in a paper from an online paper mill. Instructors know what to look for when evaluating student papers for plagiarism. When students cannot answer questions about sections of their papers, the evidence is stronger. At many schools, screening software also is used to detect plagiarism. Some schools require students to submit papers in electronic format using a plagiarism-detecting platform. The platform scans and flags potential examples of plagiarism before the instructor even reads the paper.

Students can use search engines to assist in the research process, but they should resist the temptation to avoid the work of writing the research paper altogether. Not only are the consequences severe when cheating is caught, but turning in one's own work is a matter of honor.

For more information on plagiarism, use a search engine to search for *plagiarism and paper mills*.

Chapter Review

During the search process, you must choose the best search tool for the job, formulate the search query, examine the search results, and evaluate the credibility of the webpages listed in the search results list.

Search tools generally are classified as directories, search engines, and metasearch engines. A directory is a human-compiled index of webpages organized into hierarchical categories and subcategories. In contrast, a search engine uses a software program called a web crawler to browse the web and compile a searchable index without human intervention. Today, most search tools are hybrids, offering both directory categorization and the ability to search their index of webpages using a search query.

A search query can be one or more keywords, a phrase, or a complete sentence or question. You enter a search query in a search engine's Address box or search text box. The search engine then returns a search results list of relevant webpages or hits from its index of pages.

Many search engines provide shortcuts to quickly retrieve information, and some include advanced search forms that make creating complex search queries easier. An advanced search form might allow the user to restrict search results not only by what keywords are included or excluded, but also by date, language, geographic region, domain, file types, and so forth. You can access various search engines at their respective websites or through the Search box in the browser.

Specialized search engines are useful for finding people, businesses, news, videos, social media, and shopping websites. To find more scholarly or in-depth information, you can use specialized electronic databases and collections. The Deep Web includes web-based resources that do not appear in search engine indexes.

TERMS TO KNOW

After reading this chapter, you should know each of these Key Terms.

Boolean operator (112)
bot (105)
breadcrumb trail (101)
broken link (98)
crawler (92)
Deep Web (132)
directory (99)
drilling down (100)
full-text searching (105)
hashtag (126)
hit (95)
index (100)
Invisible Web (132)
keyword (94)
meta tag keywords (105)
metasearch engine (109)
natural language search (93)
open-ended search (96)

primary source (98)
search engine (105)
search engine algorithms (92)
search engine optimization (SEO) (93)
search query (94)
search results list (95)
search text box (95)
shopping aggregator (128)
shopping bot (128)
social media aggregator (126)
spider (105)
stop word (96)
Surface Web (132)
targeted search (96)
web crawler (105)
wiki (98)
white pages directory (124)
yellow pages directory (124)

TEST YOUR KNOWLEDGE

Complete the Test Your Knowledge exercises to solidify what you have learned in the chapter.

True or False

Mark T for True and F for False. (Answers are found on page numbers in parentheses.)

____ 1. Using multiple keywords in a search query narrows the scope of the query. (95)

____ 2. All search engines clearly mark paid or sponsored links in search results. (105)

____ 3. If you misspell a keyword, the search results return an error. (96)

____ 4. *How often do whales come to the surface?* is an example of a natural language search. (93)

____ 5. Spiders are a type of search engine. (105)

____ 6. A metasearch engine uses human editors to compile an index of webpages. (109)

____ 7. The Boolean operators AND, NOT, or OR are used in advanced search techniques to include or exclude keywords. (112)

____ 8. Search engines publish their search engine algorithms in order to improve the search results. (93)

____ 9. Search engine optimization refers to the creation of search indexes. (93)

____10. Unlinked webpages, password-protected webpages, and product catalogs are all part of the Invisible Web. (132)

Multiple Choice

Select the best answer. (Answers are found on page numbers in parentheses.)

1. For the most effective search results, choose keywords that are _____. (94)

   a. Boolean

   b. specific

   c. general

   d. stop words

2. To search for a webpage that contains a specific phrase, _____. (95)

   a. no special action is required

   b. surround the phrase with brackets

   c. insert the word, AND, between every word

   d. surround the phrase with quotation marks

3. A list of hits typically contains _____. (95)

   a. a link to each website

   b. a description of the webpage or a sample of text from the page

   c. websites that are sponsored or that have paid to have their pages placed at the top of the list

   d. all of the above

4. The most popular search engine in the United States is _____. (108)

   a. Google

   b. Bing

   c. Yahoo!

   d. Internet Explorer

5. A social media _____ searches online tools that allow users to communicate ideas, share links, contribute personal commentary, and interact online with other web users. (128)

   a. consolidator

   b. search engine

   c. aggregator

   d. crawler

6. _____ keywords appear in a webpage's HTML code and are readable by the web crawler but invisible to the user. (105)

   a. Meta tag

   b. Boolean

   c. Natural language

   d. Hashtag

7. _____ is an example of a website you can use to search for, manage, and track hashtags. (126)

   a. Dogpile

   b. Twubs

   c. StumbleUpon

   d. Shopzilla

8. You can use the _____ bar to locate information on the current webpage. (125)

   a. Toolbar

   b. Keyword

   c. Address

   d. Find

9. A(n) _____ is a webpage listed in search results. (95)

   a. stop word

   b. bot

   c. hit

   d. operator

10. Which of the following should you do to exclude a word from search results? (112)

    a. type NOT before the word

    b. include the word in brackets

    c. do not include the word in the search terms

    d. Any of the above will work.

TRENDS

Investigate current Internet developments with the Trends exercises.

Write a brief essay about each of the following trends, using the web as your research tool. For each trend, identify at least one webpage URL used as a research source. Be prepared to discuss your findings in class.

1 | Search Engine Algorithms

Search for *search engine algorithm trends*. Sort or filter your results, if possible, to search for the most recent articles or blog posts. Find information regarding any of the following topics: personalized searches; localized or geographic searches; use and impact of social media trends; natural language searches; and unethical SEO practices. Submit your findings in the format requested by your instructor.

2 | Hashtags

Search for *hashtags marketing examples*. Sort or filter your results, if possible, to search for the most recent articles or blog posts. Find an example of a marketing campaign or other business strategy involving hashtags. What was the business or organization? Who was the target audience? How was social media used? What results were you able to find about the effectiveness of the campaign? Submit your findings in the format requested by your instructor.

Challenge your perspective of Internet technology with the @Issue exercises.

Write a brief essay in response to the following issues, using the web as your research tool. For each issue, identify at least one URL used as a research source. Be prepared to discuss your findings in class.

1 | Deep Web

Search for *deep web criminal activity*. Sort or filter your results, if possible, to search for the most recent articles or blog posts. Find articles discussing concerns about possible or actual criminal activity in the Deep Web. What types of crime does or could occur? Are there examples of people being caught? What can be done to monitor the Deep Web? Submit your findings in the format requested by your instructor.

2 | SEO

Search for *seo marketing techniques*. Sort or filter your results, if possible, to search for the most recent articles or blog posts. Find and read at least two articles or blog posts that list common, current SEO practices. List five practices for using SEO techniques effectively. List five SEO practices that are considered unethical. Why? Should search engines publish their search engine algorithms? Why or why not? Submit your findings in the format requested by your instructor.

Use the web to obtain more information about the concepts and skills taught in the chapter with the Hands On exercises.

1 | Online Scavenger Hunt

1. Start your browser, if necessary.

2. Find solutions to three of the following scenarios using online resources. Even if you already know the answer or can ask someone who knows, search the web to find the answer. For each scenario, complete the following steps.

   a. Choose a search engine.

   b. Determine the keywords you will use in the search query.

   c. Note whether you found the desired information using your original keywords and search engine choice, or whether you had to search again using different keywords or a different search engine.

   d. Judge the value and authenticity of the result pages the search engine returns.

Scenario 1: Your cousin recently moved to a new townhouse in Albuquerque, New Mexico. You want to send her a gift certificate to a large, chain hardware store as a housewarming gift. Select a store and visit its website. Find all locations in Albuquerque. Note the process for sending a gift certificate from the hardware store's website.

Scenario 2: You want to find out more about fan reaction to a recent sporting or current event. Select an event, and locate hashtags that were trending for the event. Find at least three hashtag examples, and describe the facts you learned with each hashtag.

Scenario 3: You are adopting a dog, and you want to find a searchable list or dictionary of pet names. Find one that allows you to search by gender, origin, and at least two other criteria, such as starting letter or number of syllables. Perform a search of names using search criteria of your choice and write down the top three recommended names for each gender.

Scenario 4: Your boss is a die-hard San Antonio Spurs fan, and you would like to impress him with your knowledge of the team. Find the current roster, and list the names of a few notable players from the past. Also, find out which year was their most successful season, and what the results were.

Scenario 5: You decide to go to the movies. Find out what film is the current number one box-office hit. Read a critic's review of the movie. See whether it is playing at a local theater and the times of the showings.

Scenario 6: A friend wants to go on a white-water rafting trip through the Grand Canyon and wants you to go along. Find out what time of year is best, what experience is necessary, what river rafting companies are available, how much such a trip costs, and how far in advance you have to make a reservation for the trip.

Scenario 7: You and your fiancé or fiancée decide to have your wedding in the Bahamas. Price the airfare and determine a range of prices for wedding packages for up to 25 guests. List the requirements for a marriage license. Find the name of a person to officiate at the ceremony in the Bahamas.

Scenario 8: You and your friends have been discussing geocaching, and now you want to know more it. Find the origins of geocaching, a geocaching club or organization, and three examples of geocaching adventures in your local area.

2 | Social Media Aggregators

1. Start your browser, if necessary.
2. Use a search engine to search for *social media aggregators*.
3. Choose one aggregator tool to use to answer the following questions.

   a. For which device(s) is the tool available? Is it available as a mobile app? A website? Both?

   b. Which social media platforms can you manage or search for using the tool?

   c. What topics currently are trending, according to the tool?

4. Submit your findings in the format requested by your instructor.

TEAM APPROACH Work collaboratively to reinforce the concepts in the chapter with the Team Approach exercises.

1 | Searching for Health Information

1. Work with a team of three to four classmates to search for and evaluate health and fitness websites and apps.
2. Start your browser, if necessary.
3. Use a search engine to search for *fitness and health websites and apps*.
4. Assign one website or app to each teammate to research. Each team member should do the following:

   a. Find out the website or app's exercise recommendations, and note any major dietary restrictions prescribed by the organization.

   b. Locate information about the sponsoring business or organization. Are they credible? Why or why not?

   c. Determine whether you can sync fitness trackers or other devices or apps with the website or app. How?

   d. Read three reviews of the website or app. Would you recommend using it? Why or why not?

5. Submit your findings in the format requested by your instructor.

2 | Internet Archive

1. Work with a team of three to four classmates to review changes to a specific website over the years.

2. Start your browser, if necessary.

3. Use a search engine to search for *the wayback machine* or enter `web.archive.org` in your browser.

4. As a group, decide on a business that has been around for at least 10 years whose website you will view using archives.

5. Use the Wayback Machine to search for the business website: 10 years ago, 5 years ago, and 1 year ago.

6. Compare the three previous website versions to the current website.

7. List three changes that were made. Why do you think the web designers changed them? What new features were added?

8. Submit your findings in the format requested by your instructor.

4 | Communicating Online

Introduction

Internet users around the world use online tools to communicate and collaborate with friends, family members, coworkers, classmates, and others. Technologies such as email, social networking, microblogging, instant messaging, IRC or web chat, cloud-based web apps, voice and video chats, mailing lists, newsgroups and web-based discussion groups, wikis, blogs, and more — help individual, professional, and business Internet users do the following:

- Share information, exchange files, and arrange appointments using email, instant messaging, chat, and microblogging.
- Broadcast messages using social networking, microblogging, or video sharing.
- Participate in web-based discussion groups or newsgroups.
- Communicate with customers, business partners, the public, and other stakeholders through blogs.
- Work together on documents using web apps.
- Collaborate on ongoing projects using wikis.
- Solicit political and charitable contributions using email and websites.
- Communicate using social networking websites, chat, instant messaging, and texting.
- Share content and media with others at social bookmarking or content-sharing websites.
- Share reviews of product or service providers at social opinion websites.

In this chapter, you will learn how continually evolving and emerging Internet and web technologies affect the way we communicate and collaborate with others.

Objectives

After completing this chapter, you will be able to:

1. Describe the components of email systems and email messages

2. Discuss and apply email etiquette

3. Use email to send, receive, and organize email messages and contacts, and discuss email viruses

4. Describe various online social media and communication tools and discuss how they are used

Email Systems

Email is one of the most efficient and commonly used online communication tools. Email communications are indispensable for businesses, schools, and other organizations. Businesses and organizations of all sizes rely heavily on email for communications among coworkers and to communicate with vendors, customers, investors, and others. People use email for nonbusiness communications with their school, organizations, family, and friends.

FACTS @HAND   According to the technology research firm Radicati, by 2017 4.9 billion email accounts will exist worldwide.

The volume of personal and business email messages sent daily is staggering, exceeding the number of pieces of paper mail handled by major national postal systems. Some email messages are spam, the unsolicited junk email you learned about in Chapter 1. Email clients block most spam email based on content, domain, and other criteria. You will learn more about recognizing and avoiding spam later in this chapter.

FACTS @HAND   The estimated percentage of unsolicited email (spam) of all email is approximately 70 percent. Malicious spam can infect your computer and use your address book to send spam to your contacts.

Using email has several distinct benefits, including speed of delivery, low cost, accessibility, convenience, and ease of management:

- Speed of delivery — A sender can compose and send an email message and deliver it to its recipient or multiple recipients in seconds. The recipient(s) can send a reply just as quickly, thus providing rapid feedback, or reply when it is convenient.

- Low cost — Email is a cost-effective way to communicate with others and to share documents quickly. For example, sending an email message is free, compared with the costs of the paper, envelope, and stamp required for writing and sending a letter. Sending an electronic file attached to an email message also is free and can save you the cost and time of sending a printed document using a courier service.

- Accessibility — You can access email messages from any computer or device with Internet access. A user can read all of the mail sent to his or her email account from any Internet-connected computer, or from a smartphone, tablet computer, or other portable device.

- Convenience — The sender can send an email message at his or her convenience, and the recipient can read it at his or her convenience. This especially is effective when users are in different time zones. Using email can promote increased collaboration among coworkers or the members of a social group.

- Ease of management — Users can manage email messages by storing them in folders on their computers or mail servers. Users can arrange and view messages by date, sender, or other criteria, and can delete emails they no longer need. Users can include the contents of the original email in their reply, creating a chain of communication to which they can refer as necessary.

In the next sections, you will learn about the components of an email system: addresses, clients, servers, and protocols.

Email Considerations

Although email messages may seem less formal than paper-based communications, they often serve as official communication or notification. Companies use email to communicate important information about customer accounts, purchases, or billing. Employers use email to distribute important information about employee health care plans or other company business. In addition, courts of law accept email information as evidence.

Keep in mind that any personal email you send using your work or school email address is the property of the company or school. Most businesses, organizations, and schools that provide email accounts and services publish a list of email rules and guidelines. These rules may include guidelines about offensive content and file size restrictions, and outline discipline for failure to abide by the rules. You must comply with company and school rules regarding the use of email. For example, if you forward an offensive email to colleagues, you risk discipline or firing for contributing to a hostile work environment. For these reasons, it is a good idea to set up a personal email account to use for nonwork or school-related correspondence. Keep in mind that many companies and schools have rules for use of their resources, including company- or school-issued computers or devices, or use of the network to send email, so some of the same parameters may apply even if you are using a personal email account. Many companies also have guidelines about personal correspondence or activity during company time.

Remember that anyone can forward your email and any file attachments to other recipients without your knowledge or permission.

Email Addresses

To reach the correct destination, an email message must have a unique delivery address consisting of a user ID and a host name, as well as a top-level domain. An example of an email address is: mariaspringer@gmail.com. In this example, *mariaspringer* is the **user name**, or **user ID**, which is a unique identifier for the recipient. The **host name**, *gmail.com*, identifies the server where the recipient's email account or mailbox resides. The host name includes a top-level domain (TLD), such as .com or .net. The @ symbol separates the user name and host name. You enter an email address in a new message window provided by your email client.

Email Clients, Servers, and Protocols

The steps in the transmission of an email message from origin to destination address, using servers instead of post offices, parallel those followed in the delivery of a letter by a traditional postal service. An email message has a unique delivery address, travels from server to server over the Internet until it reaches its destination, and then appears in its recipient's mailbox.

EMAIL CLIENTS   An **email client** is any program used to create, send, and receive email messages (Figure 4-1 on the following page). To use some email clients, you download and install the program or app on your computer or mobile device and instruct it to manage your incoming email from a server or a web-based email service. Most mobile devices have an email app installed. Some mobile devices enable you to download a different email app using your device's store, while others require you to use the installed email app. When you install an email client, you must set it up to sync and download email from your email address. If you are a student or an employee, often your school or company provides you with an email client and address. If you are using a system such as Windows Live Mail, you will need to provide your email address and password for the email client to access your email. Web-based email services, such as Gmail or Yahoo! Mail, allow users to establish an email address (such as mariaspringer@gmail.com) as well as access to the email account using a web browser and a web or mobile app. You can sync web-based email to an email client or app, or manage web-based email using tools provided by the web-based email service you are using. You will learn more about managing web-based email with an email client in this chapter.

Email Clients

Client Name	Web-based or Installed?	Description
Apple Mail	Installed	Available for Apple's OS X operating system. Supports web-based email such as Yahoo! Mail, AOL Mail, Gmail, and iCloud. Mobile version available.
Eudora	Installed	Open source program, developed by Qualcomm and others. The current version incorporates aspects of Mozilla Thunderbird.
Gmail	Web-based	Integrates with other Google services, including Google Drive and Google+. Available for free, and includes ads.
Mail.com	Web-based	Free, advertising-supported. Offers unlimited email storage, choice of over 200 domain names, online file storage, collecting of emails from other accounts, and Facebook integration.
Microsoft Outlook	Installed	Part of the Microsoft Office suite. Includes a calendar, task manager, contact manager, note taking, journal, and web browsing.
Mozilla Thunderbird	Installed	Free, open source. Offers email, chat, and news. Extensions add functionality, such as Lightning, which adds a calendar to Thunderbird.
Opera Mail	Installed	Originally a feature of the Opera browser, but now available as a stand-alone product. Includes a feed aggregator and news client.
Outlook.com	Web-based	Free email service that has similar capabilities to Microsoft Outlook. Formerly known as Hotmail. Integrates with OneDrive (cloud storage and applications) and Skype (Internet voice and video calls).
Windows Live Mail	Installed	Free, downloadable client for use with Windows operating system. Includes options to create picture email messages, as well as read web feeds and use web-based email.
Yahoo! Mail	Web-based	Free, advertising-supported. Also includes Yahoo! Business, (a fee-based business email administration services), customized domain names, and more. Advertising-free version is available for a fee.

© Cengage Learning®

Figure 4-1 Components of an email address.

Q&A

What is the difference between server- and web-based email?

Server-based email is email that is hosted by, and stored on, a mail server and managed using a program such as Microsoft Exchange. Schools, businesses, and organizations that provide you with an email address likely use a mail server. Web-based email, such as Gmail, is stored and hosted on a web server, and often is used for personal email. You can access web-based email through a browser, or using an installed email client. You access server-based email using an email client.

FACTS @HAND

Many colleges and universities provide email services for their students. Google offers free email platforms for schools to manage. Students and teachers use their Google email accounts to communicate and turn in homework or papers electronically using Google's productivity and collaboration tools.

@SOURCE

To find out which email clients are the most popular, use a search engine to search for *email client market share*.

Email clients typically offer tools to:

- Create and send outgoing email messages
- Read, save, and print incoming email messages and their attachments
- Sort, archive, and delete messages
- Create folders in which to organize messages

Individuals at home, at school, and at work use web-based email services. You access web-based email services using a web browser instead of email client software. You will learn more about using a web-based email service later in this chapter.

EMAIL SERVERS AND PROTOCOLS   Email messages travel over the Internet using the same packet-switching technology and TCP/IP suite that govern all communications over the Internet. An email client might use a number of protocols, such as **POP (Post Office Protocol)**, **SMTP (Simple Mail Transfer Protocol)**, **IMAP (Internet Message Access Protocol)**, and HTTP (Hypertext Transfer Protocol) to interact with mail servers when sending and receiving messages. Figure 4-2 on the following page illustrates the steps involved in sending and receiving an email message:

Step 1: The sender creates and sends the message using an email program on a computer or mobile device.

Step 2: The email program makes contact with software stored on the outgoing mail server.

Step 3: The outgoing mail server contacts a DNS name server to resolve the host domain name portion of the email address to an IP address, determines the best route over the Internet to the message's destination, and sends the message on its way.

Step 4: The mail server receives the message and stores it in the recipient's mailbox. A **mailbox** is a folder on the server that corresponds to the user name portion of the email address. Upon request from the user's email client, the mail server sends the new message to the client.

How an Email Message May Travel from a Sender to a Receiver

Step 1
Using an email program, you create and send a message on a computer or mobile device.

Step 2
Your email program contacts software on the outgoing mail server.

Step 3
Software on the outgoing mail server determines the best route for the data and sends the message, which travels along Internet routers to the recipient's incoming mail server.

incoming mail server

Internet router

Internet router

Step 4
When the recipient uses an email program to check for email messages, the message transfers from the incoming mail server to the recipient's computer or mobile device.

© Oleksiy Mark / Shutterstock.com; © iStockphoto / luisimmolina; Courtesy of Juniper Networks; © iStockphoto / hocus-focus; © Cengage Learning; © Cengage Learning

Figure 4-2 Several steps are involved in sending and receiving an email message.

Email clients, such as Microsoft Outlook and Windows Live Mail, use POP or IMAP incoming mail servers. Some free web-based email services, such as Outlook.com, use HTTP servers. While each type of server handles incoming messages, each server does so in a different way.

When an incoming message arrives on a POP server, the email client handles the mail management functions. For example, an email client sends a request to a POP server, downloads all new messages, and stores the messages on the user's computer. The main disadvantage of a POP server is that after the user downloads messages to his or her computer or device, the user can view and manage the messages only using that computer or device.

In contrast, an IMAP mail server provides mail management functions on the server. The server stores and manages a user's messages. Although the user reads, deletes, or sorts the messages using his or her email client, the action actually takes place on the IMAP server. The user also can work with messages locally on his or her computer or device by downloading the messages and reading them, marking them for deletion, or composing new messages. The next time the user's email client connects to the IMAP server, the server synchronizes with the email client, sending out any new mail messages and deleting messages on the server that were marked for deletion in the email client. Unlike POP servers, where a user downloads his or her messages to a specific machine, a user can access an IMAP server from different computers or devices to view his or her messages.

An HTTP server provides web-based email services that you can access through a website and a web browser. The main advantage of an HTTP server and web-based email is that you have access to email anywhere, using any Internet-connected computer or device. One disadvantage is that an email client, such as Windows Live Mail, might not support access to incoming messages stored on an HTTP server.

Anatomy of an Email Message

Most email clients provide the same basic message window features. Figure 4-3 outlines common email client features using a Microsoft Outlook 2013 email message window.

- The **To line** contains one or more email addresses of the message's recipient or recipients. The email addresses for multiple recipients typically appear separated by semicolons or commas.

- The **Cc line** lists the email addresses of recipients who will receive a courtesy copy of the message. A **courtesy copy** is a copy of the message you send as a courtesy to someone other than the primary recipients in the To line.

Q&A

When should I use the Bcc line?

One helpful use of Bcc is when you are sending a bulk email to a group of people. Bcc keeps the distribution list private so recipients cannot see the other people's names or email addresses. Bcc protects your recipients from spammers who use bulk email to collect email addresses. You also can use Bcc when you are sending an additional copy of an email to a contact or group of contacts and do not want the other recipients to know. Another benefit of Bcc is that if a recipient uses the Reply to All feature, only the original sender or anyone not in the Bcc line receives the return message.

- The **Bcc line** contains the email addresses of recipients who will receive a blind courtesy copy of the message. A **blind courtesy copy** is a copy of a message sent without that recipient's name or email address appearing in the message header. Only the sender can see the Bcc line. The Bcc recipient(s) only see his or her own email address or name, and cannot see addresses for others in the Bcc line.

- The **Subject line** contains a description of the message content.

- The **Attach line** contains the file names of any attachments. An **attachment** is a file that is sent along with the email message.

- The **message body** contains the text of the message. In addition to text, a message body can include graphics, links to webpages, or the contents of webpages.

- You can include a signature automatically to all of your outgoing email using a small **signature file**. A signature file contains standard content, such as the name, title, and contact information of the sender.

Figure 4-3 Typical components of an email message window.

The To, Cc, Bcc, Subject, and Attach lines all are part of the **message header**. You can indicate whether to compose your message as plain text or as an HTML-formatted message. An **HTML-formatted message** contains formatting, such as different fonts, font sizes, and font styles, as well as bulleted lists, indented paragraphs, and so forth. If you specify an HTML-formatted message, a Formatting toolbar might appear above the message composition box, as it does in Figure 4-3. Most email clients can read HTML-formatted messages, or can translate HTML-formatted messages into text-based ones. The figures in this book show HTML-formatted messages.

@ISSUE

Email Etiquette

The very characteristics of email that make it so popular and easy to use also can be disadvantages. For example, because email is informal, you may be tempted to send messages that you do not write clearly or word carefully. The speed and ease with which you can send an email message can create another potential problem. An individual might send an email message when tired, upset, or uninformed without carefully thinking through the message's contents. Additionally, because email is so easy to send, some individuals might send too many unnecessary, and often unwanted, email messages to their friends, family, and coworkers.

One major drawback of email and most text-based communications in general, is the potential for misunderstanding. The composer of an email message might write something with sarcasm in mind. The reader, however, might not interpret the language as sarcasm, instead reading the message as entirely sincere. The reader sees only the content of the message, and does not see the facial expressions, hear the tone of voice, or observe the body language of the sender. Following some basic email etiquette guidelines can convey an idea clearly and avoid accidentally insulting someone or causing confusion. Email etiquette guidelines include the following:

- Consider whether email is the proper communication format. A phone call may be best for urgent or sensitive communications.

- When composing an email message, do not use all capital letters for the entire message. All caps represent SHOUTING!

- When responding to a message about which you have strong negative feelings, it is a good idea to save your response for a few hours or a day before you send it. Responding with strong language or insults by email (and other online communication tools), called flaming, is improper in most online venues.

- When you want to convey a particular feeling or emotion in an email message, you can make use of an **emoticon** such as typing a colon and a right parentheses character :) to convey a smile, at appropriate points in the message to represent the emotion you are trying to convey. Email, instant messaging, and text messaging programs might provide a set of emoticon icons you can use, called **emojis**. Emoticons and emojis can help the message recipient get the full flavor of a message. Be careful, however, not to overuse emoticons or emojis: A message that contains one or more icons per sentence loses its appeal and impact. Additionally, emoticons and emojis generally are not appropriate for business email messages.

- Consider the timing and audience when responding to email. You should respond to or acknowledge time-sensitive or business-related emails right away. Do not use the Reply All feature unless you intend your message to go to the entire CC and To list.

Using Email

As you have learned, email clients provide tools to send and receive messages; reply to and forward messages; and print, organize, and delete messages. A **web-based email service**, such as Gmail or Yahoo! Mail, is an email service available to a user through a browser and a website, or a web or mobile app. Web-based email services make personal email available to anyone with access to an Internet-connected computer or device. Individuals who have Internet access at work but want to receive personal mail in an account other than one supplied by their employer also use web-based email services. In addition, some individuals set up separate web-based email accounts to use for specific types of email, such as one for correspondence with family and friends and another for buying and selling at auction websites.

Basic web-based email services generally are free, but may include advertising. A premium web-based email service usually reduces or eliminates advertising and often provides additional advanced features, such as increased message storage space, typically for a small annual fee. Popular basic and premium web-based email services include Gmail, Microsoft Outlook.com, Yahoo! Mail (basic), and Yahoo! Mail Plus (premium).

Web-based email services typically offer the same email functions as an installed email client: sending and receiving messages, maintaining contacts, sending messages with attachments, and so forth. The primary advantage of using a web-based email service is portability. Because web-based email can be sent and received from any computer, users can access their email accounts at coffee shops, libraries, and other public venues that provide Internet access. The primary disadvantage of web-based email is the inclusion of advertising on the email service's webpages that some users find annoying.

In this section, you will learn how to set up an email account and install an email client; review the features of an email client window and then receive, read, and reply to an email message; open an attachment; compose and send a message with an attachment; and organize email messages.

Note: The figures and steps in this book use Windows Live Mail as an email client and Gmail as the email service. Your steps should be similar if using a different client or platform. In order to complete the steps in this section, you must ensure that you have both an email client and email address, or use the following steps to create a web-based email account using Gmail.

Creating a Web-Based Email Account

To create a web-based email account, you must have access to a computer or mobile device with an Internet connection and a web browser. Your mobile device may have an email app installed to which you can sync your web-based email. You access your account by signing in with your user name and password using your browser or the email app.

In this section, you will set up an email account with a user name and password. Take care to write down your user name and password and keep them in a safe place in case you need them later. Next, you will access your new email account and read a Welcome message automatically sent to your account's Inbox folder. As with other activities in this text, your screen might look different from the figures in this section.

To Create a Web-based Email Account

The following steps access the Gmail website and create a new account.

1

- Start your browser and enter **gmail.com** in the Address bar.

- Press the ENTER key, or tap or click the necessary button to open the Gmail home page (Figure 4-4).

Q&A

What if I already have an email account?

If you already have a web-based email account, such as Gmail or Yahoo! Mail, and you do not want to create an additional account, you can use that address to work through the exercises in this chapter. In that case, do not complete the steps To Create a Web-Based Email Account. Instead, begin with the following set of steps, To Sync a Web-Based Email Account with an Email Client.

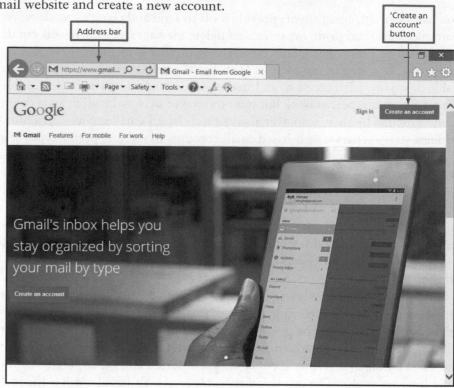

Figure 4-4

2

- Tap or click the 'Create an account' button to open the Gmail registration page.

- Enter your name and user name in the Name text boxes.

- Enter and verify a password in the 'Create a password' text box, making sure the password you choose has a rating of Strong (Figure 4-5).

Q&A

What if I get a prompt that tells me that my chosen user name is unavailable?

Common first and last name combinations likely are in use by other Gmail users. You might have to try several user names before you find one that is available, or you can choose one of the suggested alternatives. Many email services block or reserve common or generic names or word combinations to prevent spammers from guessing or generating your email address. **Spambots,** automated programs that create fake email accounts or hack into an unsuspecting user's email account to send spam, not only collect email addresses but can also generate email addresses to which to send spam. You can protect yourself further from spam by using initials and numbers to make your email address more specific and less vulnerable to spammers.

Figure 4-5

3

- Scroll the registration webpage to view the rest of the form and enter the necessary information.

- Tap or click the 'Set Google as my default homepage' check box to remove the check mark, if necessary.

- Enter the CAPTCHA as it appears on the page (Figure 4-6).

Q&A | **What is a CAPTCHA?**

A CAPTCHA (Completely Automated Public Turing Test to Tell Computers and Humans Apart) is a commonly used testing feature to ensure that a real person, not a programmed bot, is attempting to enroll in or set up an account. A user must enter in the characters that appear in the CAPTCHA box as part of the confirmation process. Users with visual or other disabilities may find it difficult to read and retype the CAPTCHA, as the letters often appear distorted.

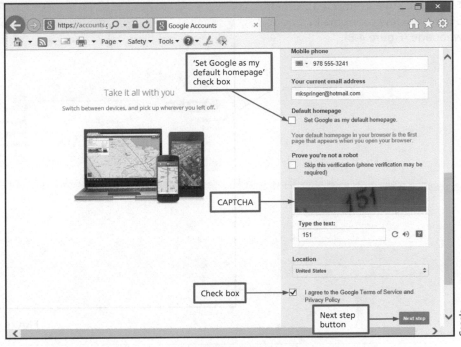

Figure 4-6

4

- Read the Terms of Service, Privacy Policy, and other links as desired, and tap or click the check box to accept them.

- Tap or click the Next step button to create the account and open the profile setup webpage.

- Tap or click the Next step button to complete the account creation process. (Figure 4-7).

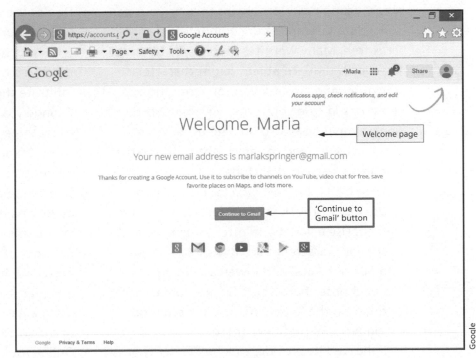

Figure 4-7

5

- Tap or click the 'Continue to Gmail' button to view your email account webpage (Figure 4-8).

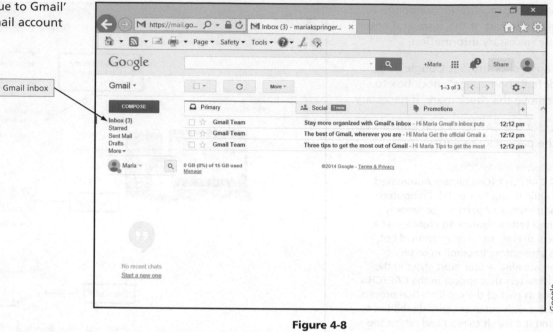

Gmail inbox

Figure 4-8

Google

Creating Passwords

Using strong passwords helps to keep your personal data safe and your computer or device virus-free. Many websites require you to create passwords that are at least eight characters in length, and also ask you for verification questions in case you forget your password. Some simple password guidelines for your email account, and for any website or app that requires a password, include:

- Even if there is no character requirement, use passwords that are at least 8 characters long. Use a variety of letters, numbers, and special characters, such as # or &, and use a mix of capital and lowercase letters. Do not choose characters that are close to each other on the keyboard, or use a common sequence of numbers or letters.
- If the website provides a menu of security questions for verification, choose questions and provide answers that cannot easily be found out by hackers, such as the name of your school or pet.
- Do not save your passwords in a file on your computer or device, or write them down where anyone can find them.

- Do not use the same password for all of your accounts. If one account or website is hacked, hackers look at all of your programs, accounts, and apps to attempt to infiltrate them as well.
- Change your passwords frequently, such as every three months. Change all of your passwords immediately if you suspect you have been hacked.
- Do not use any personal information, such as your name or phone number, as part of your password.
- Consider using a passphrase instead of a password, if it is an option. A **passphrase** is a sequence of words separated by spaces. If using a passphrase, misspell or replace some of the words.
- Online tools exist that test the strength of passwords. If the website, account, or app does not indicate the strength of your password, use a reputable online tool to test it.

Following these guidelines will help prevent identity theft, and protect you from hackers and viruses.

Syncing Web-based Email with an Email Client

One advantage of using an email client to manage and view your email is that you do not need to be online in order to use the email client to view email you have received and downloaded previously, or to compose new email. You must be online to send and receive new email. Another advantage of email clients is that you can sync multiple web-based or other email accounts to the email client, enabling you to receive personal and work or school email in one Inbox.

Windows Live Mail is an email client available for free for the Windows platform. The steps and figures in this book use Windows Live Mail 2012 on Windows 8. If you are using another operating system, check to see if Windows Live Mail is available. If not, use a different email client to perform the steps. You may need to adapt the steps slightly, but the capabilities should be similar.

To Sync a Web-based Email Account with an Email Client

The following steps sync your newly created Gmail account with Windows Live Mail.

1

- Open Windows Live Mail.

Q&A **What if I do not have Windows Live Mail?**
You might need to download and install Windows Live Mail and Windows Essentials to complete the steps in this chapter. Windows Live Mail is free, but you need permission from your instructor if using a school-owned computer or device. The steps and figures in this chapter use Windows Live Mail to teach email skills. If you install Windows Live Mail or Windows Essentials, accept any and all license agreements.

- Enter your Gmail address, password, and display name (Figure 4-9).

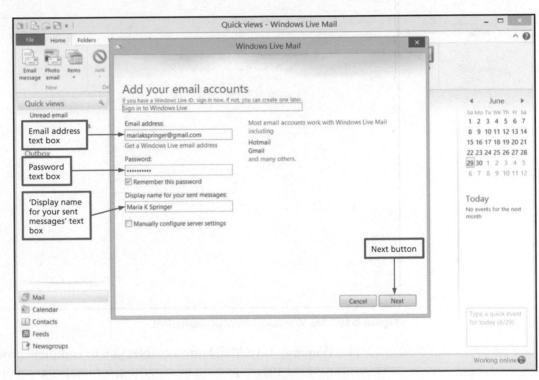

Figure 4-9

Q&A **What if I get a message telling me to enable IMAP for my Gmail account?**
You might need to enable IMAP services from within your Gmail account. Click the message link to access Google Help and read the necessary instructions.

2

- Click the Next button to open your Windows Live Mail inbox.

Reviewing the Email Window

The Windows Live Mail window (Figure 4-10) includes common email client elements, such as an inbox, folders, and viewing panes, as well as a program interface that is similar to other Windows or Microsoft Office programs and applications, such as the ribbon. If you are using a different email program or app, your features and locations might differ, but you should have similar capabilities.

The left pane contains links to your unread mail, your outbox, and the email folders established by your email client. In the middle pane, you will see your Inbox messages and the Search box. You can use the Search box to search the address, subject, and body text of messages in the open mail folder.

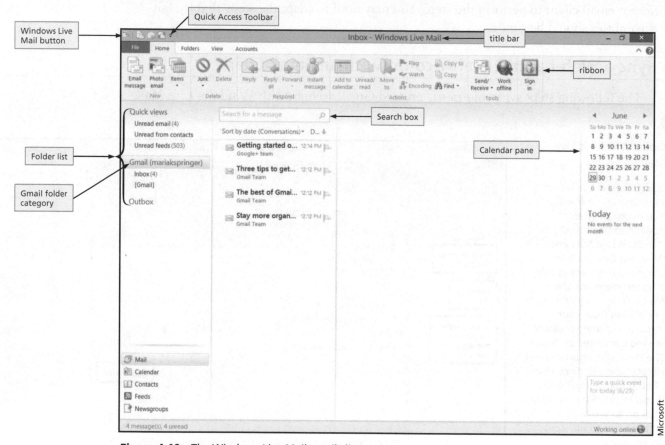

Figure 4-10   The Windows Live Mail email client.

The Windows Live Mail button enables you to complete program-specific tasks, such as printing, saving, importing or exporting, setting program options, getting Help, and exiting the program.

The ribbon is located below the title bar. The tabs, groups, and buttons on the ribbon differ depending on what type of item you are currently viewing. When you are viewing mail items, the ribbon contains the following tabs: Home, Folders, View, and Accounts. The Home tab contains the following groups and default buttons (Figure 4-11):

Figure 4-11   The Home tab.

- **NEW GROUP** The New group contains the Email message button, which opens the New Message window you use to address and compose an email message; the Photo email button, which creates a photo album using Windows Live Photos on a Windows Live SkyDrive to send a message; and the Items button, which opens a menu of options you can create, such as events, contacts, and news messages. **Contacts** are those users whose email or other information you have access to; their address information is stored in the Contacts folder.
- **DELETE GROUP** The Delete group contains the Junk button and Junk button arrow, which you use to move spam to the Junk mail folder as well as block senders and domains; and the Delete button, which you use to delete selected messages.
- **RESPOND GROUP** The Respond group contains the Reply button and the Reply all button, which open the Re: message window and address the reply message to all addresses in the incoming message (the sender plus anyone receiving a copy of the message); the Forward button, which opens the Fw: message window you use to forward an incoming message to one or more recipients; the Forward button arrow, which enables you to forward a message as an attachment; and the Instant message button, which you use to open an Instant Message window.
- **ACTIONS GROUP** The Actions group contains several buttons that you can use to manage messages, including the 'Add to calendar' button, which creates a calendar item based on the selected message, as well as buttons you can use to move, flag, mark as unread, and copy a message. Also in the Actions group is the Find button, you use to search for contacts, message folders, or the contents of the current message.
- **SIGN IN BUTTON** The Sign in button enables you to sign in to your email account. If you are using a shared computer or device, you might need to sign out of another user's account and sign in with your own information. If you are using a public or shared computer or device, ensure that you log out of your account when you are done using Windows Live Mail to protect your privacy.
- **TOOLS GROUP** The Tools group contains the Send/Receive button and the Work offline button, which disconnects Windows Live Mail from the Internet.

The Folders tab contains buttons that enable you to move, flag, copy, and navigate through messages and folders. You can use the View tab to change the layout of the panes in the Windows Live Mail window, sort or filter the current view or folder, or follow a conversation. You will learn about watching and ignoring conversations later in this chapter. The Accounts tab contains buttons that help you manage your email accounts and newsgroups.

Four viewing areas — the Folder list, Message list, Preview pane, and Calendar — appear below the ribbon.

The Folder list contains the Windows Live Mail mail folders used to store messages. The Quick views category enables you to view all unread messages and newsgroup items. Each email account appears as a separate category, such as in the example used in this chapter, which uses Gmail as the email account connected to the Windows Live Mail client.

Depending on the account(s) you have installed, for each account you may have some or all of the following folders: Inbox, Outbox, Sent items, Deleted items, Drafts, and Junk email folder, as well as any other default folder or folders you create. You can delete or create folders to suit your own needs. An **Inbox folder** contains incoming messages. An **Outbox folder** is a temporary storage folder for outgoing messages. Once you send an outgoing message, a copy appears, by default, in the **Sent Items folder** or **Sent Mail folder**. The **Deleted Items folder** or **Trash folder** contains deleted messages. Just as you can restore deleted files sent to the Windows Recycle Bin until you empty it, you can retrieve deleted messages from the Deleted items folder until you empty it manually. You also can set an option to have the folder emptied each time you close Windows Live Mail. The **Drafts folder** contains messages that you create and save to work on again, usually with the intention of sending them later.

Because you can customize the Folder list to add or delete folders, the folders you see in your Windows Live Mail window might vary from those shown in the figures in this chapter. The **Junk email** or **Spam folder** contains messages marked as unsolicited commercial email or spam based on the junk email options you set. You will learn more about setting junk email options later in this chapter. To access any folder, tap or click it in the Folder list.

The **Message list** displays individual messages. The messages appear sorted by date in the Message list by default. Tap or click the Sort by date button to change the sort order. The Preview pane displays a preview of the selected message in the Message list. As you receive new email messages, you also might see an email notification icon in the notification area on the taskbar. The Calendar pane shows the current month, as well as a list of tasks, events, or appointments for that day.

Receiving and Replying to an Incoming Email Message

Most email clients check for new email messages on the assigned mail servers at regular intervals and then display them in your Inbox. At any point, however, you can tap or click the Send/Receive or Refresh button to check for new email messages and sync all mail and newsgroup items.

To Check for Incoming Mail

The following step checks for incoming email and views an email message sent to you by your instructor.

1

- Tap or click the Send/Receive or Refresh button to download an incoming message from your instructor and send any outgoing messages temporarily stored in the Outbox folder.

- Tap or click the message from your instructor to select it and view the message contents in the Preview pane (Figure 4-12).

Q&A

What if I did not receive a message from my instructor?
If your instructor did not send a message to you, open any message in your Inbox that contains an attachment to complete the following steps. If you do not have any messages with an attachment, read through the next sets of steps to learn how to send a message with an attachment. Send an email to yourself that contains an attachment, and then complete the steps.

Figure 4-12

A standard feature of any email client is the reply feature, which allows you to respond to an incoming message. Replying opens an Re. message window addressed to the sender of the original message. The window includes, on the Subject line, a reference to the subject of the original message preceded by Re:. Most email clients include the text of the original message for reference by default. The Re: message window also enables you to perform a variety of tasks, such as send the message; cut, copy, and paste message contents; check spelling; set message priority; undo a previous action; and more.

To Reply to an Email Message

The following steps reply to the email message you just received.

1

- Tap or click the Reply button to open the Re: message window (Figure 4-13).

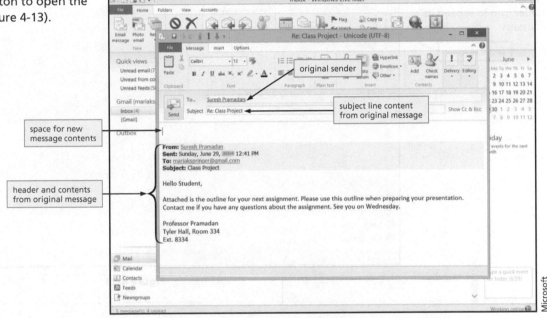

Figure 4-13

2

- Enter **Received** in the message window at the insertion point on the blank line above the original message header and text.

- Press the ENTER key to move to a new line.

- Enter your name on the current line.

- Press the ENTER key to complete the message (Figure 4-14).

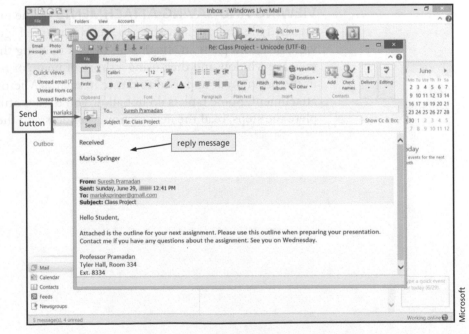

Figure 4-14

3

- Tap or click the Send button to close the Re: window and send the message.

- Tap or click the Sent Mail or Sent items folder to see the sent message (Figure 4-15).

Q&A

What if I do not see the Sent Mail folder? You might need to expand the Gmail folder icon to expand its contents.

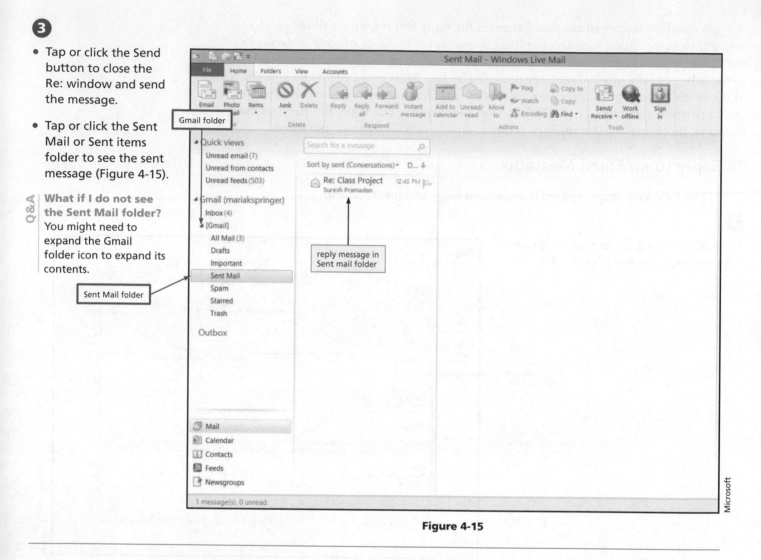

Figure 4-15

VIEWING AND SAVING ATTACHMENTS The message from your instructor has an attached file, indicated by the paper clip icon (see Figure 4-12 on page 160). You can preview, save, and print an attachment by first opening the message with the attachment in a message window and then using a shortcut menu or menu commands to open the email in the program or app used to create it, such as Microsoft Word, or to save or print the attachment. Some tablets do not allow you to save attachments. If you are unable to complete the steps, read the next section to understand the capabilities.

To View and Save an Attachment

The following steps view the file attached to your instructor's message and then save the attached file in a folder specified by your instructor. The message contents and attachment file name might vary from those shown in the figures.

1

- Verify that the email window or app is open, tap or click the Inbox folder icon if necessary, and then select the message from your instructor in the Message list.

- Double-tap or double-click the message from your Instructor to open the message in its own window (Figure 4-16).

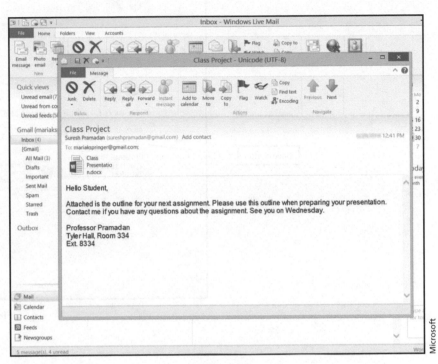

Figure 4-16

2

- Right-click or press and hold the attachment's file name to display the shortcut menu (Figure 4-17).

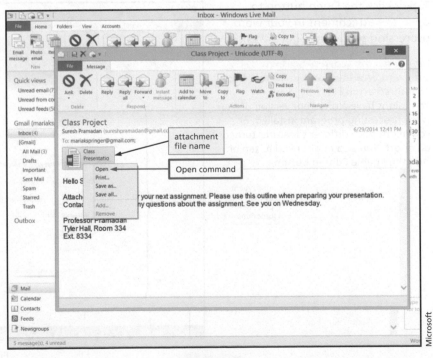

Figure 4-17

3

- Tap or click the Open command, if it is available, to open the Mail Attachment dialog box (Figure 4-18).

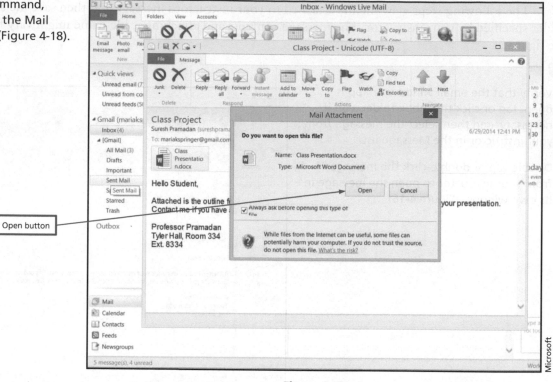

Figure 4-18

4

- Tap or click the Open button to open the attachment in your word processing program (Figure 4-19).

Q&A

Why does my word processing program window look different from the illustration?
You might have a different version of the word processing program installed, or you might have different features turned on or off. You also might need to tap or click the Enable Editing button.

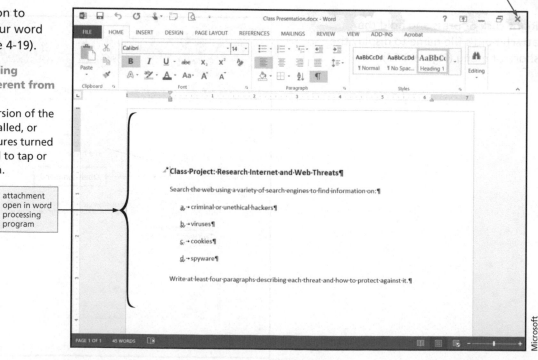

Figure 4-19

5

- Tap or click the Close button on the word processing program title bar to close the document and return to Windows Live Mail.

- Display the message from your instructor, if necessary.

- Right-click or press and hold the attachment icon to open the shortcut menu (Figure 4-20).

attachment icon

Save as command

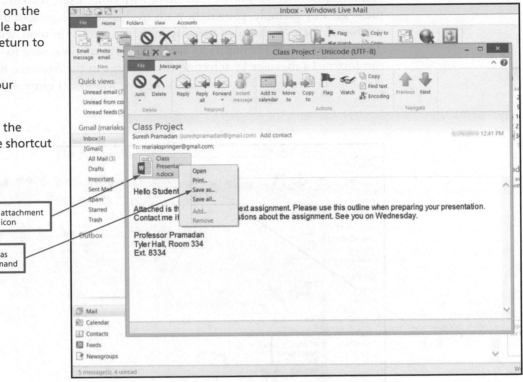

Figure 4-20

6

- Tap or click the Save as command to open the Save Attachment As dialog box.

- If necessary, tap or click the Browse button to navigate to the drive or folder specified by your instructor (Figure 4-21).

- Tap or click the Save button to close the Save Attachment As dialog box and save the attachment.

- Tap or click the Close button on the message window title bar and leave Windows Live Mail and the Inbox folder open.

Save button

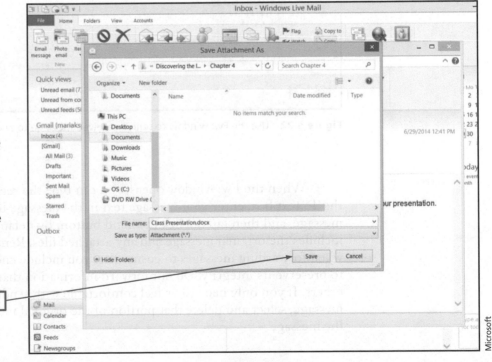

Figure 4-21

FORWARDING AN EMAIL MESSAGE You might receive an email message that contains information you want to share with other users who did not receive the original message. For example, you might want to share a message sent to one person with information about a rescheduled meeting, either in part or in total, with all meeting attendees. To **forward** a message means to send a message that was sent to you to someone else. You can forward a message by selecting the message in the Message list and then tapping or clicking the Forward button to open the Fw: window (Figure 4-22).

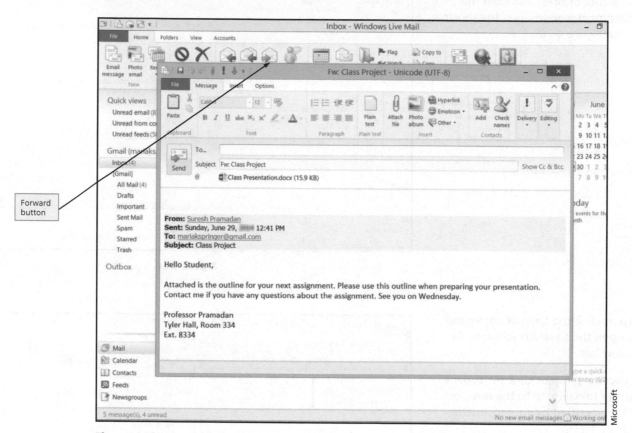

Figure 4-22 Use the Fw: window to send a received message to another person.

When the Fw: window opens, you can type the recipient's email address in the To text box, enter your message text in the message body area above the original message, and then tap or click the Send button. By default, a forwarded message includes the original message and any attached files. Remember to use good judgment when forwarding messages to ensure that you include enough of the original message to preserve its integrity. Do not forward information that you should not share with others. If you only need to or feel comfortable with sending part of the original message, select and delete that portion of the original message before forwarding the message.

Cyberbullying

Cyberbullying includes any Internet content created or distributed with the intent of hurting or humiliating someone. Cyberbullying includes circulating cruel and spiteful email, photos, instant messages, and social networking messages. Anything designed to hurt and humiliate the messages' target or recipient — perhaps a former girlfriend or boyfriend, a classmate, a coworker, or even a stranger — for entertainment or revenge is bullying or harassment. Examples of cyberbullying abound. The pictures of a young girl's horrific death in an automobile accident are widely circulated online, tormenting the girl's family. Students harass another student continually with hateful messages until she ultimately quits school. A young girl commits suicide because of a social networking hoax. Intimate pictures circulated among classmates result in a teenager's prosecution for child pornography and a lifetime as a registered sexual predator.

The cyberbullying statistics for kids and teens are astounding. According to Dosomething.org, 43 percent of kids have been victims of online bullying, and 58 percent have had hurtful things said about them online. Only one in ten kids informs a parent or other adult of the abuse.

You cannot protect yourself fully against cyberbullying. Take precautions to avoid putting yourself at risk by blocking contact with offenders and being aware of who you connect and share information with while using social networking and other online communication tools. Keep personal information private, and enable security and privacy settings on all of your online accounts. When necessary, ask for help from school officials, a parent, a responsible adult, or the police. For more information on protecting against cyberbullying, visit Dosomething.org or use a search engine to search for *cyberbullying protection tips.*

PRINTING AN EMAIL MESSAGE   Although email messages are stored and read electronically, many people prefer to work with paper and pen for certain tasks. Sometimes you may want to keep a hard copy of an email as part of a record of communication. Most email clients provide printing capabilities that allow users to create a hard copy of an email message, assuming you have access to a network printer. Before printing an email message, set any necessary print options, including the number of copies to print.

Composing and Sending an Outgoing Email Message

Many of the email messages you send will be replies to messages you receive. You often will need to send a new, original message to communicate news, updates, or event details. As you compose a message, keep in mind the following guidelines to ensure that your messages are well-received by your intended audience:

- Put a meaningful phrase in the Subject line to get the reader's attention or to identify the message's content.
- Add a greeting. Although the email header shows the recipient's email address or name, it is good form to include a greeting on the first line. The greeting can be a formal one (Dear Ms. Patil:) or a casual one (Hi, Julia!), depending on the nature of the message.

- Keep the message brief, but make sure its wording is clear. Make the point quickly, but provide enough information so the recipient understands the required background information. If the message contains requests, clearly state them in the first sentence or two, if possible.

- Instead of typing or retyping information, use hyperlinks to link to a website or network folder to which you reference in your email, or include an attachment file that contains information.

- When replying to an email, you should leave the message to which you are replying at the bottom of your message. Maintaining a message thread in this way can provide background information and make it easier for the recipient to understand the latest message in the thread.

- Use a personalized closing and include a signature file in case the recipient needs to know alternative ways to contact you.

CREATING A SIGNATURE FILE   Most email services enable you to create a signature file. A signature file includes standard information automatically inserted at the end of email messages. For example, you often might need to provide your contact information and title, particularly with business email. A signature file can contain basic contact information, such as your name, company, phone number(s), website, Twitter handle, and email address (Figure 4-23). You also could add a confidentiality agreement, logo, inspirational quotation or motto, or more.

Figure 4-23   You can create email signatures to display information automatically in every email message you send.

When deciding whether to create and include a signature in your email messages, consider how you usually use email. If most messages you create do not need a signature, then you might prefer to include a signature on a message-by-message basis, instead of automatically including it in all email messages. Some email clients allow you to set up multiple signatures so that you can use one for business communications, one for personal messages, and so on. If you want to insert a signature file on a message-by-message basis or be able to select from multiple signatures, do not turn on the option to add the signature file to all new messages. Instead, create the signature file or files. Then, after composing a new message, locate and select the desired signature.

COMPOSING A NEW MESSAGE WITH AN ATTACHMENT   You can send an electronic file — such as a document, spreadsheet, or photo — to someone by attaching the file to an email message. Be aware, however, that some mail servers limit attachment sizes to ensure that extremely large files do not bog down the email system. Additionally, some networks block incoming email messages that have certain types of attachments to reduce the risk of viruses.

It is a good idea to check the spelling of your message before you send it. To check the spelling, tap or click the Spelling button to identify any spelling errors. Most email clients alert you to potential spelling errors by using red squiggly lines or other indicators. Many also include an Autocorrect feature, which might change words you did not want to change. In addition to checking spelling, you also should thoroughly read emails before sending them.

FACTS @HAND

To Compose and Send a Message with an Attachment

The following steps compose a new email message and attach a small file as an attachment. For these steps, assume that you have asked a classmate, Emma Griffin, for her email address. Your instructor should have provided you with a digital photo file to use as an attachment. You compose a new email message to Emma Griffin, attach the file, and send the message.

1

- Verify that your email client website or app is open.

- Tap or click the Email message button to open a new email message window (Figure 4-24).

Email message button

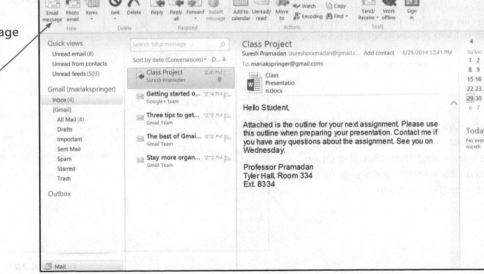

Figure 4-24

2

- Enter `Emma.Griffin@Cengage.com` in the To text box to enter the recipient's email address.

- Enter `Class Assignment` in the Subject text box to describe the message contents.

- Enter `Hi Emma,` to create the greeting line in the message body area, and then press the ENTER key twice to add space between the greeting and the message body.

- Enter `Let's get together before class to work on the attached assignment.` to enter the message text, and then press the ENTER key (Figure 4-25).

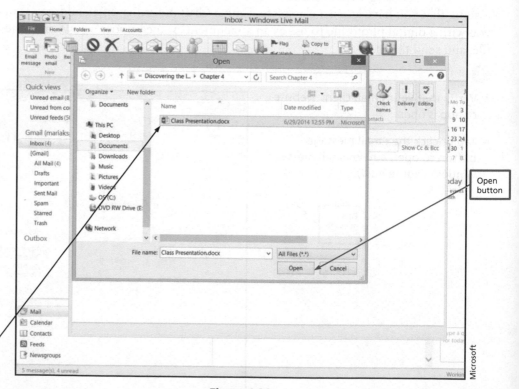

Figure 4-25

3

- Tap or click the Attach file button to display the Open dialog box.

- Navigate to the location in which you saved the attachment from your instructor.

Q&A

What do I do if I did not receive an attachment from my instructor?
You can access the file on the webpage with student resources for this book, or use a low-resolution (small file size) photo to which you have access and own the copyrights.

4

- In the Open dialog box, double-tap or double-click the Class Presentation file name, and then click the Open button to attach the document to the message (Figure 4-26).

Figure 4-26

5

- Tap or click the Send button. You should receive Emma's reply soon. Tap or click the Update all button if necessary to view the incoming reply message from Emma Griffin (Figure 4-27).

Q&A

Is Emma standing by to return my message?

No. The reply you receive from Emma is an automated reply sent in response to your email. You can set up an automated reply to inform people that you will be out of the office and provide alternate contact information, or to inform them of a change to your email account.

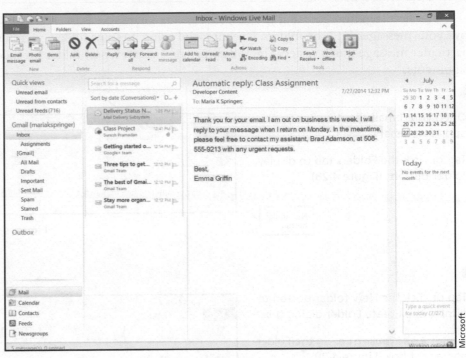

Figure 4-27

Managing Messages

As the number of emails you receive from friends, family members, business associates, and others grows, keeping track of them all can be a challenge. You can organize the messages to find specific messages more quickly, delete messages you do not need, and indicate which new messages need your immediate attention. With most email clients, you can create folders in which you can store your messages, access options for deleting messages, and create rules to move incoming messages automatically into specific folders. You also can flag incoming messages for follow-up and mark message conversations — multiple messages on the same topic — as watched conversations. Finally, you can rearrange messages in the Message list by sorting them in a specific order. Your exact capabilities may differ, depending on your email client and computer or device.

FACTS @HAND

You can mark a message as either read or unread — despite any previous action with the message. To mark an unread message as a read message, tap or right-click the message and tap or click 'Mark as read.'

To Create a New Message Folder

The first step in organizing your incoming email messages is to create message folders. You then can move your messages into the folders. Creating and using message folders with meaningful names makes finding a particular message much easier. The following steps create a new folder for incoming messages about class assignments.

1

• Open your email client webpage or app, if necessary.

• Tap or click the Folders tab to display folder options (Figure 4-28).

Figure 4-28

2

• Tap or click the New folder button to display the Create Folder dialog box.

• Enter **Assignments** in the Folder name text box (Figure 4-29).

• Tap or click the OK button to create the folder.

Figure 4-29

3

- Tap or click the Inbox folder arrow to view the Assignments folder as a subfolder of the Inbox folder, if necessary (Figure 4-30).

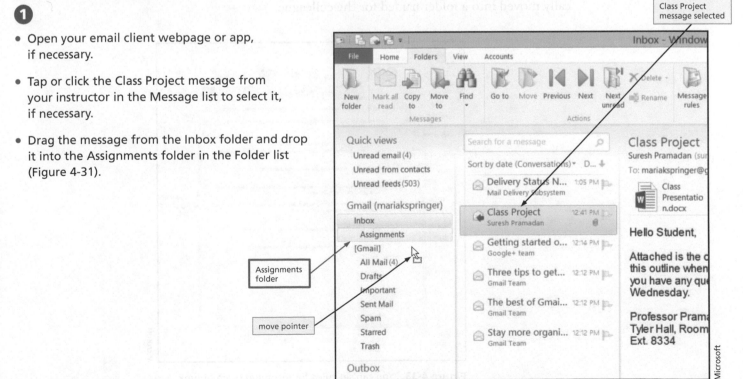

Figure 4-30

To Move a Message from the Inbox Folder into the Assignments Folder

After you create message folders, you can move incoming messages from the Message list (or from any folder) into the appropriate folder. The following steps move your instructor's message into the Assignments folder.

1

- Open your email client webpage or app, if necessary.

- Tap or click the Class Project message from your instructor in the Message list to select it, if necessary.

- Drag the message from the Inbox folder and drop it into the Assignments folder in the Folder list (Figure 4-31).

Figure 4-31

2

• Tap or click the Assignments folder in the Folder list to open the folder (Figure 4-32).

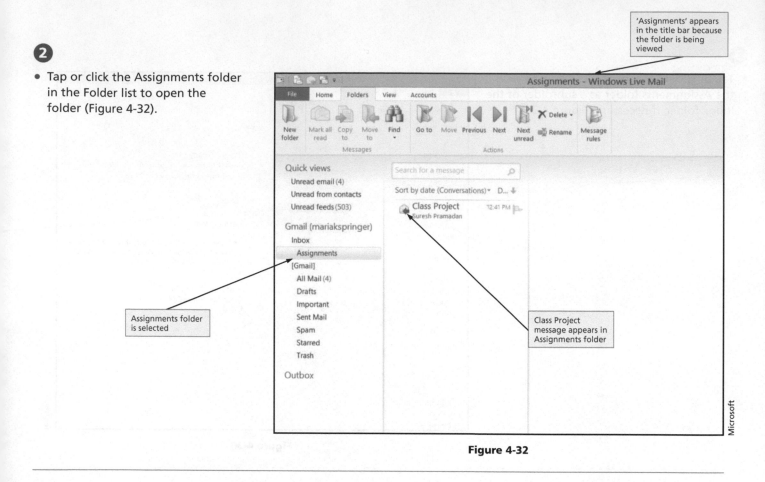

'Assignments' appears in the title bar because the folder is being viewed

Assignments folder is selected

Class Project message appears in Assignments folder

Figure 4-32

MANAGING YOUR INBOX You can specify a **message rule** that instructs your email client to move certain messages to specific folders automatically (Figure 4-33). For example, you might choose to have all incoming messages from a business colleague automatically moved into a folder named for the colleague.

Figure 4-33 You can set rules for incoming spam or junk messages in the Safety Options dialog box.

In addition to keeping messages organized using folders, you can keep the number of incoming messages manageable by deleting selected messages when you no longer need them. You can delete selected messages by tapping or clicking the Delete button. To select multiple adjacent messages for deletion using a Windows PC or laptop, tap or click the first message, press and hold the SHIFT key, and tap or click the last message. To select nonadjacent messages using a Windows PC or laptop, press and hold the CTRL key and tap or click each message to delete. If using a different email client or a mobile device, you likely will have check boxes next to messages that you can tap or click to select a message. Deleted messages move to your email system's deleted mail folder or storage area.

You can retain messages in the Deleted items folder and then retrieve them, as necessary, by moving them to another folder, such as the Inbox folder. Emptying the Deleted items folder saves space on your computer's hard drive or your mobile device; most web-based email services limit email storage. Once you empty the Deleted items folder, you no longer can retrieve any of the messages stored in the folder.

To Delete a Message

The following steps delete a message from your Inbox folder.

1

- Open your email client webpage or app, if necessary.

- Double-tap or double-click the message from Emma Griffin to open it (Figure 4-34).

Figure 4-34

2

- Tap or click the Delete button to move the message to the Trash or Deleted items folder.

- Tap or click the Deleted items or Trash folder to verify that it contains the message from Emma (Figure 4-35).

Q&A

How do I delete a message on an iPad?

To delete a message using an iPad and some other devices, tap or click the message checkbox from the Inbox, and then tap or click the Trash or Deleted items folder icon.

3

- Tap or click the Inbox folder to open it and confirm that the message from Emma does not appear.

Figure 4-35

FLAGGING AND WATCHING MESSAGES   Some messages require further action. Many email clients enable you to mark an incoming message with a flag icon, indicating that the message requires your attention. You then can leave the flagged message (Figure 4-36) in your Inbox folder until you have completed the required action. To **flag** or unflag a message, tap or click in the flag column to the right of the message in the Message list.

Figure 4-36   You can flag a message for further action.

It is common for people to exchange multiple messages on the same topic or in the same conversation by replying to and forwarding messages. To more easily identify all the messages in a conversation, you can mark the original message and all of its replies as part of a **watched conversation**. Messages in a watched conversation appear in color in the Message list. You also can add a Watch/Ignore column to the Message list to display a watch symbol or an ignore symbol for each message in a watched conversation.

By default, Windows Live Mail organizes all messages that originate from the same message, such as replies and forwards, into a conversation. This helps you keep your Inbox organized by subject. To turn conversation view on and off, tap or click the View tab, tap or click the Conversations button in the Arrangement group, and then tap or click On or Off.

PRIORITIZING MESSAGES   Many email clients enable you to prioritize email messages to help you determine which you need to respond to first. For example, Windows Live Mail allows you to assign a message a High, or Low Priority. By default, all outgoing messages are Normal Priority. If you want a message recipient to take immediate action when he or she receives the message, you can specify the message priority by tapping or clicking the Delivery button arrow when composing the email message, and then clicking the High importance or Low importance command (Figure 4-37). You can indicate that a message has a low priority for action by Tapping or clicking the Low importance command.

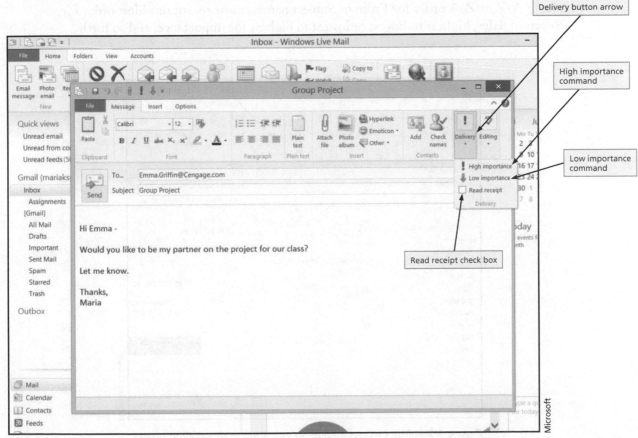

Figure 4-37   You can specify a High or Low importance status for an outgoing message, or specify a Read receipt.

If the message recipient is using Windows Live Mail, a red exclamation point appears in the Priority column in the Message list when a high-priority message appears in his or her Inbox folder. A low-priority incoming message has a downward-pointing blue arrow. As with any feature, think carefully before setting the importance of a message. What is important to you may not seem as urgent to the recipient. Marking your message as a high priority does not guarantee that he or she will respond immediately. If you send all of your messages with High importance, eventually people will ignore the indicator.

ADDING A READ RECEIPT   Many email clients let you request that the email client sends you a message when the recipient opens the email (see Figure 3-37). This feature can help track when a recipient receives and opens the message. Usually the recipient receives notification that the message has a read receipt. You should use this feature sparingly. A recipient could check your message while he or she is on personal time or otherwise busy, and may become annoyed or feel pressure to respond right away. Recall that one benefit of email is that recipients can respond at their own convenience. A recipient may need time to research or respond to the original message, and might not appreciate the notification and the implied pressure to reply quickly.

SORTING MESSAGES   You also can rearrange messages in the Message list by sorting the messages in a specific order. The most common way to sort is by the received date — either most recent or earliest. To select a different sort order and/or column, tap or click the Sort order button in the Arrangement group on the View tab. You also can tap or click the Sort by button arrow in the message pane, and then tap or click an option (Figure 4-38). The sort order options depend on the contents of the column. For example, by A–Z or Z–A order for From or Subject names, most recent or oldest order for Received dates, highest to lowest or lowest to highest for importance, and so forth.

Figure 4-38   You can sort a folder in ascending or descending order.

Managing Contacts

All email clients have an electronic address book in which you can store the email addresses and other information for your contacts, often called a **Contacts folder**. In the Contacts folder, you can enter names, addresses, email addresses, and other important information about those with whom you correspond. Mobile devices enable you to access your phone or device's contacts from within your email app.

CREATING CONTACTS   In the Contacts folder, you can add, modify, or delete a contact. Most email clients and web-based email services allow you to create a nickname or an alias for a contact. You then can simply enter the nickname in the To line instead of typing the entire email address or selecting a contact from the Contacts folder. Additionally, email clients and web-based mail services often provide an AutoComplete-style feature that remembers commonly typed text, such as email addresses. The AutoComplete-style feature offers a list of suggested email addresses as you begin to type in the To, Cc, or Bcc lines of a message header.

To Create a Contact

The following steps open the Contacts folder and add Emma Griffin as a contact.

1

- Open your email client webpage or app, if necessary.

- Tap or click the Contacts folder button in the left pane to open the Contacts folder (Figure 4-39).

Q&A

Why does my Contacts folder look different?
In the illustrations in this section, the Folder list in the left pane appears hidden and the right pane, which shows the contents of the Contacts folder, is in List view. Your Contacts folder display settings might be different. Additionally, your list of contacts will be different.

Figure 4-39

2

- Tap or click the Contact button in the New group on the Home tab to display the Add a Contact dialog box.

- Enter **Emma** in the First name text box to enter the first name of the new contact.

- Enter **Griffin** in the Last name text box to enter Emma's last name.

- Enter **Emma.Griffin@Cengage .com** in the Personal email text box to specify Emma's email address (Figure 4-40).

Q&A **Why does the text box say Personal?** The Add a Contact dialog box opens, by default, with the Quick add view, which offers limited contact information. To add or specify additional contact information, use the other views, such as Work to add a work email and work address and phone, or IDs to include a contact's digital IDs (such as Twitter handle).

First name text box

Last name text box

Personal email text box

Add contact button

Figure 4-40

3

- Tap or click the Add contact button to add the new contact and view the new contact in the Contacts folder (Figure 4-41).

- Tap or click the Mail folder icon in the left pane to return to the Mail folder.

new contact

Mail folder link

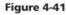

Figure 4-41

To Send an Email Message to a Contact

You can create a new message and tap or click the To button to open the Send an Email dialog box to select a contact's email address. The following steps send an email message to Emma Griffin using the Contacts folder. If you are using a tablet or other mobile device, your steps might differ. Use your mail app or device's Help feature if necessary to complete the steps.

1

- Open your email client webpage or app, if necessary.

- Tap or click the Email message button in the New group on the Home tab (Figure 4-42).

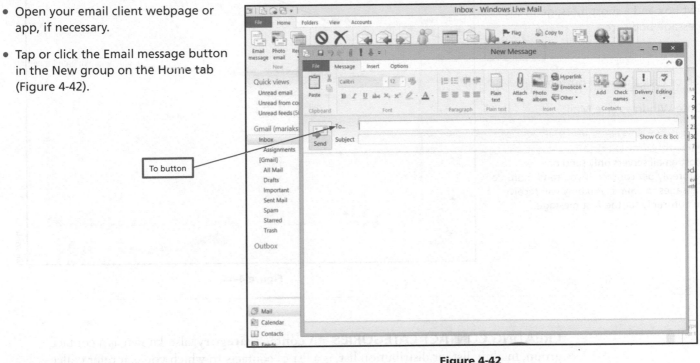

Figure 4-42

2

- Tap or click the To button in the message header to open the Send an Email dialog box.

- Tap or click Emma Griffin to select the contact.

- Tap or click the To button in the lower part of the dialog box to add Emma Griffin to the To text box (Figure 4-43).

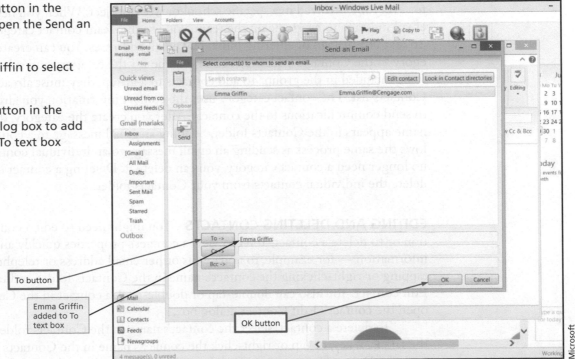

Figure 4-43

3

- Tap or click the OK button to add Emma Griffin's address to the To text box in the message header (Figure 4-44).

- Compose the message of your choice by typing a subject in the Subject text box and a short message in the message body area.

4

- Tap or click the Send button.

- Close Windows Live Mail.

Why do I not receive another autoreply from Emma?
Most email servers only send one autoreply per contact. If you send multiple messages to Emma, you only will receive an autoreply for the first message.

Figure 4-44

CREATING CONTACT CATEGORIES A **contact category**, also known as a contact group, mailing list, or distribution list, is a list of contacts to which you can refer collectively by a single name and to whom you can easily address a single email. For example, a contact category named Team could contain the email addresses and contact information for everyone involved in a specific school or work project. When you need to send an email message to everyone on the team, you use the Team contact category name in the To text box instead of entering individual email addresses. You can create a contact category in the Contacts folder. You enter a name for the category and select the contacts to be included in the group. To add contacts to a group, they must already exist in your Contacts list. The contact category uses the contact information you already have entered to send communications to the contacts. After you create the category, the category's name appears in the Contacts folder. Sending an email message to a contact category follows the same process as sending an email message to an individual contact. When you no longer need a contact category, you can delete it. Deleting a contact category does not delete the individual contacts from your Contacts folder.

EDITING AND DELETING CONTACTS You might need to edit a contact's information or to delete a contact. You can view a contact's properties quickly and then edit the information — for example, to update his or her email address or telephone number — by tapping or right-clicking the contact's name in the Contacts folder and tapping or clicking Edit contact. You also can double-tap or double-click a contact in the Contacts folder to open the contact's Edit Contact dialog box.

To delete a contact, select the contact's name in the Contacts folder and then press the DELETE key, or tap or right-click the contact's name in the Contacts folder and tap or click the Delete Contact command. In each case, you will need to confirm the deletion.

Email Viruses and Worms

For all its benefits, email also can be a host to computer viruses and worms. Email attachments are one way a computer can distribute a virus. Viruses and worms that arrive in an email message might damage files on the computer or device or copy themselves to other computers or devices on a network. Some may access a user's address book, passwords, or personal information.

Email worms also can send out viruses. Unlike a virus, which attaches itself to programs and documents, an email **worm** is self-replicating. A mass mailing worm harvests the email addresses stored on an infected computer and then sends an infected email message to each address it harvests.

An email message also might include, as an attachment, a program that appears to be something useful, but actually does something harmful. For example, a **Trojan horse** creates a way for a hacker to breach network security. Spyware is a different type of threat. In Chapter 2, you learned about spyware, which is software installed on your computer without your permission that gathers personal information. Most often, you unknowingly download spyware as part of other software. Sometimes just tapping or clicking a link at a website triggers spyware to download without your knowledge. HTML-formatted email also can deliver spyware without your knowledge.

Because of the risk of email viruses, worms, Trojan horses, and spyware, you must always be cautious when opening email messages. Make certain that you install virus protection software on your computer and keep it updated. Set the email software options, as well as change the settings on your antivirus software, to scan all incoming email. Do not open attachments unless they are from a trusted source. As an added precaution, open an attachment only from a trusted source and only if you are expecting the attachment. An email worm can send infected messages from a user's address book without his or her knowledge.

Unscrupulous people continually attempt to identify and exploit security flaws in email client software. Because of this, email client software manufacturers frequently publish security updates for their software. It is very important that you keep your email client software current with the latest security updates. You can generally download these security updates — called patches — from the manufacturers' websites. Often, you can set your software or apps to update automatically to ensure you receive all new releases or fixes.

Another area of concern is virus hoaxes. Sometimes unsuspecting people receive email from family, friends, or other associates describing a new virus threat. Be aware that these types of email warnings often are hoaxes. Before you send the message on to someone else or attempt to follow any instructions for removing the "virus," check it out. Antivirus software manufacturers, such as Symantec, maintain lists of legitimate viruses, worms, and other threats and hoaxes at their websites. You can also use websites such as snopes.com to search for and verify that such a threat is a hoax.

Junk Email Options

Because email is inexpensive to send and easy to use, it is a perfect medium for bulk email advertisements and spam. The large volume of unsolicited commercial email strains computing resources, frustrates technical support personnel, and consumes bandwidth. Some people consider all marketing messages to be spam. Most marketing messages, such as from companies with whom you do business, are not harmful.

Financial fraud perpetrated by spammers includes deceitful requests for money and phony products or services for sale. Malicious spam types include:

- **Phishing** — Attempts to collect personally identifiable information, credit card numbers, bank account numbers, and so forth

- **Stock-manipulation schemes** — Scams encouraging unwary investors to buy a specific stock, thereby artificially inflating the stock's value

- **"Nigerian Sting" operations** — Fraudulent requests for money

Other types of spam messages include advertisements for prescription drugs, mortgage or home refinancing, software, dating websites, and pornography. To protect against spam, many ISPs and most web-based email services provide **spam-filtering services** — services that filter out and either block or move to the Spam folder messages that do not meet certain criteria, such as messages from senders whose addresses are not in the recipient's address book. Most email clients filter spam. Additionally, many network routers or firewalls include a spam filter (Figure 4-45). You can set options on the various tabs to block junk email and to set exceptions to the blocking process.

Figure 4-45   You can set security options and more on the Security tab in the Safety Options dialog box.

Spam and the CAN-SPAM Act

You might be wondering, because spam is such a problem, what are governments doing about it? The CAN-SPAM Act of 2003 set standards for defining spam, and authorized the Federal Trade Commission (FTC) to monitor spam. The acronym, CAN-SPAM, stands for Controlling the Assault of Non-Solicited Pornography and Marketing.

The act does not prevent users from sending spam or allow for prosecution of spammers. Although intended to define, regulate, and lessen spam, it has had little effect on the volume of spam sent and received on the Internet. One major reason is that the bots used to gather email addresses and send spam are located outside of the United States.

For more information about spam, its costs, and how to protect against it, as well as the CAN-SPAM Act, use a search engine to search for *spam costs and prevention* and *CAN-SPAM*.

By default, blocked messages bypass the Inbox and go straight to a Junk, Trash, or Spam email folder. You also can set your email client to delete blocked or spam messages automatically instead of delivering them to a Junk email folder. Take care when automatically deleting blocked messages. Depending on the level of blocking you set in the Options dialog box, you may inadvertently be deleting legitimate messages. It also is a good idea to periodically check the Junk email folder for legitimate messages. Email clients might identify a message as spam if it is from an unknown contact, has no subject line, or uses Bcc.

Social Media

Social media tools are an integral part of the way Internet-connected individuals interact with family, friends, and others who share their professional, personal, or political interests. In previous chapters you learned that **social media** refers to online tools that allow people to communicate, collaborate, and share over the Internet.

Social networking websites and apps, such as Facebook, LinkedIn, and Google+, provide a medium in which friends, colleagues, and school alumni can share personal information or photographs, résumés and networking opportunities, or information about events. Public figures, organizations, and businesses such as Target also use social networking websites and microblogging sites such as Twitter to build interest or connect with their fans, members, employees, and customers (Figure 4-46).

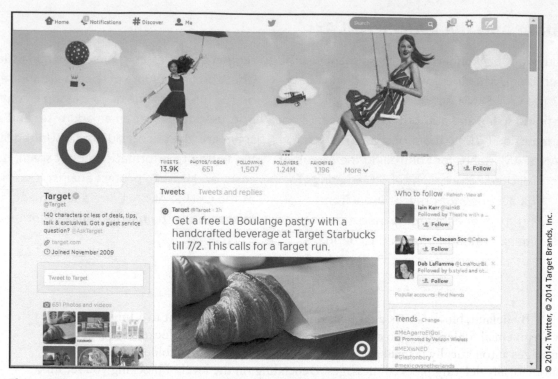

Figure 4-46 Businesses use social networking and microblogging to connect with customers.

Social Networking

Individuals who maintain connections with other people to share information or participate in activities of common interest are involved in a process called **social networking**. Social networking websites typically offer a combination of online communication tools: email, discussion groups, blogs, instant messaging, P2P networking, and real-time chat. Members use these tools to build and maintain their own personal networks of friends. Schools such as Westchester Community College (Figure 4-47) and other organizations use Facebook groups and pages to establish and communicate with interested parties.

Figure 4-47 Schools and other organizations connect with students and others using social media.

Social networking websites use members' profiles as hubs for members' personal networks. When an individual joins one of these social networking sites, he or she first creates a personal profile that describes his or her hobbies and interests. This profile then becomes the center point from which the member builds his or her network of friends. Profile information includes some or all of the following: name, location, photos, interests, status updates, likes, and a timeline. Users typically have a news feed in which they can view status updates, photos, and links posted by their contacts or liked pages.

A new member uses the website's online communication tools to invite friends to join his or her network. Friends who join the new member's network then post messages to members' webpages, post comments to discussion groups or blogs, chat with each other in real time, exchange digital files, and invite their other friends to join the network. The new member's personal network grows larger and larger as current friends connect to new friends and friends of friends.

FACTS @HAND According to a survey by the Pew Internet & American Life Project, 73 percent of online adults use Facebook, 17 percent use Instagram, and 22 percent use LinkedIn.

Business, medical, and technology professionals use online social networking to make new career contacts, find sales leads, locate job opportunities, and hire new employees. Social networking websites such as LinkedIn (Figure 4-48) and Spoke focus on career networking. These websites offer online communication tools to create and build career-oriented personal networks plus information about offline educational and networking events, online job search tools, career tips, classified ads, and sales leads. Additionally, employers looking for new hires can join and search members' profiles to locate qualified prospective employees.

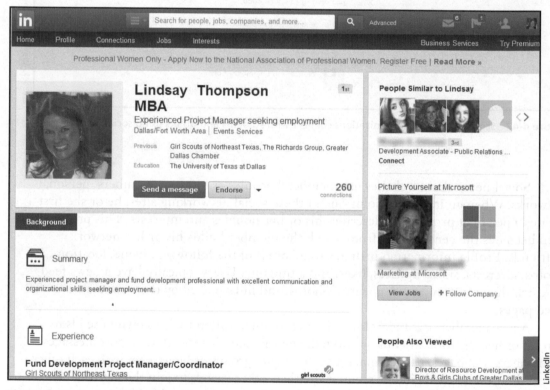

Figure 4-48 Professionals often use social networking websites to make career contacts, search for jobs, qualify sales leads, and hire new employees.

Smart and Safe Online Social Networking

A university expels a college student in Massachusetts. A California auto club fires several employees. A recent college graduate in Illinois does not receive an important summer internship. A job hunter in North Carolina waits for that critical and anticipated first interview. What do all of these people have in common? All were participants in online social networking, and all failed to recognize the dangers of posting inflammatory, harassing, or indiscreet comments and photos at social networking websites.

School administrators and employers commonly review the websites' postings to assess reported inappropriate student activities or to gather information about prospective employees. In the previous examples, the Massachusetts college student made inflammatory and, in the judgment of school administrators, threatening comments about a college security guard, resulting in expulsion. Prospective employers rejected the Illinois and North Carolina job applicants after discovering comments about drug and alcohol use and explicit photos posted in the applicants' social networking profiles. After an employee complained to management about workplace harassment through postings to a social networking blog, the auto club fired the employees.

The temptation toward unlimited self-expression within a personal network of friends through social networking website postings can be great. Social networking site postings — yours or the postings of friends who know you — might not be kept private, and the cost of indiscreet comments or photos posted at these sites can be very high.

Personal safety is another issue for participants in an online social network. As you learned in Chapter 2, being online can expose you to certain safety risks, such as loss of personally identifiable information, exposure to objectionable material, or interactions with people who might not be who they say they are. Smart and safe participation in online social networking requires following a few simple rules, such as those outlined at the OnGuard Online website sponsored by the FTC and other federal agencies. For example, you should:

- Carefully review the type of participants allowed at a social networking website before you join.
- Control access to your profile, if possible, and be careful not to include any personally identifiable information in your profile.
- Post only those comments or photos you are willing to share with anyone, not just your network of friends.
- Keep in mind that with screen capturing software, anyone with access can take a picture of your profile or activity on a social networking website and post the picture to his or her blog or send it to the media.

Blogging and Microblogging

In Chapter 1, you learned about online diaries called blogs. Blogs are highly popular and powerful tools for sharing thoughts and ideas across a wide spectrum of interests and audiences. The variety of blogs available is collectively referred to as the **blogosphere**. To find blogs to which you want to contribute, you can use the search tools at blog portals or directories, such as Technorati or Bloglines (Figure 4-49).

Q&A

What is a troll?

Bloggers and other web content publishers use the term **troll** to refer to those who intentionally post inflammatory comments on a blog or article, in order to provoke a response. If a troll comments on your blog, you can delete the comment, and block the user name from posting further comments to your blog. Most blogging tools enable you to approve comments from unknown user names before they appear on your blog.

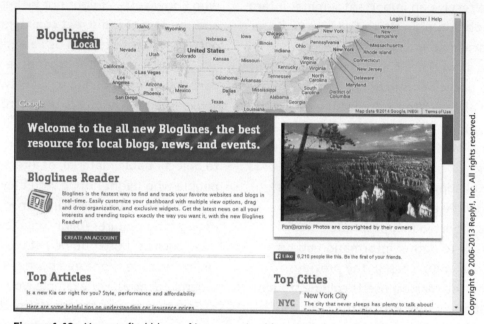

Figure 4-49 You can find blogs of interest using blog platforms and aggregators.

You also can create and publish your own blog using tools, such as Blogger, WordPress, Drupal, and Joomla. Wordpress and other blog platforms include options to analyze views, comments, and other statistics using a dashboard (Figure 4-50).

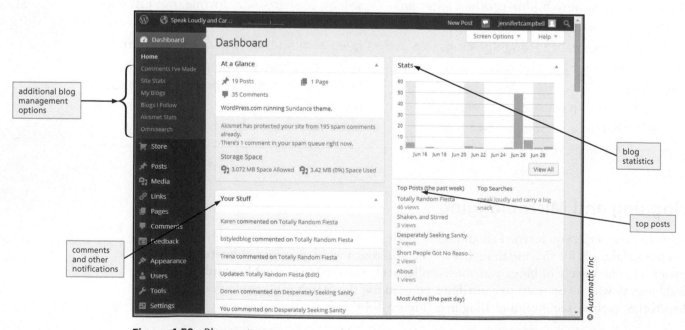

additional blog management options

comments and other notifications

blog statistics

top posts

Figure 4-50 Blog content managers enable you to track statistics for your blog.

Microblogging, which resembles a combination of blogging and instant messaging, involves broadcasting brief (typically 140 characters or less) messages to a public website, or sending email or text messages, to subscribers. Individuals and professionals use microblogging to broadcast status updates about their thoughts, current activities, or current location to friends, family members, and other constituencies. Businesses, such as Priceline.com, Southwest Airlines, and IBM, use microblogging to broadcast special offers to customers, conduct informal customer surveys, provide customer service, and promote collaboration among employees. The most popular microblogging tool is Twitter. In addition to posting messages, users can employ hashtags to indicate that their message is part of a trending topic included in the service's search engine, as you learned previously. Hashtags can appear within or at the end of a message. Microblogging and other social media websites group related messages by hashtags (Figure 4-51).

Figure 4-51 Microblogging websites use hashtags to group related posts or content.

Although discussed separately, microblogs, blogs, and social networking websites share many of the same features. For example, a microblog post on Twitter is called a tweet. Facebook uses status updates to enable users to share short thoughts or links. LinkedIn offers ways for users to post microblogs. In addition, there are services that can share your microblog posts to multiple platforms at once, including one by Twitter that updates your Facebook status as you tweet. Social media integration tools, embedded in most social media platforms, enable you to sync your Twitter feed, Instagram photos, Facebook status, blog, and more.

Text Messaging

Text and multimedia messaging, also called **Short Message Service (SMS)** and **Multimedia Messaging Service (MMS)**, respectively, allow users to send short messages containing text only or text, audio, and video. Typically, users send and receive text messages using smartphones (Figure 4-52), but some services enable you to access and use texting services on your computer or other mobile device. Some ISPs, such as

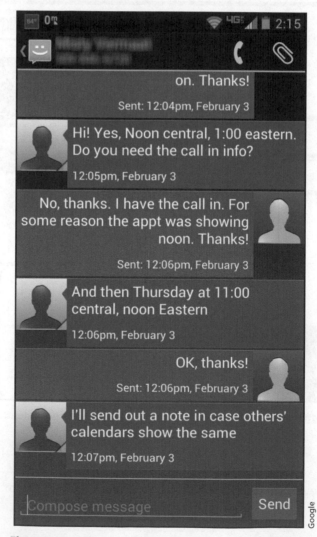

Figure 4-52 Most text messages are sent and received using smartphones.

Verizon Wireless, allow users to send a text or multimedia message to a cell phone from a webpage. You also can find a number of online SMS services that provide messaging services from a webpage, such as MightyText or AirDroid. Text messaging character limits vary. Some services have done away with character limits in messages received or sent. Other services cut off messages at a certain character count, such as 160 characters, in messages the user sends and receives. The way text messaging services handle character limits varies. Some cut off the message at the character limit; others break the message into multiple messages. Because the amount of text sometimes is limited, and to save time, users often use short abbreviations, known as **text speak**. An example of text speak is: "CU L8R K?" for "See you later, OK?"

Chat

Chat is a facility that allows two or more people to exchange text or multimedia messages in real time, using either a special client, or a mobile or web app. To chat, users need a special client software or app. Depending on the network and platform, users may be able to chat with those using other platforms or networks. A **channel**, or **chat room**, is a specific chat discussion that might be on a given topic or with a certain set of participants. Users also can set up private channels in which access is by invitation only, thus restricting who can participate.

Web-based chat allows for real-time communication using a web browser or web or mobile app. Web-based chat allows users to exchange both text and multimedia messages. Some chat facilities also allow users with a microphone to exchange voice messages in a chat room instead of, or in addition to, text messages. Some web-based chat sites provide the ability to share video between two participants who have web cameras. New users might find that it takes some time to learn how to follow a conversation online. If a chat room has many participants, many conversations might be going on at once, which makes following one particular chat thread very difficult.

Before jumping into a chat room discussion, a new user should read the rules and FAQs webpages. Because many chat rooms have regular participants, a new member can become familiar with the group by **lurking**, remaining quiet, and not participating in the chat discussion at first. Because the exchange of text often is rapid, participants use the same abbreviations and shorthand as in text speak — for example, typing LOL instead of the phrase, "laughing out loud" — to express laughter in response to another's post. Flaming also can occur in a chat room, just as it does in asynchronous discussions taking place with email, mailing lists, or newsgroups.

To maintain privacy and security, chat participants should adhere to these guidelines:

- Do not disclose your real name and address or any information of a sensitive nature. Use a nickname rather than your real name.

- Avoid using websites or apps that display your IP address along with your nickname.

- Remember that other participants might misrepresent themselves — she might not be a woman, and he might not be a teen — and that some predators are online, seeking the unwary. Therefore, be careful about arranging to meet online chat participants in person.

Some e-commerce websites use chat for real-time customer service, providing the user with a chance to talk to a customer service representative electronically in real time. Unlike when communicating by phone, a customer service representative can chat with multiple customers at once, increasing the speed of resolving customer issues.

Another very popular form of chat is **instant messaging (IM)**, a private means of exchanging real-time messages with one or several people using the Internet. Many social networking websites, including Facebook, provide IM messaging tools (Figure 4-53). Several IM programs are in popular use, including AOL Instant Messenger (AIM), ICQ, Windows Live Messenger, Yahoo! Messenger, and Gchat (Figure 4-54). Although all of these IM programs offer similar features, an individual using one IM program might not be able to communicate with another individual using a different IM program, such as Yahoo! Messenger. For this reason, many people choose to install and use several different IM programs so they can send instant messages to all of their contacts who use IM. Alternatively, users can install and use Pidgin, an instant messaging program that consolidates messages from these dissimilar IM programs into a single interface.

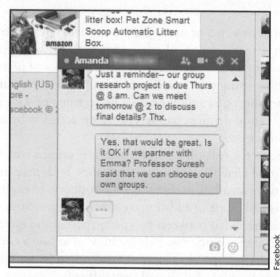

Figure 4-53 Chat is a feature of many social media websites.

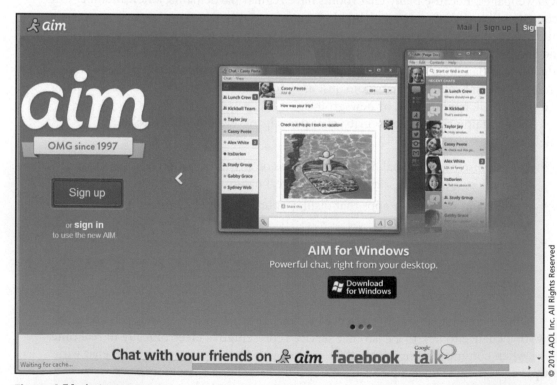

Figure 4-54 Instant messaging is a popular form of real-time communications over the Internet.

Asynchronous communication does not require users to be online at the same time and includes email, mailing lists, and newsgroups. Chat is an example of **synchronous communication**, or real-time communication, in which two or more users are online at the same time.

Collaboration and Sharing

Millions of people share their knowledge, research, opinions, photos, and video clips with others online using websites that allow them to collaborate on content, share favorite news stories, share image files, and share webpage bookmarks. Online tools for collaboration and sharing include wikis, social bookmarking, content-sharing, and opinion sites.

WIKIS Most websites you visit do not permit you to add to or edit content. A **wiki** consists of webpages in which authorized users can make edits to content, such as supplementing or deleting. One popular example of a wiki is the free online encyclopedia Wikipedia (Figure 4-55). The Wikia wiki service is a popular wiki platform, and host to many large and small wikis, searchable by topic (Figure 4-56).

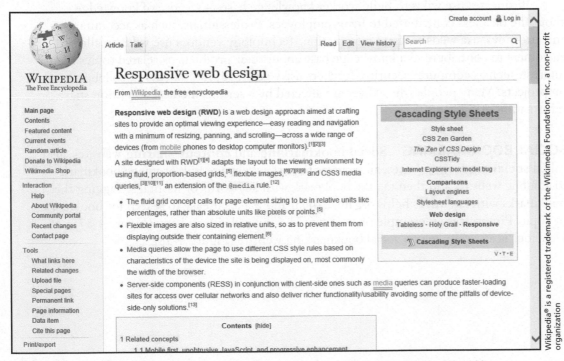

Figure 4-55 A wiki consists of webpages whose content can be edited, added to, or deleted by approved contributors.

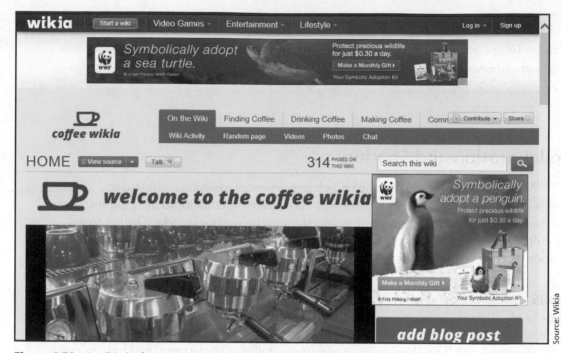

Figure 4-56 A wiki platform enables users to create, edit, and search for wikis.

@SOURCE

Despite the popularity of Wikipedia, users should take care to review the accuracy and authenticity of information posted to webpages at the Wikipedia site just as they would any other website.

Businesses use wikis to build worker knowledge bases — a core of knowledge about the business contributed to by its employees. Professionals, such as accountants and attorneys, use wikis to share information. Technology vendors use wikis to allow customers to contribute to a knowledge base about their products or related topics of interest, such as computer security. Teachers use wikis to allow students to collaborate on projects. Many people whose lives are affected by a serious medical condition share information using wikis.

SOCIAL BOOKMARKING   **Social bookmarking** and **content-sharing** websites, also called **social tagging** websites, allow users to post a webpage link or image bookmark to a public website, and then tag the bookmark with keywords or hashtags. Tagging the bookmarks with keywords helps organize them and makes it easy to search for bookmarks by topic. Pinterest is an example of a content-sharing website and app (Figure 4-57). Delicious is an example of a social bookmarking website (Figure 4-58).

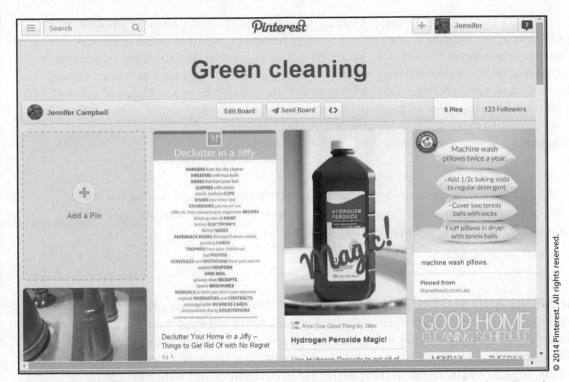

Figure 4-57 Content-sharing platforms enable you to tag, organize, and post links, text, and media and share with your followers or the public.

#typography is the current search

#typography search results

Delicious

Links for #typography
0 links this week

SUBSCRIBE

Popular   Recent   All Time

Putting the Sans in Comic Sans | IconicHipster.com - Your Muse into the 22nd Century
iconichipster.com
1088   N   documentaries   typography   10/12/

Sign Generator 1.0 abstraction-now.at
1219   design   generator   typography   eps   symbol   norm   generative   signs   lines
                                                                                  10/11/

FFFFOUND! | Lovely Type by Beato | Allan Peters ffffound.com
1219   RD   typography   10/10/

Zf3TS.png (996×667) imgur.com
1120   design   post   tools   typography   10/7/

30 Free Serif Fonts to Download | Vandelay Design Blog vandelaydesign.com
2010   fonts   free   serif   good   typeface   serifs   typography   design   freefonts   font
                                                                                  10/6/

How it happened « Bits and Pieces bitsandpieces.us
1241   comedy   design   post   typography   10/5/

Q #typography
Sign in
Network
Discover
+ Add Link

help · apps · tools · blog
© Delicious Science, LLC

Figure 4-58 Social bookmarking websites allow you to tag your bookmarks by keyword and share content with others.

Using tags, such as a Twitter hashtag described earlier in the chapter, a poster or collaborator can indicate that an article, a video, or other content includes information about a certain topic. For example, an article shared to a social bookmarking website on the release of a new documentary about whales might include tags such as whales, ocean, documentary, and other tags that indicate where the documentary was filmed or other relevant information. Social tagging allows users to find information that is interesting and relevant to them and provide others with their opinions in the form of ratings and comments.

FACTS @HAND   U.S. government agencies are successfully harnessing the power of social media to get their messages to the public and to improve internal operations. One example includes the Library of Congress's photostream project at the Flickr photo-sharing site.

@SOURCE

To learn more about the social collaboration and sharing websites discussed in this section, use a search engine to search for *social bookmarking, content sharing, and social opinions.*

SHARING AND STORING PHOTOS ONLINE   Many people use photo sharing websites or apps to manage their photo collections using websites such as Flickr, Shutterfly, Instagram (Figure 4-59), and Picasa, and then share access to the photos and photo slide shows with family members and friends. The increase in broadband Internet access, together with access to inexpensive video equipment and webcams, has made creating personal video clips and sharing them online a very popular activity. Businesses and organizations, as well as individual professionals and topic experts also post videos to websites such as YouTube. YouTube includes many professionally created video clips. Many companies, such as Google, post frequent videos to YouTube on the company's official YouTube channel (Figure 4-60).

Figure 4-59 Instagram is a social media sharing website and app used to share pictures and short videos.

featured video playing on Google channel

Figure 4-60 Video sharing websites offer a venue for sharing personal video clips as well as professionally created videos designed to broadcast messages to a wide audience.

SOCIAL OPINION   Consumers visit **social opinion websites** to check out user reviews for products, movies, books, travel accommodations, local restaurants, appliances, and local service providers. Social opinion websites, such as Angie's List and Yelp (Figure 4-61), aggregate thousands of individual reviews of products and services into well-organized and easily accessible categories. Some sites, such as Yelp, offer reviews of services by locality. Users who join social opinion sites can add their own reviews and rate the reviews posted by other users. E-commerce websites, such as Amazon.com and TripAdvisor, integrate social opinion features (reading list recommendations, book reviews, hotel and restaurant reviews) into their e-commerce operations to attract visitors.

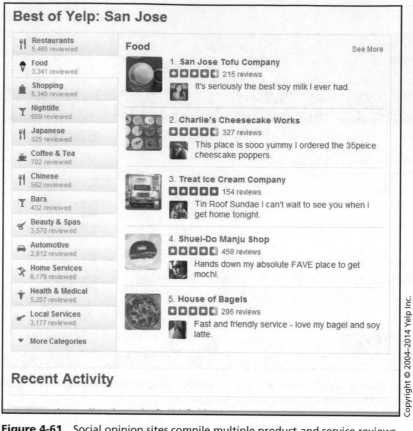

Figure 4-61   Social opinion sites compile multiple product and service reviews into categories.

FACTS @HAND   Related to social opinion sites, knowledge-sharing websites offer community-based answers (generally free, but sometimes for a fee) to user questions on a variety of topics. Yahoo! Answers and Ask.com are examples of knowledge-sharing sites.

FACTS @HAND   Web-based interactive games, such as World of Warcraft and EverQuest, allow players from around the world to play together. People can create alternative identities in virtual worlds, such as Second Life.

Email Marketing and Online Survey Technologies

Other replacements for mailing lists include email marketing and online survey technologies. Companies, schools, churches, and nonprofits use online marketing companies, including Constant Contact (Figure 4-62) and Lyris to communicate and solicit information or feedback. **Email marketing software** helps organizations send email and track the success of a marketing campaign by keeping track of the number of users who read the email, how many times the recipients tapped or clicked a link in the email, and how many times the recipients purchased a product or enrolled in a service. In addition to email services, these services can help you promote events and reach customers using social media. Unlike spam, email marketing relies on users to **opt-in** to receive emails. A user opts-in to an email marketing list by providing his or her email address during an enrollment, solicitation, or purchase, usually from the company or organization's website. Opt-in email marketing typically is more successful and welcomed because the users have expressed an interest in receiving communications from the company or organization.

© Constant Contact, Inc. 1995-2014

Figure 4-62   Email marketing enables the sender to disseminate information to a group who has opted-in.

Online survey technology companies, such as SurveyMonkey (Figure 4-63) and LimeSurvey, offer companies and organizations the ability to send an online survey using email. Recipients typically tap or click a link in the email or on the company's social media profile, to open the survey in their browser. Surveys are useful tools to collect and analyze opinions about products, services, or any other topic. Some survey companies allow you to create a free survey with limited functionality or to subscribe for a premium version of the service, which gives additional analytical and formatting capabilities. You can share your survey through blogs, email, and social media in order to reach your target survey audience.

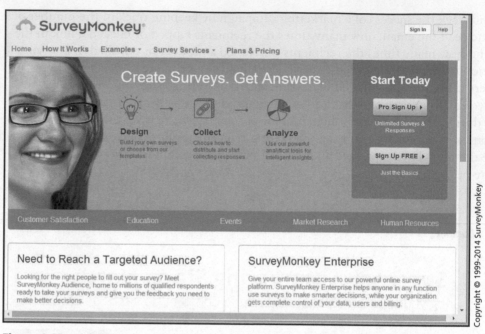

Figure 4-63   Online survey technology enables the creation, dissemination, and analysis of a survey.

VoIP

VoIP (**voice over internet telephony**) is a technology used to make phone calls over the Internet. In order to use VoIP, you must have a broadband connection, a microphone, and a speaker. In addition, you need software or an app, such as Skype (Figure 4-64) to facilitate the phone call. You may need to purchase or install an additional VoIP router. Some VoIP services are fee-based, while others are free. You must have another user's contact information or account name in order to initiate a VoIP call. You will learn more about VoIP in a later chapter.

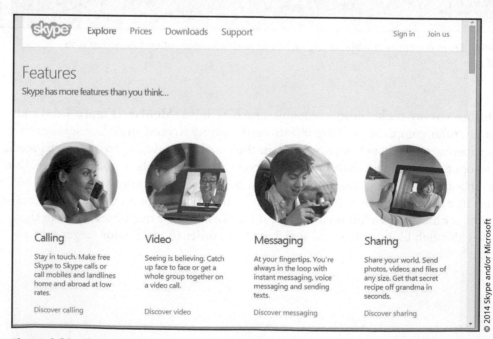

Figure 4-64   Skype enables users to communicate using video, chat, and voice calls.

Newsgroups and Web-Based Discussion Groups

Web-based discussion groups are online discussion forums often hosted by a portal. Discussion groups are an outgrowth of **newsgroups**, which are online bulletin boards that were first made available in the 1980s over the **Usenet network**. Usenet consists of a number of servers that use the **Network News Transfer Protocol** (**NNTP**) to send newsgroup messages over an IP network. Each Usenet server, also called a **news server**, acts as a host to a number of newsgroups. In addition, each news server subscribes to any number of newsgroups from other news servers.

Each news server stores the messages of the newsgroups it hosts. The server also polls the other news servers at fixed intervals to find the new messages for its subscribed newsgroups from those servers. The servers then download the new messages to be able to provide them locally. Each group exists in a permanent home on one server. Copies of messages in other groups appear on other servers that subscribe to those groups. Some ISPs maintain a news server, or provide access to a news server, for their subscribers.

Newsgroup postings include text postings and image, video, and movie file postings. Some ISPs limit or prohibit Usenet newsgroup services to avoid the increased cost of transmitting image, video, and movie file postings and to avoid the transmission of illicit images, such as pornography, or unauthorized copyrighted material, such as movies.

Each newsgroup has a unique name that identifies it, such as rec.pets.dogs or humanities.lit.authors.shakespeare. The names are multilevel, and each level provides more detail about the purpose of the newsgroup. The multilevel hierarchy is based on content.

A user can access newsgroup content using a **newsreader**, which is software or an app that allows a user to read newsgroup messages. Some online newsgroup services, such as Newsville and Google Groups (Figure 4-65), provide access to newsgroups using a web browser.

Figure 4-65   Online newsgroup services provide access to newsgroups using a browser.

Mailing Lists

As you learned in Chapter 1, mailing list subscribers use email to exchange information, opinions, and ideas about particular subjects with other subscribers. Mailing lists have diminished in popularity with the rise in usage of social networking tools. Because mailing lists are easy to use, offer free or inexpensive options, and have none of the privacy concerns of social networking websites, they still are used.

Q&A

How do I find mailing lists?

Users can find mailing lists through work or professional associations or while searching the web. Some websites provide mailing list directories with a search tool you can use to find mailing lists on specific topics.

A mailing list must have a **moderator** or **list owner** who handles administrative tasks. Some universities, such as the University of Georgia, offer list servers to host mailing lists for faculty and students (Figure 4-66).

Figure 4-66   Users rely on mailing lists to exchange information, opinions, and ideas with other subscribers.

To receive email from a mailing list, you first must join, or **subscribe** to, the list. When subscribing to an **open list**, the subscription begins automatically upon receipt of the subscription email message. Subscriptions to a **closed list** require approval by the list moderator.

You also can send messages to the **list address**, which is an email address used to send messages for distribution to list subscribers. If the list is an **unmoderated list**, the message goes out immediately to all subscribers. If the list is a **moderated list**, the moderator reviews the message and then either approves and sends it, makes or requests edits, or discards it. **Posting** is the process of sending a message to the list. Each mailing list might follow different rules for posting messages to ensure that subscribers can contribute to the list in a productive manner and do not offend other subscribers by sending inappropriate material to the list.

Chapter Review

Email is one of the most popular online communication tools and is indispensable for businesses and other organizations. An email client, such as Windows Live Mail, is software installed on a computer you use to send, receive, forward, and manage email messages, and create and manage a list of contacts.

Web-based email, such as Gmail or Yahoo! Mail, uses a web browser and a webpage to send, receive, forward, and manage email messages. The benefit of web-based mail is portability; a user can access his or her web-based mail account from any computer that has a web browser installed and an Internet connection. You can sync your web-based email with an email client to take full advantage of its capabilities.

Social media — newsgroups, web-based discussion groups, chat, blogs, microblogs, and wikis, along with social networking, bookmarking, content-sharing, and opinion websites — are an integral part of the way Internet-connected individuals interact with family, friends, and others who share their professional, personal, or political interests. VoIP is one technology used to make phone calls over the Internet.

Email marketing and online survey technologies enable organizations and companies to send, track, and analyze e-marketing and survey campaigns. Mailing list subscribers use email to exchange information, opinions, and ideas about particular subjects with other subscribers.

TERMS TO KNOW

After reading this chapter, you should know each of these Key Terms.

asynchronous communication (191)
Attach line (147)
attachment (147)
Bcc line (147)
blind courtesy copy (147)
blogosphere (185)
Cc line (147)
channel (189)
chat (189)
chat room (189)
closed list (200)
contact (155)
contact category (178)
Contacts folder (175)
content-sharing (192)
courtesy copy (147)
cyberbullying (163)
Deleted items folder (155)
Drafts folder (156)
email client (143)
email marketing software (196)
emoji (148)
emoticon (148)
flag (172)
forward (162)
host name (143)
HTML-formatted message (148)
IMAP (Internet Message Access
    Protocol) (145)
Inbox folder (155)
instant messaging (IM) (190)
Junk email folder (156)
list address (200)
list owner (200)
lurking (189)
mailbox (145)
message body (147)
message header (148)
Message list (156)
message rule (170)
moderated list (200)
moderator (200)
Multimedia Messaging Service (MMS) (188)
Network News Transfer Protocol
    (NNTP) (199)

news server (199)
newsgroup (199)
newsreader (199)
"Nigerian Sting" operations (180)
online survey technology (197)
open list (200)
opt-in (197)
Outbox folder (155)
passphrase (152)
phishing (180)
POP (Post Office Protocol) (145)
posting (200)
Sent items folder (155)
Sent Mail folder (155)
Short Message Service (SMS) (188)
signature file (147)
SMTP (Simple Mail Transfer Protocol) (145)
social bookmarking (192)
social media (181)
social networking (182)
social opinion websites (195)
social tagging (192)
spam-filtering services (180)
Spam folder (156)
spambot (150)
stock-manipulation schemes (180)
Subject line (147)
subscribe (200)
synchronous communication (191)
text speak (189)
To line (147)
Trash folder (155)
Trojan horse (179)
troll (186)
unmoderated list (200)
Usenet network (199)
user ID (143)
user name (143)
VoIP (voice over Internet telephony) (198)
watched conversation (173)
web-based chat (189)
web-based discussion group (199)
web-based email service (149)
wiki (191)
worm (179)

Complete the Test Your Knowledge exercises to solidify what you have learned in the chapter.

True or False

Mark T for True and F for False. (Answers are found on page numbers in parentheses.)

___ 1. Email is an informal tool you use for personal communication, not to deliver important or official information. (143)

___ 2. Twitter is a microblogging platform. (187)

___ 3. Cyberbullying occurs infrequently. (163)

___ 4. You can use an emoji to flag a message with high priority. (148)

___ 5. Chat is an example of asynchronous communication. (191)

___ 6. Instagram is an example of a photo-sharing service. (194)

___ 7. A contact category allows you to send messages to multiple people at one time. (179)

___ 8. You should use a read receipt with most email communications to ensure the recipient opens the message. (174)

___ 9. Facebook is an example of a social bookmarking website. (192)

___10. Yelp is an example of a social opinion website. (195)

Multiple Choice

Select the best answer. (Answers are found on page numbers in parentheses.)

1. The B in Bcc stands for _____. (147)

    a. before

    b. the letter, b, as in the second choice in a list

    c. blind

    d. broadband

2. For what purpose is VoIP used? (198)

    a. To send and receive email messages

    b. To identify spam

    c. To moderate newsgroups

    d. To make phone calls over the Internet

3. To keep email organized, you should _____. (170)

    a. print out each message

    b. create folders for different topics and move messages to them

    c. add a flag to each message

    d. attach electronic sticky notes to the messages

4. A valid email address includes _____. (143)

   a. html://, the user name, an @ symbol, and the host name

   b. http://, the user name, the password, and the mail server name

   c. the user name, an @ symbol, the password, and the mail server name

   d. the user name, an @ symbol, and the host name

5. A(n) _____ enables multiple users to create, add, and edit website content. (191)

   a. wiki

   b. channel

   c. mailing list

   d. newsgroup

6. _____ is an example of email marketing software. (196)

   a. Survey Monkey

   b. Gmail

   c. Constant Contact

   d. Yahoo! Mail

7. Which of the following is a photo-sharing website? (195)

   a. Lyris

   b. Delicious

   c. Angie's List

   d. Flickr

8. New users to a chat room often stay quiet and observe before jumping in, known as _____. (189)

   a. lurking

   b. spoofing

   c. surfing

   d. spying

9. _____ is an example of a blogging platform. (186)

   a. Wordpress

   b. Bloglines

   c. Facebook

   d. Constant Contact

10. _____ is the use of spam to attempt to collect personally identifiable information, credit card numbers, bank account numbers, and so forth. (180)

    a. Spoofing

    b. Phishing

    c. Hacking

    d. A "Nigerian Sting" operation

Investigate current Internet developments with the Trends exercises.

Write a brief essay about each of the following trends, using the web as your research tool. For each trend, identify at least one webpage URL used as a research source. Be prepared to discuss your findings in class.

1 | Microblogging

Use a search engine to search for *microblogging statistics*. Sort or filter your results, if possible, to search for the most recent articles or blog posts. Make a list of four statistics you found. Did any statistic surprise you? Why or why not? How do the statistics compare with your experience with following microblogs, or using a microblog platform? What new developments or platforms relating to microblogging did you find? Join Twitter, if necessary, and view the postings of at least five people, including a local newsperson, a television or movie personality, a blogger, a politician, and an individual user (such as a friend or classmate). Summarize your findings about microblogging and how each person uses microblogging to communicate with his or her followers. For each person, include the following: an example of a post; the average daily number of posts; the number of followers; and the number of people the person follows. Submit your findings in the format requested by your instructor.

2 | Social Bookmarking

Use a search engine to search for *social bookmarking*. Sort or filter your results, if possible, to search for the most recent articles or blog posts. Read at least three articles discussing social bookmarking platforms. What are the advantages and disadvantages of sharing your bookmarks and favorite content with others? What are the benefits of reviewing other people's bookmarks and shared content? Which platform(s) do or would you use? Why? Submit your findings in the format requested by your instructor.

Challenge your perspective of Internet technology with the @Issue exercises.

Write a brief essay in response to the following issues, using the web as your research tool. For each issue, identify at least one URL used as a research source. Be prepared to discuss your findings in class.

1 | Phishing and Spoofing

Use a search engine to search for recent articles discussing spoofing cases. Describe the event and its effect on the company or organization hosting the website. Were there any known security flaws that contributed to the attack? Were the offenders caught? How? Use a search engine to search for articles and blog posts about protecting yourself from phishing attacks. What changes, if any, should you make to your Internet activities to protect yourself? Evaluate, if possible, any protections offered by your antivirus software, firewall, or browser. Submit your findings in the format requested by your instructor.

2 | Evaluating Wikis

Start your browser, if necessary, and visit wikia.com or another source to find a wiki on a topic that interests you and with which you have experience or knowledge. Read several links or articles on the site. Evaluate the information for its credibility and determine whether any information is missing or inaccurate. Locate the Help link for Wikia to find guidelines for editing content and other rules for participation, and then read through them. What is your school or instructor's policy on using wikis for research? Have you used a wiki for research? Why or why not? Submit your findings in the format requested by your instructor.

HANDS ON

Use the web to obtain more information about the skills taught in the chapter with the Hands On exercises.

1 | Using Email

1. Start your email client, if necessary.

2. Partner with a friend or classmate, if possible, to send and receive emails using the following criteria. Alternatively, you can send the emails to yourself.

   a. Send an email with a photo attachment. Look at the attachment you receive. Can you view it from within the email message?

   b. View the same message using another device, or using web-based email if you are not using web-based email already. Does the email look different from when viewed in your email client? If so, how?

   c. Create a new email folder. Use your email client Help feature to determine how to set up a message rule so that any incoming emails from your classmate (or from yourself) automatically move to the new folder. Test the new rule to see if it works.

   d. Use your email client Help feature to determine how to create a signature file. Create a signature file, and send a message using it.

   e. Check your email client's spam-filtering options. Evaluate whether they are adequate. Would you change them? Why or why not?

2 | Social Opinion Websites

1. Start your browser, if necessary.

2. Use a search engine to search for *social opinion websites,* and select one or multiple websites to use to answer the following questions:

   a. What Mexican restaurant within 10 miles of you is most highly rated?

   b. Find a pet-sitting or dog-walking service in your neighborhood or city. Are the reviews favorable?

   c. Locate a business with a negative review. Has the business owner responded to the review? How?

   d. Read the policies for the social opinion website regarding account setup, making reviews or comments as a user, and responding to reviews as a business owner.

   e. What other features does the website offer? Can you view restaurant menus or make a reservation? Does the website offer contact information and websites?

3. Submit your findings in the format requested by your instructor.

Work collaboratively to reinforce the concepts in the chapter with the Team Approach exercises.

1 | Social Networking Security

1. Work with a team of three to four classmates to learn more about keeping safe using social networking websites.

2. Assign one social networking website or app to each teammate to research using information published by the website or app, such as its privacy policy, and a search engine to find additional information. Each team member should do the following:

   a. Find the social networking website's security tips and privacy policy.

   b. If possible, evaluate your own account on the social networking website to ensure you are following the recommendations. What changes should you make?

   c. Locate one instance where legal action or criminal charges occurred, or examples of hackers taking advantage of flaws in the social networking website's security protocols or firewalls.

   d. If possible, determine what changes the social networking website has made over the years to its privacy and security policy. Why might the website have made these changes?

3. Submit your findings in the format requested by your instructor.

2 | Online Communication Etiquette

1. Work with a team of three to four classmates to come up with a list of guidelines for etiquette when using online communication tools, such as email, IM, chat, and text.

2. As a team, brainstorm or research answers to the following questions:

   a. In what occasions do you recommend communication using online communication tools? How formal should you be? How does your answer differ when using different platforms?

   b. Have you encountered an example where a recipient misunderstood a message you sent? If so, describe the occurrence, and what you could do to avoid it in the future. What actions did you take to clear up the situation?

   c. Rank the communication tools mentioned in this chapter from least to most appropriate for formal or business communications.

   d. List guidelines for the following: Bcc, emoticon or emoji use, and text speak.

   e. Come up with an example of a sentence or scenario that may be misinterpreted when sent as a message, rather than delivered in a conversation.

3. Submit your findings in the format requested by your instructor.

5 Getting More Out of the Internet

© Google

Introduction

Websites that you visit daily or multiple times a day likely contain complex, useful, interesting, and timely content. Possibly, some of your favorite websites are portals, similar to those you first learned about in Chapter 2. In this chapter, you will learn more about different types of portals and the role they play in providing appropriate content to various target audiences, including the general public, employees, vendors, customers, and business partners. You also will learn how to get immediate notification of breaking news from a major news source, learn about traffic or weather problems, listen to Internet radio, look up the definition of a new technical term, verify your bank balance and pay bills, and perform many more tasks using the Internet and the web.

Objectives

After completing this chapter, you will be able to:

1. Describe and give examples of different types of portals and their target audiences

2. Identify and use online news, sports, weather, and traffic resources

3. Discuss streaming media, watch video clips, and listen to Internet radio

4. Use online research and reference tools

5. Explore health, entertainment, hobby, and other special-interest websites

6. Use online tools for managing personal finances

7. Describe online educational resources

8. Describe the consumer marketspace and online auctions

9. Identify types of online games

10. Share files over the Internet

Portals

In Chapter 2, you learned that a portal is a website that provides access to a wide variety of web content and services. A portal can be a single web-based interface to a company's general business information, intranet, and extranet, or a gateway to information about a specific area of interest or a specific industry. You can determine the portal type by identifying the target audience. Portal examples include general consumer portals, personal portals, vertical portals, industry portals, and corporate portals.

Consumer Portals

General consumer portals offer a broad range of content, including search tools, current news and weather, stock quotes, sports scores, links to reference tools and links to shopping. Some portals also provide communication tools such as email, file sharing, or social media. By offering varied content, a general consumer portal appeals to a very large audience, thus becoming a more attractive venue for other organizations wanting to advertise and promote their websites on the portal. Several popular general consumer portals evolved from more humble beginnings. For example, Yahoo! began as a list of links that developed into a search tool, and MSN originated from the default home page for the Internet Explorer web browser. By expanding their content, these early search tool and default browser home page websites have increased their audiences by attracting new users and encouraging users to visit their websites repeatedly. Over time, these websites developed into general consumer portals.

Personal portals, also called **horizontal portals**, are consumer portals whose content you customize to meet your specific needs. Personal portals exploit the interactive nature of the web to tailor web page content to your specific interests. Using your personal preferences to customize a consumer portal makes the portal content more interesting and useful. My Yahoo! and My MSN (Figure 5-1) are examples of customized personal portals. As you learned in Chapter 2, you can change the settings in your web browser to make a customized personal portal your browser's default home page.

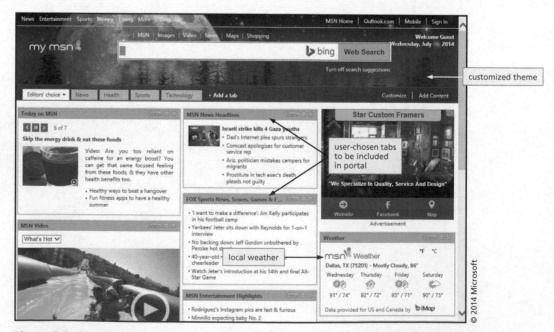

Figure 5-1 Personal portals allow viewers to customize content to their specific interests.

Vertical, Hyperlocal, and Industry Portals

Vertical portals, sometimes called **vortals**, provide a web gateway for visitors with more specific interests, such as gardening, children's activities, social issues, ethnic interests, and government information. Examples of vertical portals include:

- USA.gov Senior Citizens' Resources and the Kids.gov websites (federal pages of interest to seniors and children)
- SuzySaid (websites for specific areas that include events, ads, coupons, reviews, and more)
- National Resource Directory (resources for U.S. service members, veterans, and their families)
- MSN Latino (Hispanic interests)
- Export.gov (export issues)
- Huffington Post (general interest website/blog, with multiple independent and contracted contributors; includes sub-websites including BlackVoices, which covers African American interests)

Hyperlocal portals are specific to a certain geographic location and provide content about that area, written for and by local citizens. Websites such as The Daily Voice (Figure 5-2) and SuzySaid provide a platform where local citizens and businesses can advertise, blog, and write articles about their specific area. Hyperlocal portal platforms are available through franchising; website managers contract with the owner of the platform to use its name, templates, and guidelines to manage local content.

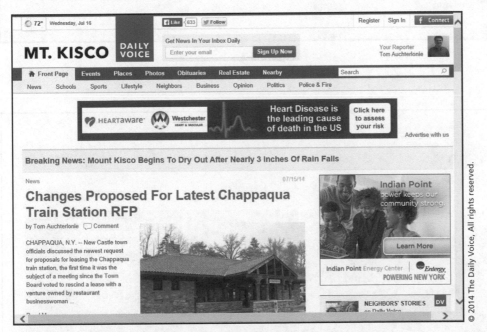

Figure 5-2   Hyperlocal portals provide content for and about a certain location.

Industry portals are vertical portals that target viewers interested in a specific industry. Some industry portals also aggregate information about a specific industry and provide a marketspace where businesses can buy from and sell to each other, creating a **B2B exchange**. Other industry portals simply provide industry information, news, links, and advertising.

Examples of industry portals include Farms.com (agribusiness), Web Host Industry Review (web hosting industry), MFG.com (manufacturing industry), COMMREX (commercial real estate industry exchange), billboard (entertainment industry), and BusinessUSA (small business).

To Explore Portals

The following steps explore various portals, and the wide range of interests these portals cover.

1

- Start your browser and enter **kids.gov** in the Address bar.

- Press the ENTER key, or tap or click the necessary button to open the kids .gov home page (Figure 5-3).

- Scroll the webpage and review its content.

- Tap or click the links of your choice to review at least two subsidiary pages at the Kids.gov website.

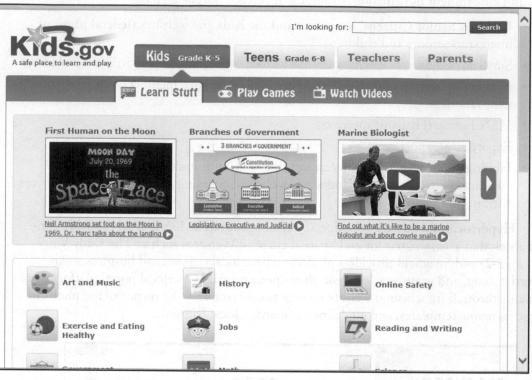

Kids.gov

Figure 5-3

2

- Open a new tab if necessary, and then enter **latino .msn.com** in the Address bar.

- Press the ENTER key, or tap or click the necessary button to open the MSN Latino home page (Figure 5-4).

- Scroll the webpage and review its Spanish-language content.

- Tap or click the links of your choice to review at least two subsidiary pages at the MSN Latino website.

© 2014 Microsoft

Figure 5-4

3

- Open a new tab if necessary, and then enter `business.ca.gov` in the Address bar.

- Press the ENTER key, or tap or click the necessary button to open the California Governor's Office of Business and Economic Development home page (Figure 5-5).

- Scroll the webpage and review its content.

- Tap or click the links of your choice to review at least two subsidiary pages at the California Governor's Office of Business and Economic Development website.

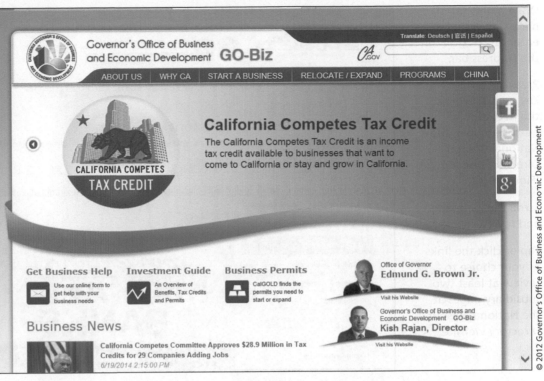

Figure 5-5

4

- Open a new tab if necessary, and then enter `billboard.com` in the Address bar.

- Press the ENTER key, or tap or click the necessary button to open the billboard entertainment industry home page.

- Scroll the webpage and review its content.

- Tap or click the links of your choice to review at least two subsidiary pages at the billboard website (Figure 5-6).

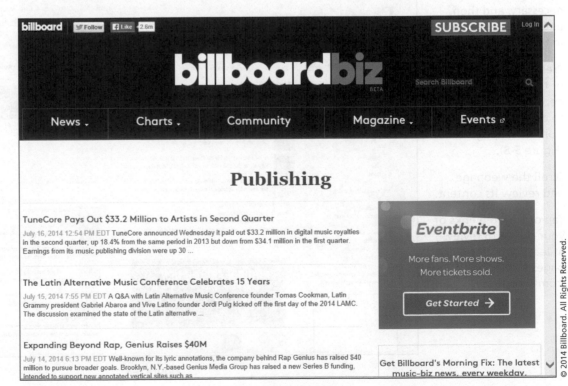

Figure 5-6

5

- Open a new tab if necessary, and then enter `nrd.gov` in the Address bar.

- Press the ENTER key, or tap or click the necessary button to open the National Resource Directory home page (Figure 5-7).

- Scroll the webpage and review its content.

- Tap or click the links of your choice to review at least two subsidiary pages at the National Resource Directory website.

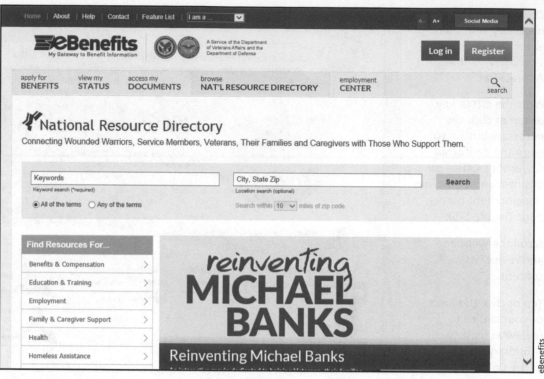

Figure 5-7

6

- Open a new tab if necessary, and then enter `farms.com` in the Address bar.

- Press the ENTER key, or tap or click the necessary button to open the Farms .com home page (Figure 5-8).

- Scroll the webpage and review its content.

- Tap or click the links of your choice to review at least two subsidiary pages at the Farms .com website.

Figure 5-8

7

- Open a new tab if necessary, and then enter `thewhir.com` in the Address bar.

- Press the ENTER key, or tap or click the necessary button to open the Web Host Industry Review (WHIR) home page (Figure 5-9).

- Tap or click the links of your choice to review at least two subsidiary pages at the WHIR website.

Figure 5-9

8

- Open a new tab if necessary, and then enter `danbury.dailyvoice.com` in the Address bar.

- Press the ENTER key, or tap or click the necessary button to open The Daily Voice portal for Danbury, Connecticut (Figure 5-10).

- Scroll the webpage and review its content.

- Tap or click the links of your choice to review at least two subsidiary pages at The Daily Voice website.

Figure 5-10

9

- Open a new tab if necessary, and then enter **blackvoices.com** in the Address bar.

- Press the ENTER key, or tap or click the necessary button to open the BlackVoices home page (Figure 5-11).

- Scroll the webpage and review its content.

- Tap or click the links of your choice to review at least two subsidiary pages at the BlackVoices website.

Figure 5-11

10

- Open a new tab if necessary, and then enter **sba.gov** in the Address bar.

- Press the ENTER key, or tap or click the necessary button to open the SBA home page (Figure 5-12).

- Scroll the webpage and review its content.

- Tap or click the links of your choice to review at least two subsidiary pages at the SBA.gov website.

- Close the browser and close all open tabs, if necessary.

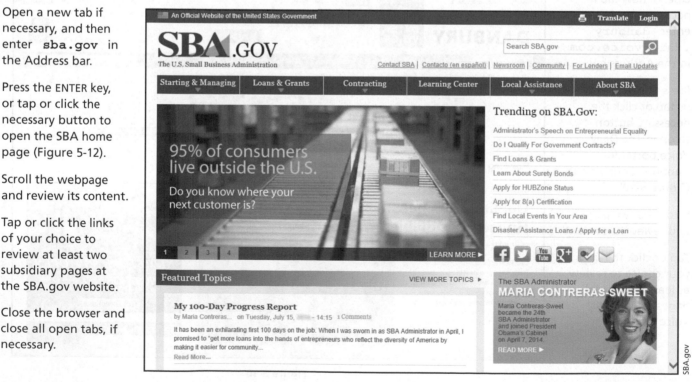

Figure 5-12

Developing Portals

Businesses create portals for a variety of reasons, such as to provide a corporate portal for its employees on a company intranet. Companies such as Oracle and IBM (Figure 5-13) provide customizable portal software packages that a company modifies to fit its unique needs. Portal software enables customization, controlled access, and multisystem integration.

Figure 5-13 Portal software packages can be customized to fit a company's needs.

The goal of portal development is to create a single webpage or website that can present content from multiple sources and contributors, in a uniform design. While large portals may be incredibly complex to create and manage, the idea is to create a design and layout that makes it easy for return visitors to find new and updated content on topics in which they are interested. Search features, navigation, carousels, and customization are all key components in portal development.

Corporate Portals

Employees, customers, vendors, and other business partners can use a **corporate portal**, or an **enterprise information portal (EIP)** to access a company's business information, work with others using email and other internal collaboration tools, or conduct business transactions. Most corporate portals are private, password-protected websites not found using a search engine. Corporate portals control access to company information and business processes based on each user's personal profile. Some corporate portals also permit customization — news on specific job-related topics, stock trackers on specific stocks, and so forth — based on user preferences.

When an employee uses the corporate portal to log on to the company intranet, the content he or she sees and is able to access differs based on his or her employee profile and position. By personalizing portal content, an employee in the Accounts Payable

Q&A

What is meant by UX (user experience)?
UX incorporates elements of good web design, including structure, use of text and color, value-added images and media, navigational elements, and more, with the goal of enhancing the user's website experience. Web designers, including those in charge of portals, incorporate UX principles to make information easy to find, and to create customizable websites and webpages.

Department, for example, can log on and track vendor invoices, company purchase orders, and company receiving reports. However, he or she cannot access any information from other departments, such as Purchasing or Marketing. Other general information, such as industry and company news, company stock performance, links to search tools, and general employee information, also may be included in the employee's portal content. Similarly, when a customer, vendor, or business partner logs on through the corporate portal, personalized content allows access only to specific information based on his or her profile.

News, Sports, Weather, and Traffic Resources

Before the Internet became a source of readily accessible information, most people used newspapers, magazines, radio, and television to stay informed about current events, follow their favorite sports teams, keep an eye on the weather, or learn about traffic problems. Users supplement these traditional print and broadcast news media sources with websites and apps they access from computers and mobile devices, such as CNN.com and the CNN mobile app (Figure 5-14).

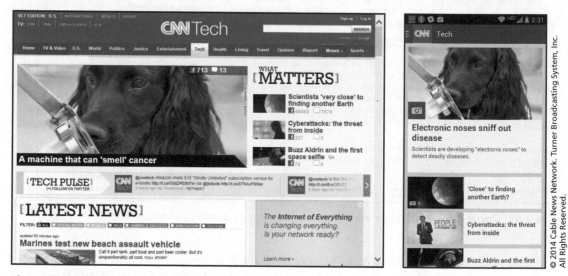

Figure 5-14 Websites and mobile apps can replace print resources for traffic resources and more.

In Chapters 2 and 3, you learned how to subscribe to web feeds for headline stories and other news articles, and how to use online search tools to locate and read news stories from news-oriented websites. Most U.S. and international newspapers publish online editions. Some offer a limited amount of free content; to read selected articles or access archived content, you must be a subscriber (for a fee, such as *The Wall Street Journal*) or register (for free, such as boston.com). Some newspaper websites give print subscribers additional online content and services.

Websites published by newspapers commonly include the same type of content found in the corresponding print versions: headline news, top stories, feature articles, current weather, sports scores, entertainment reviews, classified ads, editorials and opinion columns, and so forth. Many new websites and apps offer frequently updated coverage on topics, enabling them to keep their audience continually informed. Many offer services that send text or email messages to users for breaking news or news related to sports, entertainment, or other criteria the user selects. Some media websites include reader polls and most allow visitors to post comments on articles, which help them to track visitors' interest in and reaction to the news.

Television and radio networks, such as National Public Radio (NPR), NBC, CBC, BBC, CNN, FOX News, and local television network affiliates, publish websites and provide apps that provide a combination of headline news, sports, weather, blogs, videos, podcasts, and other news and entertainment features. Often these websites include content that promotes their broadcast programming and on-air personalities.

According to a Pew Internet survey 50 percent of smartphone users use their devices to find news information.

While sports, weather, and traffic reports usually are available at news-oriented websites, you also can find a number of websites devoted specifically to these topics. For example, online editions of ESPN, FOX Sports (television), and *Sports Illustrated* (magazine) cover a wide range of sports around the world, often in conjunction with existing cable news networks, such as CNN.

Websites such as the Weather Channel, AccuWeather.com, and Intellicast provide local and worldwide weather forecasts, weather-related travel advisories, and weather maps. Websites such as NAVTEQ, Google Maps, and local television station websites provide updated traffic reports that highlight routes with congestion, construction, or accidents that might cause delays.

Q&A **What is a podcast?** A **podcast** is digital audio or video available to listen to remotely. Originally called webcasts, they more commonly are known as podcasts because of the popularity of the Apple® iPod® and iPad®.

According to Journalism.org, 50 percent of social networking users have shared or reposted news stories.

Characteristics of News-Oriented Websites

Internet users rely on news, sports, weather, and traffic websites and apps for the following reasons:

- Availability — You can access them easily from almost anywhere, at anytime

- Authority — Legitimate news websites follow common journalistic practices to ensure integrity

- Immediacy — News websites offer breaking news, sports scores, or weather and traffic updates

- Interactivity — You can interact with the editorial staff by posting comments, and react or respond to articles

- Customizability — Each viewer can customize the information he or she sees based on location and interests

- Connectivity — Users share news and articles with their contacts by posting links using social media, or by sending links using text or email

The following sections review each of these characteristics in detail.

AVAILABILITY   Local, national, and international news-oriented websites often are more readily available than broadcast news sources. For example, if you are away from home, you might be unable to conveniently access television or radio, but you might have access to the Internet by using a computer or mobile device at work or at school. The immediate availability of Internet access from multiple locations makes it very easy for you to check the latest news, sports scores, or changing weather quickly.

AUTHORITY   Authoritative news coverage comes from reliable, informed contributors and journalists, and includes facts, citations, quotes, attribution, and supporting media. In addition, all news sources have a responsibility to provide content that has integrity. News sources should avoid showing bias, and not use lurid or misleading headlines.

IMMEDIACY   News-oriented websites offer updated content of breaking stories as the events unfold, thus providing you with immediate access to the latest information. Print news media, of course, cannot be constantly updated and distributed, and can contain only information about events that occurred prior to the last publication deadline.

INTERACTIVITY   Interactive features help make any type of website stickier and more interesting. A **sticky website** is one that users visit often and browse for long periods of time. Many news-oriented websites provide interactivity by allowing you to submit questions and comments to their editorial staff, commentators, and reporters by email, or to join other users in posting questions and comments in web-based discussion groups or on blogs. If the news source has a corresponding print or broadcast media presence, these questions and comments often are answered or shown in print or on the air. Another way in which these websites provide interactivity and create stickiness is by allowing viewers to participate in an online survey on a current topic and then quickly see how their opinions compare with those of other viewers. Sports-oriented websites often use a similar technique to allow viewers to vote for a league's most popular players, or to vote for members of an All-Star team.

CUSTOMIZABILITY   The ability to customize website content plays a major role in the growing popularity of news-oriented websites. For example, the websites for MSNBC, CNN, and BBC allow you to customize content based on a series of preferences. These preferences can include the following:

- Location — Uses postal code or other identifying information to customize content for local news, weather, and traffic
- News region preference — Used to customize content for a specific geographic area, such as the United States, Europe, or Asia
- Sports preferences — Used to include news and scores for favorite sports or teams
- Stock portfolio — Used to include activity reports and current quotes on the individual investments in a personal portfolio

CONNECTIVITY   News websites use Twitter or Facebook to entice users to read more about interesting or relevant stories by clicking links in their Twitter or Facebook news feeds to open articles in their original news webpages. You can also share news content with contacts and friends through social media links. Some of these websites allow viewers to subscribe to updates so that they can receive brief email or text messages about breaking news and a link to the website for more details. Many also offer apps that aggregate and publish content and provide alerts to a user's smartphone or tablet.

To Explore News and Traffic Websites

The following steps explore several news and traffic websites to view the latest news and information. Because you are reviewing websites that contain current content, the content on your screen will vary from the figures in this section.

1

- Start your browser and enter `nytimes .com/technology` in the Address bar.

- Press the ENTER key, or tap or click the necessary button to open the *New York Times* technology webpage (Figure 5-15).

- Scroll the webpage to review its major headlines and links to subsidiary pages.

Figure 5-15

2

- Open a new tab if necessary, and then enter `latimes .com/business/ technology` in the Address bar.

- Press the ENTER key, or tap or click the necessary button to open the *Los Angeles Times* technology webpage (Figure 5-16).

- Scroll the webpage to review its major headlines and links to subsidiary pages.

Figure 5-16

❸

- Open a new tab if necessary, and then enter **maps. google.com** in the Address bar.

- Press the ENTER key, or tap or click the necessary button to open the Google Maps home page.

- If necessary, enter your current ZIP code or address into the Search box, and then tap or click the Search button or press the ENTER key (Figure 5-17).

Q&A | **What if I live in a rural area?**
If you live in a rural area, you might not see certain features, such as location icons. Choose a medium- to large-sized city, such as Birmingham, Alabama, to explore the map features in this set of steps.

- Scroll the webpage and click the 'Explore this area' or 'Getting around' links to view attractions and transportation options.

Figure 5-17

❹

- Tap or click the Traffic link to display current traffic conditions (Figure 5-18).

- Use the arrow buttons, finger swipes, or click and drag to see surrounding areas.

Figure 5-18

5

- Tap or click the Typical traffic option button, if available, to see typical traffic patterns (Figure 5-19).

- Change the time of day or day of the week to view changes in the traffic patterns.

Satellite button

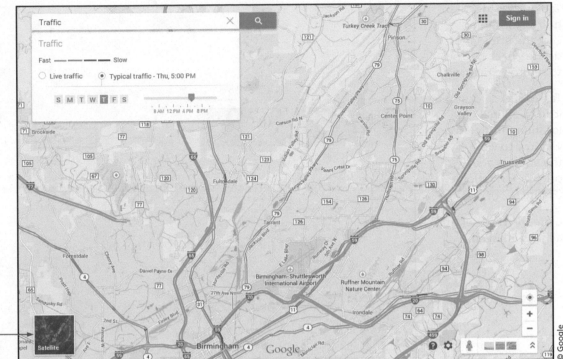

Figure 5-19

6

- Tap or click the Satellite button to view the satellite traffic feed, and then tap or click the Zoom button to zoom in to see a closer view (Figure 5-20).

Figure 5-20

7

- Tap or click the Map button, or tap or click the browser or device's back button to return to map view.

- Tap or click a location icon to open a location information window to view the address and other information (Figure 5-21).

- Close the browser and all tabs, if asked.

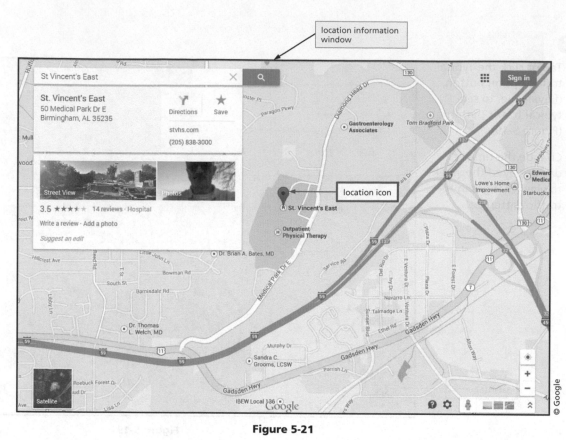

Figure 5-21

Streaming Media

Website audio and video content can enhance text-based content by providing interviews and reports from newscasters, subjects, or eyewitnesses. Audio and video that you can view in a web browser without downloading it is **streaming media**. Many news websites, such as CNN.com, provide video clips of timely news commentaries or important newsmaker interviews. Sports websites provide video clips of game highlights or postgame interviews with players and coaches. Radio websites provide short audio clips of interviews or make entire broadcasts available as audio over the Internet. Television networks, such as ABC, show clips or entire episodes on their websites. Hulu is a website that collaborates with multiple entertainment studios to provide clips, episodes, and movies from a variety of sources (Figure 5-22). Amazon Prime and Netflix have thousands of videos available to subscribers. Some websites enable you to purchase, rent, or subscribe to media that you can download to your computer or device. The advantage of streaming media is that you do not use storage space to store the media. Many news media content only is available through streaming to protect the copyright of the source. One way to experience streaming media is to listen to a radio broadcast over the Internet. A number of traditional radio station broadcasters, such as NPR, as well as local radio stations, broadcast over the Internet directly from their websites.

To access streaming media, your computer or device must have a sound card, speakers, and a media player. The Windows operating system comes with the Windows Media Player. You can download other media players, such as RealNetworks' RealPlayer, Apple's QuickTime Player, and the open-source SMPlayer, free from the vendors' websites. Most mobile devices include a media player. A number of websites that offer video, such as

Figure 5-22 Streaming media includes audio and video continuously delivered from a web server to a browser.

CNN.com, MSNBC, and the TODAY show, stream the media in their own media player. The TED (technology, entertainment, design) website offers free streaming online and prerecorded conferences and speeches on numerous topics by industry experts.

To View a Web-Based Video

The following steps allow you to experience streaming media by viewing a video about technology innovator and inventor Ray Kurzweil using a built-in website media player.

1

- Start your browser and enter `ted.com` in the Address bar.

- Press the ENTER key, or tap or click the necessary button to open the TED home page (Figure 5-23).

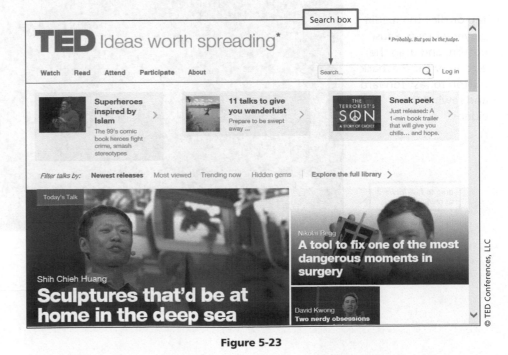

Figure 5-23

②

- Enter `ray kurzweil` in the Search box, and then press the ENTER key, or tap or click the necessary button to open the search results for Ray Kurzweil (Figure 5-24).

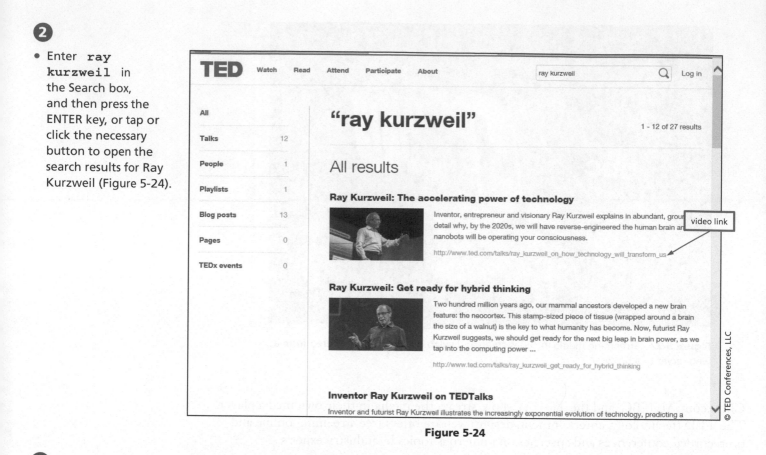

Figure 5-24

③

- Tap or click any video link to open it, then tap or click the Play button to start the video (Figure 5-25)

- Tap or click the media player window Pause button, and drag the arrows or the Playback button to fast-forward and rewind the videos.

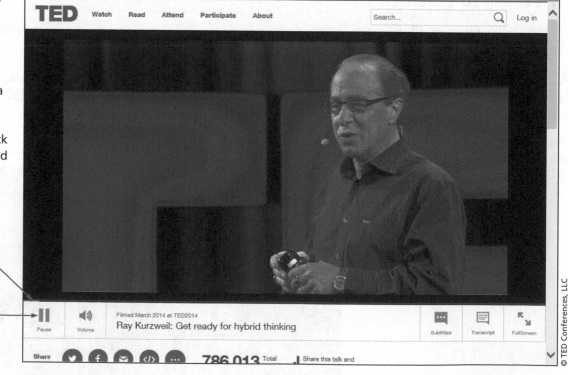

Figure 5-25

4

- Tap or point to the right side of the screen to view a menu of buttons, and then tap or click the Rate button to open the rating window (Figure 5-26).

- If desired, tap or click a ratings option to contribute to the video's ratings, then tap or click the Submit button or tap or click the Close button to close the window without submitting a rating.

- Close the browser and close all open tabs, if necessary.

Figure 5-26

According to comScore, Inc., over 186 million Americans watched online videos in a recent month. Top video sources in order were Google Sites, Facebook, and AOL.

FACTS @HAND

Research and Reference Tools

As you learned in Chapter 3, the web includes numerous websites that provide access to specialized information collections, such as LexisNexis, FindLaw, and Hoover's, and government websites, such as the Census Bureau (Figure 5-27 on the following page) and the Bureau of Labor Statistics. In addition to these specialized information collections, the web also includes numerous general reference websites, such as online encyclopedias, dictionaries, reference desks, and trip planners. Charity Navigator (Figure 5-27) is a reference tool to find information about a charity's mission, finances, and more. Remember to use the criteria and tools you learned about in Chapter 3 to evaluate the credibility of the content on reference websites.

Q&A

How can I ensure I am citing and crediting my research sources properly?
Websites such as easybib .com and bibme.org help you organize web resources, and assist you in creating a bibliography to list all of your sources.

Figure 5-27   Reference websites provide access to specialized information collections.

Online Encyclopedias

You can access a number of online encyclopedias, such as Encyclopedia.com (which aggregates information from multiple encyclopedias), Encyclopædia Britannica (a premium service), Bartleby.com, Infoplease, and Encyclopedia Smithsonian to research topics, verify facts, and find credible sources of information.

To Explore an Online Encyclopedia

The following steps use an online encyclopedia to perform a keyword search for a specific topic.

1

- Start your browser and enter `encyclopedia.com` in the Address bar.

- Press the ENTER key, or tap or click the necessary button to open the Reference.com home page.

- Enter `Molly Pitcher` in the Search box, and then tap or click the Search button to find links to information about the American Revolutionary War heroine.

- Scroll through the search results to see suggested links (Figure 5-28).

Q&A **Why do I see a drop-down list of search query suggestions?**
Like some of the search engines you learned about in Chapter 3, Encyclopedia .com provides a list of search suggestions based on the characters you are typing in the Search box. You can tap or click a search suggestion in the list to search using that search suggestion.

Figure 5-28

2

- Tap or click any link to view the article (Figure 5-29).

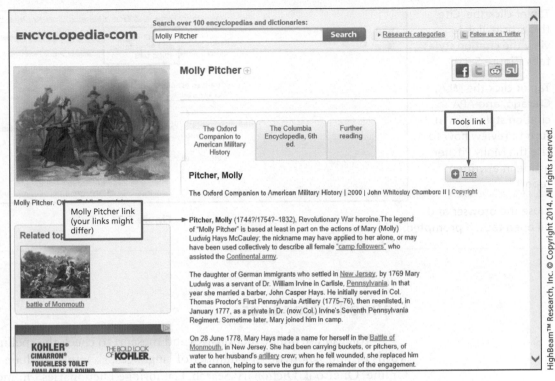

Figure 5-29

3

- Tap or click the Tools link to view online tools for printing, citing, and sharing the search results (Figure 5-30).

Figure 5-30

4

- Tap or click the 'Cite this article' link to view the citation styles tabs (Figure 5-31).

- Tap or click the MLA, Chicago, and APA citation styles tabs in turn to review how to cite the Molly Pitcher article in a written report.

- Close the browser and all open tabs, if prompted.

Figure 5-31

Online Dictionaries

You can use online dictionaries and thesauri to check the spelling and meaning of words or find synonyms in a number of languages. Examples include Merriam-Webster Online, OneLook Dictionary Search, Cambridge Dictionaries Online, and Thesaurus.com. You also can find dictionaries devoted to specific topics, such as law, biology, or technology. The NetLingo and Law.com dictionary websites, for example, provide definitions of thousands of technical and legal terms, respectively.

Some websites, such as OneLook, enable you to do **wildcard searches**. Wildcard searches use characters such as * or ? to replace letters, or use : (the colon character) to narrow your search by subject (Figure 5-32).

Wildcard Searches

Search Term	Finds Words or Phrases That
*ball	End with *ball*
ball*	Start with *ball*
b????? ball	Start with *b*, end with *ball*, and have five characters between, such as *basketball*
:ball	Are related to *ball*

Figure 5-32 Sample wildcard search terms and results.

To Explore an Online Dictionary

The following steps use an online dictionary to search for the definition, part of speech, and phonetic pronunciation of a specific word. You will open the website's home page link to open the web page in a new tab. You also will perform wildcard searches.

1

- Start your browser and enter `merriam-webster.com` in the Address bar.

- Press the ENTER key, or tap or click the necessary button to open the Merriam-Webster home page (Figure 5-33).

Figure 5-33

2

- Enter `meme` in the Search box.

- Tap or click the Search button to search for a definition.

- Review the main entry, which is the definition of meme as a noun (Figure 5-34).

Figure 5-34

3

- Tap or click the sound icon to open the Merriam-Webster Pronunciation page in the same tab and hear the pronunciation (Figure 5-35).

Q&A **Why am I prompted to accept a pop-up window from this webpage?**
The pronunciation option opens in a new window. Tap or click the OK button or other option to open the window.

4

- Tap or click the 'Listen to the audio pronunciation again' link on the Pronunciation page to listen to the pronunciation a second time.

- Tap or click the pronunciation window Close button to close the window.

Close button

Merriam-Webster Pronunciation - Internet Explorer

http://www.merriam-webster.com/audio.php?file=meme001s&word=meme&text=%

"meme"

Listen to the audio pronunciation again ← 'Listen to the audio pronunciation again' link

\'mēm\

Having trouble hearing a pronunciation?
* Click here to listen with your default audio player.

© 2014, Merriam-Webster, Incorporated

Figure 5-35

5

- Open a new tab if necessary, and then enter **onelook.com** in the Address bar.

- Press the ENTER key, or tap or click the necessary button to open the web page in a new tab.

- Enter **cyber*** in the Search box (Figure 5-36).

OneLook
Dictionary Search

Word, phrase, or pattern: [cyber* ✕] [Search] ← Search button

Example searches ↑ Search box

bluebird	Find definitions of *bluebird*
blue*	Find words and phrases that start with *blue*
*bird	Find words and phrases that end with *bird*
bl????rd	Find words that start with *bl*, end with *rd*, with 4 letters in between
bl*:snow	Find words that start with *bl* and have a meaning related to *snow*
bl*:adjective	Find any adjectives that start with *bl*
*:snow or :snow	Find any words related to *snow*
*:winter sport	Find words related to the concept *winter sport*
winter	Find phrases that contain the word *winter*
expand:nasa	Find phrases that spell out *n.a.s.a.*

Advanced help with wildcards and the reverse dictionary is available.

19,633,003 words in 1061 dictionaries indexed — Today's word is **pursue**

Reverse Dictionary   Browse Dictionaries   Privacy   Blog   Help

g+1 1.3k

OneLook

Figure 5-36

6

- Tap or click the Search button to view the search results (Figure 5-37).

- Tap or click one of the links in the search results to view the webpage.

- Close the browser and all open tabs, if prompted.

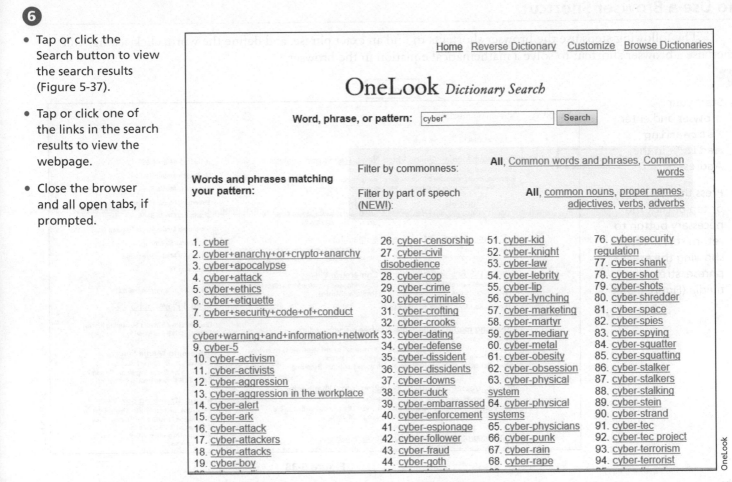

Figure 5-37

In Chapter 3, you learned several search engine shortcuts, such as to use quotations to include an exact phrase. Another use of browser shortcuts is to solve mathematical equations. When you enter an equal sign (=), the browser knows you are starting an equation. You enter the numbers and operators, such as × or +, and then start the search. Another shortcut is the define: shortcut, which you can use to return a search results list that contains webpages with a definition for a specific word or phrase. Simply enter the shortcut **define:** followed by a word or phrase in the Address bar, and then press the ENTER key or tap or click the necessary button to start the search. The browser then returns a search results list of webpages containing a definition of the word or phrase, or a message indicating that no web page meets the criteria.

To Use a Browser Shortcut

The following steps use the browser shortcuts to find an exact phrase, and define the word, clickjacking. You then use a browser shortcut to solve a mathematical equation in the browser.

1

- Start your browser and enter **"streaming media"** in the Address bar.

- Press the ENTER key, or tap or click the necessary button to return search results showing the exact phrase, streaming media (Figure 5-38).

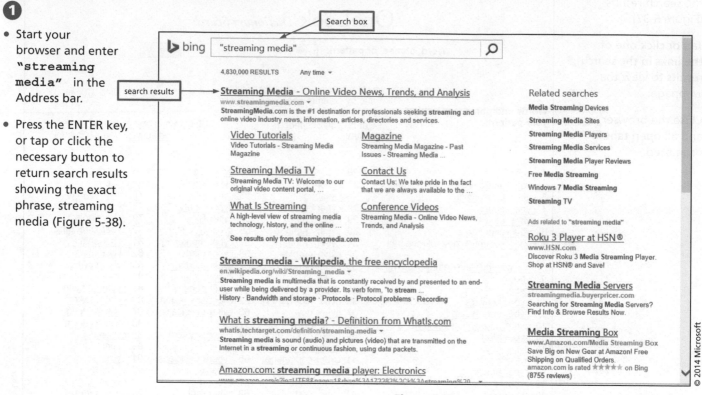

Figure 5-38

2

- Enter **define: clickjacking** in the Address bar.

- Press the ENTER key, or tap or click the necessary button to return search results showing the definition of clickjacking (Figure 5-39).

- Tap or click the link of your choice to review the definition's source.

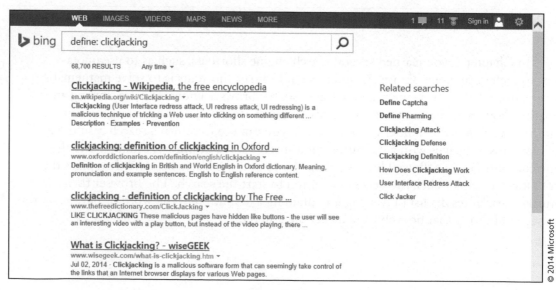

Figure 5-39

3

- Enter `=425×19` in the Address bar (Figure 5-40).

- Press the ENTER key, or tap or click the necessary button to solve the equation (Figure 5-40).

- Close the browser and all open tabs, if prompted.

Q&A **Why do I see a calculator in the browser window?** Depending on your browser, when you enter an equation to solve, the browser may display a calculator that you can use to perform additional equations.

WEB   IMAGES   VIDEOS   MAPS   NEWS   MORE

bing   `=425×19`   🔍

187,000 RESULTS   Any time ▾

425×19=

8075

Inv	Deg	x!	(	)	C	⌫
In	sin	%	7	8	9	÷
log	cos	√	4	5	6	×
^	tan	1/x	1	2	3	−
Exp	π	e	0	.	=	+

© 2014 Microsoft

Figure 5-40

Online Reference Desks

Do you need to know what time it is in Bahrain? What important event took place on today's date in history? How to translate text into another language? You can find this information at an online reference desk website, such as the Internet Public Library, refdesk.com, LibrarySpot.com (Figure 5-41), and iTools. An **online reference desk** is a collection of links to online resources.

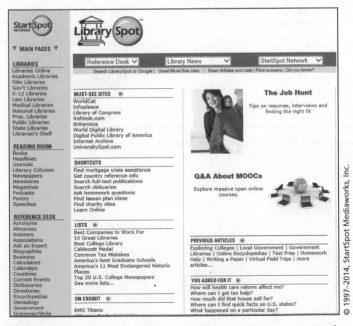

© 1997–2014, StartSpot Mediaworks, Inc.

Figure 5-41 Online desk references provide access to a range of information resources.

Online reference desks offer links to dictionaries, thesauri, language translators, fast fact finders, and other traditional library reference desk resources. Additionally, many college, university, public, and government libraries offer online reference desk resources. Examples include the Michigan eLibrary, the Duke University Libraries Research Support and the Chicago Public Library Online Research websites.

Most online dictionary, reference desk, and encyclopedia websites, such as the websites you explored in the previous sections, offer free information. Some websites, such as the Encyclopædia Britannica and the Britannica Kids websites, offer premium websites requiring a subscription fee to access some or all of the information available at the website.

User-Generated Content

By enabling users to review and rate restaurants and other services, websites such as Yelp (Figure 5-42), OpenTable, and Urbanspoon provide research tools that enable you to find local venues and read reviews by people who have been there. **User-generated research tools** can use GPS or a user-entered ZIP code, as well as criteria you select to provide you with specific results. You can find specific diet or allergy information such as gluten-free or vegetarian, a type of food such as Mexican or Indian, and a price range to find suggested restaurants and more.

Figure 5-42   Yelp provides reviews of local venues from users.

To Explore a User-Generated Research Tool

The following steps explore Urbanspoon to find options for fondue restaurants in Los Angeles.

1

- Start your browser and enter **urbanspoon.com** in the Address bar.

- Press the ENTER key, or tap or click the necessary button to open the Urbanspoon home page.

- Tap or click the Los Angeles link at the top of the webpage to view results for that city (Figure 5-43).

- Scroll the webpage to review the reference desk resources available.

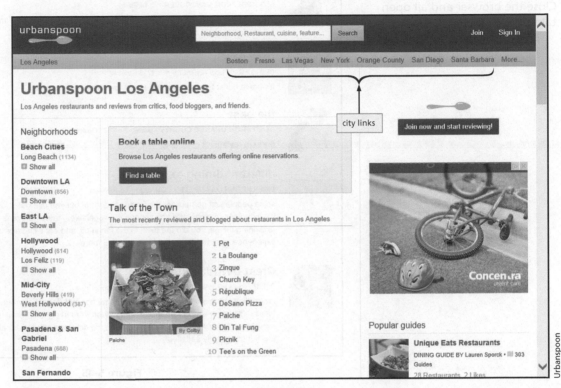

Figure 5-43

2

- Enter **fondue** in the Search box, and then press the ENTER key, or tap or click the Search button to display the search results (Figure 5-44).

Figure 5-44

3

- Scroll the webpage to see reviews of the restaurant (Figure 5-45).

- Close the browser and all open tabs, if prompted.

Follow Me Foodie

BLOGGER FROM VANCOUVER • 14 Posts

We came here strictly for dessert, so I'm curious to try their cheese fondue next time. Neat and fun idea, and great... Full Review

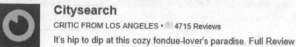

Citysearch

CRITIC FROM LOS ANGELES • 4715 Reviews

It's hip to dip at this cozy fondue-lover's paradise. Full Review

the best

DINER FROM ORANGE COUNTY • Darwin F • 26 Reviews   • FAVORITE

the best restaurant of all time

different dining experience!

DINER FROM LOS ANGELES • Chloexp • 5 Reviews   • LIKES IT

some people just go here for the fondue desserts, but you can eat a full course meal here. they have choices of meat, and you choose the vegetables. the employees are very good at explaining things. you dip the meat in the fondu oil, and eat with vegetables. a fun dining experience, may not fill up the big eaters out there

Great birthday dinner!

DINER FROM LOS ANGELES • Terrapinzero • 3 Reviews   • FAVORITE

I recently went to this location with my wife for her birthday. They made it such a special night for us. We sat in a very romantic booth, hidden from everyone. It wasn't so much dinner, but an experience. We were there over two hours, ate delicious cheese, steak and chocolate fondue and left completely satisfied!

Urbanspoon

Figure 5-45

Online Route Planners

Online route planners such as FreeTrip, MapQuest, Google Maps, Yahoo! Maps, and Expedia Maps enable you to plan a driving or walking route, calculate mileage, and find locations to stop for food or gas along the way. Many online route planners use GPS or your identified current location to identify your starting point. When you use an online driving trip planner, you specify a starting location and an ending destination, and then indicate your preferences, such as a scenic route or the shortest-distance route. Some trip planners also provide information about restaurants, shopping, and accommodations along the desired route. Many have corresponding mobile apps that you can use to either perform the same searches, or send the route and details to your smartphone from the website or web app.

To Explore Online Route Planners

The following steps explore an online driving trip planner to find a driving route of your choice.

1

- Start your browser and enter `freetrip.com` in the Address bar.

- Tap or click the FreeTrip link to open the web page in a new tab.

- In the Step 1: Origination area, tap or click the 'Select State/Province' box arrow, and then select your state. If you do not live in the United States, click Oregon.

- Enter the name of your city or enter `Portland` in the 'Step 1: Origination Enter City/Town/Place' text box.

- Tap or click the 'Step 2: Destination Select State/Province' box arrow, and then tap or click Utah.

- Enter `Moab` in the 'Step 2: Destination Enter City/Town/Place' text box (Figure 5-46).

Figure 5-46

2

- Tap or click options to select or deselect route and lodging preferences (Figure 5-47).

Figure 5-47

3

- Choose options in the 'Step 5: Road Advisory Display Options' section.

- Enter your email address in the 'Step 6: Email Address' text box to receive a copy of your itinerary by email, if desired.

- Scroll to view the 'Step 7: Submit Trip Request' area near the bottom of the page (Figure 5-48).

- Read the disclaimer about the accuracy of the trip planner's results.

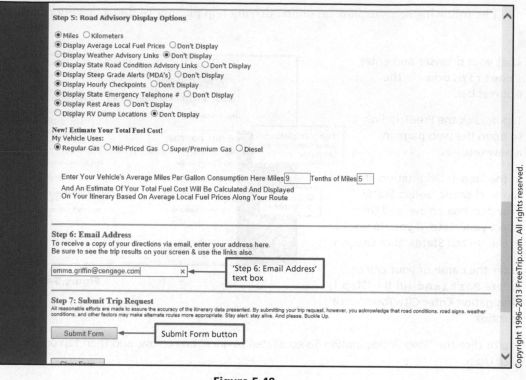

Figure 5-48

4

- Tap or click the Submit Form button.

- Scroll your personal itinerary page to view the driving instructions and suggestions for accommodations (Figure 5-49).

- Close the browser and all open tabs, if prompted.

		Start South on I-5 for 67mi			
15	0:16	La Quinta Inn Wilsonville -WILSONVILL $$(OR)	more info	1581	31:59
18	0:19	BEST WESTERN WILLAMETTE INN -WILSONVI $$(OR)	more info	1578	31:56
18	0:19	PHOENIX INN Sts WILSONVILLE -WILSONVI $$(OR)	more info	1578	31:56
19	0:21	Rest Stop		1577	31:54
30	0:31	Super 8 Motel Woodburn Or -WOODBURN $$(OR)	more info	1566	31:44
38	0:40	**Approaching Vicinity of Salem OR**		1558	31:35
		Avg Regular Gas Price for Next 307 Mi: [3.98]			
43	0:45	BEST WESTERN PACIFIC HIGHWA -SALEM $$(OR)	more info	1553	31:30
45	0:48	Cozzzy Inn -SALEM $$(OR)	more info	1551	31:27
45	0:48	Super 8 Salem Or -SALEM $$(OR)	more info	1551	31:27
48	0:50	HoJo Inn Salem -SALEM $$(OR)	more info	1548	31:25
57	1:00	Driving Checkpoint: 1 hr		1539	31:15
59	1:02	Rest Stop		1537	31:13
67	1:11	QUALITY INN ALBANY -ALBANY $$(OR)	more info	1529	31:04
67	1:11	Phoenix Inn Suite Albany -ALBANY $$(OR)	more info	1529	31:04
67	1:11	Best Western Albany Inn -ALBANY $$(OR)	more info	1529	31:04
67	1:11	La Quinta Albany -ALBANY $$(OR)	more info	1529	31:04
67	1:11	**Junction With Rt 99e**		1529	31:04
		Cont. South on Rt 99e for 1.3mi			
69	1:13	**Junction With US 20**		1527	31:02

Figure 5-49

Special-Interest Websites

No matter how obscure your hobby or special interest might be, there likely is at least one website or wiki dedicated to it. Thousands of special-interest websites are devoted to topics such as health, diet, and fitness; entertainment news and movie reviews; home decorating and repair; museums; or genealogy. The next few sections explore just some of the wide range of health, entertainment, hobby, and other special-interest websites available online.

Health, Diet, and Fitness Information

The epidemic of obesity in the United States, coupled with rising health care costs, may have you thinking about ways to ensure that you are eating a healthy diet, getting the proper exercise, and staying informed on health, diet, and fitness issues. You also might need information about a specific illness or medical condition. Your primary source of health, diet, and fitness information should be your doctor or another health care professional. If you are looking for general health, diet, and fitness information online, however, you can choose from hundreds of websites, such as Discovery Health, MayoClinic, and WebMD (Figure 5-50).

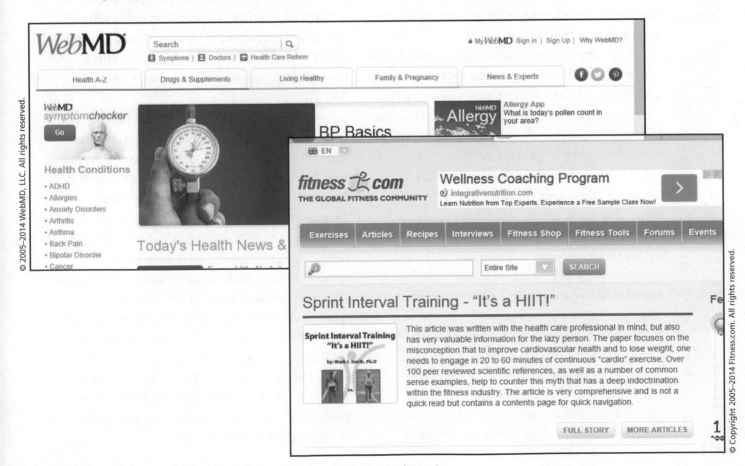

Figure 5-50 Diet, fitness, and health-related websites provide general information.

Several popular commercial diet and fitness websites, such as Fitness.com (Figure 5-50 on the previous page) and MyFitnessPal, help you plan and execute a personal diet and fitness program. These websites offer a variety of features, including:

- Restricted-calorie meal plans
- Grocery shopping lists
- Exercise plans, complete with text and graphic instructions
- Daily food and exercise diaries
- Databases of food items with nutrition information that users can select to create a food diary to track calories, protein intake, and more.
- Support discussion groups

You can find almost everything you need to create a personal diet and fitness plan at one of these commercial websites for a fee. For free diet and fitness information, you can turn to government websites such as Fitness.gov (sponsored by the President's Council on Fitness, Sports, and Nutrition) and Nutrition.gov.

@ISSUE Credibility of Online Health Information

Because of the large numbers of American Internet users who search for health information online, many health care professionals and Internet users are concerned about the credibility of online health information that might be unclear or inaccurate.

With these concerns in mind, how should you evaluate health-oriented websites? The credibility of the content at these websites first should be evaluated using the steps you learned in Chapter 3, including identifying the sponsoring organization or author, establishing that the content is timely and objective, and comparing the content with that from other, similar websites. Most people who go online to find health information rely on popular search tools to locate health-oriented websites; however, some health care professionals suggest that you ask a trusted source, such as your doctor or medical information professional, to recommend health-oriented websites. Another resource to help you evaluate health-oriented websites is the CAPHIS (Consumer and Patient Health Information Section) website. The nonprofit Medical Library Association sponsors and publishes content provided by medical information professionals on the CAPHIS website. CAPHIS evaluates health-oriented websites based on a number of criteria, including credibility, disclosure, sponsorship and authorship, and design, and then lists the top 100 highest-evaluated websites as part of the CAPHIS Top 100.

Another alternative is to look for accredited websites. Two agencies that offer accreditation for health-oriented websites are the URAC website and the Health On the Net Foundation HONcode accreditation program. The website standards required by these agencies include the full disclosure of financial relationships, an editorial review process to ensure content accuracy, and internal processes to ensure privacy, security, and website quality. Websites that adhere to the standards established by these agencies are entitled to display the URAC or HONcode symbols on their websites, as shown in Figure 5-51. For more information about the URAC and HONcode programs, use a search engine to search for *URAC and HON accreditation*.

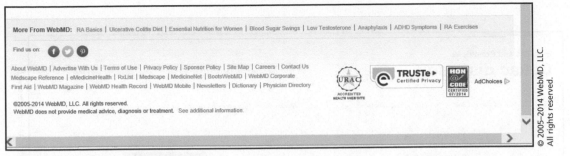

Figure 5-51 The URAC and HONcode symbols indicate that the information at a health-oriented website, such as WebMD, meets strict quality standards.

In addition to researching specific health topics, you can review hospital websites to check out services; go to health insurance provider websites to evaluate enrollment options and coverage; and fill prescriptions at online drugstores. Websites such as CarePages enable people with a health condition to create a web page where they can post information about their health and treatments, and receive comments from friends and family. You also can go online to learn about and sign up for medical clinical trials or to locate a doctor in your area. Websites such as CenterWatch, ClinicalTrials.gov, AMA DoctorFinder, and MedlinePlus offer these services. Many health care organizations, such as the American Diabetes Association, also provide online information about a specific disease and its treatment and how to find support groups.

To Explore Health-Related Websites

The following steps explore health-related websites. You will open each website's home page link to open the web page in a new tab.

1

- Start your browser and enter **mayoclinic .org** in the Address bar.

- Press ENTER or tap or click the necessary button to open the Mayo Clinic home page.

- Enter **celiac disease** in the Search box (Figure 5-52).

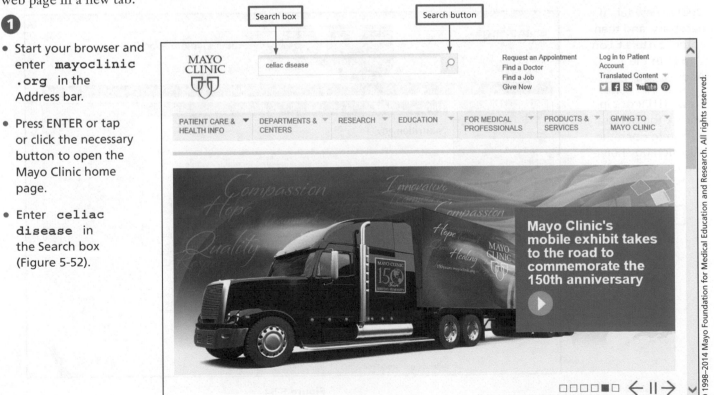

Figure 5-52

2

- Tap or click the Search button to view a search results list for the keywords, celiac disease.

- Tap or click the Celiac Disease – MayoClinic .com link or another link of your choice to learn more about celiac disease (Figure 5-53).

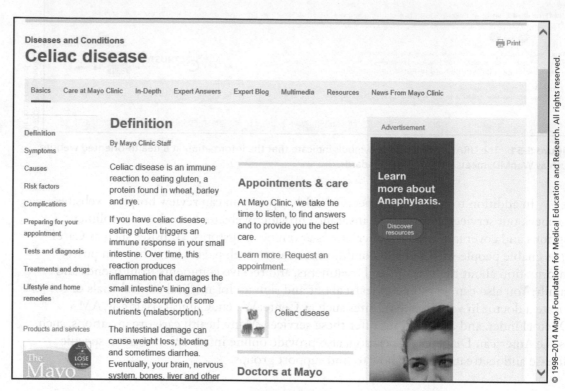

Figure 5-53

3

- Open a new tab, if necessary, and then enter `nutrition .gov` in the Address bar.

- Press ENTER or tap or click the necessary button to open the Nutrition.gov home page (Figure 5-54).

Smart Nutrition 101 link

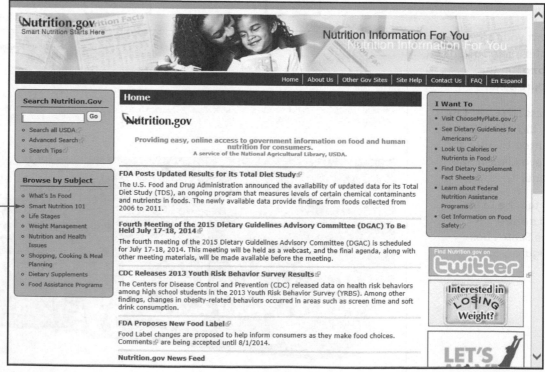

Figure 5-54

4

- Tap or click the Smart Nutrition 101 link in the Browse by Subject area to display the Smart Nutrition 101 page.

- Tap or click the 'MyPlate & Food Pyramid Resources' link, and then tap or click the ChooseMyPlate.gov link in the Smart Nutrition 101 section to view links to information about the MyPlate food guide program (Figure 5-55).

- Scroll the webpage to view the resources for creating a healthy eating and fitness plan.

- Close the browser and all open tabs, if prompted.

ChooseMyPlate.gov

Figure 5-55

Personal Finance Resources

Using online tools to help manage your personal finances —checking your bank balance, making a deposit, paying bills, financing a new car, reviewing investment opportunities, and more — makes managing your personal finances more convenient. In this section, you will learn about the benefits of various online personal financial management tools.

Banking, Bill Presentment, and Bill Payment Services

Using online banking and banking apps allows you to complete traditional time-consuming and paper-based banking activities, such as those required to transfer money from one account to another, quickly and easily. If you use your bank's or financial institution's online banking features or an app, you already might be familiar with how easy it is to go online and check your bank balance, or view a list of paid items from your account. Some financial institutions offer apps to manage your banking. Some banking or finance apps enable you to take a picture of a check with a mobile device and instantly make a deposit without going to the bank or ATM.

In the past, a bank was largely a **brick-and-mortar business**, meaning that customers conducted transactions primarily in person at a physical location, over the phone, or using paper-based transactions. Today, large banks, such as Chase (Figure 5-56 on the following page), Citibank, the RBC Royal Bank (Canada), and the National Australia Bank, as well as smaller regional banks, local banks, and credit unions are **brick-and-click businesses** — that is, they offer online banking in addition to the services offered at the physical banks. A brick-and-click business is any business that allows customers to conduct business or complete transactions at a physical location as well as online at a website.

Figure 5-56   Online banking extends your banking capabilities beyond having to go to the ATM or brick-and-mortar bank.

 FACTS @HAND   According to the U.S. Federal Reserve, 69 percent of mobile banking users check their account balances using their mobile device, and 24 percent of these users track expenses and purchases using mobile banking apps.

Online banking can allow you to complete some or all of the following tasks:

- View real-time account balances and recent transactions
- View a history of account activity
- Deposit checks
- Search for individual transactions
- Pay your bills
- Transfer funds between accounts
- Download transactions into personal financial management software, such as Quicken
- Issue a stop payment on a check
- Order checks
- Report a lost or stolen ATM card and request a replacement
- Change personal information, such as your address, telephone number, and email address

Fees for online banking services vary from one institution to another. For example, some banks offer free online checking with no minimum account balance requirement, while other banks may require that you maintain a minimum balance to avoid paying service fees. Some banks also charge additional fees for specific types of online transactions, such as transferring money from account to account. Before you open an online bank account, you should compare the services and fees of several online banking services.

A common concern about online banking is the security of online banking transactions. Although no online transactions are 100 percent secure, and instances of online banking fraud do occur, the banking industry has been involved with the security of electronic transactions for more than 40 years, starting with the electronic funds transfer (EFT) systems originating in the 1960s. Today, you can expect your bank to use sophisticated Internet security technologies to protect your personal information and to secure your online transactions. When shopping for an online bank, you should carefully review a bank's privacy policies and any security statements it provides.

One of the most valuable uses of online banking is online bill payment services. A **bill payment service** allows you to log on to a website and pay any number of bills from a range of vendors. In addition to online banks, e-businesses such as MSN Bill Pay and PayTrust (Figure 5-57) offer bill payment services. To pay a bill online using your bank or a bill payment service, simply log in to your account with the bank or service, select a vendor from a list you created when you first set up your bill payment service, enter a payment amount, and specify a payment date. On the scheduled payment date, the bank removes the payment from your bank account and transmits it to the vendor either by an electronic funds transfer or with a paper check. You also can set up recurring monthly payments so that you can pay bills, such as your phone bill or car payment, automatically on a specific day each month.

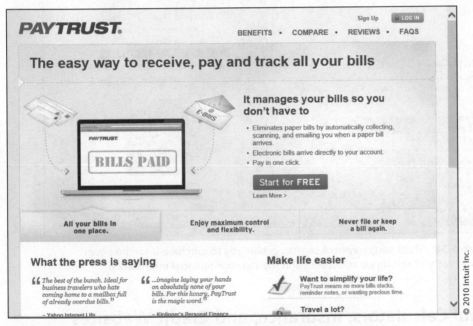

Figure 5-57 Bill payment services enable you to set and track all payments.

Many utilities, credit card companies, auto finance companies, and other businesses use **bill presentment**, the process of sending bills electronically, instead of mailing paper bills or statements to customers. Using bill presentment to send electronic bills, also called **e-bills**, instead of sending paper bills can reduce a company's billing costs substantially, and is a more environmentally friendly approach than sending paper bills through the postal service. You can arrange to receive e-bills and then pay them electronically through your online bank account or bill payment service. For many consumers, receiving bills online is a convenient way to pay bills while away from home. If you receive an e-bill while traveling, you can log on to your bill payment service from a laptop or mobile device and pay the bill on time.

Some banks offer online bill payment and bill presentment services for free, while others charge monthly service fees as well as transaction fees. You should research several banks and bill payment services and compare their fees before selecting an online bank.

One way to take advantage of the ease and speed of online bill presentment and payment without paying a fee is to pay your bill directly at the vendor's website. Many utility and credit card companies allow you to set up payment information that includes a user ID, password, and bank account information at the company's own website. Then, you simply log on to the website each month, view your monthly statement, and make your payment. Although this method is less expensive than paying for a bill presentment and payment service, it lacks the advantage of using a single website to pay all your bills. For example, to pay bills directly to a credit card company or utility company website, you must remember multiple user IDs and passwords.

One way to manage online payments securely is to use a trusted third-party payment service. Many online merchants enable you to pay using PayPal (Figure 5-58) or other services. You create an account with the third-party service, which stores and encrypts your payment and contact information. When making a purchase online, especially with an unknown vendor, using PayPal protects your information.

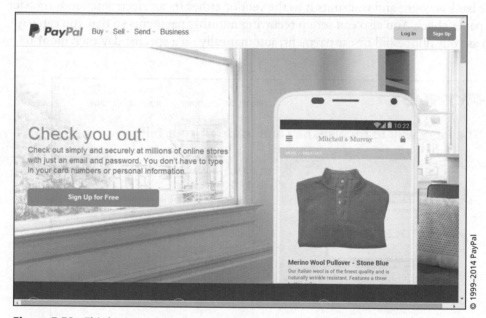

Figure 5-58   Third-party payment services enable you to purchase from unknown vendors without setting up an account and sharing your financial information.

Financial Calculators, Insurance, and Credit Websites

Online information sources can help you make important personal financial decisions, such as buying a new automobile, selecting the right home mortgage, getting the best insurance value, tracking your expenses to stay within a budget, or accepting a credit card offer. Online mortgage loan calculators and auto loan calculators can help you decide how much you can afford to pay each month for a home mortgage or how big of a down payment you should make when buying an automobile. Savings calculators can help you budget and plan for a major purchase or your eventual retirement. These types of financial calculators and apps are available through a number of financial institutions, such as Chase, or through other vendors, such as CardRatings.com (Figure 5-59) or Kiplinger .com. Unless you decide to do business with a company and have thoroughly checked out its reliability and security, you should not provide any personal, financial, or contact information to any website. Some financial websites exist to attempt to capture sensitive data to commit identity theft or other crimes.

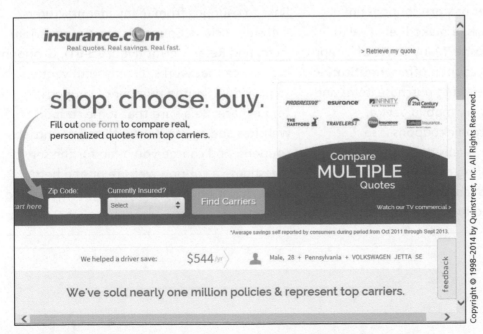

Figure 5-59 Financial institutions offer savings calculators and other financial tools.

If you own a vehicle, auto insurance likely is one of your major expenses. Shopping for auto insurance offline often requires that you personally contact several different insurance agents and then manually compare each agent's policies, terms, and quoted rates. Websites such as Insweb, Insure.com, or Insurance.com (Figure 5-60), make it easier to comparison shop for auto insurance by providing competing quotes from multiple insurance companies in just a few seconds. You simply submit your auto and personal information, along with information about the insurance coverage you want, using an online form. You also can get online comparative quotes on other types of insurance, such as homeowner's, renter's, and life insurance.

Figure 5-60 Insurance agencies' websites enable you to get quotes for services.

Websites provide similar comparison shopping for credit cards. Because a wide range exists in the payment terms, fees, and services associated with different credit cards, it is a good idea to shop for a credit card in the same way that you shop for other products and services. You can compare credit card offers at comparison shopper websites, such as BillSaver.com, or credit card information websites, such as CardRatings.com. Additionally, before you accept a credit card offer, you may want to learn more about the advantages and disadvantages of using credit cards, learn how to protect yourself from credit card fraud, and learn how to budget your credit card spending. Many credit card issuers provide online credit card education. For example, banks Wells Fargo and Citibank include student financial services and credit education webpages at their websites.

Protecting your credit also involves being aware of your credit history, and knowing what to do if you are a victim of credit card fraud or identity theft. The three major U.S. consumer credit reporting agencies — TransUnion, Experian, and Equifax — provide options for reviewing your credit reports online. By conveniently and routinely reviewing your credit reports online, you easily can detect an error or an instance of possible fraud and take immediate action to have the error corrected or the fraud uncovered. If you are a victim of credit card fraud or identity theft, the U.S. Federal Trade Commission (FTC) website provides useful information on steps you should take to protect yourself and correct your credit records.

@ISSUE   Coupon Websites

When considering finances and saving money, couponing comes to mind. Printed coupons, available in weekly flyers from the grocery store or mailed as promotions, have been widely used since the early 1900s when the Post cereal company started printing them on cereal boxes. Manufacturer or store coupons email coupons to customers or make them available on the vendor's website. Many stores offer apps that provide special coupon offers, notification of sales, and enable you to purchase items and view reviews from your mobile device.

The use of electronic coupons is so prevalent that many websites exist for the sole purpose of sharing coupons or links to coupons. To take advantage of the coupons, sometimes you need to print a copy to bring to a brick-and-mortar store, or copy a code to enter when shopping online. If you have a coupon app, or received an email or text with the coupon, often the store can scan the coupon at the register.

Examples of coupon websites that provide links to coupons from many manufacturers' websites include Coupons.com, CouponMom.com, and RetailMeNot (Figure 5-61). Groupon is a service that works directly with vendors to provide a limited number of coupons to purchase. Be aware that some coupon websites and apps offer outdated or unusable coupons, and charge you a fee for the service. Investigate a coupon website or app before accessing or downloading it, or before paying any fees.

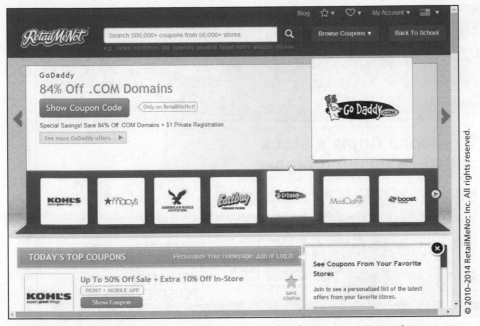

Figure 5-61 Couponing websites enable users to search for, review, print, and use coupons for groceries, clothing, and more.

Investing Online

The availability of quick access to online investment information and the proliferation of investment-oriented websites empower people to handle or receive advice on their own stock portfolios and other investments. Online sources such as MarketWatch (Figure 5-62), Hoover's, CNNMoney, Morningstar, MSN Money, and The Motley Fool provide investors with current market information and stock quotes. Online brokers, such as E*TRADE and Charles Schwab, offer a variety of investment accounts, some with low start-up costs and small per-trade transaction fees. Most online brokers also offer premium financial services, including financial planning and market research. Increasingly, online brokers are offering a full line of financial services, including e-bill presentment and payment from your investment account. Many of these online brokers provide apps that enable you to manage your investments, and also provide notifications of changes in your stock value through text, email, or alerts sent to your mobile device. If you are considering investing online, websites such as the Investing Online Resource Center (IORC) can help by providing tips on how to select an online broker and how to open an online account. The IORC website also provides an online investing simulation in which you can practice managing an investment account before you actually open one. Many investor information websites also offer a portfolio feature that you can use to create a mock portfolio and practice managing it over time.

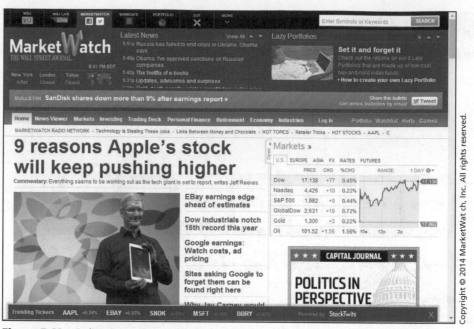

Figure 5-62   Online investment websites enable people to manage their own stock portfolios, use online brokers, and research investments.

Entertainment, Hobby, and Other Special-Interest Websites

Whether your interest is cooking, learning about your family's genealogy, finding a job, making new friends, reading a movie review or the latest celebrity gossip, or visiting the world's great museums, thousands of entertainment, hobby, and other special-interest websites exist. For example, using one of the numerous entertainment, hobby, and other special-interest websites, you can:

- Learn to make gazpacho at Vegweb
- Exchange family history with distant cousins at FamilySearch
- Review résumé-writing tips and post your résumé at Monster
- Check out colleges, universities, graduate schools, and financial aid choices at Peterson's
- Enjoy movie reviews at Rotten Tomatoes
- Discover the beauty of Native American art by touring online exhibits at the National Museum of the American Indian

FOOD AND COOKING   Just as news media publish related websites, food and cooking print and broadcast media also publish websites to promote their magazines and television shows, and famous chefs publish websites to promote their restaurants and cookbooks. Websites such as Emerils (Emeril Lagasse, world-famous chef and restaurateur), Epicurious (*Gourmet* and *Bon Appétit* magazines), and Vegetarian Times (*Vegetarian Times* magazine) (Figure 5-63) tempt you with recipes, easy-to-follow cooking tips, products to purchase at online stores, and information about associated restaurants.

If you love to cook and want to try something different, you can find a wide variety of food and cooking websites that offer recipes and cooking tips from around the world.

For example, you can learn how to make a range of Indian dishes with recipes at the Sify Food website, or learn to cook specialty dishes at chef Jamie Oliver's website. Many blogs are dedicated to exploring and cooking different types of food. You can find blogs that include general recipes, or blogs specific to barbecue, salads, soups, Southern cuisine, and more.

Figure 5-63 Food-related websites provide recipes, ingredient lists, reviews, and more.

MUSEUMS Perhaps you enjoy touring museums and viewing natural science exhibits, paintings, sculpture, or ancient artifacts from around the world. With Internet access, many of the world's museum exhibits — great and small — are as close as your computer screen. At museum websites, such as that of The Metropolitan Museum of Art in New York (Figure 5-64 on the following page), you can learn about current exhibits, operating hours, and membership opportunities. You also can view portions of ongoing special exhibits at many museum websites. Many museum websites offer interactive games or apps that engage the visitor in a topic or exhibit currently on display. Examples of online museum exhibits include the following:

- Archaeological and anthropological exhibits at the American Museum of Natural History in New York
- An animated tour of treasures from the world's greatest libraries at the National Library of Australia
- An exhibit of American colonial coins at the Colonial Williamsburg Museum
- Illustrations of African American life in Philadelphia from colonial days to the middle of the nineteenth century at the African American Museum in Philadelphia

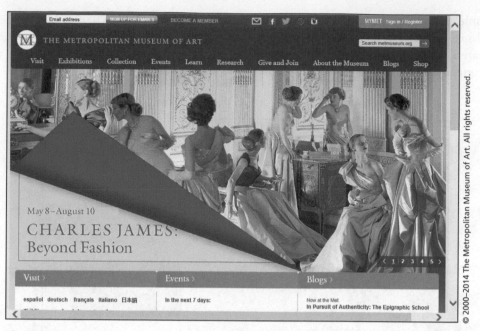

Figure 5-64 Museum websites provide information about exhibits, hours, and memberships.

GENEALOGY To learn more about your family's history, you can use the Internet to find U.S. census data, federal land grant information, state and county court records, death and cemetery records, marriage records, immigrant ship manifests, diary transcripts, historical and genealogical society records, and other genealogical information online. Similar information from other countries around the world is available online as well.

For a subscription fee, commercial websites such as Ancestry (Figure 5-65) provide you with access to a variety of databases. Data recorded in these databases includes the U.S. and U.K. censuses, U.S. county and U.K. parish records, the U.S. Social Security Death Index, and family tree submissions by other subscribers. Rootsweb is a free

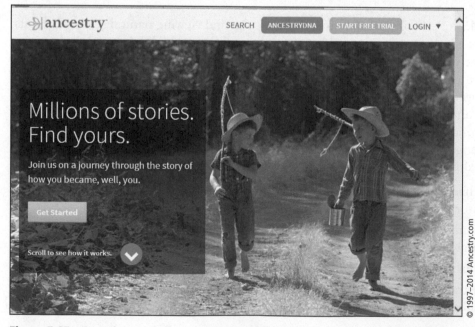

Figure 5-65 Genealogy websites connect you with information about your family's history.

genealogy website that focuses on surname searches and general information on how to research family history. Hobbyist-supported websites, such as Cyndi's List of Genealogy Sites on the Internet, publish free directories of online genealogical information from around the world. Many government archives, such as Canadian Genealogy and Family History on the Library and Archives Canada website, Gov.uk, the National Archives of Australia, and the U.S. National Archives, publish websites offering a wealth of tips on how to gather genealogy information, including how to order copies of archived military pension, naturalization, and immigration documents.

SENIORS The web offers specific resources related to health and aging issues. A number of websites, such as the AARP website (Figure 5-66) and SeniorNet, cater exclusively to the interests of older adults. Senior-oriented websites offer a variety of content, including articles on aging, continuing education courses, retirement planners, and updates on legislation that affects seniors. Government websites, such as the USA.gov Senior Citizens' Resources website, the Public Health Agency of Canada Seniors Health website, and the Australian Seniors.gov.au website, offer information about health and aging and about government programs designed for seniors.

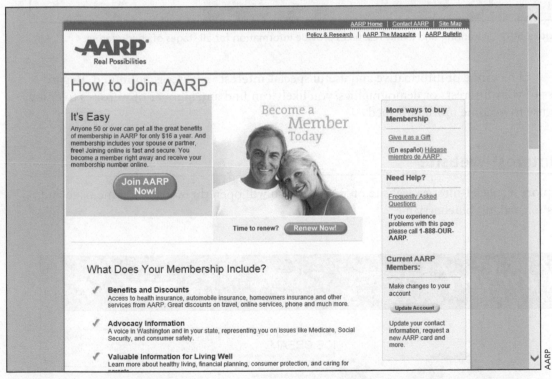

Figure 5-66 Senior-oriented websites include articles on aging, retirement planners, and more.

PARENTS AND FAMILIES Websites exist for parents and prospective parents to find information for every step of the child-rearing process: pregnancy and adoption, planning a baby shower or choosing a name, finding a pediatrician, and locating local events such as concerts and playgroups. Totspot, babble, and BabyCenter (Figure 5-67) are just a few of the many options available for new or seasoned parents and families to find, comment, and share advice and tips on raising a child.

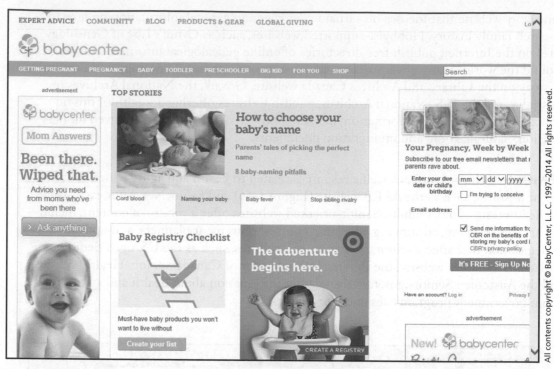

Figure 5-67   Parenting and family resources provide information for all stages of child-rearing.

The range of informative and useful special-interest websites is unlimited. Regardless of your interests or demographics, you likely can find any number of websites to enjoy or use to become more informed.

To Explore a Special-Interest Website

The following steps explore a special-interest website on cooking. You will open the website's home page and find a recipe and cooking tips for making blueberry pie.

1

- Start your browser and enter **gourmet.com** in the Address bar.

- Enter **blueberry pie** in the Search box (Figure 5-68).

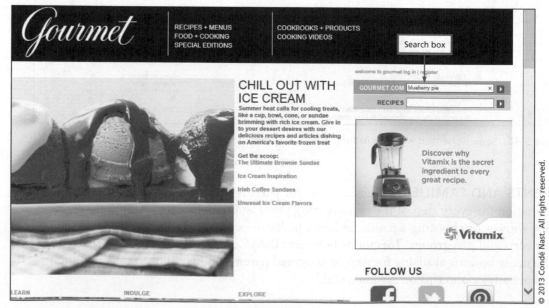

Figure 5-68

2

- Press the ENTER key or tap or click the Search button to open the search results (Figure 5-69).

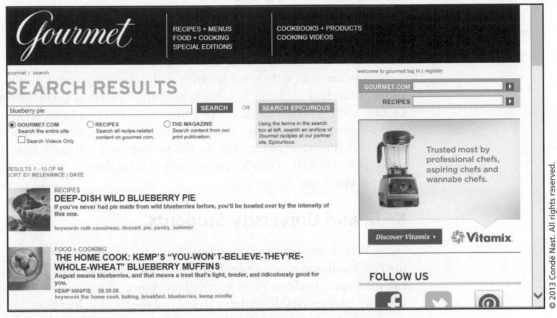

Figure 5-69

3

- Tap or click any link to view the recipe.

- Scroll the webpage to view its content (Figure 5-70).

4

- Close the browser and all open tabs, if prompted.

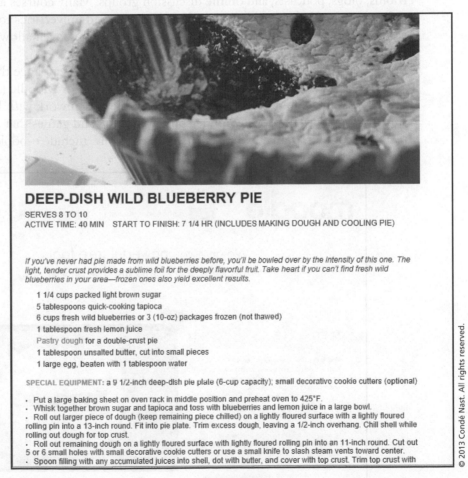

DEEP-DISH WILD BLUEBERRY PIE

SERVES 8 TO 10
ACTIVE TIME: 40 MIN   START TO FINISH: 7 1/4 HR (INCLUDES MAKING DOUGH AND COOLING PIE)

If you've never had pie made from wild blueberries before, you'll be bowled over by the intensity of this one. The light, tender crust provides a sublime foil for the deeply flavorful fruit. Take heart if you can't find fresh wild blueberries in your area—frozen ones also yield excellent results.

    1 1/4 cups packed light brown sugar
    5 tablespoons quick-cooking tapioca
    6 cups fresh wild blueberries or 3 (10-oz) packages frozen (not thawed)
    1 tablespoon fresh lemon juice
    Pastry dough for a double-crust pie
    1 tablespoon unsalted butter, cut into small pieces
    1 large egg, beaten with 1 tablespoon water

SPECIAL EQUIPMENT: a 9 1/2-inch deep-dish pie plate (6-cup capacity); small decorative cookie cutters (optional)

- Put a large baking sheet on oven rack in middle position and preheat oven to 425°F.
- Whisk together brown sugar and tapioca and toss with blueberries and lemon juice in a large bowl.
- Roll out larger piece of dough (keep remaining piece chilled) on a lightly floured surface with a lightly floured rolling pin into a 13-inch round. Fit into pie plate. Trim excess dough, leaving a 1/2-inch overhang. Chill shell while rolling out dough for top crust.
- Roll out remaining dough on a lightly floured surface with lightly floured rolling pin into an 11-inch round. Cut out 5 or 6 small holes with small decorative cookie cutters or use a small knife to slash steam vents toward center.
- Spoon filling with any accumulated juices into shell, dot with butter, and cover with top crust. Trim top crust with

Figure 5-70

Education Tools

Web-based learning, also called **online learning** or **distance learning**, involves the delivery of educational material over the Internet to users, who view and use the material using a web browser or web or mobile app.

You can find web-based learning and training opportunities in every educational venue, from K–12 schools to adult continuing education at colleges and universities. Online adult professional development courses and employee training courses abound. Additionally, you can enjoy noncredit online courses on almost any topic for your personal enrichment or just for fun. In this section, you will learn how schools, colleges, and universities, as well as employers wishing to train their employees, teach using the Internet and web-based learning.

K–12 and University Students

Web-based learning programs open up a broad vista of educational opportunities for K–12 and university students. Rural schools with limited enrollment and resources can offer their students more curriculum choices through web-based learning. Web-based learning courses enable students to control the timing, location, and learning pace of the course. Today, hundreds of colleges and universities offer online courses in which students interact with their instructors and other students through social media, text, email, chat rooms, blogs, podcasts, and online discussion groups. Many courses and schools offer online testing. Web-based learning allows colleges and universities to offer working adults courses that are flexible enough to fit into their busy lives, even allowing them to complete degree programs without setting foot on campus.

The same tools used to teach online classes also can enhance the regular curriculum at all levels of education. Companies such as Blackboard or Moodle (Figure 5-71) offer course management systems. Publishing companies often work with Blackboard and other similar companies to provide online content, testing, and games that correspond with textbook content. Many textbooks, including this one, include e-book options that enable

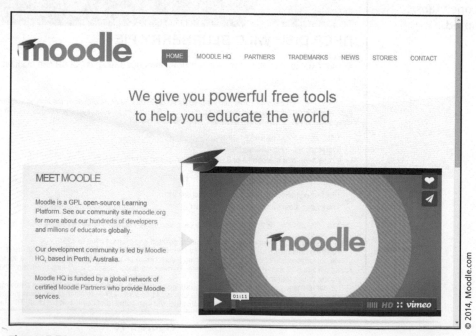

Figure 5-71 Online course management systems are used to manage virtual classes and enhance learning.

you to read the textbook through an e-reader or browser. Some schools offer students accounts at websites to practice math or other skills at home, such as IXL or Typing Pal. Teachers can track students' progress and activity at these websites, and can assign activities as homework.

Homeschoolers can access a variety of free and subscription-based online learning platforms on any subject, broadening their learning experience and enabling them to work at their own pace. Homeschool platforms such as K^{12} (Figure 5-72) also can send progress reports to the student's local school district to ensure the student is staying on pace with his or her grade level.

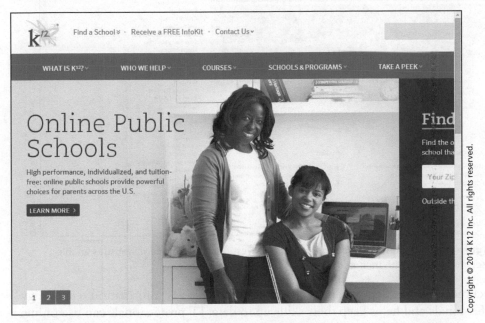

Figure 5-72   Free and subscription-based learning platforms help homeschoolers track and expand their education.

Online Employee Training and Professional Development

Diverse business, nonprofit, and government organizations use web-based learning to deliver employee training programs. Internet tools such as online video conferencing, self-paced training programs, apps, and prerecorded video and audio lectures can deliver training opportunities. Using online training can save organizations millions of training dollars each year by reducing travel costs, keeping their employees on the job, reducing the need for trainers and centralized training facilities, and promoting customer service. For example, General Motors has used web-based learning to introduce new vehicle models to auto dealership salespeople, and to train dealership mechanics on how to repair them. By delivering new vehicle training online, General Motors avoided the expenses involved in sending thousands of sales and service trainers to auto dealerships around the country each new model year. Additionally, General Motors provides web-based driver training for its large commercial van customers. The U.S. Army offers soldiers the chance to enroll in online courses and degree programs from colleges and universities around the country through the Army's GoArmyEd web-based learning program. The GoArmyEd program promotes enlistment among potential recruits and keeps enlistees in the service longer — thus reducing recruitment and turnover costs.

Teachers, accountants, doctors, nurses, and other professionals also go online to meet their professions' continuing education requirements. For example, e-businesses such as Checkpoint Learning offer online continuing professional education (CPE) courses for accounting and financial professionals, who must take several courses each year to keep their licenses updated. Doctors and other health professionals can log on to the Medscape CME page (Figure 5-73) and take online courses to complete their continuing medical education requirements.

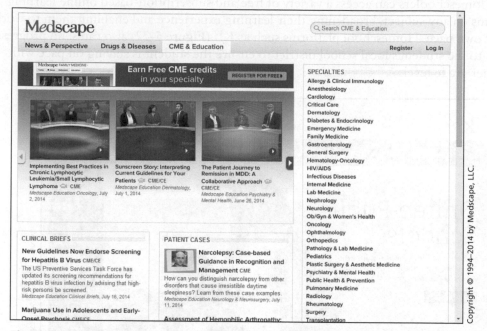

Figure 5-73 Online employee training and professional development websites enable users to keep up with their education.

Technical certification enhances career opportunities for information technology (IT) professionals and helps keep their skills up to date. IT professionals can use online courses provided by colleges, universities, and training companies, such as SkillSoft and New Horizons (Figure 5-74), to prepare for CompTIA A+ and Network+ certification, the Microsoft Certified Systems Engineer (MCSE) certification, the Cisco Certified Network Associate (CCNA) certification, and other technical certification examinations.

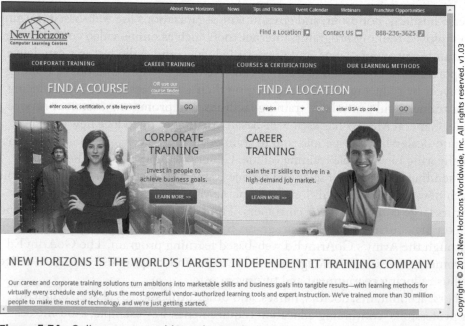

Figure 5-74 Online courses enable professionals to participate in training and obtain new certifications.

Adult Continuing Education Websites

Participating in online courses provides learning for personal growth, lifestyle enrichment, and professional advancement opportunities. Many colleges and universities, such as the University of California, Berkeley, offer a variety of credit and noncredit courses online. Fees for online courses at e-business websites such as these can range from free for short, non-interactive courses to around $100 for interactive, instructor-led courses. Fees for college- and university-sponsored online continuing adult education courses vary by the length of the course and whether you earn college credit. MIT Open Courseware (Figure 5-75) and EdX are examples of **massive open online courses (MOOCs).** A MOOC is a college- or graduate-level course created by an instructor or school, and offered for free online. MOOCs do not count for educational credit.

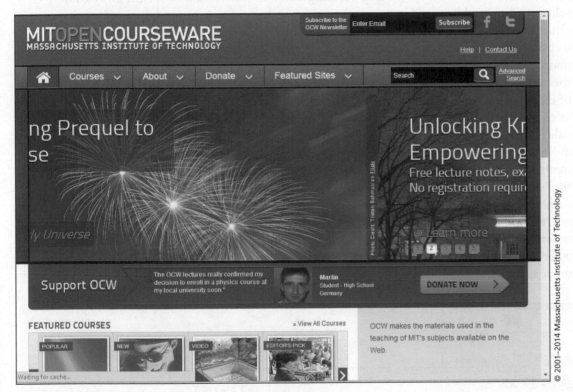

Figure 5-75 MOOCs offer free online learning opportunities.

Shopping Websites

You can purchase, sell, auction, and bid on almost any type of item or service online. Online stores do not have to worry about renting storefronts, creating displays, or deciding what hours to run their business. Broadband Internet access allows consumers to view feature-rich web stores, and permits quick processing of online inquiries and transactions. Online store websites keep shoppers' needs in mind and are easy to use. Shoppers can take advantage of the ability to compare products and prices online without making trips to one or more brick-and-mortar stores.

According to Statista, the B2C mobile retail market recently was measured at $1,251.4 billion. Amazon.com alone accounted for $67 billion of these sales.

The Online Consumer Marketspace

The term **marketspace** distinguishes the virtual location where e-business is conducted — such as an online bookstore — from the conventional physical marketplaces in which business takes place — such as the bookstore in the local mall. As you learned in Chapter 3, if you want to buy consumer electronics, such as an MP3 player or a digital camera, you can use a shopping bot or shopping aggregator to compare features and prices at multiple online retailers, avoiding traffic hassles and tedious checkout lines at brick-and-mortar stores. Additionally, online retailers may offer discounted prices, free shipping, and other incentives that could make your consumer electronics purchase a real bargain.

Some consumers shop online to compare product features and prices, and then buy the products at brick-and-mortar locations. Using the Internet and the web to gather product information before making a buying decision leads to a power shift away from sellers and toward buyers. One example is the purchase of new or used cars and trucks. Online shoppers in the market for a new or used vehicle can use third-party automotive websites, such as Edmunds.com, autobytel, Kelley Blue Book, and CARFAX, to get information on factory and dealer pricing, trade-in values, financing deals, auto ownership histories, and other factors that go into buying a new or used vehicle. Armed with this kind of information, vehicle buyers then are better able to negotiate with sellers at the point of sale — either online or at a dealership. Online auction websites attract millions of individuals with something to sell or a desire to buy. Computer equipment, hand-crafted jewelry, quilts, collectible items, autos, books, and numerous other items can be found on websites that specialize in overstocked items, such as Overstock.com (Figure 5-76), on online auction websites, such as uBid and eBay (Figure 5-76), or on consumer-to-consumer websites such as Etsy (Figure 5-76). In addition to major auction websites, some companies such as Dell Auction conduct online auctions of refurbished, marked-down, and closeout computer equipment at their own websites. Other companies provide B2B auction websites where business buyers and sellers can use the online auction model to buy and sell equipment and other products.

Figure 5-76   Online discount, auction, and C2C websites are popular ways to shop online.

At most online auction websites, the general processes for selling and buying items are similar. First, you register at the website as a seller, a buyer, or both. As a seller, you post the items you want to sell and indicate the specific time period during which each item is available for purchase. Sellers can set a **reserve price**, which is the lowest price at which a seller will or must sell an item. As a buyer, you search the website for an item you want to buy. When you find the item, you indicate how much you are willing to pay for it, an amount called a **bid**. At the end of the specified time frame, the item is sold to the highest bidder. Finally, the seller and buyer arrange for payment and shipping.

The main advantages of buying items at an online auction include access to a variety of items, some of which may be hard to find elsewhere, and the opportunity to get products at lower prices. Unfortunately, a darker side to online auctions also exists, such as sellers who collect payment but either do not send the item, or who deliver a used or damaged item. Most reputable auction websites provide tips for their prospective sellers and buyers on how to reduce the risk of auction fraud. The OnGuard Online.gov website also provides helpful tips on reducing this risk.

Online Gaming Websites

While early online gamers were likely to be males ages 15 through 30 involved in role-playing games, today, online gaming appeals to a much wider group of participants, including young women and older adults of both genders. You can play card games, arcade games, and word games, or you can log on to an online game room and join a friend — from across town or across the world — in playing a board or tile game. You can test your gaming skills by competing with other players in online game tournaments, or you can experience an exciting alternative universe by participating in a strategy or role-playing game. Devices such as the Xbox or Playstation enable users to play using their Internet-connected console, a television, a game, and controller(s), with connections or with random users. Gaming apps are available for download to your mobile device. Although online gaming can be fun, it also can be quite addictive.

Many online games are free. For example, some gaming websites offer free word or trivia games as an incentive for viewers to return to their websites frequently, or include advertisements for their products or sell ads to other companies to generate revenue. Gaming portals, such as Yahoo! Games and MSN Games, offer free online and downloadable games for players who register at their websites. A number of websites directed toward children, such as PBS Kids and webkinz, offer online games. Some online games are subscription based; gamers buy the software and install it on their computers and then pay a subscription fee for premium features or to play online with other players. Popular strategy or role-playing games, often called **massively multiplayer online games (MMOGs)**, in which thousands of players from around the world assume personas and play either on a turn-by-turn basis or in real time, are subscription-based games. A **virtual world**, such as Second Life, in which players assume a persona that lives in an alternate virtual existence, is another type of role-playing game.

Online gaming is not without its risks. Many gaming web or mobile apps contain malware, which exposes your computer or device to viruses, hacking, and more. Because virtual worlds offer anonymity, unscrupulous users can create false personas to create and exploit relationships with other users. Many games offer social networking features, which can access your contacts list or other information, and post on your behalf when you are playing or reach an achievement. Many social networking users find these social networking posts obtrusive and annoying.

Online Gambling

Online gaming should be about fun — enjoying the challenge of the game and interacting with other players in multiplayer games. When it comes to online gambling, however, the stakes and consequences can be much higher than simply losing a game to a friend. As losses mount, online gambling can have a detrimental effect on the personal lives of gamblers.

Regardless of your personal opinions about gambling, gambling websites are prevalent on the web. Online gambling offerings include casino games, such as poker or bingo, betting on horses or sports, and participating in lotteries.

No U.S. federal law prohibits online gambling, although in 2006, the U.S. Congress passed legislation that made it illegal for financial institutions, such as banks or credit card companies, to transfer money to online gambling websites. Bitcoin is one example of an online currency that gamers use to avoid this law and enable them to participate in online gambling.

New Jersey became the first state to legalize certain forms of online gambling. New Jersey's law requires the gamer to be a current resident, or be physically present in the state. State-authorized gaming websites use GPS to track a user's whereabouts, and will kick off a user if they do not meet the requirements. As of this writing, eight other states are pursuing legislation to legalize aspects of online gambling.

Many Internet analysts and social scientists are concerned about the addictive quality of online gambling and its detrimental effect on a user's health and finances. Gambling on the web is convenient, and is accessible to any user, including underage minors, who have a credit card or use a third-party payment service. Because it cannot be regulated like other forms of legal gambling, it is more open to fraud and other crimes, such as money laundering. Websites such as Google and Yahoo! prohibit online gambling ads.

Before you begin gambling online, you should consider the ethical, social, and financial ramifications for you and your family. For more information on gambling issues, use a search engine to search for *online gambling risks*.

Download and File-Sharing Websites

Downloading paid content, such as music files, software, stock photos, and so forth, is one of the most popular Internet activities. For example, music download websites, such as Apple iTunes and Rhapsody (Figure 5-77), typically offer either subscription-based services or pay-per-song services, while software vendors offer all types of software downloads for which you pay a licensing fee. In addition to paid content websites, the Internet also has numerous websites where you can search for and download freeware or shareware programs, including games or utilities.

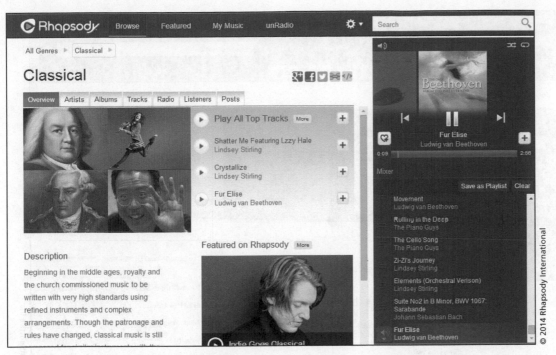

Figure 5-77 Music download websites offer subscription-based or pay-per-song services.

Transferring files between Internet-connected computers is another widely used and convenient activity. In Chapter 4, you learned how to transfer a file by attaching it to an email message. Two other ways to transfer files over the Internet are by using FTP (File Transfer Protocol) or by using a peer-to-peer (P2P) file-sharing network. In this section, you will learn about freeware and shareware download websites, the basics of using FTP to download and upload files, and how P2P file-sharing networks are used.

Commercial file downloading uses HTTP (Hypertext Transfer Protocol), FTP (File Transfer Protocol), or other technologies specifically developed for file transmission over a network.

Download Websites

Freeware is software that the author allows you to download and use without charge. Although free, you still must follow copyright laws and restrictions, meaning you can use it only in the ways permitted by the author, manufacturer, or copyright owner. For example, you cannot distribute it to someone else unless given permission to do so. **Shareware** is software that you can download and try out, but you are expected to pay for the software if you decide to use it on a permanent basis. You can search websites, such as tucows, and CNET Download.com (Figure 5-78), for freeware or shareware screen savers, games, utilities, file compression programs, and more.

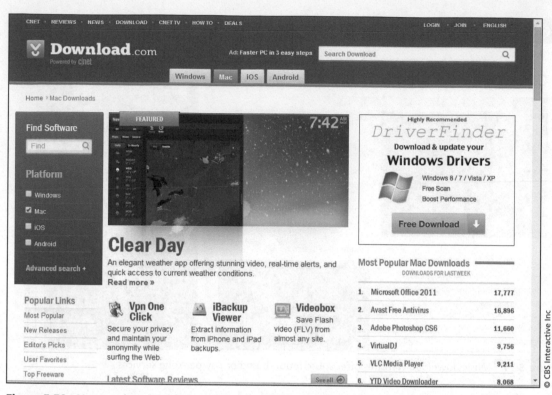

Figure 5-78 You can download freeware and shareware from websites.

File Transfer Protocol (FTP)

As you learned in Chapter 1, FTP is an Internet standard that allows you to download or upload files to and from other computers connected to the Internet. You can use FTP to view a directory of files located on a remote computer, called an **FTP website**, and then open or download a file. You also can upload a file to an FTP website.

To access an FTP website, you log on with a username and a password. Public FTP websites, such as those provided by government agencies, some colleges and universities, and other organizations, are called **anonymous FTP websites** because anyone can log on to these websites using "anonymous" as their username. As a courtesy to the website administrator, anonymous users often enter their email addresses at the password prompt, although a password is not required for a public FTP website. Private FTP websites, such as those operated by a private company for its employees' use, restrict access to authorized users, who must enter a unique username and a unique password.

You can download or upload files using FTP by typing instructions using an FTP client program, using your web browser, or using your operating system's file management program, such as Windows Explorer for Windows 8. Some browsers offer compatible FTP client software, such as Mozilla's FileZilla.

An **FTP client**, such as FileZilla (Figure 5-79), is a program that offers an easy-to-use graphical user interface containing menu commands and toolbar shortcuts. FTP clients generally use an interface similar to other file management programs with which you already may be familiar, such as Windows Explorer. To upload or download files, you simply:

1. Start the FTP client. Select or enter the information for the FTP website to which you want to connect.

2. Enter your username and password, and connect to the website.

3. Specify the source location (where the file is stored) and the destination location (where the file is to be downloaded or uploaded).

4. Select a file or files.

5. Tap or click a menu command or toolbar button to begin the download or upload process.

Figure 5-79   FTP clients and tools enable you to transfer and share files.

The FTP client automatically issues the necessary FTP commands to download or upload the selected file(s). To navigate to an FTP website using your web browser, you type the FTP website's URL in the Address box in the same way in which you type a website's URL. FTP websites' URLs start with ftp://, to represent the File Transfer Protocol (FTP), instead of the http:// used for websites' URLs. An FTP website can require a user to enter a username and password information to access an FTP folder or download or upload content.

P2P File-Sharing Networks

Another way to share or transfer files is over a peer-to-peer (P2P) file-sharing network. A **peer-to-peer (P2P) file-sharing network** allows files to be transferred between individual personal computers located on the same local area network (LAN) or between individual personal computers connected to the Internet. P2P file-sharing networks exploded in popularity as a means for individuals to share music, video, and other files stored on their personal computers. Unfortunately, many users of these P2P file-sharing networks might be sharing material — music, movies, and software — that is protected

What is BitTorrent?
BitTorrent is the most commonly used protocol for P2P public or private sharing of large website files, and accounts for a high percentage of Internet traffic, although its exact usage is difficult to predict.

by U.S. copyright law. In fact, the music and movie industries, through the Recording Industry Association of America (RIAA) and the Motion Picture Association of America (MPAA), are working to stop the piracy of copyrighted material over P2P file-sharing networks.

Many legitimate P2P uses exist. Dropbox is a popular filesharing tool used by academics and professionals to share work and other files. Sharing personal files publicly or privately is an acceptable use of P2P file sharing. P2P file sharing of copyrighted material accounts for job loss and revenue, and opens you to potential litigation.

@ISSUE
Responsible Internet Access

Many workers assume that no one gets hurt if they spend time on the Internet for personal reasons while at work, and some companies allow moderate personal use of company computers. However, **cyberslacking**, or the excessive use of the Internet and the web for personal use at work, can result in lost worker productivity and reduced IT network capacity. For example, downloading music and video files eats away at a company's expensive Internet access bandwidth, slowing down legitimate business activities. Sending and receiving personal email and downloading files can expose a company's network to viruses and other security breaches. Viewing pornography websites or hate websites at work creates a hostile work environment and increases a company's liability for expensive and embarrassing lawsuits.

Increasingly, companies are protecting themselves from cyberslacking in several ways, including:

- Formulating clear Internet use policies
- Educating employees about Internet use policies, and then following through with appropriate action when an employee violates those policies
- Controlling which employees have Internet access

- Installing monitoring software that provides information on individual employee's Internet activities
- Installing filtering software that blocks access to nonbusiness websites and filters email

What should you do to access the Internet at work responsibly? Carefully read and understand your company's Internet access policies and follow them. When in doubt, ask your supervisor for clarification on the policies. Resist the urge to shop, chat, play online games, send personal email, visit social media websites, or send instant messages to friends during work hours, unless your company permits these kinds of activities. Remember that downloading copyrighted music, videos, and software — either at work or at home — without paying for the downloaded material is piracy and a violation of U.S. copyright law.

Read your company's policy on using personal devices during work hours to do any personal, entertainment, or other nonwork activities. Companies find it difficult to track employee's usage of privately owned devices, but keep in mind that misuse of or wasting company time is equivalent to stealing, and can lead to discipline or termination of employment.

Music and video file sharing, while popular, are not the only uses of P2P networks. Commercial applications of P2P file-sharing networks include sharing product information among several thousand employees and researchers, and distributing training materials to employees. Many Internet analysts expect more organizations to use P2P technologies in the future to distribute network processes to individual users.

Chapter Review

Portals for every interest and need are available online, including general consumer portals, personal or horizontal portals, hyperlocal portals, vertical portals that focus on more narrow interests, and corporate portals.

Internet users go online to get news, weather, sports, and traffic information from news-oriented websites, and/or download corresponding apps, because these websites share six primary characteristics: availability, accuracy, immediacy, interactivity, customizability, and connectivity. Streaming media is audio and video transmitted continuously from a web server to your browser.

Online dictionaries, encyclopedias, reference desks, and trip planners provide you with convenient, immediate access to information on specific topics, fast facts, word definitions, and driving directions. Internet users, including seniors and parents, go online to find health, diet, and fitness information; enjoy entertainment information; practice their hobbies; look for jobs; make new friends; trace their family tree; and many other activities.

Managing your personal finances with online tools, such as online banking and bill payment, is fast, easy, and convenient. Web-based financial calculators help you determine how much you can afford to spend and estimate a monthly mortgage or auto payment.

Millions of people around the world are taking advantage of web-based learning opportunities made possible by the Internet and the web. K–12 schools and universities, homeschoolers, employers, and professionals are embracing web-based learning.

Consumers shop online because of the availability of Internet access, the design of online stores, trust in the online purchasing process, and increasing satisfaction with their shopping results. You can play card games, board games, casino games, word games, trivia games, arcade games, and strategy or role-playing games online — either alone, with a friend, or with thousands of other players.

Downloading paid content, such as music files, is a popular Internet activity. You also can download software from vendors' websites, and several popular websites offer freeware and shareware software downloads. You can use FTP to download and upload files. Another way to transfer files is over a P2P file-sharing network, where files can be transferred from one computer to another over a local area network (LAN) or the Internet. When downloading or sharing files online, be aware of copyright laws and only share files to which you own the rights.

TERMS TO KNOW

After reading this chapter, you should know each of these Key Terms.

anonymous FTP website (266)
B2B exchange (211)
bid (263)
bill payment service (247)
bill presentment (247)
brick-and-click business (245)
brick-and-mortar business (245)
corporate portal (217)
cyberslacking (268)
distance learning (258)
e-bill (247)
enterprise information portal (EIPs) (217)
freeware (265)
FTP client (266)
FTP website (266)
general consumer portal (210)
horizontal portal (210)
hyperlocal portal (211)
industry portal (211)
marketspace (262)

massive open online course (MOOC) (261)
massively multiplayer online game (MMOG) (263)
online learning (258)
online reference desk (235)
peer-to-peer (P2P) file-sharing network (267)
personal portal (210)
podcast (219)
reserve price (263)
shareware (265)
Smart TV (224)
sticky website (220)
streaming media (224)
user-generated research tool (236)
vertical portal (211)
virtual world (263)
vortal (211)
web-based learning (258)
wildcard search (230)

TEST YOUR KNOWLEDGE

Complete the Test Your Knowledge exercises to solidify what you have learned in the chapter.

True or False

Mark T for True and F for False. (Answers are found on page numbers in parentheses.)

____ 1. A website that viewers visit often and browse for longer periods of time is called a sticky website. (220)

____ 2. Many news-oriented websites provide the ability to customize content, which means they can display information tailored to the user's locality and interests. (220)

____ 3. A hyperlocal portal provides general information on global news, entertainment, and other topics. (211)

____ 4. All health information on the web has been evaluated and certified as accurate by health care professionals. (242)

____ 5. A MOOC is a type of online group game. (261)

____ 6. A podcast is digital audio or video available to listen to remotely. (219)

____ 7. Yelp! is an example of a P2P network. (226)

____ 8. A brick-and-mortar location is one that offers both an online store and a physical location, such as in a mall. (245)

____ 9. The term, marketspace, is used to distinguish the virtual location in which e-business is conducted from the conventional physical marketplaces in which business takes place. (262)

____10. Software you can download and use for free on a permanent basis is called shareware. (265)

Multiple Choice

Select the best answer. (Answers are found on page numbers in parentheses.)

1. File-sharing networks that allow users to transfer files between individual personal computers located on the same LAN or between Internet-connected individual computers are called _____ networks. (267)

   a. FTP

   b. P2P

   c. C2C

   d. NPR

2. A(n) _____ can provide employee or client access, and can be used to manage a company's human resources or accounting activities. (217)

   a. EIP

   b. FTP client

   c. hyperlocal portal

   d. B2C website

3. Which of the following wildcard searches returns search results related to the word, snow? (230)

   a. *snow

   b. :snow

   c. ?snow

   d. snow*

4. Which of the following can you do using browser shortcuts? (233)

   a. define a term

   b. solve mathematical equations

   c. search for an exact phrase

   d. All of the above.

5. FTP stands for _____. (266)

   a. Full Torrent Protocol

   b. Free Transfer Portal

   c. File Transfer Protocol

   d. Forward Telephone Packet

6. A reserve price is often used with _____. (263)

   a. consumer-to-consumer sales

   b. discount shopping

   c. brick-and-click websites

   d. online auction websites

7. _____ is an example of a company that provides online educational tools for homeschoolers. (256)

   a. eSchool

   b. Moodle

   c. K^{12}

   d. iTools

8. When evaluating a health care website, if it includes the _____ symbol, it is likely a credible source for general health information. (242)

   a. CAPHIS

   b. HONcode

   c. URAC

   d. either b or c

9. A public FTP website also is called a(n) _____. (266)

   a. anonymous FTP website

   b. open FTP website

   c. nameless FTP website

   d. unknown FTP website

10. Audio and video content transmitted continuously from a web server to a web browser is called _____ media. (224)

    a. downloaded

    b. virtual

    c. freeware

    d. streaming

TRENDS

Investigate current Internet developments with the Trends exercises.

Write a brief essay about each of the following trends, using the web as your research tool. For each trend, identify at least one webpage URL used as a research source. Be prepared to discuss your findings in class.

1 | Massive Open Online Courses

Visit the MIT OpenCourseWare website. Look for a course you might want to take. What requirements or materials must you have to take the course? Investigate the registration process, but do not sign up for the course. Is it easy to register? What information is required? Use a search engine to search for *MOOCs*. List industries or users who might take advantage of a MOOC, and explain why. Describe the benefits of using a MOOC. Submit your findings in the format requested by your instructor.

2 | User-Generated Content Tools

Use Yelp! or another user-generated content tool to find reviews of a local restaurant. Are the reviews positive? If not, did the company respond to any negative reviews? How? Investigate, but do not create a new account, the process for registering to submit a review or comment. Use a search engine to search for *negative online reviews* to find examples of cases where a venue took action, legal or otherwise, against a user who submitted a negative review. What was the outcome? Should venues, such as restaurants, be able to remove negative reviews? Why or why not? Submit your findings in the format requested by your instructor.

Challenge your perspective of Internet technology with the @Issue exercises.

Write a brief essay in response to the following issues, using the web as your research tool. For each issue, identify at least one URL used as a research source. Be prepared to discuss your findings in class.

1 | Evaluating the Credibility of Online Health Information

Use a search engine to search for *online health information credibility*. Find articles or blog posts that discuss issues regarding misleading or incorrect health information online. Visit a credible online health website, such as WebMD. Search the website for disclaimers and other language pertaining to the sources of information, what the information is to be used for, and any other information that can be used to guide the user in evaluating the information. Have you gone online to research health information? Why? What were your findings? Submit your findings in the format requested by your instructor.

2 | Online Gambling

Use a search engine to search for *online gambling laws*. What current or pending legislation in your state or a nearby state exists to address the legality of online gambling? Do the laws seem fair? If possible, find an article or webpage opposing the legislation. What are the concerns listed? Use a search engine to search for *online gambling risks and statistics*. Name two risks not already mentioned in the chapter that are associated with online gambling. List three statistics of online gambling's negative effects. Would you participate in legal online gambling? Why or why not?

Submit your findings in the format requested by your instructor.

Use the web to obtain more information about the skills taught in the chapter with the Hands On exercises.

1 | Customizing a Personal Portal

1. Start your browser, if necessary and visit the yahoo.com portal webpage.

2. Tap or click the My Yahoo link.

3. Tap or click the 'Customize your page' button to open the customization options.

Note: If you do not have a Yahoo! account, you will be asked to create one.

4. Select options to change the content, appearance, location, and other options for your personal My Yahoo! webpage.

5. If requested by your instructor, take a screenshot of your customized webpage.

6. Sign out from your My Yahoo! account when you are finished.

2 | Using Online Resources to Research a Report Topic

1. Start your browser, if necessary, and visit an online encyclopedia such as encyclopedia.com.

2. Use the encyclopedia to answer the following questions.

   a. Where is Mali located? Who are its geographical neighbors? Where can you find a map of Mali and its geographical neighbors? What are its major cities and towns?

   b. List three major events in Mali's history.

c. What is the current population of Mali?

d. What is the basis of Mali's economy?

3. Use the encyclopedia's resources to cite your online sources.

4. Submit your findings in the format requested by your instructor.

TEAM APPROACH

Work collaboratively to reinforce the concepts in the chapter with the Team Approach exercises.

1 | Exploring Special-Interest Websites

1. Work with a team of three to four classmates to search for and evaluate special-interest websites and apps.

2. Decide on a special-interest topic or demographic.

3. Use a search engine to search for websites related to the special-interest area.

3. Assign one website or app to each teammate to research. Each team member should do the following:

   a. Evaluate the credibility of the information, including its contributors and any certifications, reviews, or endorsements.

   b. Does the website have an associated mobile app? Download and explore the app, if possible, or read reviews to determine the features and ease-of-use of the app.

   c. Does the website or app give the option to connect using a social network to share user information? What might the risks be with doing so?

   d. Find an article or post on the website on an agreed-upon topic.

4. As a team, compare your findings. Which website would you recommend? Why? Compare the different articles to determine which has the most helpful or interesting information.

5. Submit your findings in the format requested by your instructor.

2 | P2P File Sharing

1. Work with a team of three to four classmates to research legitimate uses of P2P file sharing.

2. As a team do the following:

   a. Find three legal and acceptable uses for P2P file sharing. Why are these legal?

   b. List at least three P2P file-sharing platforms.

   c. Research BitTorrent. Define its purpose and describe its uses.

   d. Identify one case where someone was prosecuted for illegal P2P file sharing.

3. Submit your findings in the format requested by your instructor.

6 | Understanding Internet Technologies and Security

© s-cyther5/Shutterstock.com

Foursquare © 2014

© Cengage Learning®

Microsoft

Introduction

The Internet and the web include the networking technologies that make it possible to use Internet-based services. In Chapters 1 and 2, you learned about circuit switching, packet switching, the TCP and IP protocols, the Domain Name System (DNS), IP addresses, URLs, and other fundamental networking and Internet technologies. In this chapter, you will learn about local, metropolitan, and wide area networks and the devices that connect them; the structure of IP addresses; how the DNS server hierarchy resolves domain names to IP addresses; and how network service providers facilitate the exchange of data across the Internet backbones. You also will learn about wireless web location-based services, how the Internet communicates with traditional telephony and conferencing technologies, and about network security threats and security technologies.

Objectives

After completing this chapter, you will be able to:

1. Discuss basic networking technologies

2. Describe the infrastructure of the Internet, including network service providers, the TCP/IP stack, IP addresses, and the Domain Name System (DNS)

3. Discuss GPS and identify wireless location-based services

4. Explain the convergence of the Internet with telephony and conferencing

5. Discuss internal and external network security threats, transactional risks, and virtual private networks

Networking Basics

To better understand the Internet, you need to begin with knowledge of basic networking technologies. As you have learned, a network connects two or more computers, printers, or other devices using wireless media or cables. A network makes it possible for users to share data, hardware such as peripheral devices, software and apps, and other network resources such as an Internet connection. Networks can be simple or complex, local or worldwide. A simple network for a small business or home office might have only two or three computers or mobile devices and a single printer, connected by cable or, more often, using wireless transmission. A large, complex network can have thousands of computers and devices in multiple worldwide locations communicating with each other using a combination of transmission media.

Local, Metropolitan, and Wide Area Networks

You can categorize modern networks by the physical area they cover: a local area, a metropolitan area, or a wide area.

LOCAL AREA NETWORKS　As discussed in Chapter 1, a local area network (LAN) is a network supporting users in a small geographical area, such as a home, an office, a single building, or several buildings, such as on a college campus. Each computer or other device on a LAN is a **node**. Nodes communicate with each other with cables or wireless media, such as radio waves. LANs typically use one of two basic structures: peer-to-peer or client/server.

In Chapter 5, you learned about peer-to-peer (P2P) file-sharing networks that allow Internet-connected users to transfer files between individual computers and devices. The term, peer-to-peer, also describes the way in which a simple LAN connects computers and devices. A **peer-to-peer LAN** consists of a small number of computers and devices (generally 10 or fewer) linked together. One or more of the computers or devices also might have a printer, a scanner, or an external storage device attached to it (Figure 6-1). To connect to the peer-to-peer LAN, each computer or device must have built-in networking capabilities or use a network interface card or other expansion tool. A **network interface card (NIC)**, sometimes called a **network card**, is an internal expansion card that enables a computer or other device to access a network. Most computers and devices come with Ethernet or other networking capabilities built in. You will learn more about Ethernet, a common network access method, later in the chapter. The computers and devices on a peer-to-peer LAN can use, at minimum, one main cable. More commonly, a peer-to-peer LAN connects the computers and devices on a common connection point on the network, using a hub. A **hub** is an inexpensive hardware device used to connect multiple nodes on the same network.

Users on a peer-to-peer LAN can access files stored on any of the networked computers and devices and use any peripheral devices connected to the networked computers or devices. For example, if your computer or device is part of a peer-to-peer LAN, you can open a file stored on another user's computer or device, save it to your hard drive, and then send the file to a printer attached to any networked device.

A peer-to-peer LAN is an attractive networking choice for a home office or for a small business or other organization with minimal networking needs because it is simple to configure and inexpensive to use. A peer-to-peer LAN is not a practical option to connect more than a few computers or devices, however. An organization thus may outgrow a peer-to-peer LAN quickly, as more computers and devices need to be added or file- and device-sharing becomes more complex. Additionally, a peer-to-peer LAN lacks robust security options.

Most large organizations use a client/server LAN. In Chapter 2, you learned about client/server computing, in which client computers and devices request resources

Q&A

How can I set permissions to protect my data from access from others on the network?

You can control access to files and printers by setting options in the operating system of the individual computers or devices connected to the peer-to-peer LAN. You can set a password for the computer or device, or only for certain folders, files or apps; you can create an administrator account that has additional access and control over the network; you also can set up accounts with parental controls that limit access to programs, apps, files, and the Internet.

wireless access point is center of wireless network

wired network

Internet

high-speed Internet connection

Figure 6-1 A small number of personal computers can be connected in a peer-to-peer LAN.

from servers. A **client/server network** consists of multiple computers and devices or workstations (clients), one or more servers, and other devices such as printers (Figure 6-2).

client

client

server

client

printer

Figure 6-2 Multiple personal computers, servers, and printers can be connected on a client/server network.

As previously mentioned, the servers enable the clients to share data, software and apps, file storage space, peripheral devices, and an Internet connection. A client/server LAN uses a **network operating system** to manage data storage, printer access, communications, Internet connections, security, and network administration. Examples of network operating systems include Microsoft® Windows® Server®, OS® X Server, Novell® NetWare®, Cisco® IOS, UNIX®, and Linux®. Figure 6-3 describes the different types of services provided by a network operating system.

Network Operating System Services

Service	Benefit
File Services	Permit the centralized storage of files on a file server, which can be accessed by any authorized user on the network. Maintain backup copies of critical files and protect against accidentally deleted files, damaged files, or files lost to natural or man-made disasters. Files stored centrally on a file server are backed up more easily than files stored on individual computers or devices.
Print Services	Enable users to share printers across a network. Replacing multiple individual printers with one or two high-speed networked printers can reduce equipment costs and increase productivity.
Mail Services	Manage the sending, receiving, routing, and storage of email messages. Email is a critical component of any organization's communications with employees, clients, and vendors. Enable email communications to flow smoothly.
Communications Services	Allow authorized users to connect to the network when out of the office. Communications services permit remote users to connect to the network.
Internet Services	Manage internal web-based services, external Internet access, and other Internet-based services such as web servers, web browsers, and email. Organizations use email to send and receive messages from clients or vendors outside the organization. Many organizations also use internal webpages to support internal business operations. External webpages are used to sell products and services and provide customer support. Internet services help manage these critical operations.
Management Services	Enable network administrators to manage the security and operation of the network by determining the level of network activity, monitoring network access and activity, detecting and solving network hardware and software problems, and distributing software to users.

© Cengage Learning®

Figure 6-3 A network operating system provides a variety of services on a client/server network.

The ability of a client/server LAN to support shared data storage, provide network maintenance tools, and promote more efficient data backups offers advantages over a peer-to-peer LAN. Client/server network operating systems also offer extensive built-in security features. Setting up and maintaining a client/server network is more difficult and more expensive than administering a peer-to-peer LAN, and requires much more technical expertise to manage. For these reasons, a client/server LAN is the best networking choice for.an organization with multiple users and the financial resources to hire technical staff or consultants to develop and maintain the LAN.

METROPOLITAN AREA NETWORKS A **metropolitan area network (MAN)** connects clients and servers in a region that is larger than a single office or building. A MAN might connect multiple buildings across a city or multiple educational, research, or government facilities across a state. MANs generally are owned by a consortium of users or by a single network provider that sells high-speed network services to multiple users.

WIDE AREA NETWORKS A **wide area network (WAN)** — a network covering a very wide geographical area — can be a single network or multiple connected LANs located across the country or around the world (Figure 6-4). For example, a business with branch offices in England, Australia, Canada, and the United States could use a WAN to connect the individual LANs in each branch office. Most WANs are corporately owned and private. The Internet, which is the world's largest WAN, is a public WAN.

Figure 6-4 A wide area network can be a single network or can connect LANs around the world.

Network Topologies, Access Methods, and Transmission Media

A network's **physical topology** is the arrangement of computers and mobile devices, printers, and other devices. A network's **access method** specifies how data travels from node to node across the network. The network's **transmission media** are the communication media — physical or wireless — used to carry these transmissions. These three characteristics help define a network's **throughput** — that is, the amount of data that can travel from one node to another node in a specified amount of time.

PHYSICAL TOPOLOGIES Three basic LAN physical topologies are the bus, the ring, and the star (Figure 6-5). Today, however, many LANs use a hybrid physical topology that combines some elements of these three basic physical topologies.

Q&A

What is a BAN?
A **body area network (BAN)** is a set of devices that function as a network on a human body. Devices can be implanted, wearable, or portable. A primary use of BANs is for medical use, such as to monitor glucose input and blood sugar levels in a diabetic patient to alert the user or medical personnel to potential health risks. Other possible uses include sports and military applications.

Network Topologies

Topology	Description	Layout
Bus	Connects all nodes on a peer-to-peer LAN to a single connection, called a bus, shared by all nodes. Only one transmission is allowed at a time.	
Ring	Connects each node to the next node using a single circle of cable. A transmission moves from node to node around the circle in a clockwise direction.	
Star	Connects each node to a central device, such as a hub or switch. A transmission passes from the originating node, through the hub, directly to the destination node.	

Figure 6-5 Overview of three LAN toplogies.

ACCESS METHODS   A network's access method (sometimes called its **logical topology**) is the way in which data travels between nodes. The two most common network access methods are Ethernet and token ring. **Ethernet** is a network access method in which a node that is attempting to transmit data first must determine if any other node is sending a transmission. If so, the node waits a short period of time and then checks again. When the network is available, the node sends its transmission. When two nodes check and then transmit at the same time, their two transmissions collide. Both nodes then stop transmitting, wait a random amount of time, check again, and then send their transmissions.

Networks using a bus or star topology commonly use the Ethernet access method, which can transmit data from 10 Mbps to 100 Mbps. High-speed networks might use Gigabit Ethernet, which transmits from 1 to 100 gigabits of data.

A **token ring** network passes **tokens**, small packets of data, clockwise in a circle from node to node. Only one free token is available per network. A node cannot transmit until it has the token. When a node is ready to transmit, it intercepts the token, adds data and the destination node's address, and then sends the token on to the next node. When the token reaches the destination node, the destination node intercepts the token and alerts the originating node. The originating node then sends a free token to the next node. Because a node cannot transmit unless it has the token, two nodes cannot transmit at once, avoiding the transmission collisions that may occur on an Ethernet network. A token ring network generally is more expensive to install.

TRANSMISSION MEDIA   As you learned in Chapter 1, data travels over modern networks using a variety of physical media, such as cable, and wireless media, such as cellular and radio waves, Bluetooth and near field communications (NFC).

Examples of wireless media used in networks include cellular, microwave, infrared, and radio frequency. As you learned in Chapter 1, microwave transmissions provide high-speed connectivity to the Internet where DSL and cable are not available. WAN transmissions also use microwaves transmitted by satellite.

Cellular transmissions travel wirelessly over land cells, using transceivers, or cell sites. Cellular transmissions can operate under various frequencies to avoid interference from other cellular users. Cellular networks can transfer voice and data over a large, almost limitless area (Figure 6-6).

@SOURCE To learn about the role IEEE plays in set networking standards, visit ieee.org.

@SOURCE Researchers and IT analysts are discussing and developing terabit (1,000-gigabit) Ethernet standards and technologies. Some experts feel the terabit standard is not necessary. To learn more, use a search engine to search for *terabit Ethernet*.

Figure 6-6   Cellular technology enables a mobile phone user to make a phone call while driving by transferring radio signals from the base station in one cell to the base station in another cell.

Infrared (IR) transmissions use infrared light-wave signals as a short-range transmission medium between computers and devices equipped with infrared ports. IR transmissions are line-of-sight transmissions, meaning that the sending and receiving devices must have an unobstructed path for the infrared signal.

Near field communication (NFC) transmissions use radio waves to connect devices that are touching or nearby (generally within 10 centimeters). NFC enables users to exchange contact data with other users, complete sales transactions, connect with social networking, participate in gaming, and more (Figure 6-7).

Figure 6-7   Some objects, such as smartphones, are NFC-enabled.

Radio frequency (RF) transmissions use broadcast radio waves to transmit data over short distances, such as between two smartphones or between a laptop computer and a printer. RF transmissions require a transmitter for sending data and a receiver for receiving it. They are not line-of-sight transmissions. Some wireless devices send and receive RF transmissions using a **transceiver** — a single component that both sends and receives transmissions.

Bluetooth is an example of a short-range RF technology that sends and receives wireless transmissions between devices such as computers, smartphones, tablets, headsets (Figure 6-8), and more. Many cars come with Bluetooth capabilities and enable you to play music, access GPS, and more through a Bluetooth-enabled device. A Bluetooth-enabled device contains a transceiver that sends and receives low throughput radio transmissions. Bluetooth devices are designed for small **wireless personal area networks (WPANs)**, and have a range of approximately 33 feet (10 meters) or less. To enable two Bluetooth devices to work together, you must **pair** them. Pairing devices typically requires modifying the device's settings, and can require a device ID or other information to complete the pairing.

Figure 6-8 Bluetooth is a short-range RF technology that sends and receives wireless transmissions between devices such as a headset and a smartphone.

A **Wi-Fi network**, or **wireless LAN (WLAN)** uses a wireless medium — such as radio frequency transmissions — to connect computers and mobile devices, printers, and other devices. A Wi-Fi network in an office, for example, can use radio frequency transmissions to allow communication between computers and devices and printers equipped with wireless network interface cards (NICs) or those with built-in wireless capabilities. To ensure that the devices on the network communicate, Wi-Fi networks follow IEEE 802.11 wireless networking standards. The IEEE 802.11 family of Wi-Fi network standards specifies data transmission speeds and the radio frequencies over which the WLANs can communicate.

FACTS @HAND

802.11 was the original standard, but now is obsolete. Each subsequent version (starting with 802.11a in 1999) is an amendment to the standard, upon which the members of the IEEE Standards Association vote. Each amendment not only includes updated standards, but also the original standards and the requirements of the previous amendments. To find the current version of 802.11 standards, use a search engine to search for *current IEEE 802.11 standard.*

Some wired LANs also provide wireless access for laptops, tablets, smartphones, and other devices through wireless access points. As you learned in Chapter 1, a wireless access point is a hardware device with an antenna that sends and receives radio signals to and from a mobile device and a wired LAN.

In addition to wireless networks set up for home or office use, libraries, coffee shops, hotels, and other public spaces offer free access to their Wi-Fi network for customers or patrons. Laptops and mobile devices can recognize when they are near a wireless network, and either connect automatically or prompt the user for a password to access the Wi-Fi network.

Examples of physical media used in networks include coaxial, twisted-pair, and fiber-optic cable. Coaxial cable was the transmission medium of choice for many early networks and still is found in cable television connections. **Coaxial cable** (Figure 6-9), pronounced *coax (KO-ax)*, consists of a single copper wire surrounded by insulating material, woven or braided metal, and a plastic outer covering. Coaxial cable can carry network traffic for long distances and is resistant to interference. It is not used in most modern networks, however, because it does not transmit data as fast as other media.

plastic outer coating   woven or braided metal   insulating material   copper wire

© Cengage Learning®

Figure 6-9   Coaxial cable can carry network traffic for long distances and is resistant to interference, but does not transmit data as fast as other media.

Twisted-pair cable (Figure 6-10) consists of insulated copper wires twisted around each other in pairs and then enclosed in a plastic covering. The original use of twisted-pair cable was for telephone transmissions. Today LAN transmissions use it because it is easier to install than other types of cable and can handle the faster transmission speeds required by modern networks.

twisted-pair wire

twisted-pair cable

© Cengage Learning®

Figure 6-10   Twisted-pair cable is commonly used as a LAN transmission medium because it is easy to install and can handle faster transmission speeds.

Fiber-optic cable (Figure 6-11), which contains glass fibers surrounded by a layer of glass cladding and a protective outer jacket, is used to carry voice, video, and data transmissions over very long distances. Because of its capacity and reliability, fiber-optic cable is a popular transmission medium for high-speed long-distance transmissions. While fiber-optic cable is too expensive to be used as a transmission medium for a small LAN, it is the transmission medium of choice for MANs and WANs.

cable contains many optical fibers

outer covering jacket

optical fiber core

glass cladding

protective coating

© Cengage Learning®

Figure 6-11   Fiber-optic cable is a popular transmission medium for high-speed long-distance transmissions.

Connectivity Hardware and Software

As discussed in Chapter 1, packet switching involves breaking up data into packets at its source and then transmitting the individual packets across various networks to their destination, and reassembling the packets. Hardware connectivity devices, such as hubs, bridges, data switches, and routers, and hardware or software gateways are at the heart of this process. These devices and software connect nodes on the same network, connect nodes across multiple networks, and forward packets between nodes.

Segments are multiple groups of computers or devices that share a common function. In a business LAN, the Marketing Department computers and devices might be on one segment and the Sales Department computers and devices might be on another segment. Bridges, data switches, routers, and gateways connect different network segments and control transmissions between segments (Figure 6-12). Most large networks use a combination of network hardware and software to help move packets efficiently and quickly to their destinations.

Figure 6-12   Large networks often are broken up into network segments.

HUBS

As you learned earlier in this chapter, a hub is an inexpensive hardware device used to connect multiple nodes on the same network. A **passive hub** cannot determine how to direct a packet; it simply sends the same signal to all of its connected nodes or segments. An **intelligent hub**, however, can perform a variety of tasks, such as filtering data or permitting a network administrator to monitor hub traffic.

BRIDGES

A **port** is an opening in a device that connects it to another device. A **bridge** is an intelligent connectivity device with one input port and one output port that connects two segments on the same LAN or two separate LANs. Each node on a network has a **MAC (Media Access Control) address**, which is a unique physical address, assigned to its network interface card (NIC) by the card's manufacturer. A bridge creates a database of all the MAC addresses for nodes on its segment or LAN. It then uses the database to determine whether to forward a packet to another segment or LAN. Bridges originally only could connect segments or LANs that used the same access method — either Ethernet or token ring. Today, more sophisticated bridges can connect, forward packets, and translate the packets between Ethernet and token ring LANs. Modern data switches and routers are replacing bridges in some cases.

Q&A

What is the Seven-Layer OSI Model?

The Seven-Layer OSI Model illustrates the flow of data in a network and defines the networking protocols at each step in the flow. To learn more about the Seven-Layer OSI Model, use a search engine to search for *Seven-Layer OSI Model.*

DATA SWITCHES

A **data switch** is an intelligent device that also interprets MAC addresses and filters and forwards packets to other network segments. A data switch has multiple ports, with each port acting as a bridge. Using multiple ports to direct packets helps ease congestion and makes a data switch a less-expensive choice than a bridge for networks with a large number of nodes.

ROUTERS

Like a data switch, a **router** is an intelligent device with multiple ports. A router is much more powerful than a switch. A router is a specialized computer that can connect LAN segments, two LANs, or multiple LANs on a WAN — all transmitting at different speeds and using different protocols. In addition to keeping track of all the nodes on a network, a router can determine the best route for a packet to take to its destination and switch the packet to an alternate route, if necessary. Routers fall into one of three categories, depending on the type of service they provide: wireless, mobile, or broadband.

A router can use one of two methods of directing packets: static routing and dynamic routing. A network administrator programs a router using **static routing** to route packets over specific paths between nodes. **Dynamic routing** allows a router to determine the best route between two nodes automatically and then store this information in a **routing table**, which is a data table stored on the router or on a network computer that includes a list of routes to network addresses. To route a packet dynamically, the router opens an incoming packet, compares the packet's destination address with the routing table, and then the packet travels to its destination using the route specified in the routing table. Dynamic routing also allows a router to detect trouble on a specific route and reroute packets when necessary.

The routers used to route packets on the Internet are complex, fast, and expensive devices that can search through routing tables quickly enough to correctly forward millions of packets per second. Internet routers ensure that packets reach their destination — across town or across the world — by sending packets from one router to another until the packets reach their destination network. A **hop** occurs when a packet travels to the next Internet router. The more hops, the longer it takes for data to go from the sending computer to the destination computer.

Most operating systems provide a utility that you can use to trace hops from your computer to another computer over the Internet. In the Windows operating system, this program is the **tracert utility**, and is available through the Command Prompt window. The tracert utility can test the path to a destination Internet site and see if any problems exist with making a connection at a particular point along the route.

Note: To trace hops using a Macintosh computer, open the Network Utilities, and tap or click the Traceroute link or icon. If you are using a mobile device, you may not be able to trace hops. Use a search engine to search for how to trace hops using your device. If you are unable to complete the steps, read through the set of steps to understand the capabilities.

To Use the Tracert Utility to Trace Hops

The following steps use the Windows 8 Command Prompt window and the Windows tracert utility to identify the number of hops from your computer to a Cengage web server. If you are using a previous version of Windows, tap or click the Start button, point to All Programs, tap or click Accessories, and then tap or click Command Prompt.

1

- Press and hold or right-click the Start button on the Windows taskbar.

- Tap or click the Run menu command to open the Run dialog box.

- Enter `cmd` in the Open text box in the Run window (Figure 6-13).

- Tap or click the Open button, or press the ENTER key to open the Command Prompt window.

Figure 6-13

2

- Enter **tracert www.cengage.com** at the command-line prompt to instruct the operating system to trace the number of hops between your computer and the destination computer (Figure 6-14).

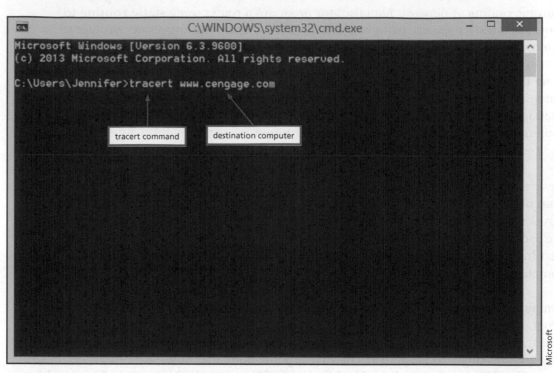

Figure 6-14

3

- Press the ENTER key to view the path from your computer to the Cengage destination server as packets are sent from router to router over the Internet (Figure 6-15).

- Tap or click the Close button on the Command Prompt window title bar.

```
Microsoft Windows [Version 6.3.9600]
(c) 2013 Microsoft Corporation. All rights reserved.

C:\Users\Jennifer>tracert www.cengage.com

Tracing route to www2.cengage.com [69.32.208.74]
over a maximum of 30 hops:

  1     1 ms    <1 ms    <1 ms  192.168.1.1
  2    10 ms    11 ms     9 ms  L100.BSTNMA-VFTTP-86.verizon-gni.net [98.110.150
.1]
  3     9 ms    17 ms     8 ms  G0-10-3-6.BSTNMA-LCR-22.verizon-gni.net [130.81.
212.180]
  4    32 ms    69 ms     8 ms  ae0-0.BOS-BB-RTR2.verizon-gni.net [130.81.209.94
]
  5    16 ms    16 ms    16 ms  0.ae11.XL4.NYC1.ALTER.NET [152.63.20.117]
  6    15 ms    15 ms    16 ms  0.xe-9-0-0.BR1.NYC1.ALTER.NET [152.63.19.213]
  7     *        *        *     Request timed out.
  8    47 ms    48 ms    52 ms  vlan51.ebr1.NewYork2.Level3.net [4.69.138.222]
  9    52 ms    51 ms    53 ms  ae-38-38.ebr2.Washington1.Level3.net [4.69.201.8
5]
 10    52 ms    54 ms    47 ms  ae-62-62.csw1.Washington1.Level3.net [4.69.134.1
46]
 11    54 ms    51 ms    83 ms  ae-61-61.ebr1.Washington1.Level3.net [4.69.134.1
29]
```

each computer along route identified by IP address and/or name

number of hops appears in Command Prompt window; your information will differ

time between hops in milliseconds

Figure 6-15

GATEWAYS   A **gateway** is a hardware device or software that runs on a mainframe computer, a server, an individual workstation, or a router. Gateways connect two or more networks or network segments that use different packet formatting, different communication protocols, and different access methods. Gateways not only forward packets, they also translate packets to be readable by the destination network. Because of this translation capability, gateways are more expensive than routers and transmit packets more slowly than bridges, switches, or routers. Most routers have a gateway, although a PC or network server can act as a gateway. Figure 6-16 lists different types of gateways.

Types of Gateways

Name	Description
Cloud gateway	Integrates standard networking protocols with cloud services to connect to the cloud.
Email gateway	Converts email messages created by one type of email system so that they can be read by a different type of email system.
Internet gateway	Allows LAN users to access the Internet. Can be used to define which users have Internet access or to restrict access to certain Internet services or websites.
LAN gateway	Connects LAN segments that use different access methods and communication protocols.
SMS gateway	Enables a computer to send SMS (short message service) messages, such as text messages. Many include the capability to convert text messages to email.
Voice/data gateway	Allows data packets to be sent over a voice network or voice to be sent over a data network by translating between voice circuit switching and data packet switching.
Wireless gateway	Integrates wireless devices such as laptops, PDAs, and cell phones with a wired network.

© Cengage Learning®

Figure 6-16   Gateways can connect two or more divergent networks.

Internet Infrastructure

From a user's perspective, accessing the Internet and downloading a file, viewing a web-page, or sending an email may seem quite simple. In a few seconds, the file downloads, the web page appears in your browser, or the email message reaches its destination. The processes that occur behind the scenes, however, are quite complex and rely on your computer and device's ability to communicate with computers and devices on other networks. Each computer and device must be operational and have the proper protocols, programs, and gateways to complete the process. The processes also rely on the ability of your Internet service provider (ISP) to exchange data with other providers, and on the ability of network hardware and software to break down data into properly addressed packets that arrive at their destination error-free and correctly reassembled.

In this section, you will learn about network service providers and how they interact to exchange data at specific points on the Internet backbones. You also will learn more about the TCP/IP suite of protocols that is instrumental in addressing and delivering data packets, how IP addresses are constructed, and how the DNS resolves domain names to IP addresses.

Network Service Providers (NSPs)

Recall that the NSFnet provided the original Internet backbone, which used transmission media from AT&T. In the mid-1990s interconnected backbones or networks provided by several telecommunications companies, including AT&T replaced the NSFnet Internet backbone. Today, AT&T, Sprint, Verizon, T-Mobile, and others, called **network service providers (NSPs)**, provide the public and private network infrastructure for the Internet that enables wireless, cellular, and other capabilities.

INTERNET EXCHANGE POINTS   An **Internet exchange point (IXP)** is a physical infrastructure that enables ISPs to communicate among their networks, which limits the upstream traffic an ISP must handle. Each ISP has at least one network switch, to which each participating ISP connects. The use of an IXP reduces the costs for running an ISP because it uses a shared connection. IXP usage also improves an ISP's bandwidth. Participating ISPs typically share costs for operating an IXP.

FACTS @HAND   IXPs range in size from around 10 members to several hundred. One of the largest IXPs in operation is the Equinix Internet Exchange, which connects major cities in Europe, the United States, Asia, South America, and Australia.

A **Metropolitan Area Exchange (MAE)** is a specific type of IXP. An MAE provides a high-speed Ethernet connection within a metropolitan area.

FACTS @HAND   Network service providers (NSPs) provide the public and private network infrastructure (backbones) for the Internet. ISPs sell Internet access to individuals, businesses, and other organizations. An ISP might sell Internet access locally to individuals and businesses, regionally to other ISPs, or worldwide to a varied customer base. An ISP can be an NSP; several NSPs, however, are also ISPs.

PEERING   **Peering** is the exchange of Internet traffic and router information between NSPs and ISPs at an exchange point, such as an IXP. Peering agreements specify the terms under which NSPs exchange data and can include the amount of traffic, the type of network the peering entities must have, and other requirements such as transit fees. Public peering involves exchanging Internet traffic at a public connection, such as an IXP. Because network access points (NAPs) can experience delays during the Internet's peak traffic periods, some NSPs and ISPs set up dedicated **private peering** connections to each other's networks. These private peering arrangements and connections enable Internet traffic to bypass congested public peering points.

TCP/IP Stack

As you learned in Chapter 1, the Transmission Control Protocol/Internet Protocol (TCP/IP) suite, or the **TCP/IP stack**, is the set of standard Internet protocols on which communications across the Internet and many private networks rely. The TCP/IP stack encompasses multiple subprotocols. Figure 6-17 provides an overview of several subprotocols. Of these protocols, TCP, IP, and UDP are the core subprotocols required for all TCP/IP transmissions. Other subprotocols accomplish various network communication tasks such as downloading files or sending and receiving email.

TCP/IP Stack

Subprotocol	Description
Address Resolution Protocol (ARP)	Converts a computer's IP address to its physical MAC address.
Dynamic Host Configuration Protocol (DHCP)	Automatically assigns IP addresses to network devices.
File Transfer Protocol (FTP)	Enables uploading and downloading of files between a local and remote computer.
Hypertext Transfer Protocol (HTTP)	Allows web servers and web browsers to communicate.
Internet Control Message Protocol (ICMP)	Sends error messages to routers and host computers when problems occur with data transmissions.
Internet Message Access Protocol version 4 (IMAP4)	Provides remote access to a mail server, allowing users to manage their stored messages; functions similar to POP3.
Internet Protocol (IP)	Sends packets and provides routers with the address information needed to deliver the packets.
Post Office Protocol version 3 (POP3)	Manages storage of email messages on a mail server and forwarding of email messages from a mail server to a user's mailbox.
Reverse ARP (RARP)	Converts a computer's physical MAC address to its IP address.
Simple Mail Transfer Protocol (SMTP)	Routes email messages from mail server to mail server across an IP network such as the Internet.
Telnet	Allows a computer to act as a terminal for logging on to remote devices such as a computer or router.
Transmission Control Protocol (TCP)	Breaks data into packets, verifies packet integrity, and reassembles error-free packets at their destination.
User Datagram Protocol (UDP)	Sends packets without checking for errors or verifying receipt of the packets. UDP is used to broadcast live video or audio over the Internet.

© Cengage Learning®

Figure 6-17 The TCP/IP stack includes several subprotocols on which communications across the Internet and private IP networks rely.

Most current network operating systems use the TCP/IP stack as their default networking protocols. **IP network** is another name for a network running TCP/IP.

IP Addresses

Every network node must have its own unique identifier to ensure that data transmitted over a private or public IP network reaches its correct destination. Earlier in this chapter, you learned that each network device has a MAC address, which is a physical address set in its network interface card (NIC). In addition to a physical address, each node on an IP network also has a **logical address**, called an IP address. The IP subprotocol uses this address to deliver packets to the correct destination.

The current IP standard, called **IPv6**, lengthens IP addresses from 32 bits to 128 bits and thus increases the number of available IP addresses from the IPv4 standard, which it replaced. Figure 6-18 compares IP addresses based on the IPv4 and IPv6 standards.

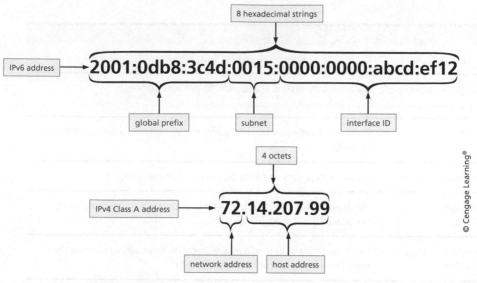

Figure 6-18 The IPv6 standard lengthens IP addresses to 128 bits, increasing the number of available IP addresses.

An IPv6 address includes eight 8-bit numbers. Each 8-bit number in the IP address is an **octet**. In IPv6, a colon (:) separates each octet. The IPv6 standard enables more nodes, networks, and domains to have a unique logical address. A node that has an IPv4 address does not need to update to an IPv6 address as the two are compatible.

The IP address for any node on a network consists of two components: one that identifies the network connection, and one that identifies the node itself. The IP addresses for nodes on the same network have the same network identification component, and each node has a unique node identifier. Originally, a **classful routing system** assigned IP addresses by classifying networks as Class A through Class E to maximize the number of available IP addresses for each network. The network class defined which octets in the IP address identified the network, and which octets identified the specific node. However, most networks were not using the full amount of IP addresses available to them, making the classful system wasteful.

The explosive demand for IP addresses strained the capabilities of this classful routing system, leading to the development of a **classless routing system**, called **Classless Inter-Domain Routing (CIDR)**. CIDR is a notation system that allows network administrators to expand the number of network nodes assigned to an IP address. The Internet and large private networks use CIDR extensively. CIDR address blocks have an assigned ISP, which then can use one IP address for thousands of customers by assigning them subnetwork addresses. Subnetworks reduce the number of unique IP addresses needed, yet each node has its own identifier based on an IP address and a subnetwork prefix.

FACTS @HAND Some IP subnets are specific to certain occasions or circumstances. For example, network administrators sometimes use IP subnets to troubleshoot TCP/IP-related problems on an individual computer, or for broadcasting messages to multiple computers and devices. Other groups of IP addresses are internal IP addresses reserved for private networks.

To View a Networked Computer's IP Address

As previously discussed, every computer and device on a network has a unique IP address, including tablets, printers, game consoles, smart TVs, and more. In Windows 8, you can use the Command Prompt window and the `ipconfig /all` command to display your own computer's IP address. The following steps use the Command Prompt window to view the IP address of your computer. To complete the steps, you must have a network-connected computer or device. The contents of your Command Prompt window will be different from the figures in these steps.

Note: If you are using a Macintosh computer, open the Applications folder, tap or click Utilities, and then tap or click the Terminal app. Use a search engine to search for steps specific to your device. If you are using a mobile device, you might not be able to perform the steps. If you are unable to complete the steps, read through the set of steps to understand the capabilities of the ipconfig /all command.

1

- Open the Command Prompt window.

- Enter `ipconfig /all` at the command-line prompt to instruct the operating system to display all IP information about your networked computer (Figure 6-19).

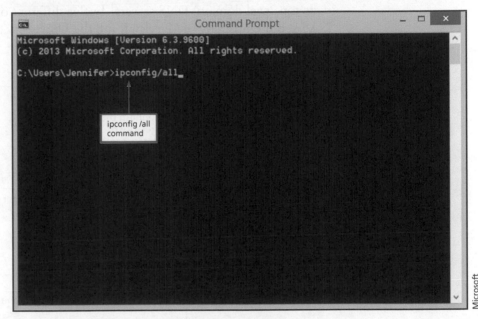

Figure 6-19

2

- Press the ENTER key to display your computer's host name, IP address, and other IP information (Figure 6-20).

Q&A Why do I not see IP information?
If your computer is not connected to a network, no IP information appears.

- Scroll the Command Prompt window, if necessary, to view the information.

- Click the Close button to close the Command Prompt window.

Figure 6-20

Domain Name System (DNS)

In Chapter 2, you learned about domain names, ICANN, and the DNS. ICANN (Internet Corporation for Assigned Names and Numbers), through its agreement with the U.S. Department of Commerce, oversees the assignment of IP addresses, the accreditation of domain name registrars, and contracts with TLD (top-level domain) registries as part of the DNS. The DNS also consists of a hierarchy of servers used to translate domain names into IP addresses in a process called **resolving** the domain name.

DNS SERVERS   At the top of the DNS hierarchy (Figure 6-21) are the DNS **root name servers** that publish a directory of the next level of DNS servers, called the **root zone file**. The root zone file lists the addresses of all the TLD and ccTLD (country code top-level domain) DNS servers. Twelve different organizations, including VeriSign, NASA, the University of Maryland, and the University of Southern California, operate the root name servers.

Figure 6-21   DNS servers consist of root name servers, authoritative servers, and local caching servers.

At the next level are the DNS **authoritative servers**, which contain the IP information for the TLD and ccTLD domains and their registrants. At the bottom of the hierarchy are thousands of local DNS **caching servers** operated by ISPs and company IT departments containing stored domain name and IP address information developed from previous domain name resolution inquiries. The **DNS namespace** consists of all of the information in the DNS databases, including the top-level domain, country code top-level domain, domain name, and IP address information.

The process of resolving a domain name to an IP address (Figure 6-22) begins with a local caching server, which may reside on your company or with your ISP. In most cases, a local caching server quickly can resolve a domain name to its IP address based on the server's cached or stored resolution inquiries. In some cases — for example, the first time the caching server attempts to resolve a specific domain name or if the caching server has just been started and its cache is empty — the caching server must contact authoritative or root name servers in the DNS to resolve a domain name.

Assume you have entered the URL mynewsite.biz in your browser. Your browser first contacts the local caching server to resolve the mynewsite.biz domain name to its IP address. If the local caching server cannot resolve the domain name, it can contact the authoritative server for the .biz TLD for a list of other authoritative servers that can resolve the mynewsite.biz domain name. The caching server then queries one of the appropriate authoritative servers for the mynewsite.biz domain and returns the IP address to the browser. If the caching server does not know the address for the .biz TLD authoritative server, it can contact a root name server for the address. Figure 6-22 illustrates the process of resolving the mynewsite.biz domain name assuming the local caching server cannot resolve the domain name and does not know the address of the appropriate authoritative server.

Figure 6-22   The process of resolving a domain name using the DNS begins with a local caching server.

You can use the Command Prompt window and the **nslookup** command to find the numeric IP address that corresponds to a domain name and vice versa.

To Look Up Corresponding IP Addresses and Domain Names

As you have learned, IP addresses are the numerical equivalent of domain names. The following steps use the Command Prompt window to look up corresponding IP addresses and domain names.

Note: If you are using a Macintosh computer, open the Applications folder, tap or click Utilities, and then tap or click the Terminal app. Use a search engine to search for steps specific to your device. If you are using a mobile device, you might not be able to perform the steps. If you are unable to complete the steps, read through the steps to understand the capabilities.

①

- Open the Command Prompt window.

- Enter **nslookup cnn.com** at the command-line prompt to display the IP address or addresses for the cnn.com domain name (Figure 6-23).

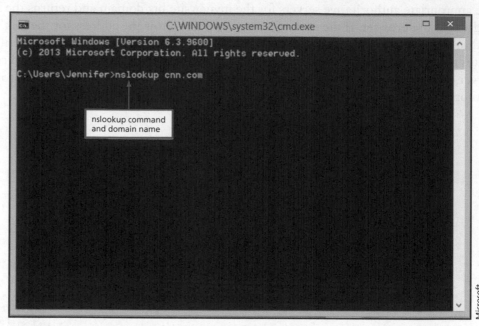

Figure 6-23

②

- Press the ENTER key to see that the cnn.com domain name corresponds to multiple IP addresses (Figure 6-24).

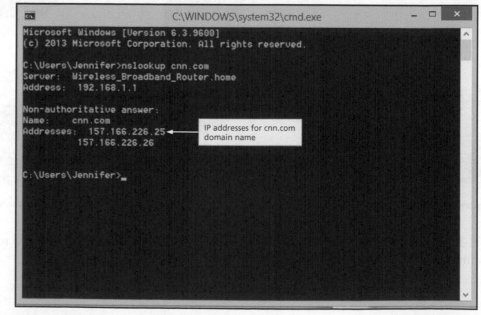

Figure 6-24

3

- Enter `nslookup 207.171.182.16` at the command-line prompt.

- Press the ENTER key to see that the IP address 207.171.182.16 corresponds to the Amazon.com domain name (Figure 6-25).

- Close the Command Prompt window.

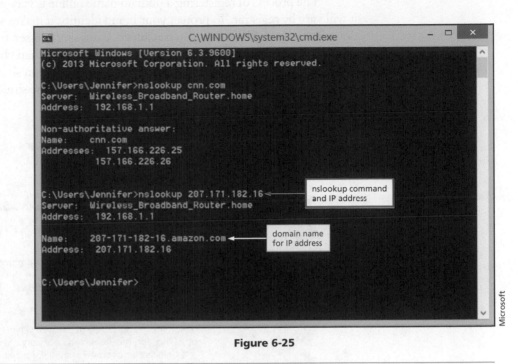

Figure 6-25

DNS REGISTRATION The **Shared Registration System (SRS)** is the registration system that allows private companies to handle the registration of domain names. These private companies, called **accredited registrars**, ensure that an organization's unique domain name appears on the appropriate DNS servers for a small annual fee. Examples of accredited registrars include Network Solutions, Register.com, Name.com, and GoDaddy.com (Figure 6-26). ICANN is responsible for managing the SRS.

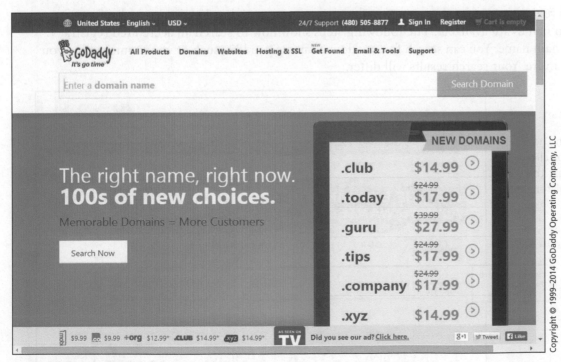

Figure 6-26 Accredited registrars can help you locate and register a domain name.

The process of registering a domain name online is very easy (Figure 6-27), although it will vary by registrar. To protect your brand identity, it makes sense to register for as many domain names and TLDs as you can afford. Choosing a lesser-used or known TLD, such as .biz may give your website a less professional impression than choosing .com or a better-known TLD. If the .com TLD of your chosen website is taken, you should reconsider your website name to avoid any confusion between your website and the similarly named .com website.

Step 1: Visit an accredited registrar's website.

Step 2: Enter a desired domain name including the top-level domain, such as .com, .net, or .biz. The website searches a database of registered domain names to determine whether the domain name you entered is available, and for what TLDs.

Step 3: Select an available domain name and enter the purchaser information, which usually consists of the name, address, telephone number, and email address of the person responsible for the domain name.

Step 4: Provide the IP address(es) of the web servers of the company or ISP hosting the website, if necessary. (See your network administrator or contact your ISP for this information, if necessary.)

Step 5: Pay for the domain name using a credit card or third-party payment service.

© Cengage Learning®

Figure 6-27 The domain name registration process.

To Search for an Available Domain Name

If you are considering registering a domain name, you first may want to search a domain name database to see what appropriate domain names are available. The following steps show how to search an accredited registrar's database for an available domain name. You can search for any domain name you like, such as your name, a blog you are interested in starting, or more. Your search results will differ.

1

- Start your browser if necessary.

- Enter **register.com** in the Address bar, and then tap or click the necessary button or press the ENTER key to open the Register.com webpage (Figure 6-28).

Q&A
Do all domain name registrars have access to the same domain names?
Register.com, Go Daddy, and others are ICANN-accredited registrars. They pay ICANN fees to access the list of available domain names and help their clients secure the proper names.

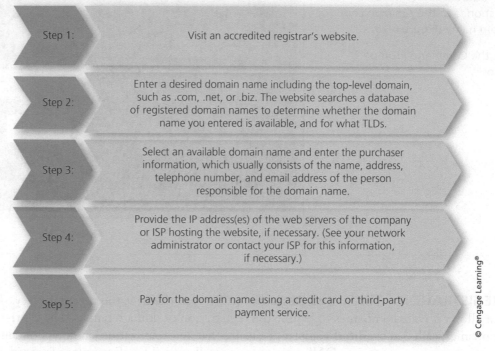

'Start your search for a domain name' text box

© 1995–2014 by Register.com®

Figure 6-28

- Enter `mynewblog` in the 'Start your search for a domain name' text box (Figure 6-29).

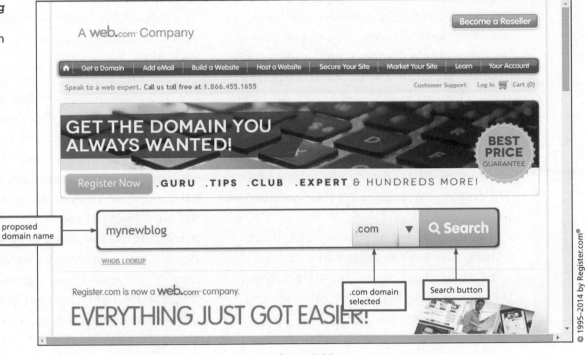

Figure 6-29

3

- Tap or click the Search button to determine whether your domain name is available (Figure 6-30).

- Close the browser.

Q&A **Why are my choices of TLD extensions different?** The search results might include a few choices of extensions. Your results may vary.

Figure 6-30

Selecting a Domain Name

Careful selection of a domain name is critical. Most likely, you will need to purchase or reserve multiple domain names and multiple TLDs to help protect your brand, decrease market confusion, and reach more customers. If your website gains popularity and you have not secured the name under other, common TLDs, you risk confusion if a cybersquatter, or even just another website owner, purchases and creates a website using your website name and another TLD.

When choosing a domain name, select a short, easy-to-remember name that ties in to the products or services the e-business sells. Avoid using hyphens or other spacing characters. Remember that your URL will not be case sensitive, so ensure that users will be able to distinguish your company name from your URL.

Consider any alternative names or abbreviations for your company, or marketing slogans, and purchase those domain names as well. You can redirect the alternate names to the main company website to ensure that your customers can reach you. For example, BN is a common nickname for the bookstore Barnes & Noble. If you type www.bn.com in the Address bar and press the ENTER key, the web site www.barnesandnoble .com is displayed. If you type www .breakfastofchampions.com, your browser redirects to the Wheaties cereal website.

Q&A

Do I need to create and manage separate websites for all of the TLDs I purchase? No. You can instruct the host to redirect all related TLDs and other URLs you register to the main website.

Location-Based Services and GPS

Handheld wireless devices, such as smartphones and tablets, have become commonplace. You might use one or more of these devices to communicate with friends and coworkers, connect to the Internet and check your email, download games, get driving instructions, or view other web content or access location-based services.

A **location-based service (LBS)** is a wireless service offered to customers based on their physical location. An example of a noncommercial location-based service is the wireless 911 emergency service mandated by the FCC in its Enhanced 9-1-1 (E9-1-1) initiative. The E9-1-1 initiative allows emergency call centers to use a location-based service to identify the location of the caller accurately, thus helping to eliminate the delay caused by asking users to describe their location. Other uses of LBS include in-vehicle navigation systems that can pinpoint your location and provide you with step-by-step directions to a new location. Many in-vehicle navigation systems provide maps, street view, real-time traffic updates, weather alerts, and even assistance with backing up the vehicle.

At the heart of this and other LBSs are the **Global Positioning System (GPS)** satellite network and receivers mounted in automobiles or placed in mobile phones, watches, tablets, or other handheld devices. The GPS is a navigation system that consists of one or more Earth-based receivers that accept and analyze signals sent by small satellites orbiting approximately 11,000 miles above Earth. There are approximately 32 satellites operating at any time. Four to six satellites always are visible above the horizon, and each of these satellites constantly beams down a signal containing the exact time and its own position in the sky. A GPS receiver in a ship, airplane, pet collar or other wearable device, automobile, or smartphone uses these signals to calculate the receiver's location on Earth to within a few feet (Figure 6-31).

Figure 6-31 A GPS receiver in a ship, airplane, pet collar or other wearable device, automobile, or smartphone uses satellite signals to calculate the receiver's location to within a few feet.

GPS tracks the time and satellite position of the GPS device, and pinpoints its exact location, including longitude, latitude, and even elevation. There are many commercial, emergency, and personal uses for GPS, including:

- An emergency service provider can identify the physical location of a person with a GPS-enabled device and then offer assistance with safety or health issues

- Locating the nearest ATM or store (Figure 6-32), or tracking a package's exact location to determine its approximate delivery time

- Social networking services, which can alert you when a friend is nearby and available to get together

Geosocial networking is a term used to describe the combination of LBS with social networking providers. For example, Foursquare (Figure 6-33) is an app that pinpoints a user's location using a GPS, and enables the user to "check in" to the location, such as a restaurant, and alert others using social networking tools,

Figure 6-32 GPS apps use your location to provide you with information and options.

LBS and GPS services raise a number of privacy concerns. Security experts warn that using these services can give law enforcement, government, or criminals the ability to track your whereabouts without your knowledge to create a digital profile of your activities, including your schedule, frequently-visited locations, purchases made, and more. To learn more, use a search engine to search for *LBS and GPS privacy concerns*.

such as Facebook or Twitter. Using geosocial networking tools, users can provide information to others about their current location, including reviews, menus, photos, and their own activities. Other uses include networking for a new job, location or trip planning, shopping for the best price and ensuring the item is available at the store, public safety, and news.

Geosocial networking, like all social networking, has some privacy concerns. For example, by sharing information about your whereabouts, you are not only enabling others to find you, but are also alerting them that you are not home, exposing yourself to potential home robberies.

search results for pizza restaurants in Springfield, IL

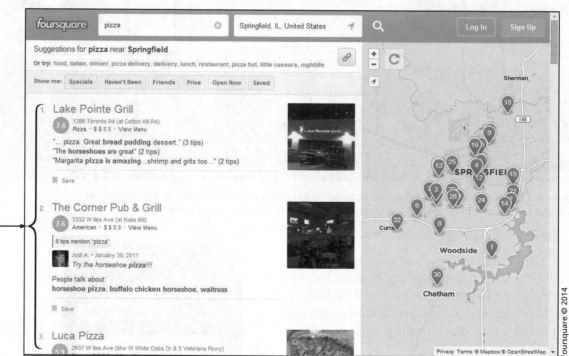

Figure 6-33   FourSquare is a geosocial networking application.

Internet Telephony and Web Conferencing

In addition to being a large-scale network, the Internet also enhances two traditional modes of communication: the telephone and business conferencing. In this section, you will learn how to conduct telephone calls over the Internet, and how the Internet enables businesses to conduct employee and client meetings and conferences.

Internet Telephony

In Chapter 1, you learned about the circuit-switching technologies that establish and maintain private circuits for telephone calls over the Public Switched Telephone Network (PSTN). A private circuit maintains a connection for the duration of a call even during conversation pauses when neither party is talking. **Internet telephony**, also called **IP telephony** or **Voice over IP (VoIP)**, uses TCP/IP and packet switching to send voice transmissions over a private or public IP network. Using IP packet-switching technologies to make telephone calls is more efficient than old circuit-switching technologies because packet switching minimizes the connection time for each call, thus allowing more calls to occur during the same time period in which a single circuit-switched call must maintain its connection. VoIP customers can make calls from their computer or telephone by installing a VoIP router or adapter between their cable or DSL modem and their computer or telephone, as shown in Figure 6-34, and subscribing to a VoIP service.

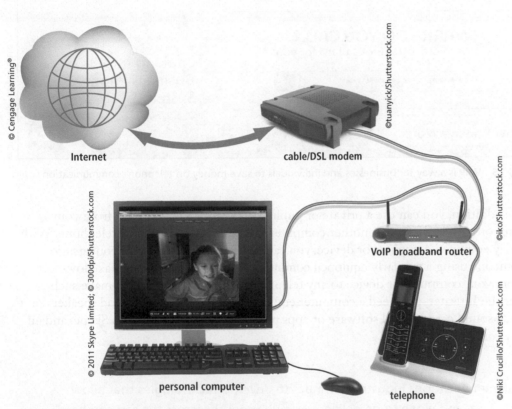

Figure 6-34 VoIP customers can make calls from their computer, device, or telephone by installing a VoIP router or adapter between their cable or DSL modem and their computer, device, or telephone, and subscribing to a VoIP service.

VoIP is a popular option for home telephone service because of reduced service costs and free or inexpensive long-distance calls. VoIP allows businesses to take advantage of packet-switching efficiencies, centralize the management of their private voice and data networks, and increase productivity. VoIP business services typically include a PBX (private branch exchange) switching service that manages incoming and outgoing calls and calls between extensions. VoIP service providers, such as Vonage (Figure 6-35), Nextiva, and Xfinity Voice offer telephone services to homes and businesses over broadband Internet connections.

Figure 6-35 VoIP is a way for businesses and individuals to save money on telephone communications.

In addition, you can use a private or public IP network to make calls from your computer or mobile device to another computer or device or directly to a telephone. With a properly equipped computer or device, you can participate in a toll-free conversation with someone using a similarly equipped computer or device, or you can make low-cost calls from your computer or device to any telephone around the world. To make such a call over the Internet, you need a computer equipped with a microphone and speakers or a headset, a sound card, special software or apps provided by vendors such as Skype, and an Internet connection.

FACTS @HAND The communications industry continues to develop technologies that allow voice, data, and video to be delivered simultaneously across the same network using a combination of computers and devices, telephones, and television. Network engineers refer to these modern networks as **converged networks**.

Virtual Meetings, Conversations, and Web Conferencing

A **virtual meeting** allows collaboration between participants, such as a group of employees, by allowing invitees to log on to their network and sign in to a meeting in which they communicate with each other as well as view, share, and work collaboratively on files. Virtual meeting participants typically communicate with each other using a combination of text, audio, whiteboard, and video.

Video conferencing, an expanded virtual meeting that sometimes includes hundreds or thousands of participants, involves the real-time transmission of video and audio between two locations. Today, most video conferencing uses streaming video over a private or public IP network. Because of transmission quality concerns, commercial video conferencing over an IP network (video over IP) most frequently occurs over private IP networks, which have more control over traffic and bandwidth availability. Examples of commercial video conferencing include employee training sessions, customer support activities, and meetings involving employees who work in different locations (Figure 6-36). Government agencies, colleges, and universities with access to Internet2 use it for video conferencing and for broadcasting instructors' lectures to numerous different classrooms.

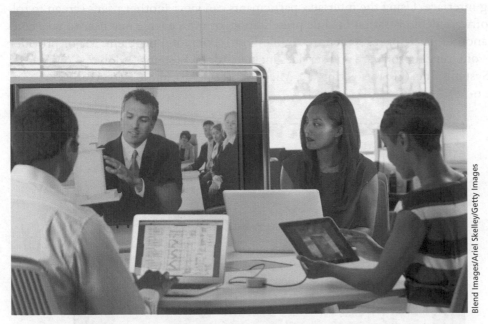

Figure 6-36   Video conferencing is the real-time transmission of video and audio between two locations.

To listen and watch a video conference using your computer, your computer or device must have speakers, a monitor, a sound card, and video conferencing software or app. If you are going to participate in the video conference, you also must have a microphone or headset and a camera connected to your computer or device.

A **virtual conversation** is a video chat using services such as Google Hangouts, or FaceTime (Figure 6-37). Unlike video conferences, virtual conversations typically occur between two users and are for communications with your personal and business contacts.

Figure 6-37   Virtual conversations take place using services such as FaceTime.

Web conferencing is a virtual meeting conducted using a browser and the web. Web conferencing can save time and money and improve productivity by allowing participants at various geographic locations to come together online to communicate as though they were all sitting around the same physical conference table. In addition to the video, chat, and audio capabilities of video conferencing, web conferencing provides a controlled meeting interface. Using the interface, participants can view another user's screen to follow a software demonstration or slide presentation, or even enable one user to take control of another participant's screen to troubleshoot a computer problem. Major providers of web conferencing software and services include Adobe Systems (Adobe® Connect™), Citrix Systems, Inc. (GoToMeeting™), Microsoft (Lync™), and Cisco (WebEx®) (Figure 6-38).

© 2014 Cisco

Figure 6-38   Web conferencing can save time and money and improve productivity.

Network Security Issues and Technologies

Network security involves protecting network equipment and data from accidental or deliberate damage. Threats to network and website security can originate both internally from within the organization and externally from outsiders. If a business conducts sales transactions over the network, fraudulent transactions and failure to protect transaction information pose additional risks. In this section, you will learn about the internal and external threats to network security, transactional security risks, and network security practices and technologies.

FACTS @HAND   Most security analysts agree that the greatest threat to network security is from human ignorance and error. One simple but amazingly effective strategy for gaining unauthorized access to a network or network facilities is social engineering. **Social engineering** simply relies on a network user divulging his or her username or password to someone, or allowing someone to enter a network facilities room without the proper authorization.

Internal Network Security Threats

Internal threats to network security can include management failure to support organization-wide security awareness, inadequate security policies, unenforced security procedures, unhappy employees or disgruntled former employees, failure to make backup copies of critical data or failure to store the copied data off-site, and missing or untested disaster recovery plans. These are just a few examples of the failure to protect against threats to internal network security and data security — the results of which can be catastrophic. Two important ways to protect against internal network security threats are (1) clearly stating and enforcing network security policies and procedures, and (2) ensuring that network access is restricted to authorized users. Equally important is ensuring backup of critical data, which is stored in a secure off-site location, and having a concrete plan for coping with a natural or human-caused disaster.

SECURITY POLICIES AND PROCEDURES After a thorough assessment of an organization's network security risks, management should develop and enforce appropriate security policies and procedures. All employees should receive the training necessary to understand fully an organization's network security policies and how to implement specific security procedures. These procedures might be as simple as not divulging the physical location of network facilities to visitors, or they could be more complex, such as requiring all users to encrypt sensitive emails sent outside the organization.

AUTHORIZED NETWORK ACCESS Network operating systems have built-in security features that allow network administrators to restrict user access to the network or to specific network functions. For example, a network administrator can configure the network so that each user must enter a unique user ID and password before he or she can log on to the network. As you learned in Chapter 4, a user ID is necessary to access an email account. A user ID is also a unique identifier used along with a password to log on to a network. A password is a group of secret characters that identifies you as an authorized network user. When a network user leaves an organization, the network administrator eliminates that user's logon information.

Unauthorized internal users or outside intruders often attempt to guess legitimate passwords to break into a network. Passwords that contain a mix of at least six letters and numbers are much more difficult to guess than those with fewer characters or with only letters. Mixing uppercase and lowercase letters or adding some nonreserved special characters (such as & or $) also can help to make a password more secure. Additionally, avoid passwords consisting of names, birth dates, and common words that might be easy to guess. Finally, users should regularly change passwords. Figure 6-39 illustrates some effective passwords.

Effective Passwords

Do This	Do Not Do This
Z89$33Q	Wilson (last name)
D33f084	012664 (birthday)
66G13b9	apple
7y3MF98F	user

© Cengage Learning®

Figure 6-39 Passwords containing a mix of letters, numbers, and special characters are harder to guess.

Other methods used to restrict network access are biometric identification and smart card identification. **Biometrics** involves using devices to measure biological data to identify a user. Biometric devices and software reads or scans a user's fingerprints, voiceprints, iris or retina image, or other biological data to allow network logon or permit entrance to a network's physical facilities (Figure 6-40). A smart card provides authorization for a remote user to access a network or for an employee to enter a network's physical facilities. A **smart card** (Figure 6-41), a plastic card the size of a credit card, contains memory chips that can store special access codes or biometric information.

Figure 6-40   Biometric devices can verify a user's identity.

Figure 6-41   Smart cards provide additional security.

WIRELESS NETWORK SECURITY   Wireless networks require the same security tools, such as encryption and passwords, and for the same reasons, such as privacy and risk of exposure to malicious code, as wired networks. Wireless networks are vulnerable to more threats than traditional wired networks. One of these threats is **LAN jacking**, or **war driving**, which is the act of driving around with a laptop, antenna, and wireless card, looking for unsecured wireless networks to access. LAN jacking not only exposes a network to viruses and other risks, but can tie up a network's bandwidth and impact its performance. **Spoofing** is when a hacker accesses a network to set up a fake website or send mail that looks like it is coming from an internal server. In addition, a hacker can create a **rogue WLAN** by installing a wireless router that uses network resources and exposes the network to security threats.

DATA STORAGE, BACKUP, AND RESTORE   Data backup and restore policies and procedures identify the location, schedule and methods/media for copies of critical data, and procedures to restore backed-up data to a network following an equipment failure or loss of data. You can back up copies of critical data and software to storage media, such as optical discs or magnetic tape, which you should then store off-site. Companies determine backup policies based on several factors, including recovery time for critical data and systems, cost of storage, and how much data a company can afford to lose if the system fails. Many businesses and individuals use **cloud storage**, which involves saving files and data to a folder on the cloud, rather than on a computer hard drive, or other device or media. Cloud storage provides access to files from any other computer or device, as long as the user has an Internet connection and the proper logon credentials. Some cloud storage services, such as Microsoft One Drive and Google Drive (Figure 6-42), also provide collaboration tools, as well as productivity web apps. In addition, files stored to the cloud are backed up using the cloud service's backup system, providing extra security.

Figure 6-42   Google Drive provides productivity and collaboration tools, as well as file storage.

A number of companies, such as Mozy® and Carbonite™ (Figure 6-43) provide cloud storage services.

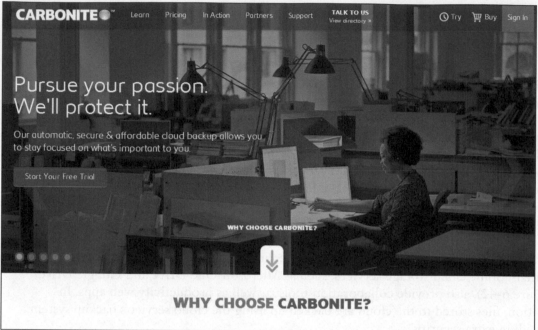

Figure 6-43   Backup copies of critical network data and software should be stored off-site using cloud storage, optical disks, magnetic tape, or other storage media.

Data backup procedures should be a normal, regularly scheduled part of network operations. Business should test data restore procedures periodically to ensure that the backed up data is correct and complete, and that the storage media or cloud-based storage service works properly. Data backup and restore policies and procedures are an important part of an organization's disaster recovery planning.

DISASTER RECOVERY PLANNING   Networks and data also are at risk for physical damage from natural causes such as fire or flood, as well as from deliberate destruction by employees or outside intruders. IT managers and network administrators use a variety of techniques to protect against accidental or deliberate physical damage to network equipment and data, including storing equipment in locked, tightly controlled, and monitored rooms; removing room numbers and door signs so that network facilities are not marked clearly; using specially designed fire suppression systems; providing backup electrical power; and following sound data backup and restore procedures. Additionally, very large organizations might maintain duplicate network facilities in different geographical areas.

Despite the use of these techniques, disasters that compromise network operations still occur. A **disaster recovery plan** covers how an organization deals with a natural or man-made disaster to ensure the organization's viability. The portion of a disaster recovery plan that covers network operations should define how an organization plans to manage equipment failure, electrical outages, data loss, security breaches, and damage to physical facilities. Companies should test all components of a disaster recovery plan periodically to make certain the plan covers new contingencies.

External Network Security Threats

External network security threats are those that originate from outside the network, such as natural disasters, hackers, viruses, worms, and Trojan horses. The best preparedness for natural disasters is a sound, tested disaster recovery plan. To help protect against hackers, viruses, worms, and Trojan horses, organizations should use virus protection software and perform regular security audits to ensure network security policies are in place.

UNAUTHORIZED NETWORK ACCESS   In Chapter 2, you learned the term, hacker, which typically describes a person who uses his or her programming skills to gain unauthorized access to a network. A hacker might attack a network for any number of reasons, including accessing and perhaps stealing valuable information or planting malware.

To attack a network, a hacker might break into a home computer or break into multiple computers and devices on a corporate network to plant software that allows the hacked computers and devices to launch difficult-to-trace attacks on other networks. These types of attacks, called **distributed denial of service (DDoS)** attacks, involve sending a continuous stream of server requests that ultimately overload a server's capacity to respond. Some hackers launch DDoS attacks just for fun and bragging rights. Other DDoS attacks are the result of criminals attempting to extort businesses with threats of further attacks or for revenge against business rivals.

Hackers also may break into a network to steal account information, such as credit card numbers, user passwords, and other personal information to steal a person's identity, make unauthorized purchases using a credit card, or open accounts in a user's name for illegal purposes.

The term hacker originally described any especially gifted software programmer. Today, the term refers to malicious hackers, also called crackers or black-hat hackers, who compromise networks to steal information or disrupt network services. Some hackers who voluntarily use their skills to find network vulnerabilities and publicize them prefer the term ethical hackers or white-hat hackers.

FACTS @HAND

COMPUTER VIRUSES   Hackers often exploit well-known security vulnerabilities in popular software to spread destructive programs such as viruses, worms, and Trojan horses. As you have learned, a computer virus is a small, destructive program that infects other files on a computer. Viruses, which usually infect executable program files, spread to other files when the infected program executes. Email headers or files attached to email messages can spread viruses as part of a computer worm.

A computer worm is a special kind of virus that spreads across a network, such as the Internet, by replicating itself. A worm does not attach itself to other programs. Worms replicate continuously, ultimately consuming network resources, slowing server response, and crashing infected networks. Another type of destructive program that might be part of a virus or worm is a Trojan horse. A Trojan horse is a program that appears to do something useful or fun, but actually does something destructive, including destroying files, creating a way for a hacker to breach network security, stealing passwords, downloading files to the user's computer and then executing them, or recording user keystrokes. Recording your keystrokes enables a hacker to capture your passwords and other sensitive information, enabling them to breach your financial, email, social networking, and other accounts. A Trojan horse program may be part of a standard virus, an infected webpage, a worm, an email message, or a downloaded file. An example of a Trojan horse is the JS/Downloader-BNL Trojan that downloads and executes files from a remote website, creating and installing malware that can affect your computer's ability to operate.

Protecting individual personal computers and devices connected to the Internet or network computers and devices, servers, and routers involves a combination of security tools, including hardware and software designed to guard against intruders and software designed to detect and destroy viruses, worms, and Trojan horses. Additionally, network administrators must be vigilant about installing software patches that plug security holes, and management should consider periodic security audits to detect network security vulnerabilities.

Several vendors, such as Symantec Corporation and McAfee, sell software and apps that detect known viruses, worms, or Trojan horses as a computer or device downloads a file or receives an email message. The antivirus programs then clean the infected file or email message by removing the destructive program. To be effective, virus protection software and apps require continual updates with information on recently discovered viruses. Most virus protection software programs perform automatic virus definition updates through downloads over the Internet. To protect your mobile device from unauthorized access, follow the best practices for any Internet usage, including safe downloading, passwords for your accounts and device, and more. Many mobile devices, including Samsung tablets, enable you to program a swipe code that provides an extra security method beyond a password (Figure 6-44).

users must swipe the buttons in a specific pattern to gain access to the device

Figure 6-44   Swipe codes prevent unauthorized access to a device.

FACTS @HAND   Another element in disaster recovery planning is the development of a formal network security plan. A security plan identifies policies and procedures designed to prevent an attack, determines how to respond in the event of an attack, and documents how the business will interact with employees, clients, and other interested parties as it handles the consequences of an attack.

To Review Current Virus, Worm, and Trojan Horse Threats

The following steps review current virus, worm, and Trojan horse threats using information found on Symantec's website. Your exact search results will differ.

1

- Start your browser, if necessary.

- Enter `symantec.com` in the Address bar, then press the ENTER key or tap or click the appropriate button to open the Symantec webpage.

- Tap or click the Security Response link to open the webpage (Figure 6-45).

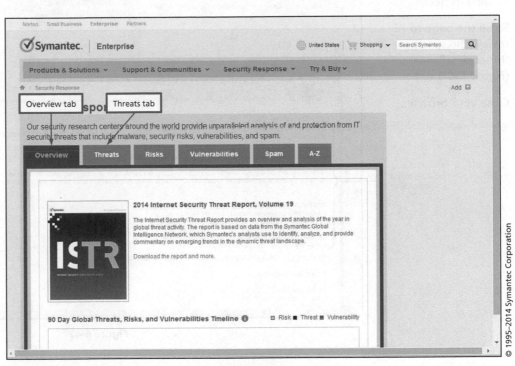

© 1995–2014 Symantec Corporation

Figure 6-45

2

- Tap or click the Threats tab.

- Scroll down to view a list of vulnerability threats (Figure 6-46).

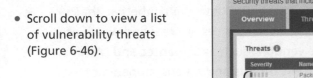

latest identified software vulnerabilities

© 1995–2014 Symantec Corporation

Figure 6-46

3

- Tap or click the linked threat name or any item in the Threats list to view its details.

- Scroll the page to review the specific threat details (Figure 6-47).

- Close your browser.

details about selected threat

Figure 6-47

© 1995–2014 Symantec Corporation

FACTS @HAND

False warnings about viruses — called virus hoaxes — often are shared from person to person through email or social networking. Before you take any action regarding an email virus warning, you should determine whether that warning is a hoax. To help users determine which viruses are real and which are hoaxes, major virus protection software vendors, such as Symantec and McAfee, maintain up-to-date information on current threats and an encyclopedia of known viruses, worms, and Trojan horse programs at their websites. You can also visit the web site Snopes.com to determine the veracity of a threat.

WEB PAGE HACKING   Webpages or databases accessed from webpages are also targets for hackers. For example, hackers have done the following:

- Stolen customer data from Target
- Hacked the USAJOBS government website and stolen personally identifiable information from a jobs database
- Distributed microblogging worms targeting celebrities' Twitter postings
- Hacked the NBC website and added a malicious JavaScript that downloaded to user's computers or devices when viewed

Hijacking a website occurs when hackers redirect a URL to an alternate website. Hackers also at times deface websites by adding graffiti, distorting graphics, or replacing or manipulating webpage text. A good resource for learning about web application security and recent hacker attacks is the Web Application Security Consortium and its sponsored Web Hacking Incidents Database (Figure 6-48).

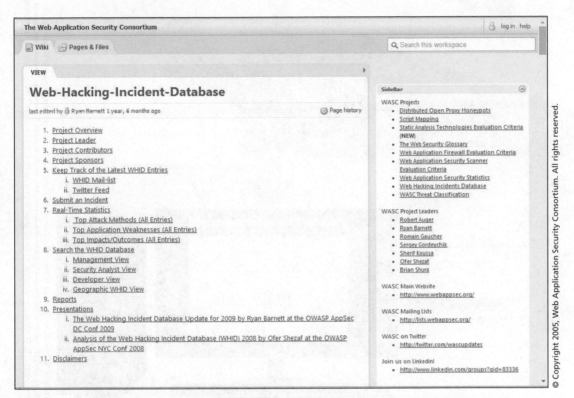

Figure 6-48 Reading about web hacking incidents can help prepare you to take necessary security measures.

FIREWALLS AND PROXY SERVERS In Chapter 2, you learned about personal firewall software, such as ZoneAlarm® PRO, which protects home computers and devices with DSL or cable modem "always on" Internet connections. A **network firewall** is a combination of hardware and software that filters traffic between private networks or between a private network and a public network, such as the Internet (Figure 6-49). Network firewalls can monitor and report suspicious network traffic, and can filter out or block incoming or outgoing network traffic based on a set of predetermined rules established by the network administrator. For example, a network firewall might block outgoing server requests for certain webpages or block incoming email from specific sources.

Figure 6-49 A network firewall is a combination of hardware and software that filters traffic between private networks or between a private network and a public network, such as the Internet.

A common type of network firewall is a **packet-filtering firewall**, which compares information contained in an IP packet header, such as the packet's source and destination IP addresses, with a set of predetermined filtering rules. The firewall allows packets that agree with the filtering rules to pass through to the network and blocks packets that do not agree with the filtering rules. Another security device often used in conjunction with a packet-filtering firewall is a proxy server.

A **proxy server** is a computer or software application that hides an internal IP address from the outside world by substituting its own IP address for a source computer's IP address before sending outgoing email or webpage requests. For example, an outgoing webpage request first would pass through the proxy server, which substitutes its own IP address for the original source's IP address. The proxy server then sends the request on to the packet-filtering firewall, which validates that the source IP address (now the proxy server's IP address) and the destination IP address meet its filtering rules before sending the request on to the destination web server.

INTERNET FILTERING SOFTWARE   As you have learned, employees' inappropriate use of Internet access can increase a company's potential liabilities and network security risks. Vendors such as WebSpy and Websense sell Internet-filtering software that monitors and restricts employee Internet access.

SECURITY AUDITS   Network administrators and IT managers use network security audits, conducted by third-party auditing firms, to expose network vulnerabilities. A **network security audit** reviews overall network security policies, employee security policy and procedure training, data backup and restore policies and procedures, and the physical security of the network equipment and data. A security audit can also involve **penetration testing**, in which security audit personnel try to hack into the network. The security audit may result in a revision of security policies and procedures, improved employee training, and making necessary updates to the network's hardware and software.

Transactional Risks

When a company conducts business transactions over the Internet, risks associated with online transactions are an additional security concern. The company must ensure that all parties are really who they say they are (authentication), that transactions cannot be intercepted or corrupted during transmission (integrity), that no party to a transaction can deny its participation (nonrepudiation), and that transaction information is kept private (confidentiality). The primary tools used to provide transaction authentication, integrity, nonrepudiation, and confidentiality are encryption and digital certificates.

Encryption is the process of translating readable data into unreadable data to prevent unauthorized access or use. A special key decodes encrypted data at its destination. A **certification authority (CA)**, such as VeriSign, creates the keys for a fee. When an organization wants to use encryption, it requests a set of associated public and private keys from a CA. The **public key** encrypts data sent to the organization and is posted by the CA to a publicly accessible directory. The **private key** is known only to the organization and is used to decrypt the incoming data.

A **digital certificate** electronically authenticates an organization's or individual's identity. CAs issue, for a fee, digital certificates that contain the issuer's name, a certificate number, an expiration date, the requesting entity's public key information, and the issuer's digital signature, which validates the certificate's legitimacy (Figure 6-50). A digital certificate is located on a public directory or registry so that interested parties can look up public keys.

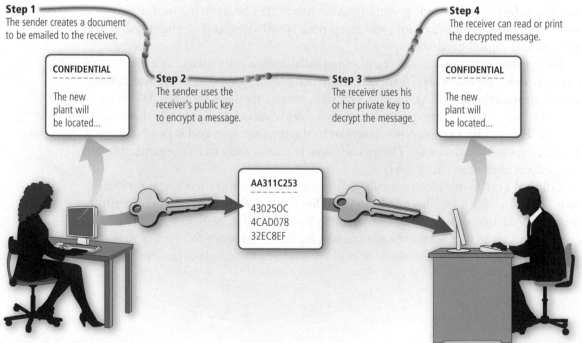

Figure 6-50   A digital certificate issued by a certification authority electronically authenticates an organization's or individual's identity.

A **public key infrastructure** is the combination of organizations or individuals sending and receiving encrypted data, their public and private keys, and the CAs that issue the keys and digital certificates. Figure 6-51 illustrates the sending and receiving of encrypted data.

An Example of Public Key Encryption

Step 1
The sender creates a document to be emailed to the receiver.

Step 4
The receiver can read or print the decrypted message.

CONFIDENTIAL

The new
plant will
be located...

Step 2
The sender uses the receiver's public key to encrypt a message.

Step 3
The receiver uses his or her private key to decrypt the message.

CONFIDENTIAL

The new
plant will
be located...

AA311C253

43025OC
4CAD078
32EC8EF

Figure 6-51   The sender encrypts data using the recipient's public key and sends the data over a public or private IP network to its destination, where it is decrypted using the recipient's private key.

Virtual Private Networks

A **virtual private network (VPN)** is a private network that uses a large public network, such as the Internet, to transmit its data. **Tunneling** is a process that encapsulates one protocol inside another protocol. VPNs use tunneling to hide encrypted data, IP addresses, and a tunneling protocol inside IP packets routed over the public network using the IP protocol. When the IP packets reach their destination LAN, VPN firewall software removes the IP protocol information, and the tunneling protocol transmits the packet to its final destination computer. VPNs also use public and private key encryption, digital certificates, and special security protocols to secure their data transmissions. Personal VPNs exist wherein mobile or wireless users can establish a private, secure network connection.

Cyber Security

@ISSUE

Cyber security — the preventing, identifying, and responding to attacks on persons or information through malicious websites, phishing, hacking, viruses, Trojan horses, worms, cyber bullying, and other threats — is a daily job. Other cyber threats include unauthorized access to mobile or Internet-based banking websites and apps; **backdoors** in software and apps that can enable hackers to infiltrate a computer or device; cloud storage vulnerabilities; and mobile botnets, which spread malicious content and viruses through unsuspecting mobile device users.

Like businesses, individuals also must recognize threats and risks and then take necessary steps to mitigate them. For example, individuals should take care to follow the same safety practices that are used by businesses: back up critical data, choose passwords carefully, consider biometric authentication tools for logon, filter out junk email, install virus protection software, and so forth. Additionally, individuals of mobile devices also should physically secure the device when it is not in use.

Chapter Review

Networks are categorized by the physical area that they cover, and include local area, metropolitan area, and wide area networks. The Internet is the world's largest public WAN. LANs are configured in one of two basic structures: peer-to-peer or client/server.

The three most common physical topologies are the bus topology, the ring topology, and the star topology. The two most common LAN access methods are Ethernet and token ring. Networks use both physical transmission media, such as twisted-pair and fiber-optic cable, and wireless transmission media, such as infrared (IR) and radio frequency (RF) transmissions. The hardware devices and software that connect network segments and multiple networks to each other are hubs, bridges, data switches, routers, and gateways.

Network service providers (NSPs) provide the interconnected Internet backbones and networks at Internet exchange points (IXPs). Peering is the exchange of Internet traffic at a public or private exchange point. NAPs and NSPs create peering agreements that regulate the exchange of Internet traffic bound for each other's networks.

The TCP/IP stack is a group of subprotocols that provides the de facto standard protocols for communications across the Internet and for many private networks. An IP address is used by the IP protocol to deliver a data packet. The DNS consists of a hierarchy of servers: root name servers, authentication servers, and local caching servers.

ICANN manages the Shared Registration System (SRS), which allows private companies, called accredited registrars, to participate in the registration of domain names.

IP telephony or voice over IP (VoIP) uses TCP/IP and packet switching to send Voice over an IP network. Web and video conferencing permit the real-time transmission of images and sounds between two locations, and are used for activities such as employee meetings and training, new product introduction, and customer support activities. Virtual conversations use similar technology, but are for personal uses.

Network security involves protecting network equipment and data from internal and external threats.

After reading this chapter, you should know each of these Key Terms.

access method (279)
accredited registrars (297)
authoritative servers (294)
backdoor (319)
biometrics (308)
Bluetooth (283)
body area network (BAN) (279)
bridge (286)
caching servers (294)
cellular transmission (281)
certification authority (CA) (317)
classful routing system (292)
Classless Inter-Domain Routing (CIDR) (292)
classless routing system (292)
client/server network (277)
cloud storage (309)
coaxial cable (284)
converged networks (304)
cyber security (319)
data switch (286)
digital certificate (318)
disaster recovery plan (310)
distributed denial of service (DDoS) (311)
DNS namespace (294)
dynamic routing (287)
encryption (317)
Ethernet (281)
fiber-optic cable (285)
gateway (289)
geosocial networking (301)
Global Positioning System (GPS) (300)
hijacking (315)
hop (287)
hub (276)
infrared (IR) transmissions (282)
intelligent hub (286)
Internet exchange point (IXP) (290)
Internet telephony (303)
IP network (291)
IP telephony (303)
ipconfig /all (293)
IPv6 (292)
LAN jacking (308)
location-based services (LBS) (300)
logical address (291)
logical topology (281)
MAC (Media Access Control) address (286)
Metropolitan Area Exchange (MAE) (290)
metropolitan area network (MAN) (278)
near field communication (NFC) (282)
network card (276)
network firewall (315)
network interface card (NIC) (276)

network operating system (278)
network security audit (317)
network service providers (NSPs) (290)
node (276)
nslookup (295)
octet (292)
packet-filtering firewall (316)
pair (283)
passive hub (286)
peering (290)
peer-to-peer LAN (276)
penetration testing (317)
physical topology (279)
port (286)
private key (318)
private peering (290)
proxy server (316)
public key (318)
public key infrastructure (318)
radio frequency (RF) transmissions (283)
resolving (294)
rogue WLAN (309)
root name servers (294)
root zone file (294)
router (286)
routing table (287)
segments (285)
Shared Registration System (SRS) (297)
smart card (308)
social engineering (306)
spoofing (308)
static routing (287)
TCP/IP stack (290)
throughput (279)
token (281)
token ring (281)
tracert utility (287)
transceiver (283)
transmission media (279)
tunneling (318)
twisted-pair cable (284)
video conferencing (304)
virtual conversation (305)
virtual meeting (304)
virtual private network (VPN) (318)
Voice over IP (VoIP) (303)
war driving (308)
web conferencing (306)
wide area network (WAN) (279)
Wi-Fi network (283)
wireless LAN (WLAN) (283)
wireless personal area networks (WPANs) (283)

TEST YOUR KNOWLEDGE

Complete the Test Your Knowledge exercises to solidify what you have learned in the chapter.

True or False

Mark T for True and F for False. (Answers are found on page numbers in parentheses.)

___ 1. Pairing is the process of connecting two Bluetooth devices. (283)

___ 2. A peer-to-peer LAN is an appropriate networking choice for a medium-sized organization with 45 users. (276)

___ 3. A proxy server sits between a user and the Internet and forwards HTTP requests using its own IP address rather than the user's IP address. (316)

___ 4. War driving is the act of driving around with a laptop, antenna, and wireless card, looking for unsecured wireless networks to access. (308)

___ 5. A virtual private network is another name for a Wi-Fi network. (319)

___ 6. VoIP uses circuit switching to send voice over an IP network. (303)

___ 7. Geosocial networking uses LBSs and tools such as Facebook to connect users. (302)

___ 8. An IXP is used by ISPs, but is expensive and has a negative impact on a network's bandwidth. (290)

___ 9. A DNS root name server publishes a directory of the next level of DNS servers. (294)

___10. A backdoor in software or an app enables hackers to infiltrate a computer or device. (319)

Multiple Choice

Select the best answer. (Answers are found on page numbers in parentheses.)

1. While _____ cable is too expensive to be used as a transmission medium for a small LAN, it is the transmission medium of choice for MANs and WANs. (285)

   a. coaxial cable

   b. infrared (IR)

   c. fiber-optic cable

   d. radio frequency (RF)

2. The Shared Registration System of domain name registrars is overseen by _____. (294)

   a. ISPs

   b. accredited registrars

   c. NSPs

   d. ICANN

3. _____ transmissions use radio to connect devices that are touching or nearby (generally within 10 centimeters). (282)

   a. Radio frequency (RF)

   b. NFC

   c. Infrared (IR)

   d. None of the above

4. The process of translating readable data into unreadable data to prevent unauthorized access or use is called _____. (317)

   a. decryption

   b. encryption

   c. tunneling

   d. private key

5. A _____ is an intelligent connectivity device with one input port and one output port that connects two network segments or two LANs. (286)

   a. bridge

   b. data switch

   c. router

   d. gateway

6. A(n) _____ is a small packet that moves clockwise in a circle from node to node on a network. (281)

   a. subnode

   b. octet

   c. router

   d. token

7. _____ is when a hacker accesses a network to set up a fake website or send mail that looks like it is coming from an internal server. (308)

   a. War driving

   b. LAN jacking

   c. Spoofing

   d. Cracking

8. Large modern networks often are broken up into _____, or multiple groups of computers and devices that share a common function. (285)

   a. LANs

   b. segments

   c. VPNs

   d. servers

9. An IPv6 address includes _____ 8-bit numbers. (292)

   a. 8

   b. 32

   c. 1,000,000

   d. 128

10. A _____ is a kind of virus that spreads across a network, such as the Internet, by replicating itself. (311)

   a. Trojan horse

   b. worm

   c. backdoor

   d. DDoS

TRENDS

Investigate current Internet developments with the Trends exercises.

Write a brief essay about each of the following trends, using the web as your research tool. For each trend, identify at least one webpage URL used as a research source. Be prepared to discuss your findings in class.

1 | NFC

Use a search engine to search for *NFC uses*. Sort or filter your results, if necessary, to search for the most recent articles or blog posts. Make a list of five specific uses of NFC for social media, data sharing, e-commerce, and more. What kinds of devices or apps use NFC? Does your device enable you to use NFC? If possible, experiment with using NFC to share contact information with another student. Describe the risks of using NFC to share data or complete e-commerce transactions.

Submit your findings in the format requested by your instructor.

2 | VPNs

Use a search engine to search for *VPN uses*. Sort or filter your results, if necessary, to search for the most recent articles or blog posts. Make a list of how a company that hires remote employees might use a VPN. What kinds of hardware and software do you need to run a VPN? List general steps to install and use a VPN. Describe security risks of using VPNs to a business. Submit your findings in the format requested by your instructor.

Use the Exercises to gain hands-on experience working with the Internet and the web.

@ ISSUE

Challenge your perspective of Internet technology with the @Issue exercises.

Write a brief essay in response to the following issues, using the web as your research tool. For each issue, identify at least one URL used as a research source. Be prepared to discuss your findings in class.

1 | Analyzing Personal Security Threats

Make a list of all of the locations and situations in which you typically access Internet resources, as well as the devices you use. Determine the three access methods or situations you use the most. For each of the three situations, identify at least one security threat. Describe any methods you can use to protect yourself from each threat. Submit your findings in the format requested by your instructor.

2 | Identifying Current Virus, Worm, and Trojan Horse Risks

Use a search engine to search for *virus, worm, and Trojan horse threats*. Sort or filter your results, if possible, to search for the most recent articles or blog posts. Make a list of 10 current viruses, worms, and Trojan horses. Create a table that lists the following information for each: Name, Risk Level, Description, Date Discovered, and Source. If possible, check your virus protection software or app to ensure you are protected from these threats. Is your virus protection up to date? If not, are your settings configured to update automatically? If possible, change your settings to ensure you receive automatic updates. Submit your findings in the format requested by your instructor.

HANDS ON

Use the web to obtain more information about the skills taught in the chapter with the Hands On exercises.

1 | Looking Up Corresponding Domain Names and IP Addresses

1. Open the Command Prompt window and use the `nslookup` command to identify the domain names that correspond to the following IP addresses:

   a. 161.225.130.163

   b. 149.48.228.139

   c. 18.7.21.110

   d. 192.168.1.1

   e. 74.125.113.106

2. Use the Command Prompt window and the `nslookup` command to identify the IP addresses that correspond to the following domain names:

   a. verisign.com

   b. zazzle.com

   c. blogger.com

   d. yelp.com

   e. garmin.com

3. Close the Command Prompt window.

4. For each of the above, make a note of the answers. Submit your findings in the format requested by your instructor.

2 | Using the Windows Tracert Utility to Trace Hops

1. Open the Command Prompt window and use the tracert command to identify the number of hops between your computer and the following locations:

   a. www.wm.edu

   b. www.cisco.com

   c. www.bbc.co.uk

   d. www.rackspace.com

   e. www.loc.gov

2. Which location required the most hops? Which location required the fewest hops? If possible, determine why one location required more or fewer hops than another.

3. Submit your findings in the format requested by your instructor.

TEAM APPROACH   Work collaboratively to reinforce the concepts in the chapter with the Team Approach exercises.

1 | Setting up a Network

1. Work with a team of three to four classmates to create a plan for installing a wireless home network to connect a personal computer, tablet, and gaming console to the Internet and each other, and that includes a printer.

2. As a team, use the Internet to search for answers to the following questions:

   a. What are the benefits of setting up a home wireless network? What is the advantage of a wireless over a wired network?

   b. What hardware resources do you need to set up a home network?

   c. How can a network enable you to share files and software applications between computers and devices?

   d. Locate a list of common networking problems. Make a list of the three that are your top concerns, and explain how you would fix them.

   e. What steps would you take to keep your network secure?

3. Submit your findings in the format requested by your instructor.

2 | Researching Past and Current Cyber Attacks

1. Work with a team of three to four classmates to research cyber attacks that made history or the news.

2. Find a list of cyber attacks, and choose one to research.

3. As a team, find the answers to the following questions:

   a. What type of attack occurred?

   b. Was an individual or group caught or credited with the attack? If so, what punishments did they receive?

   c. What vulnerabilities led to the attack occurring?

   d. What measures did the company or organization that was attacked make to increase security, inform customers, and protect data?

   e. If possible, find the estimated cost of the attack.

4. Submit your findings in the format requested by your instructor.

7 | Understanding E-Business

Introduction

As you learned in Chapter 1, the term e-commerce sometimes describes the process of conducting business transactions over the Internet, while the term e-business more often describes the broader scope of maintaining partner, customer, and employee business relationships using the Internet. Many people use these terms interchangeably. This chapter uses the term e-business to describe business activities of all types supported by Internet technologies.

In this chapter, you will learn about the early origins of e-business and the unique factors that underlie its rapid and continuing growth, as well as individual e-business successes. Multiple real-world examples will help you learn about different e-business models. Finally, you will focus on business-to-consumer retailing by learning about online store software, merchant accounts, and authorization and processing procedures for credit card transactions.

Objectives

After completing this chapter, you will be able to:

1. Describe the origins of electronic business transactions, including the electronic funds transfer (EFT) system, the electronic data interchange (EDI) standard, and value-added networks (VANs)

2. Discuss unique e-business factors and identify e-businesses that use them

3. Define common e-business models and explain how each model generates revenue

4. Describe the e-retailing storefront software, merchant accounts, and payment-processing services needed to create and operate an online store

E-Business Origins

You might be surprised to learn that the origins of some types of business transactions conducted electronically goes back more than 40 years — long before the Internet became a popular and useful business channel. Electronic business activities actually originated in the 1960s and 1970s with the banking industry's electronic funds transfer system and the electronic data interchange (EDI) networks used by large companies.

Electronic Funds Transfer

Electronic funds transfer (EFT) allows the electronic transfer of money between banks — without the exchange of paper currency. In the 1960s, banks began exchanging money electronically through a network that connects all U.S. financial institutions, called the **Automated Clearing House (ACH)** network. EFT continues to play an important role in business today. Having your payroll check deposited directly to your bank account; paying your federal income taxes, utility bills, or credit card bills online; and using an ATM all are examples of EFT (Figure 7-1) in action.

ATM

bank A

bank B

ACH network

payroll direct deposit

online bill payments

mobile banking app

credit card, utility, and other vendors

shokunin/openclipart.org

Figure 7-1   Paying bills online, having a paycheck deposited directly into an account, and using an ATM are examples of the Electronic Funds Transfer (EFT) system in action.

Electronic Data Interchange

The **electronic data interchange (EDI)** standard specifies the layout or format a company uses to exchange electronic business data — such as purchase orders, receiving reports, and invoices — with its suppliers and customers. For example, a manufacturing company could use specific EDI formats to automate the process of ordering parts from its suppliers. The participants in an EDI exchange of business data are called **trading partners**. Before the Internet became a viable alternative for transmitting data, EDI exchange of business information between trading partners occurred over private telecommunication networks called **value-added networks (VANs)**. Traditional VANs are very expensive to set up and maintain, and require the creation of costly, customized interfaces for exchanging data with trading partners. For these reasons, primarily only very large companies still use EDI exchanges (Figure 7-2).

Figure 7-2 Value-added networks (VANs) are private telecommunication networks that allow trading partners to exchange business data.

The Internet is a much less expensive network alternative to creating and maintaining VANs. Many small, medium, and large companies use the Internet rather than VANs to exchange business data. Companies can send purchase orders and invoices over the Internet to their trading partners using the XML document format and the HTTP protocols. Grid computing refers to the general processes served by VANs. **Grid computing** combines resources from many sources to reach a common goal. For example, the software, hardware, and network capabilities of a group of companies in a business process — from resource procurement to manufacturing to sales — all combine to create a grid. **Distributed computing** is a related term to grid computing, and refers to combining many networked computers and devices to create a **virtual super computer** that can perform complex tasks. Cloud computing is a type of distributed computing.

Unique E-Business Factors

Companies that conduct activities online have several business advantages, including worldwide sales opportunities, reduced transaction and purchasing costs, and access to small, niche markets. At the same time, individual and business consumers also enjoy similar advantages: access to a global electronic marketspace, wider product availability, improved customer and product support, and easy comparison shopping.

Beyond these advantages, other factors unique to conducting business activities online play an important role in the ongoing growth and success of e-business. In this section, you will learn about some of these factors, including the effects of geography, time, and space on the online marketspace; the network effect; the ability of individual e-businesses to redefine a market; and the power of personalization and customization.

Geography, Time, and Space

Geography, time, and space are limiting factors for any brick-and-mortar business. The following is a look at the role geography, time, and space can play in the operation of a brick-and-mortar store, such as a bookstore:

- Geography — A brick-and-mortar bookstore must be physically located within a modest driving distance of its targeted customer base. In addition, the store should be located in a high-traffic area to increase its visibility and attract new customers, as well as provide or have accessible ample parking for customers.

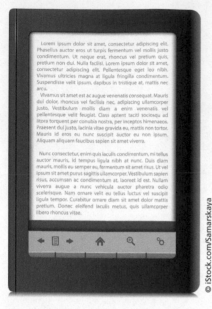

© iStock.com/Samarskaya

Figure 7-3 E-book readers enable you to download books instantly from the Internet.

- Time — A brick-and-mortar bookstore is likely to maintain the same operating hours as other stores in its area, which might be only peak shopping hours. In most areas, it is uncommon to find a brick-and-mortar bookstore open 24 hours a day.

- Space — The inventory of books available at a brick-and-mortar bookstore is limited to the store's available storage and shelf space. Because of space restrictions, a brick-and-mortar bookstore might stock only the most recently published books in the most popular categories — perhaps carrying only a few hundred titles.

Now consider the effect of geography, time, and space on the online bookstore marketspace. Suppose you just read a review of the latest book by your favorite British mystery author, and you want to purchase a copy of the book. The book currently is available only in the United Kingdom and will not be available in U.S. bookstores for several months. You can visit a website and order the book anytime it is convenient for you. You also might be able to purchase an electronic copy of the book, called an **e-book**, which you can download to a handheld device, such as an e-book reader (Figure 7-3), tablet computer, or smartphone.

Perhaps you need to find an inexpensive used copy of a classic nineteenth century novel that currently is out of print. The nearest used bookstore is several miles away and has a poor selection of these types of books. Several e-business websites — such as Amazon, Abebooks.com, and Alibris (Figure 7-4) — aggregate information about the used, out-of-print, and rare book inventories held by individual book resellers located all over the world. Websites dedicated to the sale of used books, such as Thrift Books, also exist. You even can use Amazon to sell your own used books, or trade them with other book readers using services such as PaperBackSwap.

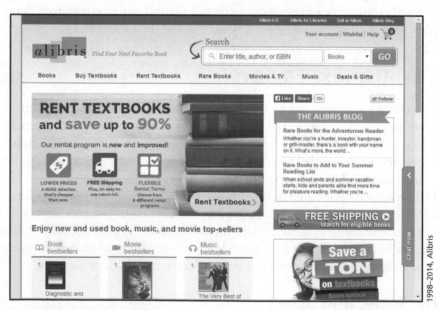

1998–2014, Alibris

Figure 7-4 Online bookstores and trading sites enable you to find used or rare books from individuals or booksellers around the world.

The Network Effect

An important e-business success factor, called the **network effect**, refers to the increasing value of a network as the network grows. The analogy often used to describe the network effect is a telephone network. Assume that your telephone is the only telephone connected to a telephone network. Your single telephone and the telephone network have little or no value because you cannot call anyone else, and no one can call you. Connect a second telephone and user to the network, however, and the value of the network increases — now you and the other user can call each other. As additional telephones and users connect to the network, the network's value continues to increase.

The rate at which Internet services such as e-business, email, and social networking have grown is an example of the network effect (Figure 7-5). For example, the value of social networks to individual users and to the business community continues to grow as the number of people who use social networking increases.

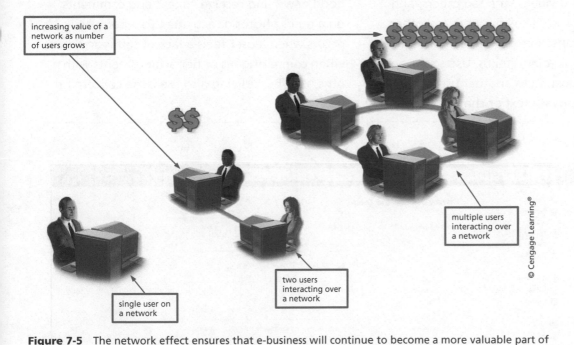

increasing value of a network as number of users grows

multiple users interacting over a network

two users interacting over a network

single user on a network

© Cengage Learning®

Figure 7-5   The network effect ensures that e-business will continue to become a more valuable part of the global economy as the number of e-businesses and their online customers grows.

Facebook and the Network Effect

CASE STUDY

If Facebook were a country, it would be the second largest country in the world, according to 2014 statistics, which list Facebook's active users as totaling over 1.28 billion. Facebook is a prime example of the network effect. The more users who are on Facebook, the more connections you can make, and the greater

the services businesses will offer to those who "like" the business on Facebook.

In 2003, Mark Zuckerberg, a Harvard University student, hacked into networks to collect and distribute student photos in a digital format that enabled students to rate other students' attractiveness. Harvard soon shut down Facemash, as he called it. Zuckerberg faced expulsion due to privacy violations, among other infractions. After the administration dropped the charges, Zuckerberg teamed with other Harvard students to create thefacebook.com, which in one month had over half of Harvard's students registered.

Since 2006, anyone with a valid email account who claimed they were over 13 years old could join. Facebook has acquired several apps and services throughout the years, including Instagram (photo sharing), and WhatsApp (instant messaging).

Facebook users create profiles that list their likes, interests, relationship status, and more; add photos and videos, and tag others; and "friend" contacts, "like" business and other pages, and "subscribe" to celebrity and other users' or organizations' feeds. Users can send messages by posting to another user's wall, or by sending a private text or chat message. A timeline lists a user's life milestones, such as schools attended, or jobs held. Users can set privacy and security settings to ensure only those with authorization can see information and photos (Figure 7-6).

Facebook's impact has been far reaching. Media sources take advantage of the social sharing offered by Facebook and other networks to promote news stories and track users' interest and comments using analytic tools. Politicians use Facebook to promote their platform, raise campaign funds, and communicate with constituents. Social impacts are both positive and negative. Being part of a social network such as Facebook enables users to connect and communicate with others, share good news, and receive "likes" and comments on a user's photos or activities. Facebook envy occurs when a user feels a lack of self-worth when comparing his or her achievements with others'. Cyberbullying also is a large concern on Facebook.

Figure 7-6   Facebook is an example of an e-business whose success was influenced by the network effect.

Redefining Markets

Another important e-business factor is the opportunity an individual e-business might have to redefine a market. Market redefinition generally takes place in one of two ways: (1) by removing traditional marketplace intermediaries or (2) by creating new ways to add value to business transactions, often by introducing new types of intermediaries to the marketplace.

DISINTERMEDIATION   An **intermediary**, or middleman, is a business entity that brings sellers and buyers together. Examples of traditional marketplace intermediaries include:

- Sporting goods industry — A retail store, selling manufactured goods to consumers
- Real estate industry — A real estate agent, marketing home owners' properties to potential buyers
- Travel industry — A travel agent, working with individuals to purchase plane tickets or reserve hotel rooms and rental cars
- Insurance industry — An insurance broker, providing clients with options from home, life, and car insurers

An individual e-business can redefine a market by allowing consumers to bypass the market's traditional intermediaries and purchase products or services directly from the e-business's website. **Disintermediation** occurs when a market removes its traditional intermediaries. Dell arguably is one of the more famous examples of disintermediation. Dell built its business by bypassing retail computer stores to sell directly to customers. Dell uses its websites to sell thousands of personal computers, printers, servers, and other consumer electronics directly to consumers around the world.

The travel industry is another example of disintermediation. In the past, planning a vacation or business trip involved calling or visiting a local travel agent who made all the arrangements, including purchasing airline tickets, reserving a car, and booking a hotel room. In turn, the agent earned a fee or commission from the airline, auto rental companies, and hotel. Today, travelers bypass the travel agent intermediary, and book and pay for their travel arrangements directly at e-business websites operated by airlines, auto rental companies, and hotels, such as Marriott, Enterprise, and US Airways, illustrated in Figure 7-7.

Figure 7-7   Examples of hotel, auto rental, and airline websites contributing to travel industry disintermediation.

Dell Inc. and Disintermediation

Michael Dell, an undergraduate at the University of Texas at Austin, founded Dell Computer Corporation (now Dell Inc.) in 1984. Michael Dell recognized that a business opportunity existed in the huge difference between the cost of individual personal computer components and the price of an assembled personal computer purchased from a retail store. He decided that by eliminating the retail store middleman, he could sell personal computers directly to consumers for much lower prices and still generate a profit. He was right. In the first year of operation, the company grossed $73 million. By 1993, Dell was a Fortune 500 company and one of the top five computer manufacturers in the world.

Dell's original, and still primary, sales channel is in the PC market (Figure 7-8). Corporate sales were the initial target, but soon Dell expanded to custom-built consumer PCs. Through product development and acquisitions, Dell's product line now includes not only computers and related products and services, but software, peripheral devices, TVs, servers, and more.

Dell has experimented with a variety of sales channels. It started selling PCs over the web in 1996. Other ventures included shopping mall kiosks and retail stores. In 2008, Dell announced it was closing all of its U.S. shopping mall kiosks to focus on direct sales and retail partnerships.

The rise in tablet sales has led to a drop in PC sales, affecting Dell and other manufacturers. Poor customer service complaints abounded after Dell moved the majority of its call centers off-shore. Dell has spent money to improve its customer service throughout the years. The firm Silver Lake Partners teamed with Michael Dell in 2013 to participate in a leverage buyout, which bought all public shares and made the company privately held. In 2013, Dell had $57 billion in revenue and more than 100,000 employees worldwide. In 2014, the company became the largest business to accept the digital currency, Bitcoin.

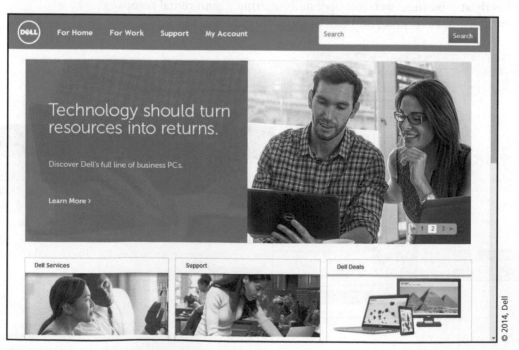

© 2014, Dell

Figure 7-8 Dell sells personal computers directly to consumers.

REINTERMEDIATION   Some e-businesses are eliminating traditional intermediaries and, in the process, redefining markets. Other e-businesses also are redefining markets through a different process called **reintermediation**. Reintermediation occurs when an e-business introduces a new type of intermediary into the marketspace. Dell, Hewlett-Packard, and even the online versions of stores such as Best Buy are examples of e-business reintermediation in the computer industry. Although it is likely that online computer sales contributed to the failure of some brick-and-mortar computer stores, such as Circuit City (with limited shelf space, and the higher business costs of renting store space and hiring store staff), disintermediation is not the culprit. E-business disintermediation in the computer industry occurs when computer manufacturers, such as Hewlett-Packard, sell computers directly to individual consumers from their websites, removing the traditional store or salesperson from the transaction.

Two examples of reintermediation in the travel industry are Orbitz Worldwide and Hotels.com. Orbitz (Figure 7-9) originally was an e-business partnership among five major airlines: American, Continental, Delta, Northwest, and United. Today, Orbitz Worldwide is a major provider of travel distribution services. Orbitz is a travel industry intermediary that uses its website and mobile apps to provide consumers with quick access to low fares for airline tickets and low rates on auto rentals and hotel accommodations.

Hotels.com, another travel industry intermediary, purchases large blocks of hotel rooms at a big discount from properties around the world. Hotels.com then marks up the discounted room rates and resells the rooms directly to consumers from its website and app.

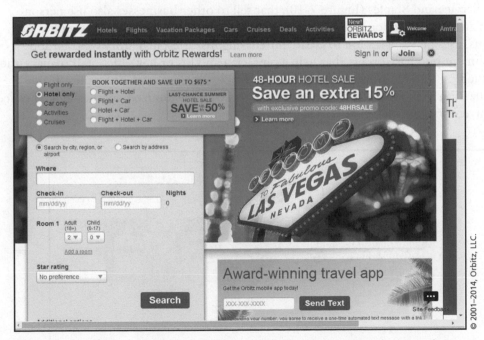

Figure 7-9   Online travel intermediary websites contribute to reintermediation in the travel industry.

Personalization and Customization

The unique interactive nature of the web that allows buyers and sellers to communicate directly is another important e-business factor. E-businesses can exploit web interactivity by personalizing and customizing web content to increase sales, provide better customer support, and encourage customer loyalty.

Sometimes people use the terms personalization and customization interchangeably. Some analysts define **personalization** as an automatic process that tailors webpage content to fit the profile of a specific target audience, or that automatically tailors webpage content for an individual visitor based on his or her actions at a site. You experience the benefits of personalization each time you shop at an online store that acknowledges you by name and suggests new items — books, shoes, food — for purchase based on your previous purchases and searches at the website.

Customization is a manual process that allows a visitor to manage webpage content by selecting viewing preferences or by creating and updating a personal profile. In Chapter 5, you learned how visitors could customize the news, sports, and weather content at a major news-oriented portal website by indicating preferences or postal codes. Customization also allows e-business customers to create individualized products, such as clothing or diet and fitness programs, designed specifically for them by indicating size, style, goals, or other preferences. Personalization and customization work together to create a unique viewing or shopping experience by using general customer purchase histories, product reviews, and target audience profile data. Personalization and customization also use individual visitor profiles to create uniquely targeted webpages with specific content, including item recommendations, and advertisements, based on the customer's past purchases.

E-businesses that sell directly to individual consumers and to other businesses use personalization and customization to develop a closer relationship with their customers that promotes increased customer loyalty. E-retail e-businesses, such as eDiets, provide customized diet and fitness plans based on consumer profiles and then track and report each subscriber's results as he or she follows the plan. E-businesses, such as Physician Sales & Service and Staples (Figure 7-10), that sell to other businesses also use personalization and customization. Physician Sales & Service, which sells medical supplies to physicians, uses personalization to create purchasing histories, inventory reports, and replenishment purchase orders that help a physician and his or her office staff manage the office's medical supply inventory. Online office supply vendors, such as Staples, also use personalization to provide their business customers with customized purchasing and office supply inventory control services.

Copyright 1998–2014, Staples, Inc.

Figure 7-10   E-businesses use personalization and customization to attract and keep customers.

E-Business Models

As you browse the web, you likely encounter many different types of commercial websites. How a commercial website generates revenue might not be obvious. A **business model** is the way a company operates to generate revenue, create profits (the excess of revenue over expenses), and continue as a viable business entity. The business model adopted by a company doing business online is its e-business model. In Chapter 1, you learned about several different e-business models, as described in Figure 7-11.

E-Business Models

Targeted Customer	E-Business Model	Description	Example
Consumers	Business-to-Consumer (B2C)	An e-business sells products or services directly to consumers.	Lands' End Amazon.com
Consumers	Consumer-to-Consumer (C2C)	A consumer sells products or services directly to another consumer.	eBay etsy
Businesses	Consumer-to-Business (C2B)	A consumer names a price for a product or service that competing businesses accept or decline.	Priceline.com
Businesses	Business-to-Business (B2B)	An e-business sells products or services to other businesses; brings multiple buyers and sellers together in a central online marketspace; sells e-business technologies; or transacts business activities over the Internet with trading partners.	Physician Sales & Service Storage Guardian
Government agencies and other businesses	Business-to-Government (B2G)	An e-business provides information about government agencies currently accepting bids for products and services; brings sellers and government agency buyers together in an online marketspace; or sells bidding and procurement technologies.	Fedmarket Onvia

© Cengage Learning®

Figure 7-11   E-business models can be defined by customer group.

Individual e-businesses optimize factors — such as geography, time, space, the network effect, personalization, and customization — within the framework of their e-business model. A number of ways to classify e-business models exist. The most common way is by targeted customer groups, such as consumers, other businesses, and government agencies. Although an individual e-business might seem to fit into one of the primary e-business model categories, many e-businesses actually operate using a mix of e-business models and revenue-generation methods. For example, an e-business's primary e-business model might emphasize selling products or services directly to consumers; however, the e-business also might generate revenue by doing one or more of the following:

- Offering subscription-based content
- Selling advertising space
- Earning referral fees by providing links to other e-businesses
- Selling proprietary e-business technologies to other companies

- Providing a channel for business partners to sell their products
- Participating in an affiliate marketing program

In this section, you will use multiple real-world e-business examples to explore common e-business models.

Business-to-Consumer (B2C)

The business-to-consumer (B2C) e-business model generates revenue in several ways, including retail sales directly to consumers, often called e-tail or **e-retail**, selling website advertising space, and charging subscription or membership fees for premium content.

E-RETAIL   Most large, traditional brick-and-mortar retailers and catalog merchants, such as Williams-Sonoma, The Container Store, and JCPenney (Figure 7-12), take advantage of their retailing experiences and existing product distribution centers to combine e-retailing websites successfully with their physical stores and catalog operations — in the process, becoming brick-and-click businesses, or e-retailers. By adding e-retailing websites to existing operations, these companies create a new business channel mix that provides increased sales opportunities and improved customer service.

Figure 7-12   Most large brick-and-mortar retailers and catalog merchants are also brick-and-click e-retailers.

Some early B2C e-retailers started life in the online marketspace as completely new businesses with no existing brick-and-mortar stores or catalog operations. These online-only retailers are **pure-play e-retailers**. Amazon.com is the most famous example of a pure-play e-retailer. Many other early pure-play e-retailers, such as Pets.com and the original eToys.com, were never able to rival Amazon.com's volume of sales or market dominance and ended as spectacular e-business failures. A **niche market** is a small segment within a larger market. Some pure-play e-retailers succeed by avoiding competition with larger e-businesses and, instead, target a niche market.

To Explore an E-Retailer

The following steps explore offerings at an e-retailer that targets a niche market, environmentally friendly cleaning products.

1

- Start your browser and enter `simplegreen.com` in the Address bar.

- Press the ENTER key, or tap or click the necessary button to open the Simple Green home page (Figure 7-13).

Household link

Figure 7-13

2

- Scroll the page to review its contents.

- Tap or point to the Household link, then tap or click All Products on the sub-menu to view the products for sale on the website (Figure 7-14).

3

- Close the browser and all open tabs.

Figure 7-14

© 2014 Sunshine Makers, Inc

© 2014 Sunshine Makers, Inc

ADVERTISING REVENUES   Some B2C e-businesses offer free content — apps, information, links, games, and so forth — and generate revenue by selling advertising at their sites. Website ads (Figure 7-15) usually link to the advertiser's own website. Visitors can go directly to the advertised website by clicking an ad in a process called a **click-through**. One method to measure the effectiveness of a particular website ad is the **per-click** revenue method, which counts the number of visitors who use it to click-through to the advertised website. Another way to generate revenue or measure an ad's success is the **cost per impression (CPI)** method. CPI counts the number of times a page that includes an ad is loaded in the browser; reimbursement for CPI is often for a certain number of impressions, such as per thousand.

Figure 7-15   Ads are one way a website generates revenue.

Google AdSense (Figure 7-16) is an example of an application that website owners can implement to include targeted advertisements on their sites. Google administers and maintains the advertisements, and site owners can include text, video, or image advertisements; this is an effective option for small e-business companies that do not have an advertising department, or individual website hosts who want to generate revenue by hosting banner ads. Social networking websites offer a large opportunity for targeted marketing. Advertisers can create ads and suggest content based on a user's social media profile, including pages the user likes; the user's location, occupation or interests; and even web searches made using an unrelated search engine.

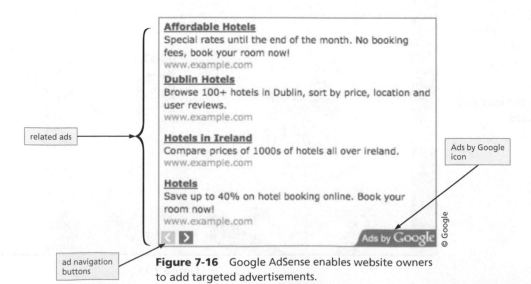

Figure 7-16   Google AdSense enables website owners to add targeted advertisements.

SUBSCRIPTION FEES   Another way the B2C e-business model generates revenue is through subscription fees for premium content or an app. Some e-businesses that generate revenue from advertising, such as Yahoo!, also might charge subscription fees for certain premium services, such as résumé posting and job search, posting personals ads, or participating in an online community.

For example, WebDesign (Figure 7-17) provides online courses, such as for WordPress, as well as access to information on web design, online marketing, and other relevant topics, such as domain names. Much of the content comes from discussions among subscribers in forums. The forums mostly are free to visitors. For an annual subscription fee, members can contribute to forums, as well as access some discussion groups only open to members.

Some nonprofit organizations also follow the B2C subscription e-business model. For example, the Consumers Union is an independent consumer product testing organization that publishes *Consumer Reports* magazine and its online version, ConsumerReports.org (Figure 7-17) and offers an app. For an annual subscription fee, you can read reviews and test results on thousands of consumer products at the ConsumerReports.org website.

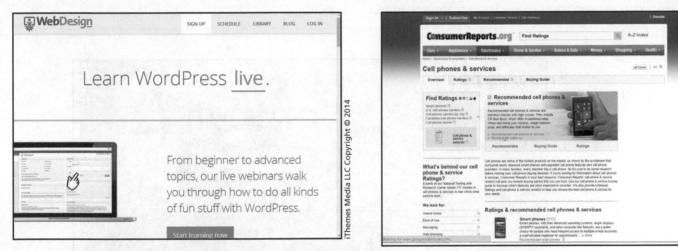

Figure 7-17   Some B2C e-businesses generate subscription-based revenues.

Netflix and the B2C Subscription Model

CASE STUDY

In 1997, Reed Hastings, a computer software entrepreneur, recognized a business opportunity in the emerging popularity of DVDs. To capitalize on this popularity, he cofounded the DVD rental e-business Netflix (Figure 7-18 on the following page), which offers various subscription plans, as well as personalized ratings. Hastings' goal was to provide a new way to rent DVDs — inexpensively delivered and then returned using a postage-paid envelope sent through the U.S. Postal Service, eliminating trips to a movie rental store. Originally, Netflix charged its customers a per-movie rental fee much like its brick-and-mortar competitors. Then, Hastings hit upon the idea of removing

specific return dates and the threat of late fees. As the story goes, Hastings had rented a movie from a video store, watched it, and then forgot to return it on time, which resulted in whopping late fees. From that costly experience was born the next Netflix e-business idea — DVDs rented on a subscription basis. Hastings envisioned Netflix customers paying a monthly subscription fee to rent as many DVDs as they wanted and keep them as long as they wanted without incurring late fees.

Netflix's original model charged customers monthly fees, which differed depending on the level of service, such as the number of movies rented at a time, with additional fees for Blu-ray rentals and streaming video. Customers can rate the movies they rent using its Cinematch five-star rating system. Netflix then uses a customer's movie ratings together with collaborative filtering software to create a list of movie recommendations based on the customer's viewing preferences.

Netflix participates in rental revenue-sharing partnerships with a number of TV and movie studios, which allows Netflix access to the studios' titles. In addition, Netflix produces original content, available only to subscribers. Netflix has been a strong supporter of independent films.

Netflix has an estimated 32 percent of the total market share for streaming video.

Subscribers can stream video over the Internet on a computer, mobile device, TV, or gaming consoles. More Netflix customers take advantage of streaming video delivery than DVD or Blu-ray rentals.

Today, Netflix has an estimated 50 million subscribers and an ever-expanding inventory of titles, including new releases, classics, hard-to-find documentaries, independent films, and original programming. Netflix has changed the way viewers watch TV shows — instead of waiting a week between episodes, many "binge" by watching multiple episodes in a day or over a short period of time.

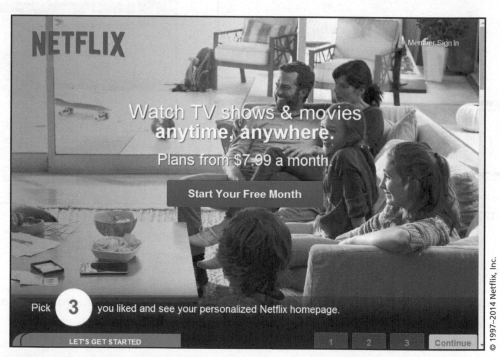

Figure 7-18 Netflix is a subscription-based streaming video and DVD/Blu-ray rental company.

SOCIAL MEDIA In previous chapters, you learned about the impact of web-based social media — social networking, social opinion, social tagging, microblogging, and more — on personal communication. Businesses also use social media to promote individual businesses and specific industries, to sell products and services to their customers, or to generate revenue by selling advertising space. For example, Facebook sells ad space; businesses actively solicit reviews of their sites by participants at StumbleUpon and other social bookmarking or tagging sites to build traffic to their sites; and companies use Twitter to broadcast a variety of business messages, or **Tweets**, announcing everything from pizza specials, to new offerings in a specific real estate market, to CEO business status updates. Businesses such as Ballard Designs create boards on Pinterest to show pictures and links to products (Figure 7-19).

Figure 7-19   Businesses can use social media sites to generate ad revenues, build traffic to their sites, and sell products and services.

Squidoo (Figure 7-20) and HubPages are platforms for user-generated websites. Without needing to know HTML, users create topic pages, which are available on the platform. Squidoo calls its webpages lenses, and the page creators are lensmasters. While lenses are informative, Squidoo pages also include click-through ads and links to generate revenue. Squidoo retains 50 percent of the revenue generated by each lens, and splits the remainder between the lensmaster and any charities the lensmaster specifies.

Figure 7-20   Squidoo relies on ads and links on user-generated content pages.

Twitter and the Social Media Business Model

Over 200 million accounts exist on Twitter, the original and most popular microblogging service available. Since its 2006 launch by Evan Williams, Biz Stone, and Jack Dorsey, Twitter has evolved into an essential marketing and communication tool for celebrities, politicians, bloggers, news outlets, businesses, nonprofit organizations such as Ocean Alliance (Figure 7-21), and personal users.

Twitter started as a text-only messaging service based on web syndication and SMS messaging technologies. Users can share photos, videos, links, and text using Twitter, and integrate their Tweets with other social networking platforms. Because of its 140-character limit per Tweet, users rely on URL shortening services when posting a link in a Tweet. A **URL shortener** is a web-based service that translates a lengthy URL into a shorter one; shorteners are available for free from several websites, including TinyURL.

To use the messaging service, individuals first create an account, from which they can broadcast messages to friends, family members, and others, who subscribe to or "follow" the individual's message feed. Twitter users also can select other Twitter users to follow. By default, Twitter accounts are public, although security features enable users to hide accounts, verify followers, and block followers.

Tweets use hashtags to group like topics together, creating trends. Trending topics might occur during a sporting event, an election, an incident from the news or entertainment, and more. Users can retweet another user's posts to increase the audience reached by the original post.

Twitter's effect on interpersonal communications has been so rapid and powerful that in 2009, *TIME magazine*'s named the three Twitter founders to the TIME 100, a list of the world's most influential people. Educators use Twitter to share articles or links with students, or to use Twitter during a lecture to enable students to ask and answer questions, and more. Twitter's impact on pop culture includes the use of hashtags during a TV broadcast to engage viewers during the broadcast of a popular show by encouraging them to Tweet about the show.

Twitter is a free service that uses paid advertisements, called "promoted Tweets," as part of its business model. In 2013, Twitter became a publicly traded company, and now is worth $664 million.

Figure 7-21 Nonprofits and other organizations use Twitter to post messages to followers.

Consumer-to-Business (C2B)

A consumer-to-business (C2B) e-business allows a buyer to name his or her own price for specific goods or services, such as airline tickets or hotel accommodations, in a process called a **reverse auction**. The C2B e-business accumulates buyer offers and then presents them to competing sellers. A buyer's offer is binding; therefore, when a seller accepts a buyer's offer, a charge immediately appears on the buyer's credit card. The C2B e-business generates revenue by earning booking fees and commissions on accepted offers.

Consumer-to-Consumer (C2C)

The consumer-to-consumer (C2C) e-business model, which brings individual buyers and sellers together in an online marketspace, generates revenue in several ways, including transaction fees, sales commissions, subscription or membership fees, and personal ad fees. C2C e-businesses, such as eBay, offer the auction services you learned about in Chapter 5 and generate revenue from listing fees, sales commissions, and advertising. Some call these auction services **forward auctions** because many buyers are bidding for an item offered by a single seller. Other C2C e-businesses offer reverse auctions, similar to the C2B model. In a C2C reverse auction, a single buyer makes an offer for a specific item, and multiple sellers compete to sell the item at the buyer's offer price.

Another type of C2C e-business, such as PaperBackSwap (Figure 7-22 on the following page) and SwapaDVD, allows members to list items of equal value they want to exchange — for example, exchanging a book for a book, or a DVD for a DVD. This type of C2C e-business might generate revenue by charging a small subscription or membership fee, selling advertising, or charging small fees for extra services, such as providing mailing labels and downloadable postage.

Still other C2C e-businesses, such as TraderOnline, sell online classified ad space to individuals trying to sell boats, cars, and other items.

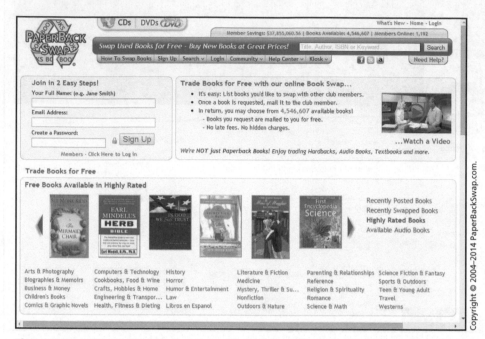

Figure 7-22 C2C auction, swap, and classified ad sites allow consumers to buy from and sell to each other.

To Explore a C2C E-Business

The following steps explore the C2C e-business website Etsy, which enables artists and craftspeople to set up online stores and sell items they have made.

1

- Start your browser and enter `etsy.com` in the Address bar.

- Press the ENTER key, or tap or click the necessary button to open the Etsy home page (Figure 7-23).

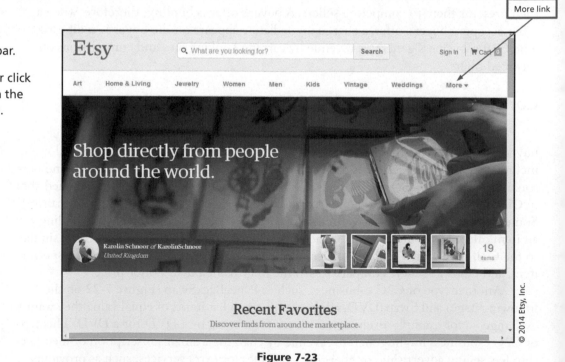

Figure 7-23

2

- Tap or click the More link, then tap or click Sell on Etsy to open the webpage.

- View the information about how and why to sell items on Etsy. (Figure 7-24).

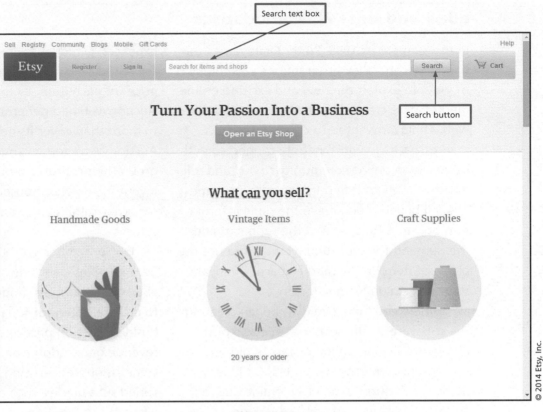

Figure 7-24

3

- Enter `recycled paper` in the Search text box, then tap or click the Search button to see the items currently for sale that use recycled paper (Figure 7-25).

- Follow the links of your choice to explore other pages at the website.

- Close the browser.

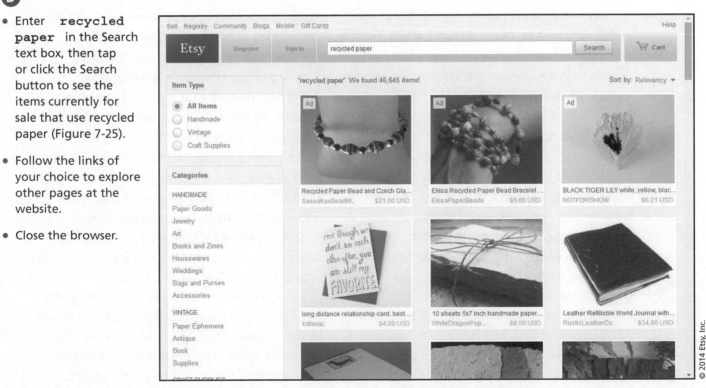

Figure 7–25

eBay and the C2C Marketspace

In the summer of 1995, Pierre Omidyar, a young Silicon Valley programmer, was thinking of ways to exploit the new and exciting online marketspace created by the Internet and the web. Omidyar wanted to create a "perfect marketspace" in which people connected with others in an online community to buy and sell a wide variety of items. In this online community, all buyers would have the same information on items for sale, and the supply of and the demand for each item would influence the prices of items in the marketspace. Omidyar's solution? An online auction.

In his spare time, Omidyar began creating the software to allow online sellers to post items for sale and online buyers to bid on those items. On Labor Day 1995, Omidyar launched AuctionWeb, a free online auction, as part of his personal website. Taking advantage of the network effect, Omidyar began advertising his free online auction through newsgroups as "The most fun buying and selling on the web." Group participants discussed the auction service and emailed their friends with the news. The first items posted for sale at the site included used computer equipment, a few health-club memberships, a couple of automobiles, and some autographed posters and other collectibles, such as Pez dispensers. Because of the effective exchange of information about the new online auction from newsgroups and email, traffic at AuctionWeb grew rapidly. In its first three months, AuctionWeb hosted hundreds of individual auctions and garnered several thousand buyer bids.

During 1995, Omidyar operated the free AuctionWeb service as a hobby. In February 1996, however, his ISP complained about the level of traffic to the site and began charging Omidyar a monthly fee for hosting a commercial site. To cover his increased expenses, Omidyar began charging sellers a fee based on a percentage of the final sales price for each item. By the end of February, AuctionWeb had generated enough in fees to more than cover its hosting expenses. AuctionWeb's fee revenue continued to grow. The profitable e-business required no inventory, no warehouse, no responsibility for order fulfillment, and no liability for item returns.

On September 1, 1997, AuctionWeb became eBay. Over time, the original eBay C2C e-business model has evolved to include both individual consumer and business auction participants, as well as revenue generation from listing fees, sales commissions, advertising, and more from its varied subsidiaries, such as StubHub (resale of event tickets), online classifieds, PayPal (online money transfer), and more. Charities can use eBay to run auction fundraisers. In 2014, eBay announced plans to permit mechanics to offer services for sale in a few select cities.

eBay sellers can opt to list items for auction, or use the Buy It Now feature. An important part of eBay is the ability to rate, and see others' ratings, of sellers in a variety of categories. The fee structure of eBay is complex, and includes vendor setup fees, item listing feeds, and a sliding scale of percentage of the final sale price. eBay prohibits many items, such as alcohol, bootlegged music or DVDs, and more. One enterprising seller attempted to auction his kidney to the highest bidder before eBay shut him down.

eBay (Figure 7-26) is one of the few early e-businesses to enjoy profitability almost from inception, and offers deals on cameras, iPads, and more. eBay now posts millions of items for auction in thousands of auction categories on any given day all over the world, and in a recent year boasted over $16 billion in revenue.

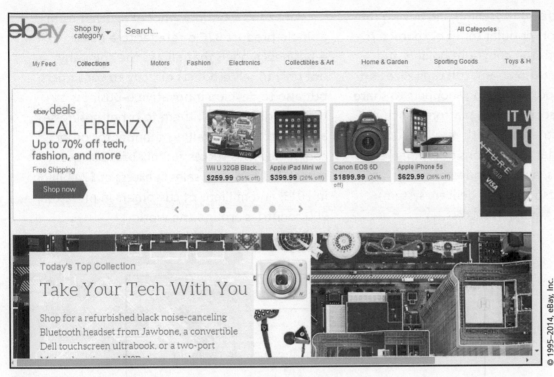

Figure 7-26   eBay has been successful since its beginnings.

© 1995–2014, eBay, Inc.

Amazon and the Evolving E-Business Model

First, think about South America's Amazon River — huge, with thousands of branches and tributaries, completely dominating its rain-forest environment. Now think about Amazon.com, the e-business named after the river — huge, with thousands of products and service for sale, becoming the world's largest online retailer.

In 1994, Amazon's founder, Jeff Bezos, reportedly observed the huge growth in the number of people using the web and decided to create an e-business to capitalize on that growth. After considerable research, Bezos opted to sell books for a number of reasons, including the enormous selection of available book titles. Bezos also reasoned that because books were inexpensive, his market risk was lower than with other products; that information about each book would fit nicely into a webpage format; and that books were easy to ship. Following a

business-to-consumer (B2C) e-business model that focused on product selection, customer service, personalization, and discount pricing, Amazon opened its virtual doors. Over the years, Amazon added music, videos, and DVDs to its offerings, as well as other retail products, including video games, toys, and electronics and much more. In 2005, Amazon launched its Prime service, which, for an annual fee, offers free, fast shipping, and streaming video options for its subscribers. (Figure 7-27).

Amazon has developed several consumer electronics, such as the Kindle e-book reader, the Kindle Fire tablet, the Internet-connected and voice-controlled Fire TV, and the Fire Phone smartphone. These devices enable users to purchase e-books, rent or purchase streaming media, download free and fee-based apps, and more. Another innovative Amazon venture was the launch of Kindle

Worlds, a platform for selling and buying fan fiction based on popular series or characters, partnering with the copyright holders and independent authors. Amazon capitalizes on social media tools, enabling shoppers to share purchases on social media platforms such as Facebook. Partnerships with retailers such as Sears Canada, acquisitions of companies such as Zappos, and expanded offerings such as Amazon Fresh (grocery delivery system) contribute to Amazon's success.

Amazon's e-business model evolved from a single-product B2C e-retailer to a mix of e-business models that allows the company not only to sell products directly to consumers, but also to develop innovative e-business technologies and sell them to other businesses, and to provide a retailing channel for other companies. This successful mix of e-business models led to annual sales in excess of $74 billion in 2013, and millions of customers in more than 200 countries around the world.

Figure 7-27 Amazon.com successfully evolved to incorporate a mix of e-business models.

Business-to-Business (B2B)

While B2C and C2C might be the most familiar e-business models, online transactions between businesses, called business-to-business (B2B) transactions, account for the largest share of total e-business revenue. Like other e-business models discussed earlier in this section, the B2B e-business model takes a variety of forms. B2B businesses generate revenue in a number of ways, including:

- Business directory listing fees
- Website advertising
- Subscription or membership fees
- Referral fees

- Transaction fees
- Sales commissions
- Website hosting fees
- File storage fees
- Software licensing and rental fees
- Affiliate marketing programs

Some B2B e-businesses aggregate business information for other businesses and generate revenue from directory listing fees and advertising. Examples include the business.com business search engine and directory and the B2B Yellow Pages (Figure 7-28) that provide business-to-business information similar to a printed telephone business directory.

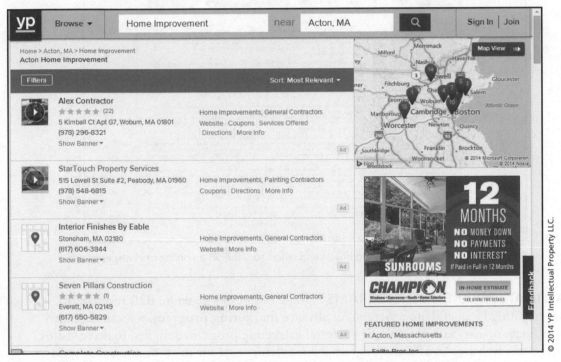

Figure 7-28   Some B2B e-businesses aggregate business information for other companies.

The term **infomediary** refers to an e-business that gathers and organizes large amounts of data and information, and then acts as an intermediary between those who want the information and those who supply the information. Infomediary examples include several B2C e-businesses, such as edmunds.com, Autobytel, AbeBooks, and Shopzilla. B2B infomediaries include business.com and the B2B Yellow Pages.

FACTS
@HAND

Other B2B e-businesses create online marketspaces in which to bring buyers and sellers together, operate reverse or forward auctions, participate in revenue-generating affiliate marketing programs, sell web hosting services, sell file storage space, or develop and sell e-business technologies.

B2B EXCHANGES   As you learned in Chapter 5, B2B exchanges create online marketspaces in which businesses can buy and sell with each other following a predetermined set of exchange rules. These rules determine how buyers and sellers communicate with each other throughout the exchange, how they negotiate prices with each other, how they make and accept payments, and also determine product delivery guidelines. B2B exchanges usually generate revenue by charging subscription or membership fees, transaction fees, and sales commissions. Examples of B2B exchanges include CATEX (Figure 7-29), a B2B exchange for the insurance and reinsurance industries, and Automotix, a B2B exchange for the auto industry.

Figure 7-29   B2B exchanges bring buyers and sellers together in an online marketspace.

AFFILIATE MARKETING PROGRAMS   Some businesses generate B2B revenue by participating in an affiliate program. An **affiliate marketing program**, sometimes called an affiliate or associate program, is a referral marketing program designed to drive visitor traffic to a website. An affiliate program is a marketing tool for the e-business that sponsors it and a source of revenue for an e-business that participates in the program. Participants in an affiliate program are affiliates or associates.

When an e-business joins an affiliate program, it places links on its website to the program operator's website or app. When a visitor to the affiliate's site clicks-through to the sponsoring e-business's site and takes some action, the affiliate earns a commission or referral fee. The commission or referral fee varies. An affiliate may receive a certain amount for the click-through, and more if the visitor makes a purchase after clicking-through to the sponsoring e-business's website.

Amazon popularized affiliate programs when it created its Amazon Associates program. Participants in the Amazon Associates program receive a referral fee each time a visitor to their site clicks-through from their e-business website to the Amazon site and makes a purchase.

TECHNOLOGY PROVIDERS   A portion of total B2B e-business occurs between e-businesses and their technology providers — companies that develop and sell the technologies that make e-business possible. Technology providers include ISPs (Internet service providers) and NSPs (network service providers) — such as AOL, Verizon, Comcast, and AT&T — that provide the Internet communications infrastructure. Other technology providers — such as Oracle, Microsoft, IBM, HP, SAP, and Cisco Systems — develop and sell the networking hardware and application software that enable buyers and sellers to conduct business activities online.

Many early B2C or B2B e-businesses, such as Amazon, modified their original e-business plans to include selling their proprietary e-business technologies. Other innovators, such as Yahoo!, added B2B technology sales to their business mix as their original e-business models matured. Still other B2B technology providers, including web hosting companies, online storage companies, application service providers (ASPs), and content delivery networks, have created completely new kinds of businesses that use Internet technologies to provide new e-business services.

Thousands of **web hosting** companies, such as Yahoo! Web Hosting and Hosting (Figure 7-30), provide e-businesses with web and database server storage and server administration services at secure, temperature-controlled storage facilities. Many e-businesses — especially smaller e-businesses — find it more convenient and less expensive to pay for services at a hosting company than to operate web and database servers at their own facilities. Monthly web hosting fees range from a few dollars for a shared hosting service to several hundred dollars for dedicated hosting or colocation services (described later).

Q&A

What is reseller hosting?
Reseller hosting occurs when a user hosts third-party websites on his or her hard drive, and then sells the host's products for a profit. To learn more, use a search engine to search for *reseller hosting*.

Figure 7-30 Web hosting companies provide storage and server administration for e-businesses.

In a **shared hosting** arrangement, multiple e-businesses share a single web server owned by the hosting company. Shared hosting services are inexpensive and attractive for small e-businesses that lack the facilities and expertise to manage their own web servers. Larger e-businesses with hundreds of complex transactions might choose to contract for **dedicated hosting** services, in which they have exclusive use of an entire server or servers. Other e-businesses might own their own servers, yet contract with a web hosting company to store their servers at the hosting company's facilities. This arrangement, called **colocation**, allows e-businesses to reduce server facility costs. Some web hosting companies, such as Rackspace, provide complete **managed hosting** services by building, customizing, managing, and supporting dedicated e-business servers for which their clients pay a flat monthly fee.

Cisco Systems B2B E-Business Model

Technology experts use the term, The Internet of Things (IoT) to describe efforts to expand connectivity between computers, mobile devices, network systems, and the Internet. Cisco Systems takes IoT one step further with its motto "The Internet of Everything."

Cisco's original purpose was to manufacture and sell networking equipment and related software. Husband and wife team Sandy Lerner and Leonard Bosack, both employees Stanford University, started Cisco in 1984. Disputes over ownership of some early company prototypes led to both Bosack and Lerner leaving Stanford. Shortly after Cisco's initial public offering in 1990, Lerner was fired from the company. Her husband resigned in protest. The couple donated approximately 70 percent of their $170 million in profit to charity.

Cisco was the first company to achieve success selling routers that serviced multiple network protocols. With the increase in reliance on the IP (Internet protocol) standard in use today, Cisco adapted its offerings to include routers optimized for IP. Cisco's main business model is providing B2B products and services for large and small businesses. Large businesses, or enterprises, look to Cisco to provide secure, high-functioning WANs or cloud-based networking services (Figure 7-31), as well as technologies that enable workers to collaborate from different locations, including IP video and phone services. Large companies can use other Cisco products to develop, maintain, secure, and integrate a remote call center for sales or customer service. Small business options include VoIP phones, cloud storage, and network security features.

Cisco runs the Cisco Networking Academy (CNA) for network and system administrators. The CNA trains, tests, and certifies networking professionals in a variety of areas and levels. Employees look for Cisco Certified Networking Associate (CCNA), and other Cisco-certified professionals, to fill a variety of jobs.

In 2000, during the peak of the dot-com bubble, Cisco was worth $500 billion, and was the most valuable company in the entire world. Today, Cisco is worth $129 billion, but remains an extremely valuable company, as well as a respected provider of technologies for networking and cloud security.

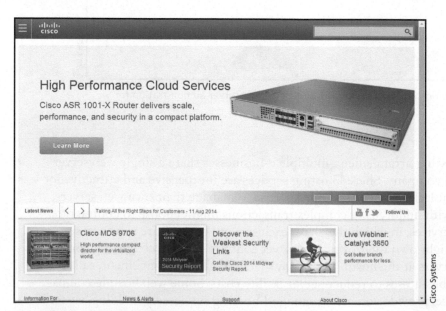

Figure 7-31 Cisco provides B2B hardware, software, and services.

In Chapter 6, you learned how important it is to create regular backup copies of critical files and then store those files off-site. Storing critical files off-site used to require manually carrying backup disks and tapes to an off-site storage warehouse. Today, for a monthly fee, an individual or business can store backup copies of critical files on the cloud or a remote server using an **online storage service** provided by e-businesses such as IBackup and Carbonite (Figure 7-32).

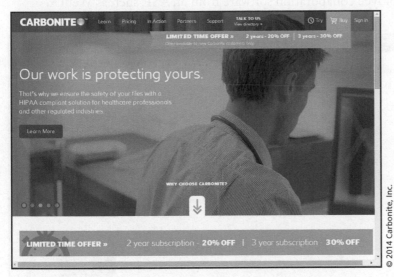

Figure 7-32 Online storage services enables businesses and personal users to store backup files on the cloud or using a remote server.

Developing e-business software applications in-house is very expensive. Many e-businesses elect to save time and money by using business software created by an application service provider. An **application service provider (ASP)** develops and maintains its own business application software — such as accounting, marketing and sales management, personnel management, and employee collaboration software — and then provides it to its customers using several business models, including pay-per-use, or an annual or monthly fee. Customers access the software over the Internet. ASP examples include AdminiTrack (software development tracking systems) and Salesforce (Figure 7-33).

Figure 7-33 ASPs develop and maintain business applications delivered over the web.

Employee collaboration software allows employees to share documents, calendars, contacts, tasks lists, and other information, and is very popular and useful. You might be familiar with employee collaboration software, such as Microsoft Outlook, which is part of the Microsoft Office suite. Software as a Service (SaaS), as mentioned in a previous chapter, is another method for encouraging collaboration. Because the software and all files reside on the cloud, employees can share and collaborate on documents easily. Microsoft Office Online (Figure 7-34) is one example of SaaS used for collaboration. E-businesses also can rent employee collaboration software from an ASP, such as WebEx.

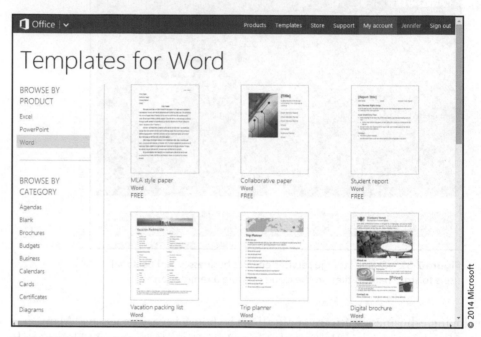

Figure 7-34 Business users rely on online software to create, collaborate on, and share files.

A **content delivery network (CDN)** is a dedicated network of servers located in different geographical areas of the country that store, or cache, webpage content from high-traffic websites for a fee. The content delivery network's servers quickly serve up the cached content on request. For example, high-traffic websites, such as Facebook, Rackspace, Adobe Systems, and JCPenney, eliminate traffic congestion at their sites by distributing their webpage content over the Akamai content delivery network. When a visitor requests a webpage from one of these sites, the Akamai server geographically closest to the visitor reads the request. This proximity speeds up the content delivery time.

SUPPLY CHAIN MANAGEMENT B2B transactions go far beyond selling products and services. Internet technologies are fostering a revolution in the way businesses interact with their partners, particularly their suppliers. Businesses can connect with their suppliers using the Internet to exchange product information, purchase orders, shipping reports, invoices, payments, and other B2B transactions. A **supply chain** consists of all the entities — raw material providers, manufacturers, distributors, wholesalers, retailers, and others — involved in creating and distributing products to end users. Many businesses conduct B2B transactions across their supply chains over an extranet. An **extranet** is a private network that uses Internet technologies to connect a business with its suppliers and business partners. Using Internet technologies and extranets to exchange information among trading partners is a less expensive option than the value-added networks (VANs) you learned about earlier in this chapter.

Business-to-Government (B2G)

The business-to-government (B2G) e-business model includes online businesses that market and sell directly to government agencies. It also includes online businesses that create a marketspace, similar to a B2B exchange, that provides other businesses with information on bidding opportunities for government agency contracts. Some B2G businesses sell the technologies used to manage the bidding and procurement process. Onvia (Figure 7-35), BidNet, Bidmain, and Fedmarket all participate in the B2G online marketspace.

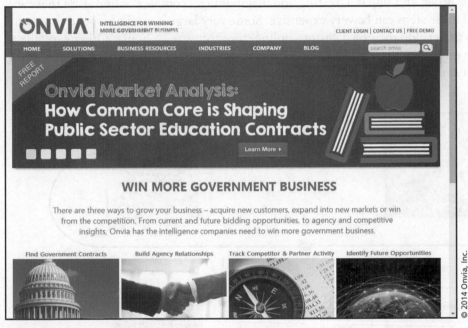

Figure 7-35   B2G e-businesses provide other businesses with government contract bidding opportunities.

An intranet is an internal network that offers employees access to resources using a website or a software interface. Because of the prevalence of remote employees, or to accommodate offices spread out over multiple sites or locations, many companies provide access to intranets over the Internet. Internal business activities related to employees and occur over a company intranet are business-to-employee, or B2E, transactions.

FACTS @HAND

Creating an Online Store

An entrepreneur is someone who both assumes the risks and responsibilities associated with starting his or her own business, and receives the opportunity to earn a profit from this business. Evan Williams (Twitter), Jeff Bezos (Amazon), Michael Dell (Dell Inc.), and Reed Hastings (Netflix) are famous entrepreneurial successes you learned about earlier in this chapter. Thousands of other men and women become e-business entrepreneurs each year, many by starting and operating their own online businesses, such as a B2C or e-retail store. In this section, you will learn about the basic elements required to operate an online store: storefront software, a payment-processing service, and a merchant account.

Storefront Software

A typical e-retail transaction (Figure 7-36) consists of several steps. First, you access the online store's website and view the store's product catalog, which is a listing of products complete with descriptions and pricing. Next, you select items from the product catalog, provide your billing and shipping information, and specify a payment method — such as by credit card or using a third-party payment service. Before filling the order, the online store must verify that your credit card number is valid and have the transaction authorized. After authorizing the transaction, the online store must then process your credit card payment, fulfill your order, and ship it. Creating and maintaining a complex online store that can handle all these steps can be very expensive. Some very large e-retailers spend thousands of dollars to develop their own custom online store software in-house. Other e-retailers choose to outsource that development by licensing storefront software packages from third-party vendors.

Step 1
buyer accesses online store and product catalog

Step 2
buyer adds items to electronic shopping cart

Step 3
buyer enters name, address, and credit card payment information

Step 4
credit card information is validated and payment is authorized

Step 5
online store processes order

Step 6
order is fulfilled at warehouse

Step 7
order is shipped

Figure 7-36   The path of an authorized e-retail transaction.

Storefront software, sometimes called **e-commerce software**, provides tools to build and maintain webpages and the underlying product databases that contain product images, descriptions, and prices. Storefront software also contains shopping cart software. **Shopping cart software** tracks items selected for purchase and handles the checkout process, including summarizing the order, calculating shipping and taxes, calculating the order's total, and processing the order's payment. High-end storefront software also might provide a number of other features, such as an interface to the e-business's order fulfillment and accounting systems or personalization features. Less-expensive storefront software might be limited to a product catalog and shopping cart.

An e-business website that already has product pages but lacks online shopping capability can add the necessary shopping features by purchasing just the shopping cart software instead of a complete storefront software package. Many content management systems enable website owners to add storefront easily to an existing website.

Choosing the appropriate storefront software package depends on the complexity of the online store and the specific features required. Medium- to large-sized e-retailers might license storefront software from vendors, such as Actinic Software, MerchandiZer, and Electric Café SEO (Figure 7-37), for a few hundred dollars. Sometimes called **installed storefront software**, this customizable storefront software resides on an e-retailer's web server, and the e-retailer uses it to create and manage a complex e-retail site.

Figure 7-37   Installed storefront software is customizable software installed on an e-retailer's server.

Smaller e-retailers with simple online store requirements often choose to use **hosted storefront software** offered by vendors such as Yahoo! Small Business and Homestead. Hosted storefront software uses webpage templates (Figure 7-38) that allow you to create a store and add products to your online catalog in just a few minutes. Fees for building and maintaining a hosted storefront can include monthly web hosting fees, per-item fees for adding products to the store's online catalog, and transaction fees.

Some hosted storefront software vendors provide software demos or allow you to review their software on a free trial basis.

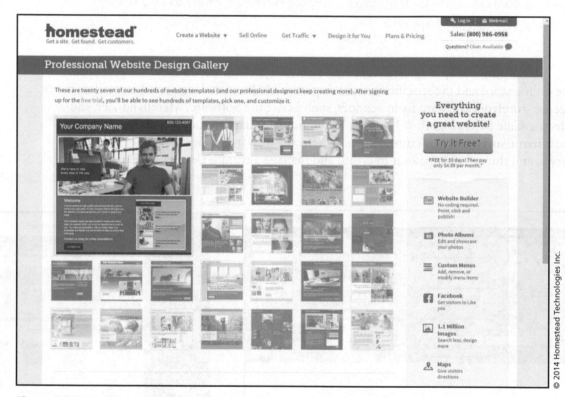

© 2014 Homestead Technologies Inc.

Figure 7-38 Smaller e-retailers with simple online store requirements often choose hosted storefront software that includes a template gallery.

Credit Card Authorization and Processing

Many online store shoppers use a credit card to complete the sale. A direct credit card payment at an online store is not the only way to pay for a purchase. Online auction sites and many online stores and mobile apps accept payments through a third-party payment processor, such as PayPal or Google Wallet (Figure 7-39). For example, a consumer can set up a personal account with PayPal, linked to his or her credit card or bank account, and then choose PayPal as the payment option when making an online purchase. PayPal processes the payment by drafting on the consumer's bank account or charging a credit card and remitting the funds to the online store's account. Online stores also might accept electronic checks and prepaid cards, such as those provided by a bank or credit card, as well as store-specific gift cards. To accept credit card payments, an e-retailer must have two things: an account with a financial institution for credit card receipt deposits and a service that authorizes and processes credit card transactions.

MERCHANT ACCOUNT An e-business account with a financial institution that stores money from credit card purchases is a merchant credit card account, or more simply a **merchant account**. Any business — whether brick-and-mortar or online — that accepts credit cards must have a merchant account. Although an e-business can withdraw funds from a merchant account, it only can deposit credit card receipts.

An e-business applies for a merchant account at a financial institution — generally a bank that specializes in e-business merchant accounts — by providing general business information, such as its size, how long it has been in business, its credit history, and the type of cards the business will accept. Fees for an approved e-business merchant account might include one-time setup fees, monthly access fees, per-item transaction fees, and a **discount rate**, which is the percentage of each transaction that the financial institution will charge the e-business. The actual fees an individual e-business pays for its merchant account depend on the financial institution's perceived level of risk on the account.

Before approving a merchant account, a bank first assesses its level of risk on the account based on the e-business's financial and operational history. The bank also evaluates its own chargeback history with similar e-business merchant accounts. A **chargeback** is a return of funds to a credit card company resulting from a card holder's refusal to pay a credit card charge. If the bank releases merchant account funds to the e-business and a chargeback later occurs, the bank must recover the funds from the e-business. The bank faces a risk that it will not be able to recover the funds from the e-business. In assessing its chargeback risk, the bank also considers the kinds of products and services the e-business sells. For example, some types of online credit card transactions — such as payments for gambling, pornography, or other such products or services — historically generate more chargebacks than other credit card transactions. E-businesses offering these types of products or services generally are a higher risk and, if approved for a merchant account, may pay higher fees.

Another merchant account risk inherent in online credit card transactions occurs because neither the credit card nor the credit card holder is physically present during the transaction. This situation increases the risk of credit card fraud and potential chargebacks. Because of the **card not present/card holder not present risk**, e-businesses may pay a higher discount rate than similar brick-and-mortar stores, where the card and card holder are present during the transaction.

PAYMENT GATEWAY An online store also must be able to connect to a payment-processing service that can verify, authorize, and process secure credit card transactions. You witness a payment-processing service in action when you use your credit card to pay for products or services at a brick-and-mortar store or restaurant. At these businesses, a card-swipe machine reads and sends your card account, and the processor sends the transaction authorization back to the store or restaurant electronically. Although it is possible to use a similar manual process to access a payment-processing service for online credit card transactions, most e-retailers use an online payment-processing service that authorizes the transaction while the customer waits. A number of vendors, such as Authorize .Net and iTransact (Figure 7-40) offer online payment-processing services, called **payment gateways**.

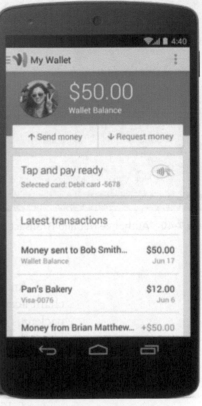

Figure 7-39 Mobile payment apps enable shoppers to pay for items using their smartphone.

Figure 7-40   Authorize.Net and iTransact are payment gateway vendors.

An important step in selecting storefront software, a payment gateway, and a merchant account is to be certain that all three are compatible. Most storefront software packages come complete with a connection to one or more payment gateway services. Hosted storefront software services, designed for small e-retailers with limited resources and experience, often provide access to both a merchant account and a payment gateway service for an additional fee.

E-retailers also must have a process for packaging and shipping products, called **order fulfillment**. Brick-and-click retailers can take advantage of existing fulfillment operations for fulfillment of online orders, while some large pure-play e-retailers build and manage their own fulfillment operations. Many e-retailers save time and money, however, by contracting with third-party fulfillment or logistics companies to warehouse, package, and ship their orders.

Chapter Review

Electronic business transactions began with the EFT system and the Automated Clearing House (ACH) network used by financial institutions to transfer money without the physical exchange of paper money. Other early electronic business transactions between trading partners were processed over private value-added networks (VANs).

The unique factors inherent in doing business online include the effects of geography, time, and space; the network effect; the ability of individual e-businesses to redefine their markets; and the power of personalization and customization.

E-businesses can capitalize on the interactive nature of the web by using website personalization and customization features to offer tailored webpage content, products, and services.

Common business models include business-to-consumer (B2C), consumer-to-business (C2B), consumer-to-consumer (C2C), business-to-business (B2B), and business-to-government (B2G). Within each e-business model classification, an individual e-business might generate revenue in a variety of ways.

To create an online store, you need installed storefront software or hosted storefront software, a merchant account to accept credit card receipts, and a payment-processing service to authorize and process credit card transactions.

After reading this chapter, you should know each of these Key Terms.

affiliate marketing program (352)
application service provider (ASP) (355)
Automated Clearing House (ACH) (328)
business model (337)
card not present/card holder not present risk (361)
chargeback (361)
click-through (340)
colocation (355)
content delivery network (CDN) (356)
cost per impression (CPI) (341)
customization (336)
dedicated hosting (353)
discount rate (361)
disintermediation (333)
distributed computing (329)
e-book (330)
e-commerce software (358)
electronic data interchange (EDI) (328)
electronic funds transfer (EFT) (328)
e-retail (338)
extranet (356)
forward auction (345)
grid computing (329)
hosted storefront software (360)

installed storefront software (359)
infomediary (351)
intermediary (333)
managed hosting (353)
merchant account (361)
network effect (330)
niche market (338)
online storage service (355)
order fulfillment (362)
payment gateways (361)
per-click (340)
personalization (336)
pure-play e-retailer (338)
reintermediation (335)
reverse auction (345)
shared hosting (353)
shopping cart software (358)
storefront software (358)
supply chain (356)
trading partner (328)
Tweet (342)
URL shortener (344)
value-added network (VAN) (328)
virtual super computer (329)
web hosting (353)

Complete the Test Your Knowledge exercises to solidify what you have learned in the chapter.

True or False

Mark T for True and F for False. (Answers are found on page numbers in parentheses.)

____ 1. Distributed computing refers to combining many networked computers and devices to create a virtual super computer that can perform complex tasks. (239)

____ 2. Amazon popularized affiliate programs with its Amazon Associates program. (352)

____ 3. Redefining a market by removing its traditional intermediaries is called intermediation. (333)

____ 4. An intranet is a private network that uses Internet technologies to connect a business with its trading partners. (357)

____ 5. A business model is the way a company operates to generate revenue and profits and remain a viable business entity. (337)

____ 6. A CDN is a dedicated network of servers that cache webpage content for a fee. (356)

____ 7. A chargeback is a fee paid by an e-business to participate in a B2B auction. (361)

____ 8. Squidoo hosts advertiser-generated topic pages, called lenses. (343)

____ 9. In the 1960s, banks began exchanging money electronically through a network that connects all U.S. financial institutions, called the Automated Clearing House (ACH) network (328)

____ 10. The CPI method of measuring an online ad's success stands for Charge Payment Instance. (340)

Multiple Choice

Select the best answer. (Answers are found on page numbers in parentheses.)

1. The term often used to describe how the growth in the number of online buyers and sellers increases the value of the online marketspace is the _____ effect. (330)

    a. network

    b. personalization

    c. affiliation

    d. infomediary

2. The process that allows money to be transferred between banks electronically is called _____. (328)

    a. ACH

    b. EDI

    c. CDN

    d. EFT

3. Visitors can go directly to the advertised website by clicking an ad in a process called a _____. (340)

    a. CPI

    b. chargeback

    c. click-through

    d. CDN

4. The C2B e-business model is sometimes called a(n) _____. (345)

    a. reverse auction

    b. forward auction

    c. e-procurement model

    d. subscription model

5. A retailer or e-retailer that specializes in providing products for a specific need or interest represents a _____ market. (338)

    a. pure-play

    b. niche

    c. channel

    d. customer-driven

6. A(n) _____ is a type of network used for EDI exchanges. (329)

    a. ACH

    b. EFT

    c. VAN

    d. CDN

7. The program designed to drive traffic to an e-business website by paying referral fees to other e-businesses is called a(n) _____. (352)

    a. supply chain

    b. shared hosting arrangement

    c. B2B exchange

    d. affiliate marketing program

8. An e-business can save money by using a(n) _____ hosting method, in which the company owns servers that they contract to store at another facility. (353)

   a. distributed

   b. colocation

   c. virtual

   d. affiliate

9. Instagram is owned by _____. (332)

   a. Facebook

   b. Amazon

   c. Twitter

   d. eBay

10. Which of the following is *not* true about value-added networks? (329)

    a. They are private telecommunication networks used for EDI exchange.

    b. They require custom interfaces for exchanging data between business partners.

    c. Extranets are an alternative to VANs.

    d. They are less expensive than Internet-only options.

TRENDS

Investigate current Internet developments with the Trends exercises.

Write a brief essay about each of the following trends, using the web as your research tool. For each trend, identify at least one webpage URL used as a research source. Be prepared to discuss your findings in class.

1 | Exploring Personalization and Customization

Visit the following websites to explore how each website integrates and offers personalization and customization for website visitors: Amazon, Netflix, My Yahoo!, and eBay. List details about the process for personalizing and/or customizing the website content for your interests. Do you need to create an account? Do you have the ability to select website content that interests you? Do a search on the website for relevant product or content. Visit the home page. Did your homepage content change after your search? If so, how? Submit your findings in the format requested by your instructor.

2 | E-commerce and Social Media Integration

Use a search engine to search for *e-commerce social media*. Sort or filter your results, if possible, to search for the most recent articles or blog posts. Look for an article or post that advises e-commerce businesses about how to best integrate social media for customers to share information about purchases or other activity at the business's website or social media account. If possible, locate an article or post that describes risks to sharing your purchases or e-commerce activities using social media, and how you can prevent this information from being shared. Have you ever shared a purchase using social media? If so, why? Would you do so in the future? Why or why not? Submit your findings in the format requested by your instructor.

@ ISSUE

Challenge your perspective of Internet technology with the @Issue exercises.

Write a brief essay in response to the following issues, using the web as your research tool. For each issue, identify at least one URL used as a research source. Be prepared to discuss your findings in class.

1 | Online Storage Services

Use a search engine to search for *online storage services* or *cloud backup.* Sort or filter your results, if possible, to search for the most recent articles or blog posts. Look for an article or post that describes available services for remote backups. List three services, and locate additional information about each, including how to enroll, costs to use, known security risks or breaches, and customer reviews. Find articles that describe how companies are adopting online storage services, and locate statistics about how many currently are doing so, as well as predictions. Have you ever used an online storage service for backup or data recovery? If so, describe the experience. Submit your findings in the format requested by your instructor.

2 | Online Auctions

Use a search engine to search for *online auction risks.* Sort or filter your results, if possible, to search for the most recent articles or blog posts. Look for an article or post that describes risks and precautions with using online auctions. Review an online auction website's selling and buying policies (such as eBay). What restrictions, requirements, or guidelines exist for both buyers and sellers? What responsibility does the auction website have to protect buyers and sellers? Have you used an online auction to buy or sell an item? Describe any experiences you have had. Find at least one article or blog post that describes a problem with an online auction transaction where the auction website needed to mediate between the buyer or seller, or restrict the item from sale. Do you agree with the actions taken? Why or why not? Would you use an online auction website? Why or why not? Submit your findings in the format requested by your instructor.

HANDS ON

Use the web to obtain more information about the skills taught in the chapter with the Hands On exercises.

1 | Evaluating Hosted Storefront Software

You are thinking about opening an online store to sell framed prints of your photographs. You have no experience running an online store, so you ask a friend how to get started. Your friend suggests that you consider using hosted storefront software to create and manage your store. (You may assume any other facts not stated here.)

1. Review the services provided by Yahoo! Small Business, Homestead, and a third hosted storefront software or service of your choice.

2. Create a table that compares the three companies' services and fees. What services (if any) are available for free? What services require added costs?

3. If possible, find articles or blog posts that describe the ease-of-use, security, reliability, and other factors of the hosting companies.

4. Choose one of the three for your online store and list the reasons for your choice.

5. Submit your findings in the format requested by your instructor.

2 | Identifying E-Business Models and Revenue-Generation Methods

1. Visit the following e-business websites:

   a. Zappos

   b. Rackspace

   c. Hometown Favorites

   d. Twitter

   e. Hulu

2. Identify each company's e-business model and revenue-generation methods.

3. Make a note of any ads that appear on the website. Do any of these ads reflect previous searches you have made? What might that mean about the company's ad generating methods?

4. If possible, locate any policies on the website for advertisers or affiliates wanting to provide ads or link to the website.

5. Submit your findings in the format requested by your instructor.

Work collaboratively to reinforce the concepts in the chapter with the Team Approach exercises.

TEAM APPROACH

1 | Redefining Markets

1. Work with a team of three to four classmates to search for and evaluate the following websites:

   a. Enterprise Rent-A-Car

   b. Dell.com

   c. Hotels.com

   d. US Airways

   e. Marriott

2. Assign one website or app to each teammate to research. Each team member should write a brief paragraph about each website, discussing whether the sponsoring business is involved in e-business disintermediation or e-business reintermediation and give the rationale for the answer.

3. As a team, discuss each student's findings. Do you agree with the conclusion? Why or why not?

4. Submit your findings in the format requested by your instructor.

2 | Exploring a C2C Website

1. Work with a team of three to four classmates to search for and evaluate a C2C website or service, such as Amazon Marketplace.

2. As a team, select a collectible, vintage, or rare item for which to search.

3. Find at least three sellers who have the item, and answer the following questions about each item/seller:

   a. What is the item's description? What, if any, are the item's distinguishing features?

   b. Is the item available for purchase, or for an auction?

   c. Who is the seller? What is the seller's rating, if rated? Where is the seller located?

   d. What payment methods are available?

   e. Who pays for shipping costs?

4. Submit your findings in the format requested by your instructor.

A Exploring Other Browsers

Introduction

The steps and exercises in this book were written to work with all browsers and devices; however, in some cases you may have encountered differences in your browser's functionality if you were not using Microsoft Internet Explorer. This appendix focuses on desktop and laptop browsers, such as Google Chrome, Firefox, Opera, and Safari, which are available for free by downloading them from their vendors' websites. This appendix also addresses general differences in mobile browsers for tablets and smartphones.

All desktop and laptop browsers share features with Internet Explorer, including menu commands, customizable toolbars, customizable search tools, tabbed browsing, RSS integration, and security features such as cookie management and phishing protection. Many browsers offer extra security features, such as untraceable browsing, and the ability to delete the browsing history and all cached files, such as cookies. Additionally, each browser has features that set it apart from the others.

Although Firefox, Google Chrome, Safari, and Opera share features with Internet Explorer and with each other, the features might have different names in each browser. For example, saved URLs are *favorites* in the Internet Explorer browser, but are *bookmarks* in Safari, Google Chrome, Firefox, and Opera. The bar that contains the text box in which URLs and search terms are entered is called the *Address bar* in Internet Explorer, Google Chrome, and Opera; it is called the *Location bar* in Firefox. Additionally, window elements similar to the Internet Explorer elements with which you are now familiar might be located in a different place in other browser windows. For example, the Safari and Google Chrome browsers position page tabs at the top of the screen in the title bar area.

Mobile browsers and browser versions, including Opera Mini, Safari, Google Android's browser, Google Chrome, Firefox Mobile, and Internet Explorer Mobile, will give you a very different user experience and you may encounter difficulty if using these browsers for some of the activities. If using a mobile device's native email client, you may have difficulty completing Chapter 4. If you cannot complete any set of steps with your browser or device, read the steps to understand the capabilities of other browsers or Internet tools.

Despite similarities between browsers, it is a good idea to carefully review a browser's window elements and Help pages to familiarize yourself with the browser's features, keyboard shortcuts, user tips, and special terminology before you begin using the browser.

Google Chrome

Developed by Google, Google Chrome for desktops and laptops (Figure A-1) presents a streamlined interface with page tabs on the title bar. Google Chrome currently is the most popular browser for desktop and laptop computers. Using the Google Chrome Address bar, called the Omnibox, you can enter URLs and conduct searches using the default Google search engine. For example, you can type a search query including Boolean operators in the Address bar, or you can select and drag text from a webpage into the Address bar to create a search query. When you create a new page tab, the new page shows thumbnails of your most frequently visited webpages, a link to History, the

Google search engine Search box, and a list of recent bookmarks. Unlike most other browsers, Google Chrome does not include RSS web feed capabilities. When you view a webpage that is written in a language other than English, Google Translate automatically offers to translate the web content into English, or your default language. Google Chrome takes advantage of Google's other social, productivity, and communication tools, such as Google+ (social network), Google Drive (document creation and storage), and Gmail (email) (Figure A-2).

Figure A-1 The Google Chrome browser.

integrated features

Figure A-2 Google Chrome integrates Google+, Google Maps, Gmail, Google Drive, and other tools.

Firefox

Firefox for desktops and laptops (Figure A-3) is developed and made available as part of the Mozilla Foundation's Mozilla open source software project, managed by Mozilla Corporation. The Mozilla open source software project is a community of software developers and software testers who create open source software. Unlike proprietary software developed by companies such as Microsoft, open source software programming code is available to software users who can then, within licensing restrictions, modify the code. The Firefox open source browser has a reputation for a high level of security for conducting online banking or shopping transactions and for protection against hackers. Like Internet Explorer, Firefox uses tabbed browsing, a separate pane for viewing bookmarks or history, and a customizable Search bar.

Firefox integrates geolocation features, which use GPS to provide targeted content and search results based on your current location. Additionally, the Firefox community of software developers has created a number of downloadable add-ons for Firefox, such as colorful Personas, or "skins," that change the browser's look (Figure A-4)

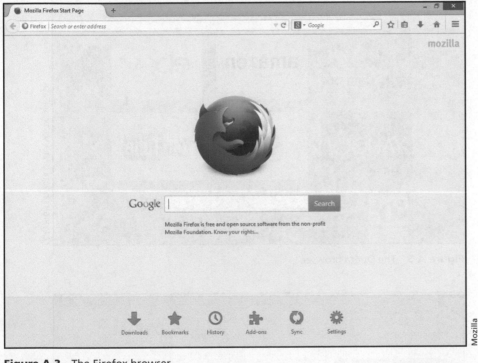

Figure A-3   The Firefox browser.

Figure A-4   Firefox with the Great Britain skin applied.

Opera

Opera is a free web browser developed by Opera Software. The Opera browser is another highly secure browser with features to protect against spyware and viruses that might infect your computer as you browse the web. Opera was one of the first browsers to offer tabbed browsing, built-in RSS integration, pop-up blocking, multiple customizable toolbars, and an easy-to-use customizable search field with different search tool options. The Speed Dial feature is Opera's New Tab feature (Figure A-5).

Opera supports voice commands, making it a great tool for users who have trouble using a keyboard and mouse. Opera also offers a built-in email client and newsreader, a chat client, and additional customizable features, such as different themes (skins) or color schemes. The Discover feature provides a built-in web feed of relevant and newsworthy content (Figure A-6).

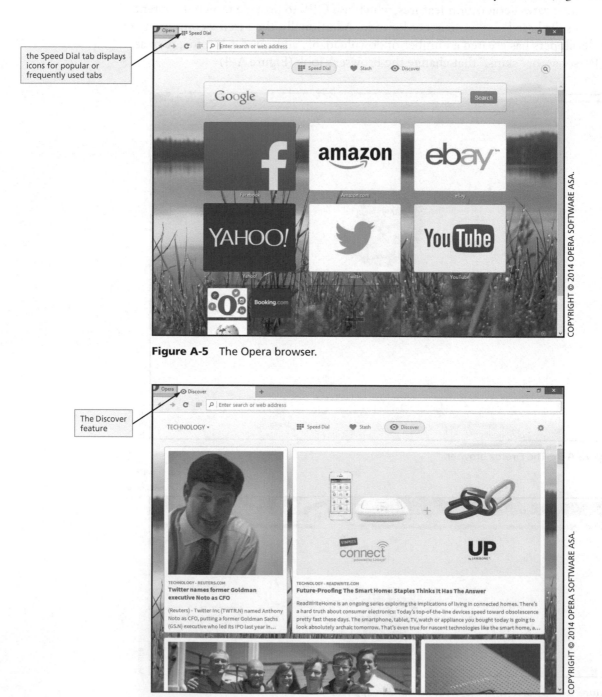

the Speed Dial tab displays icons for popular or frequently used tabs

Figure A-5   The Opera browser.

The Discover feature

Figure A-6   Opera's Discover feature is a set of built-in news feeds

COPYRIGHT © 2014 OPERA SOFTWARE ASA.

Safari

Apple Inc. developed the Safari (Figures A-7 and A-8) browser. Safari is available for the Mac OS X operating system environment. Apple no longer supports a Windows-based version of Safari. Known for fast webpage download times and adherence to programming standards, the Safari browser devotes more screen space to webpage views by placing its page tabs at the top of the screen in the title bar area, and by keeping toolbars, buttons, and so forth to a minimum. Shared Links lets you view links from people you follow on Twitter and LinkedIn. The iCloud features sync your browsing history, favorites, and other web preferences and settings with your other Apple devices, such as the iPhone and iPad. New privacy and battery-conserving features of Safari help you use your device longer and with more anonymity than with previous versions.

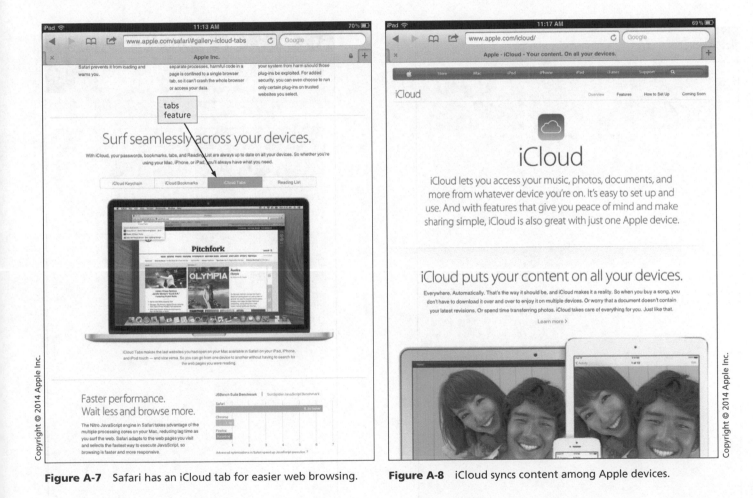

Figure A-7 Safari has an iCloud tab for easier web browsing.

Figure A-8 iCloud syncs content among Apple devices.

Mobile Web Browsers

As you learned earlier, most tablets, smartphones, and other mobile devices, such as e-readers, come with a browser installed. Some devices, but not all, enable you to download additional mobile web browsers. Mobile web browsers display web content in a format that is optimized for the limited screen size and memory capability of mobile devices. Mobile web browsers also are known as microbrowsers, minibrowsers, or wireless Internet browsers (WIBs). Manufacturers of mobile devices such as Android smartphones and Samsung Galaxy tablets have created specific mobile web browsers to work on their products. In addition, versions of Internet Explorer, Firefox (Figures A-9 and A-10), Opera, and Google are available for mobile devices. Mobile browsers share many of the same features, including the ability to zoom in and out on a webpage and use touch technology.

Figure A-9 The Firefox tablet browser.

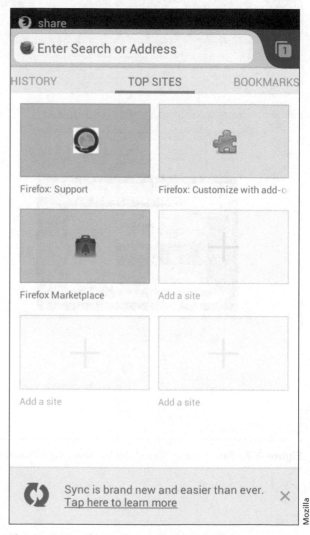

Figure A-10 The Firefox smartphone browser.

Use the Exercises to gain hands-on experience working with
the Internet and the web.

1 | Learning More About the Mozilla Foundation, the Mozilla Project, and the Firefox Browser

1. Use a search engine to search for *Mozilla project and the Mozilla Foundation*. Then answer the following questions:

   a. What is the mission of the Mozilla project?

   b. Who launched the Mozilla project, and when? What is the relationship between the Mozilla project and Netscape?

   c. Who participates in the Mozilla project?

   d. What are the primary achievements of the Mozilla project to date?

   e. What is the Mozilla Foundation, and how does it support the Mozilla project?

2. Use a search engine to search for the latest Firefox browser features. Then answer the following questions:

   a. What new features or advantages does Firefox have?

   b. What special features of Firefox would you find most useful? What features would be least useful? Why?

2 | Comparing and Contrasting User Features of Popular Web Browsers

1. Use a search engine to search for articles, reviews, and reports that compare and contrast the user features of these popular desktop and laptop web browsers: Chrome, Firefox, Internet Explorer, Opera, and Safari. Pay special attention to articles that discuss each browser's strengths and weaknesses.

2. Using your research, create a table or other tool to compare the primary user features of the web browsers. Describe the strengths and weaknesses of each browser. Indicate which of these five browsers (that you are not currently using) you would most like to download and explore in more detail, and explain why.

3. If possible, download your preferred browser, test its features, and then write a brief summary of how well the browser performed against your expectations.

3 | Investigating Web Browser Security Features

1. Use a search engine to search for articles or blog posts discussing the built-in security features of the Chrome, Firefox, Internet Explorer, Opera, and Safari browsers.

2. Using your research, write a one-page paper that describes the security features of each browser.

4 | Exploring Mobile Web Browsers

1. Using the search engine of your choice, search for information about mobile versions of the Firefox, Opera, Safari, Internet Explorer, and Google Chrome browsers, as well as the mobile web browsers available for Android and Samsung Galaxy, or other devices.

2. Choose four common capabilities of these browsers, such as search, tabs, speed, and security, and then make a table listing each mobile web browser and whether it shares the capability as well as any additional information. If you have experience using mobile web browsers, write a paragraph about your experience.

B Understanding Web Design

Introduction

Most regular Internet users visit dozens or even hundreds of websites in the course of a week. Some—but not all—of those websites will help you understand current events, hold your interest on specific topics, entice you to order products, or engage you in other ways. The goal of most websites, regardless of the website's industry or purpose, is to keep visitors' interest. The success or failure of any website relies on the quality of its design. The web design process includes planning, designing, and publishing a website. A well-planned website includes considerations such as consistency, responsive web design, and more, and contributes to a website's credibility and ease-of-use. In the field of web design, there are many roles, including creative, technical, and oversight.

The Web Design Process

The web design process can be simple or complex, depending on the needs of the website and the tools used to create it. A user who wants to set up a personal blog can use a content management system to register the domain name, select a theme and layout, and start entering content in a few hours. The planning, design, and creation of larger websites can take weeks or months, during which time the website designers determine the structure and graphic design, write the content, and ensure the security of the network and the website; often, implementation of a web database is a requirement as well.

Regardless of the scope and size of the website, the web design process typically follows these six steps:

- **Step 1: Define the website's purpose and target audience.** A website's purpose includes both the goals and objectives. Goals are the results you wish to see, such as increased sales. Objectives are the methods you use to achieve the goals, such as by offering discounts or coupons to entice customers to buy items, therefore increasing sales. Web designers keep in mind the website's target audience and their wants and expectations, and how their actions may help you reach your goals.

- **Step 2: Determine the website's general content.** Determine what content should appear on the website's home page, as well as any underlying webpages you will need. This helps influence the structure and navigation of the website. All home pages should introduce the website and entice the visitor to explore further. Underlying webpages may include product catalogs, a shopping cart, customer service, contact information, a privacy statement, a blog, and more. At this step, the web designer determines what types of content to create, including any media or graphics that need to be developed, or whether a database will supply dynamic content for a catalog.

- **Step 3: Select the website's structure.** A website's structure includes the organization of webpages and how they link together. Some web designers use storyboards or flowcharts to ensure that all webpages follow a logical structure, and that no webpages are unlinked to other webpages.

- **Step 4: Specify the website's navigation system.** A website's navigation system should take into consideration the user's experience when visiting the website, as well as the website's structure. Navigation options include hyperlinks, navigation areas (menus, tabs, or bars), breadcrumb trails that outline the path a visitor takes to reach a website, and search capability.

- **Step 5: Design the look and feel of the website.** A website should have visual consistency, meaning that typefaces, content positions, colors, and more should be consistent for all webpages. Background and text colors should provide contrast to maintain legibility. Web designers use styles and style sheets to define webpage elements and control how they appear. Some responsive websites use separate style sheets to best display content on mobile devices. Page layout, the arrangement of webpage content elements, also should be consistent across webpages for certain elements, such as a logo and navigation.

- **Step 6: Test, publish, and maintain the website.** Testing a website is a necessary step before publishing. Depending on the size and scope of your website, you may run a formal usability test with multiple users to get feedback about the website's usability. As part of testing, you should use multiple devices and platforms to ensure that your website is responsive to different screen sizes and browsers. Testing is an ongoing part of website maintenance, and does not end upon publication. Publishing a website includes determining the web server, budget and size restrictions, and frequency of allowable updates. Maintenance, like testing, is ongoing. Maintenance of a website includes keeping content updated and ensuring the continued security of web content.

Web Design Roles

People plan and develop websites of all sizes working independently, in small groups, or as part of a team. Depending on the size and scope of a website, some people take on multiple responsibilities. Web design roles fall into three general categories: creative, including design and content writing; technical, such as web programming, databases, or network security; and oversight or administrative roles.

CREATIVE ROLES   Creative input in web design contributes to the look and feel of the website, as well as its content. Content roles include writing and editing, and focus on creating and revising text that visitors read when they visit a website, and choosing the links, images, video, and media that enhances text content. Another aspect of content management includes taking into consideration SEO (search engine optimization) practices. SEO is the creation of text written specifically for the web with the goal of increasing website traffic by placing content higher in search results. Web designers use markup languages—CSS, text editors, HTML, and more—to layout and design webpages that are visually appealing, easily navigable, and meet accessibility and responsive web design goals. Graphic designers create original art, such as logos and typefaces, using special graphic hardware and software. Multimedia producers design and produce video, audio, and 2D and 3D models that enhance a website.

TECHNICAL ROLES   Technical roles play a key part in a website's functionality and security. Web programmers use sophisticated web-specific programming languages and tools, including JavaScript and Active Server Pages (ASP), to add interactivity and dynamic web content. Many websites use databases to supply dynamic web content, such as a product catalog. Web database developers integrate large, complex databases with webpages to receive new data, such as customer contact information, and provide content, such as inventory and product descriptions. Web database developers also must understand security risks with using databases and how to protect data from unauthorized access. Network and security administrators control the maintenance, upgrades, and evaluation of threats.

OVERSIGHT ROLES   A web administrator or webmaster works with all aspects of web design. For a smaller website, the web administrator may assume multiple roles, including all or most technical aspects of maintaining the website. Web administrators must be familiar with all aspects of website development in order to balance creative and technical needs. Large websites often require web architects, who determine the structure and technical needs required to build, maintain, and expand the website.

1 | Exploring Web Design

1. Use a search engine to search for articles or blog posts discussing web design and visit a website of your choice to answer the following questions.

   a. Identify two goals and objectives of the website. Describe three characteristics of the target audience profile.

   b. Review the website's homepage content. Is it easy to tell who owns this site? Is the visual identity consistent among the underlying pages?

   c. Describe the website's structure, and create an outline, storyboard, or flowchart.

   d. Identify the website's navigation system(s). Use the website's search feature, if any, to find content on an underlying webpage.

   e. Describe the visual identity elements on the website, such as logo, colors, and more. Identify, if possible, any decisions the web designer(s) made to meet accessibility guidelines, or anything that does not meet accessibility guidelines.

   f. Identify any steps you would take, as the web designer or web content editor, to maintain and update the website's content.

2 | Discover Web Career Options

1. Determine which type of web career is most interesting to you. What about the job appeals to you?

2. Use a search engine or a job search website to identify available jobs in your area. What current jobs meet your experience? What additional education, degrees, or certifications do you need, if any?

3. List and describe three responsibilities identified in the job description.

4. List the salary, or research a possible salary range for the position.

C | Exploring the Cloud

Introduction

Throughout this book you learned about the many available resources on the cloud. Cloud computing, as you learned, is the technology that provides resources that you access through the Internet. You can use cloud computing to store, create, and share documents, photos, and more, without installing or downloading additional software or apps to your computer or device. To help you fully understand how developments in cloud technology enhance your use of the web, this appendix covers several cloud topics, including advantages of cloud computing, software and apps, storage, and security.

Cloud Advantages

Business and personal users take advantage of the available resources on the cloud for several reasons, including:

- **Storage and space savings:** Using virtual servers to store data and host networking functions enables users, especially businesses, to remove or limit the amount of office space taken up by the large hardware required to perform these functions. Using cloud storage also avoids the need to purchase and maintain the storage equipment, saving costs and personnel resources.

- **Availability of data:** With the right passwords, software, and secure Internet connection, authorized users can access data and software and apps stored on the cloud from any computer or device. Cloud software enables users to collaborate and share data, documents, and other resources. One advantage to storing data and resources on the cloud is that it protects data in the event of a fire or other natural disaster that destroys the office or facility.

- **Financial savings:** Using cloud-based software and apps frees computing resources from having to host the programs. Many web-based software programs and apps are free. Data storage and network administrator devices are expensive, as previously mentioned.

Web-based Software and Apps

Software and apps available through the cloud are known as Software as a Service (SaaS). The software or app resides on an Internet server. Users can access the software or app through any Internet-connected device. Available SaaS uses include productivity software such as Google Drive/Google Docs and Office Web Apps, as well as photo-editing, and sales and marketing management programs.

SaaS delivery and sales models vary. Some, such as Google Drive, are free to individual users. Fee-based services typically use monthly or annual subscription models and typically are used by businesses or educational institutions. Other SaaS packages offer free and premium packages. A premium package might include additional apps, increased security, more storage space, and more. Organizations sometimes buy licenses to SaaS programs in order to create a community of users who can share and collaborate on documents, send email, and access storage space within a controlled, web-based environment.

Cloud Security

Cloud computing is relatively new, so some security threats are unknown or untested. Data security is the main concern with cloud computing. Hackers could gain access to data stored on the cloud without your knowledge. Because you do not control the network security procedures or firewalls, you do not receive alerts for data breaches. When sending data from a network to the cloud, experts recommend encrypting the sent data, and authenticating the received data.

Searches by law enforcement of your cloud data are another concern. Some legal experts argue that the data belongs to the owner of the cloud hosting service or server. Others claim that you have total rights over the data you upload, as well as an expectation of privacy. Another security concern is whether government or law officials have the right to search your cloud content without your permission or knowledge. Before using SaaS or cloud storage, be sure to read the contract and terms of the service to determine your rights to and ownership of your data, as well as the company's policy on retrieving your data if you no longer subscribe.

Use the Exercises to gain hands-on experience working with cloud computing.

1 | Learning More About Cloud Computing

1. Use a search engine to find information about cloud computing to answer the following questions:

   a. List and describe five uses of cloud computing. With how many of these are you familiar?

   b. Identify any cloud services you currently use, or would like to use. Why do or would you use the service? What are the advantages?

   c. What is the role of the Cloud Security Alliance (CSA)? Are there other organizations dedicated to cloud computing?

   d. Does your school or business use any cloud resources, such as SaaS?

2 | Exploring Web-based Programs and Apps

1. Use a search engine to find information about web-based programs and apps to answer the following questions:

   a. Find articles comparing the features of Google Drive and Office Web Apps.

   b. What different tools does each offer?

   c. Are there costs associated with using these resources?

   d. Do they offer any premium services?

   e. Are there any known security issues?

3 | Identifying Cloud Security Concerns

1. Use a search engine to find information about cloud security to answer the following questions:

   a. List four known threats or concerns regarding cloud security and privacy.

   b. Does using a premium or fee-based service offer additional privacy and security?

   c. Find an article describing a situation in which a company that stored data on the cloud was hacked. What was the effect on the company's customers? How did the company resolve the issue?

   d. What restrictions and privileges exist for law enforcement or government officials who want to access cloud data?

   e. In your opinion, who owns the data you store on the cloud? What responsibilities does the storage provider have to its users?

Index

hub: An inexpensive hardware device used to connect multiple nodes on the same network. 276, 286

HubPages, 343

hyperlink (link): Text or picture on webpage that can be clicked with pointer to view a different location in the same webpage, another webpage at the same website, or a webpage at a different website. 7, 8

hyperlocal portals: Portals that are specific to a certain geographic location and provide content about that area, written for and by local citizens. 211

hypertext: System of hyperlinks that allows users to click a word or image to move to another location within the same file or link to different files in the same location. 17

early history of, 16–18

Hypertext Markup Language (HTML): A set of special codes or tags that define the layout of webpage content. 5, 17

Hypertext Transfer Protocol (HTTP): Protocol that defines how HTML documents and web-based mail are transmitted to a browser. 17

I

IANA (Internet Assigned Numbers Authority), 2

IBM WebSphere portal software, 217

ICANN (Internet Corporation for Assigned Names and Numbers), 2, 297

icons, locked padlock, 79

images
saving webpage, 72
web bugs, 83

IMAP (Internet Message Access Protocol): An email delivery protocol that provides mail management functions on the server. 145

IMPs (Interface Message Processors), 14

Inbox folder: A mail folder that contains incoming messages. 155

index: Webpage information received from the spiders stored in a database on one or more servers. 105

individual messages format: Sends each message to members as a single email message.

industry portals: Vertical portals that target viewers interested in a specific industry. 211

information privacy: Right of individuals and companies to deny or restrict the collection and use of personal information. 81

infrared (IR) transmissions: The use of infrared light-wave signals as a shortrange transmission medium between computers or other devices equipped with infrared ports. 282

ingentaconnect service, 131

InPrivate Browsing, Internet Explorer, 83

InPrivate Filtering, Internet Explorer, 84

Instagram, 332

instant messaging (IM): Private means of exchanging real-time messages with others using the Internet. 9, 190

Insurance.com, 249

Insure.com, 249

Integrated Services Digital Network (ISDN): Set of standards for digital transmission of data over standard copper phone lines. 22

intelligent hub: A hub that can perform a variety of tasks, such as filtering data or permitting a network administrator to monitor hub traffic. 286

Internet: Worldwide network of computers that allows individual and business users around the world to share information and other resources and to conduct business transactions. 2

backbone, 15

communication methods (table), 9

connecting to the, 19–25, 40–41

filtering software, 317

impact of the, 12–19

infrastructure of, 289–300

negative effect, 4

network operating system services (table), 278

overview of, 2

public WAN, 279

using the, 3–12

Internet Assigned Numbers Authority (IANA), 2

Internet Corporation for Assigned Names and Numbers (ICANN): Organization that manages the DNS and controls the domain name registration system. 2, 39

Internet exchange point (IXP): A physical infrastructure that enables ISPs to communicate among their

networks, which limits the upstream traffic an ISP must handle. 290

Internet Explorer (IE)
adding browser home page using, 74–75
domains, searching for available, 298–299
favorites, using, saving, organizing, 56–60
features, 41–43
InPrivate Browsing, InPrivate Filtering features, 83, 84
pop-up blocker, turning on, 46
search feature, using, 47
starting, opening webpages, 44–45
suggested websites, 68
webpage searches, 120–122

Internet filters: Hardware or software that filters the display of web content based on user settings. 80

Internet Protocol (IP): Protocol that addresses and sends packets over the network. 14

Internet Relay Chat (IRC): Text-based communications tool. 9

Internet service provider (ISP): Company that provides Internet access for homes and businesses. 20
and information privacy, 81
overview of, 20–21

Internet telephony: Uses TCP/IP and packet switching to send voice transmissions over a private or public IP network. 302–303
See also IP telephony or voice over IP
overview of, 302–306

Internet2 (I2): High-speed network reserved specifically for research and education. 19

investing online, 251–252

Invisible web: Webpages with few or no links to and from the main core of the web. 132

IP address (Internet Protocol address): A number that uniquely identifies each computer or device connected to the Internet. 38, 39
components of, 292
looking up, 296–297
viewing networked computer's, 293

ipconfig/all: A command to display your computer's IP address. 293

iPrism web content filter, 80

IP telephony: Uses TCP/IP and packet switching to send voice transmissions over a private or public IP network. 302–303. *See also* Internet telephony or voice over IP